Cram101 Textbook Outlines to accompany:

Access to Health

Donatelle, 9th Edition

An Academic Internet Publishers (AIPI) publication (c) 2007.

You have a discounted membership at www.Cram101.com with this book.

Get all of the practice tests for the chapters of this textbook, and access in-depth reference material for writing essays and papers. Here is an example from a Cram101 Biology text:

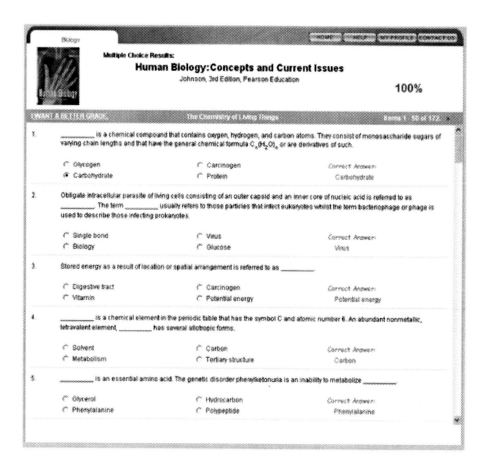

When you need problem solving help with math, stats, and other disciplines, www.Cram101.com will walk through the formulas and solutions step by step.

With Cram101.com online, you also have access to extensive reference material.

You will nail those essays and papers. Here is an example from a Cram101 Biology text:

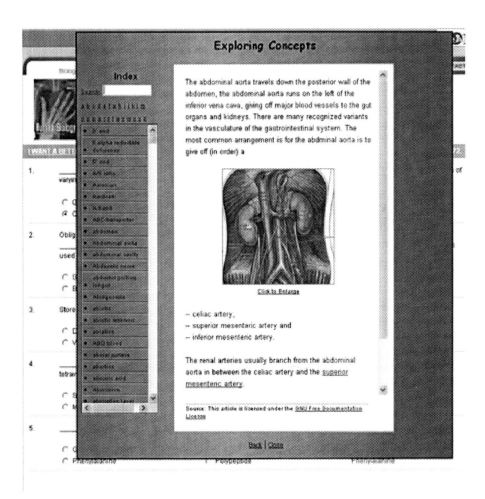

Learning System

Cram101 Textbook Outlines is a learning system. The notes in this book are the highlights of your textbook, you will never have to highlight a book again.

How to use this book. Take this book to class, it is your notebook for the lecture. The notes and highlights on the left hand side of the pages follow the outline and order of the textbook. All you have to do is follow along while your intructor presents the lecture. Circle the items emphasized in class and add other important information on the right side. With Cram101 Textbook Outlines you'll spend less time writing and more time listening. Learning becomes more efficient.

Cram101.com Online

Increase your studying efficiency by using Cram101.com's practice tests and online reference material. It is the perfect complement to Cram101 Textbook Outlines. Use self-teaching matching tests or simulate in-class testing with comprehensive multiple choice tests, or simply use Cram's true and false tests for quick review. Cram101.com even allows you to enter your in-class notes for an integrated studying format combining the textbook notes with your class notes.

Visit **www.Cram101.com**, click Sign Up at the top of the screen, and enter **DK73DW2884** in the promo code box on the registration screen. Access to www.Cram101.com is normally $9.95, but because you have purchased this book, your access fee is only $4.95. Sign up and stop highlighting textbooks forever.

Access to Health
Donatelle, 9th

CONTENTS

Health	Health is a term that refers to a combination of the absence of illness, the ability to cope with everyday activities, physical fitness, and high quality of life.
Diabetes	Diabetes is a medical disorder characterized by varying or persistent elevated blood sugar levels, especially after eating. All types of diabetes share similar symptoms and complications at advanced stages: dehydration and ketoacidosis, cardiovascular disease, chronic renal failure, retinal damage which can lead to blindness, nerve damage which can lead to erectile dysfunction, gangrene with risk of amputation of toes, feet, and even legs.
Epidemic	An epidemic is a disease that appears as new cases in a given human population, during a given period, at a rate that substantially exceeds what is "expected", based on recent experience.
Obesity	The state of being more than 20 percent above the average weight for a person of one's height is called obesity.
Cancer	Cancer is a class of diseases or disorders characterized by uncontrolled division of cells and the ability of these cells to invade other tissues, either by direct growth into adjacent tissue through invasion or by implantation into distant sites by metastasis.
Influenza	Influenza or flu refers to an acute viral infection of the respiratory tract, occurring in isolated cases, epidemics, and pandemics. Influenza is caused by three strains of influenza virus, labeled types A, B, and C, based on the antigens of their protein coats.
Virus	Obligate intracellular parasite of living cells consisting of an outer capsid and an inner core of nucleic acid is referred to as virus. The term virus usually refers to those particles that infect eukaryotes whilst the term bacteriophage or phage is used to describe those infecting prokaryotes.
Cholesterol	Cholesterol is a steroid, a lipid, and an alcohol, found in the cell membranes of all body tissues, and transported in the blood plasma of all animals. It is an important component of the membranes of cells, providing stability; it makes the membrane's fluidity stable over a bigger temperature interval.
Depression	In everyday language depression refers to any downturn in mood, which may be relatively transitory and perhaps due to something trivial. This is differentiated from Clinical depression which is marked by symptoms that last two weeks or more and are so severe that they interfere with daily living.
Stress	Stress refers to a condition that is a response to factors that change the human systems normal state.
Infectious disease	In medicine, infectious disease or communicable disease is disease caused by a biological agent such as by a virus, bacterium or parasite. This is contrasted to physical causes, such as burns or chemical ones such as through intoxication.
Stomach	The stomach is an organ in the alimentary canal used to digest food. It's primary function is not the absorption of nutrients from digested food; rather, the main job of the stomach is to break down large food molecules into smaller ones, so that they can be absorbed into the blood more easily.
Lifestyle	The culturally, socially, economically, and environmentally conditioned complex of actions characteristic of an individual, group, or community as a pattern of habituated behavior over time that is health related but not necessarily health directed is a lifestyle.
Validity	The extent to which a test measures what it is intended to measure is called validity.
Stroke	A stroke or cerebrovascular accident (CVA) occurs when the blood supply to a part of the brain is suddenly interrupted.
Blood clot	A blood clot is the final product of the blood coagulation step in hemostasis. It is achieved via the aggregation of platelets that form a platelet plug, and the activation of the humoral coagulation system
Hormone	A hormone is a chemical messenger from one cell to another. All multicellular organisms produce hormones. The best known hormones are those produced by endocrine glands of vertebrate animals, but hormones are produced by nearly every organ system and tissue type in a human or animal body. Hormone

molecules are secreted directly into the bloodstream, they move by circulation or diffusion to their target cells, which may be nearby cells in the same tissue or cells of a distant organ of the body.

Hormone replacement therapy	Hormone replacement therapy is a system of medical treatment for perimenopausal and postmenopausal women, based on the assumption that it may prevent discomfort and health problems caused by diminished circulating estrogen hormones.
Blood	Blood is a circulating tissue composed of fluid plasma and cells. The main function of blood is to supply nutrients (oxygen, glucose) and constitutional elements to tissues and to remove waste products.
Estrogen	Estrogen is a steroid that functions as the primary female sex hormone. While present in both men and women, they are found in women in significantly higher quantities.
Ulcer	An ulcer is an open sore of the skin, eyes or mucous membrane, often caused by an initial abrasion and generally maintained by an inflammation and/or an infection.
Acid	An acid is a water-soluble, sour-tasting chemical compound that when dissolved in water, gives a solution with a pH of less than 7.
Affect	Affect is the scientific term used to describe a subject's externally displayed mood. This can be assesed by the nurse by observing facial expression, tone of voice, and body language.
Intervention	Intervention refers to a planned attempt to break through addicts' or abusers' denial and get them into treatment. Interventions most often occur when legal, workplace, health, relationship, or financial problems have become intolerable.
Alcohol	Alcohol is a general term, applied to any organic compound in which a hydroxyl group (-OH) is bound to a carbon atom, which in turn is bound to other hydrogen and/or carbon atoms. The general formula for a simple acyclic alcohol is $C_nH_{2n+1}OH$.
Agent	Agent refers to an epidemiological term referring to the organism or object that transmits a disease from the environment to the host.
Statistics	Statistics is a type of data analysis which practice includes the planning, summarizing, and interpreting of observations of a system possibly followed by predicting or forecasting of future events based on a mathematical model of the system being observed.
Pneumonia	Pneumonia is an illness of the lungs and respiratory system in which the microscopic, air-filled sacs (alveoli) responsible for absorbing oxygen from the atmosphere become inflamed and flooded with fluid.
Statistic	A statistic is an observable random variable of a sample.
Kidney	The kidney is a bean-shaped excretory organ in vertebrates. Part of the urinary system, the kidneys filter wastes (especially urea) from the blood and excrete them, along with water, as urine.
Vital statistics	Vital statistics are the information maintained by a government, recording the birth and death of individuals within that government's jurisdiction. These data are used by public health programs to evaluate how effective are their programs and are the cornerstone to public health systems today.
Culture	Culture, generally refers to patterns of human activity and the symbolic structures that give such activity significance.
Value	Value is worth in general, and it is thought to be connected to reasons for certain practices, policies, actions, beliefs or emotions. Value is "that which one acts to gain and/or keep."
Wellness	A dimension of health beyond the absence of disease or infirmity, including social, emotional, and spiritual aspects of health is called wellness.
Medical model	The medical model views abnormal behavior as a disease.
Organ	Organ refers to a structure consisting of several tissues adapted as a group to perform specific functions.

Tuberculosis	Tuberculosis is an infection caused by the bacterium Mycobacterium tuberculosis, which most commonly affects the lungs but can also affect the central nervous system, lymphatic system, circulatory system, genitourinary system, bones and joints.
Cholera	Cholera is a water-borne disease caused by the bacterium Vibrio cholerae, which are typically ingested by drinking contaminated water, or by eating improperly cooked fish, especially shellfish.
Stigma	Stigma refers to a personal characteristic that at least some other individuals perceive negatively because that characteristic is different than those of the general population.
Public health	Public health is concerned with threats to the overall health of a community based on population health analysis.
Course	Pattern of development and change of a disorder over time is a course.
Pathogen	A pathogen or infectious agent is a biological agent that causes disease or illness to its host.The term is most often used for agents that disrupt the normal physiology of a multicellular animal or plant.
Antibiotic	Antibiotic refers to substance such as penicillin or streptomycin that is toxic to microorganisms. Usually a product of a particular microorvanism or plant.
Centers for Disease Control and Prevention	The Centers for Disease Control and Prevention in Atlanta, Georgia, is recognized as the lead United States agency for protecting the public health and safety of people by providing credible information to enhance health decisions, and promoting health through strong partnerships with state health departments and other organizations.
Infection	The invasion and multiplication of microorganisms in body tissues is called an infection.
Complaint	Complaint refers to report made by the police or some other agency to the court that initiates the intake process.
Medicine	Medicine is the branch of health science and the sector of public life concerned with maintaining or restoring human health through the study, diagnosis and treatment of disease and injury.
Health outcome	Any medically or epidemiologically defined characteristic of a patient or population that results from health promotion or care provided or required, as measured at one point in time is a health outcome.
Outcome	Outcome is the impact of care provided to a patient. They can be positive, such as the ability to walk freely as a result of rehabilitation, or negative, such as the occurrence of bedsores as a result of lack of mobility of a patient.
Risk factor	A risk factor is a variable associated with an increased risk of disease or infection but risk factors are not necessarily causal.
Survey	A method of scientific investigation in which a large sample of people answer questions about their attitudes or behavior is referred to as a survey.
Binge drinking	Binge drinking refers to consuming 5 or more drinks in a short time or drinking alchohol for the sole purpose of intoxication.
Binge	Binge refers to relatively brief episode of uncontrolled, excessive consumption.
Cervical cancer	Cervical cancer is a malignancy of the cervix. Worldwide, it is the second most common cancer of women.
Population	Population refers to all members of a well-defined group of organisms, events, or things.
Lung cancer	Lung cancer is a malignant tumour of the lungs. Most commonly it is bronchogenic carcinoma (about 90%).
Mental health	Mental health refers to the 'thinking' part of psychosocial health; includes your values, attitudes, and beliefs.
Young adult	An young adult is someone between the ages of 20 and 40 years old.

World Health Organization	The World Health Organization (WHO) is a specialized agency of the United Nations, acting as a coordinating authority on international public health, headquartered in Geneva, Switzerland.
Concept	A mental category used to class together objects, relations, events, abstractions, or qualities that have common properties is called concept.
Quality of life	Quality of life refers to the perception of individuals or groups that their needs are being satisfied and that they are not being denied opportunities to achieve happiness and fulfillment.
Life span	Life span refers to the upper boundary of life, the maximum number of years an individual can live. The maximum life span of human beings is about 120 years of age.
Vaccine	A harmless variant or derivative of a pathogen used to stimulate a host organism's immune system to mount a long-term defense against the pathogen is referred to as vaccine.
Mortality	The incidence of death in a population is mortality.
Morbidity rate	Measures the number of individuals who become ill as a result of a particular disease within a susceptible population during a specific time period are morbidity rate.
Morbidity	Morbidity refers to any condition that causes illness.
Adaptation	A biological adaptation is an anatomical structure, physiological process or behavioral trait of an organism that has evolved over a period of time by the process of natural selection such that it increases the expected long-term reproductive success of the organism.
Activities of daily living	Activities of daily living is a way to describe the functional status of a person.
Pain	Pain is an unpleasant sensation which may be associated with actual or potential tissue damage and which may have physical and emotional components.
Muscle	Muscle is a contractile form of tissue. It is one of the four major tissue types, the other three being epithelium, connective tissue and nervous tissue. Muscle contraction is used to move parts of the body, as well as to move substances within the body.
Criterion	Criterion refers to a standard of comparison. For performance appraisal, it is the definition of good performance.
Planning	In agreement with the patient, the nurse addresses each of the problems identified in the planning phase. For each problem a measurable goal is set. For example, for the patient discussed above, the goal would be for the patient's skin to remain intact. The result is a nursing care plan. This is the third step.
Health promotion	Any planned combination of educational, political, regulatory, and organizational supports for actions and conditions of living conducive to the health of individuals, groups, or communities is called health promotion.
Assessment	In clinical practice, the process by which a mental health professional gathers and compiles information about a client for the purpose of describing the person's problems or disorder and developing a plan of treatment is an assessment.
Anger	Anger is an emotional response often based on a sensation or perception of threat to one's needs.
Connectedness	Connectedness refers to according to Cooper and her colleagues, connectedness consists of two dimensions: mutuality and permeability.
Susceptibility	The degree of resistance of a host to a pathogen is susceptibility.
Intolerance	Intolerance refers to a type of interaction in which two or more drugs produce extremely uncomfortable symptoms.
Primary	Primary prevention is any effort to avoid the development of a disease or condition.

prevention	
Lead	Lead is a chemical element in the periodic table that has the symbol Pb and atomic number 82. A soft, heavy, toxic and malleable poor metal, lead is bluish white when freshly cut but tarnishes to dull gray when exposed to air. Lead is used in building construction, lead-acid batteries, bullets and shot, and is part of solder, pewter, and fusible alloys.
Secondary prevention	Psychological counseling, psychotropic medications, and other rehabilitation treatment programs designed to prevent repeat offenses are called secondary prevention.
Tertiary prevention	Tertiary prevention refers to treatment of a disease to avoid its worsening or the onset of any complications.
Incidence	In epidemiological studies of a particular disorder, the rate at which new cases occur in a given place at a given time is called incidence.
Chronic disease	Disease of long duration often not detected in its early stages and from which the patient will not recover is referred to as a chronic disease.
Competency	Ability of legal defendants to participate in their own defense and understand the charges and the roles of the trial participants is referred to as competency.
Rehabilitation	Rehabilitation is the restoration of lost capabilities, or the treatment aimed at producing it. Also refers to treatment for dependency on psychoactive substances such as alcohol, prescription drugs, and illicit drugs such as cocaine, heroin or amphetamines.
Poliomyelitis	Poliomyelitis refers to an acute, contagious viral disease that attacks the central nervous system, injuring or destroying the nerve cells that control the muscles and sometimes causing paralysis; also called polio or infantile paralysis.
Diphtheria	Diphtheria refers to an acute, highly contagious childhood disease that generally affects the membranes of the throat and less frequently the nose. It is caused by Corynebacterium diphtheriae.
Smallpox	Once a highly contagious, often fatal disease caused by a poxvirus. Its most noticeable symptom was the appearance of blisters and pustules on the skin. Vaccination has eradicated smallpox throughout the world.
Measles	Measles refers to a highly contagious skin disease that is endemic throughout the world. It is caused by a morbilli virus in the family Paramyxoviridae, which enters the body through the respiratory tract or through the conjunctiva.
Rubella	An infectious disease that, if contracted by the mother during the first three months of pregnancy, has a high risk of causing mental retardation and physical deformity in the child is called rubella.
Tetanus	Tetanus is a serious and often fatal disease caused by the neurotoxin tetanospasmin which is produced by the Gram-positive, obligate anaerobic bacterium Clostridium tetani. Tetanus also refers to a state of muscle tension.
Cardiovascular disease	Cardiovascular disease refers to afflictions in the mechanisms, including the heart, blood vessels, and their controllers, that are responsible for transporting blood to the body's tissues and organs. Psychological factors may play important roles in such diseases and their treatments.
Blood pressure	Blood pressure is the pressure exerted by the blood on the walls of the blood vessels.
Micronutrients	Micronutrients are essential elements only needed by life in small quantities. Vitamins and trace minerals are sometimes included in the term.
Micronutrient	Micronutrient refers to an element that an organism needs in very small amounts and that functions as a component or cofactor of enzymes.
Rickets	Rickets is a disorder which most commonly relates directly to Vitamin D deficiency, which causes a lack of calcium being absorbed. It can also arise, however, from other etiologies such as rare mesenchymal

tumors or any phosphate-wasting disease. It is a disorder which most commonly relates directly to Vitamin D deficiency, which causes a lack of calcium being absorbed.

Goiter	Goiter refers to an enlargement of the thyroid gland resulting from a dietary iodine deficiency.
Infant mortality	Infant mortality is the death of infants in the first year of life. The leading causes of infant mortality are dehydration and disease. Major causes of infant mortality in more developed countries include congenital malformation, infection and SIDS. Infant mortality rate is the number of newborns dying under a year of age divided by the number of live births during the year.
Multiple sclerosis	Multiple sclerosis affects neurons, the cells of the brain and spinal cord that carry information, create thought and perception, and allow the brain to control the body. Surrounding and protecting these neurons is a layer of fat, called myelin, which helps neurons carry electrical signals. MS causes gradual destruction of myelin (demyelination) in patches throughout the brain and/or spinal cord, causing various symptoms depending upon which signals are interrupted.
Prognosis	Prognosis refers to the prospects for the future or outcome of a disease.
Alternative medicine	Treatment used in place of conventional medicine is an alternative medicine.
Immune system	The immune system is the system of specialized cells and organs that protect an organism from outside biological influences. When the immune system is functioning properly, it protects the body against bacteria and viral infections, destroying cancer cells and foreign substances.
Longevity	A long duration of life is referred to as longevity.
Protein	A protein is a complex, high-molecular-weight organic compound that consists of amino acids joined by peptide bonds. They are essential to the structure and function of all living cells and viruses. Many are enzymes or subunits of enzymes.
Calorie	Calorie refers to a unit used to measure heat energy and the energy contents of foods.
Brain	The part of the central nervous system involved in regulating and controlling body activity and interpreting information from the senses transmitted through the nervous system is referred to as the brain.
Mutual interdependence	A condition in which two or more persons must depend on one another to meet each person's needs or goals is referred to as mutual interdependence.
Heart attack	A heart attack, is a serious, sudden heart condition usually characterized by varying degrees of chest pain or discomfort, weakness, sweating, nausea, vomiting, and arrhythmias, sometimes causing loss of consciousness. It occurs when the blood supply to a part of the heart is interrupted, causing death and scarring of the local heart tissue.
Assess	Assess is to systematically and continuously collect, validate, and communicate patient data.
Anatomy	Anatomy is the branch of biology that deals with the structure and organization of living things. It can be divided into animal anatomy (zootomy) and plant anatomy (phytonomy).
Osteoporosis	Osteoporosis is a disease of bone in which bone mineral density (BMD) is reduced, bone microarchitecture is disrupted, the amount and variety of non-collagenous proteins in bone is changed, and a concomitantly fracture risk is increased.
Trial	In classical conditioning, any presentation of a stimulus or pair of stimuli is called a trial.
Fetus	Fetus refers to a developing human from the ninth week of gestation until birth; has all the major structures of an adult.
Menstrual cycle	The menstrual cycle is the set of recurring physiological changes in a female's body that are under the control of the reproductive hormone system and necessary for reproduction. Besides humans, only other great apes exhibit menstrual cycles, in contrast to the estrus cycle of most mammalian species.

Neoplasm	Neoplasm refers to abnormal growth of cells; often used to mean a tumor.
Heredity	Heredity refers to the transmission of genetic information from parent to offspring.
Septicemia	Septicemia is sepsis of the bloodstream caused by bacteremia, which is the presence of bacteria in the bloodstream. It is also called blood poisoning.
Homicide	Death that results from intent to injure or kill is referred to as homicide.
Syndrome	Syndrome is the association of several clinically recognizable features, signs, symptoms, phenomena or characteristics which often occur together, so that the presence of one feature alerts the physician to the presence of the others
HIV	The virus that causes AIDS is HIV (human immunodeficiency virus).
Incentive	Incentive refers to an object, person, or situation perceived as being capable of satisfying a need.
Theory	Theory refers to an explanatory statement, or set of statements, that concisely summarizes the state of knowledge on a phenomenon and provides direction for further study.
Health belief model	Health belief model refers to a paradigm used to predict and explain health behavior; based on value-expectancy theory.
Clinical psychology	Clinical psychology is involved in the diagnosis, assessment, and treatment of patients with mental or behavioral disorders, and conducts research in these various areas.
Variable	A characteristic or aspect in which people, objects, events, or conditions vary is called variable.
Demographic variable	A varying characteristic that is a vital or social statistic of an individual, sample group, or population, for example, age, sex, socioeconomic status, racial origin, education is called a demographic variable.
Immunity	Resistance to the effects of specific disease-causing agents is called immunity.
Imagined rehearsal	Practicing, through mental imagery, to become better able to perform an event in actuality is called imagined rehearsal.
Cocaine	Cocaine is a crystalline tropane alkaloid that is obtained from the leaves of the coca plant. It is a stimulant of the central nervous system and an appetite suppressant, creating what has been described as a euphoric sense of happiness and increased energy.
Cognitive therapy	Cognitive therapy is a kind of psychotherapy used to treat depression, anxiety disorders, phobias, and other forms of mental disorder. It involves recognizing distorted thinking and learning how to replace it with more realistic thoughts and actions.
Albert Ellis	Albert Ellis is a psychologist whose Rational Emotive Behavior Therapy (REBT), is the foundation of all cognitive and cognitive behavior therapies.
Anthrax	Anthrax refers to an infectious disease of animals caused by ingesting Bacillus anthracis spores. Can also occur in humans and is sometimes called woolsorter's disease.
Host	Host is an organism that harbors a parasite, mutual partner, or commensal partner; or a cell infected by a virus.
Anemia	Anemia is a deficiency of red blood cells and/or hemoglobin. This results in a reduced ability of blood to transfer oxygen to the tissues, and this causes hypoxia; since all human cells depend on oxygen for survival, varying degrees of anemia can have a wide range of clinical consequences.
Hypercholest-rolemia	Hypercholesterolemia is the presence of high levels of cholesterol in the blood. It is not a disease but a metabolic derangement that can be secondary to many diseases and can contribute to many forms of disease, most notably cardiovascular disease.
Arthritis	Arthritis is a group of conditions that affect the health of the bone joints in the body. Arthritis can

be caused from strains and injuries caused by repetitive motion, sports, overexertion, and falls. Unlike the autoimmune diseases, it largely affects older people and results from the degeneration of joint cartilage.

Dementia	Dementia is progressive decline in cognitive function due to damage or disease in the brain beyond what might be expected from normal aging.
Research method	The scope of the research method is to produce some new knowledge. This, in principle, can take three main forms: Exploratory research; Constructive research; and Empirical research.
Shock	Circulatory shock, a state of cardiac output that is insufficient to meet the body's physiological needs, with consequences ranging from fainting to death is referred to as shock. Insulin shock, a state of severe hypoglycemia caused by administration of insulin.
Ratio	In number and more generally in algebra, a ratio is the linear relationship between two quantities.
Stressor	A factor capable of stimulating a stress response is a stressor.
Stress inoculation	Use of positive coping statements to control fear and anxiety is a form of stress inoculation.
Adjustment	Adjustment is an attempt to cope with a given situation.
Blocking	A sudden break or interuption in the flow of thinking or speech that is seen as an absence in thought is refered to as blocking.
Antecedents	In behavior modification, events that typically precede the target response are called antecedents.
Counselor	A counselor is a mental health professional who specializes in helping people with problems not involving serious mental disorders.
Aerobic	An aerobic organism is an organism that has an oxygen based metabolism. Aerobes, in a process known as cellular respiration, use oxygen to oxidize substrates (for example sugars and fats) in order to obtain energy.
Lifestyle changes	Lifestyle changes are changes to the way a person lives which are often called for when treating chronic disease.
Malnutrition	Malnutrition is a general term for the medical condition in a person or animal caused by an unbalanced diet either too little or too much food, or a diet missing one or more important nutrients.
Predisposition	Predisposition refers to an inclination or diathesis to respond in a certain way, either inborn or acquired. In abnormal psychology, it is a factor that lowers the ability to withstand stress and inclines the individual toward pathology.
Catalyst	A chemical that speeds up a reaction but is not used up in the reaction is a catalyst.

Mental health	Mental health refers to the 'thinking' part of psychosocial health; includes your values, attitudes, and beliefs.
Health	Health is a term that refers to a combination of the absence of illness, the ability to cope with everyday activities, physical fitness, and high quality of life.
Sexual assault	Sexual assault refers to any act in which one person is sexually intimate with another person without that other person's consent.
Depression	In everyday language depression refers to any downturn in mood, which may be relatively transitory and perhaps due to something trivial. This is differentiated from Clinical depression which is marked by symptoms that last two weeks or more and are so severe that they interfere with daily living.
Assault	Assault is a crime of violence against another person that intentionally instills fear and creates a reasonable aprehension of harm.
Conscious	Conscious refers to the thoughts, feelings, sensations, or memories of which a person is aware at any given moment.
Jealousy	An aversive reaction evoked by a real or imagined relationship involving a person's partner and a third person is a jealousy.
Anger	Anger is an emotional response often based on a sensation or perception of threat to one's needs.
Ethnicity	While ethnicity and race are related concepts, the concept of ethnicity is rooted in the idea of social groups, marked especially by shared nationality, tribal affiliation, religious faith, shared language, or cultural and traditional origins and backgrounds, whereas race is rooted in the idea of biological classification of Homo sapiens to subspecies according to chosen genotypic and/or phenotypic traits.
Value	Value is worth in general, and it is thought to be connected to reasons for certain practices, policies, actions, beliefs or emotions. Value is "that which one acts to gain and/or keep."
Introspection	Deliberate looking into one's own mind to examine one's own thoughts and feelings is called introspection.
Assess	Assess is to systematically and continuously collect, validate, and communicate patient data.
Stress	Stress refers to a condition that is a response to factors that change the human systems normal state.
Culture	Culture, generally refers to patterns of human activity and the symbolic structures that give such activity significance.
Anxiety	Anxiety is a complex combination of the feeling of fear, apprehension and worry often accompanied by physical sensations such as palpitations, chest pain and/or shortness of breath.
Arousal	Arousal is a physiological and psychological state involving the activation of the reticular activating system in the brain stem, the autonomic nervous system and the endocrine system, leading to increased heart rate and blood pressure and a condition of alertness and readiness to respond.
Grief	Grief is a multi-faceted response to loss. Although conventionally focused on the emotional response to loss, it also has a physical, cognitive, behavioral, social and philosophical dimensions.
Pain	Pain is an unpleasant sensation which may be associated with actual or potential tissue

damage and which may have physical and emotional components.

Isolation	Isolation refers to the degree to which groups do not live in the same communities.
Social isolation	Social isolation refers to a type of loneliness that occurs when a person lacks a sense of integrated involvement. Being deprived of participation in a group or community involving companionship, shared interests, organized activities, and meaningful roles causes a person to feel isolated.
Trauma	Trauma refers to a severe physical injury or wound to the body caused by an external force, or a psychological shock having a lasting effect on mental life.
Affect	Affect is the scientific term used to describe a subject's externally displayed mood. This can be assesed by the nurse by observing facial expression, tone of voice, and body language.
Concept	A mental category used to class together objects, relations, events, abstractions, or qualities that have common properties is called concept.
Longevity	A long duration of life is referred to as longevity.
Attachment	Attachment refers to the psychological tendency to seek closeness to another person, to feel secure when that person is present, and to feel anxious when that person is absent.
Engagement	Engagement occurs when the presenting part of the fetus has settled into the true pelvis at the level of the ischial spines.
Aspiration	In medicine, aspiration is the entry of secretions or foreign material into the trachea and lungs.
Interconnect-dness	A web of connections, including our relationship to ourselves, to others, and to a larger meaning or purpose in life is interconnectedness.
Mindfulness	Awareness and acceptance of the reality of the present moment are referred to as mindfulness.
Evaluation	The fifth step of the nursing process where nursing care and the patient's goal achievement are measured is the evaluation.
Conviction	Beliefs that are important to a person and that evoke strong emotion are a conviction.
Wellness	A dimension of health beyond the absence of disease or infirmity, including social, emotional, and spiritual aspects of health is called wellness.
Intimate relationships	Relationships with family members, friends, and romantic partners, characterized by closeness and understanding are intimate relationships.
Host	Host is an organism that harbors a parasite, mutual partner, or commensal partner; or a cell infected by a virus.
Immune system	The immune system is the system of specialized cells and organs that protect an organism from outside biological influences. When the immune system is functioning properly, it protects the body against bacteria and viral infections, destroying cancer cells and foreign substances.
Cortisol	Cortisol is a corticosteroid hormone that is involved in the response to stress; it increases blood pressure and blood sugar levels and suppresses the immune system.
Quality of life	Quality of life refers to the perception of individuals or groups that their needs are being satisfied and that they are not being denied opportunities to achieve happiness and fulfillment.
Blood pressure	Blood pressure is the pressure exerted by the blood on the walls of the blood vessels.
Blood	Blood is a circulating tissue composed of fluid plasma and cells. The main function of blood

is to supply nutrients (oxygen, glucose) and constitutional elements to tissues and to remove waste products.

Population	Population refers to all members of a well-defined group of organisms, events, or things.
Elderly	Old age consists of ages nearing the average life span of human beings, and thus the end of the human life cycle. Euphemisms for older people include advanced adult, elderly, and senior or senior citizen.
Control group	A group that does not receive the treatment effect in an experiment is referred to as the control group or sometimes as the comparison group.
Immune response	The body's defensive reaction to invasion by bacteria, viral agents, or other foreign substances is called immune response.
Cancer	Cancer is a class of diseases or disorders characterized by uncontrolled division of cells and the ability of these cells to invade other tissues, either by direct growth into adjacent tissue through invasion or by implantation into distant sites by metastasis.
Adjustment	Adjustment is an attempt to cope with a given situation.
Medicine	Medicine is the branch of health science and the sector of public life concerned with maintaining or restoring human health through the study, diagnosis and treatment of disease and injury.
Behavioral medicine	Behavioral medicine refers to an interdisciplinary field that focuses on developing and integrating behavioral and biomedical knowledge to promote health and reduce illness.
Psychosomatic	A psychosomatic illness is one with physical manifestations and perhaps a supposed psychological cause. It is often diagnosed when any known or identifiable physical cause was excluded by medical examination.
Brain	The part of the central nervous system involved in regulating and controlling body activity and interpreting information from the senses transmitted through the nervous system is referred to as the brain.
Public health	Public health is concerned with threats to the overall health of a community based on population health analysis.
Course	Pattern of development and change of a disorder over time is a course.
Outcome	Outcome is the impact of care provided to a patient. They can be positive, such as the ability to walk freely as a result of rehabilitation, or negative, such as the occurrence of bedsores as a result of lack of mobility of a patient.
Drug abuse	Drug abuse has a wide range of definitions, all of them relating either to the misuse or overuse of a psychoactive drug or performance enhancing drug for a non-therapeutic or non-medical effect, or referring to any use of illegal drug in the absence of a required, yet practically impossible to get, license from a government authority.
Sexual abuse	Sexual abuse is a relative cultural term used to describe sexual relations and behavior between two or more parties which are considered criminally and/or morally offensive.
Stressor	A factor capable of stimulating a stress response is a stressor.
Intervention	Intervention refers to a planned attempt to break through addicts' or abusers' denial and get them into treatment. Interventions most often occur when legal, workplace, health, relationship, or financial problems have become intolerable.
Lead	Lead is a chemical element in the periodic table that has the symbol Pb and atomic number 82. A soft, heavy, toxic and malleable poor metal, lead is bluish white when freshly cut but tarnishes to dull gray when exposed to air. Lead is used in building construction, lead-acid

batteries, bullets and shot, and is part of solder, pewter, and fusible alloys.

Helplessness	A maladaptive pattern of achievement behavior in which children avoid challenge, do not persist in the face of difficulty, and tend to attribute their failure on tasks to a lack of ability rather than a lack of effort or an inappropriate strategy is referred to as helplessness.
Learned helplessness	A model for the acquisition of depressive behavior, based on findings that organisms in aversive situations learn to show inactivity when their operants go unreinforced are called learned helplessness.
Theory	Theory refers to an explanatory statement, or set of statements, that concisely summarizes the state of knowledge on a phenomenon and provides direction for further study.
Assertiveness	Asking for what one wants while demonstrating respect for others is refered to as assertiveness.
Compliance	In medicine, a patient's (or doctor's) adherence to a recommended course of treatment is considered compliance.
Independence	The condition in which one variable has no effect on another is referred to as independence.
Conscientiouness	One of the dimensions of the five-factor model of personality and individual differences involving being organized, thorough, and reliable as opposed to careless, negligent, and unreliable is conscientiousness.
Life span	Life span refers to the upper boundary of life, the maximum number of years an individual can live. The maximum life span of human beings is about 120 years of age.
Young adult	An young adult is someone between the ages of 20 and 40 years old.
Interpersonal communication	Interpersonal communication refers to communication with another person. This kind of communication is subdivided into dyadic communication, public communication, and small-group or communication.
Developmental task	Developmental task refers to any personal change that must take place for optimal development.
Conservation	Conservation refers to according to Piaget, recognition that basic properties of substances such as weight and mass remain the same when superficial features change.
Neurotransmitter	A neurotransmitter is a chemical that is used to relay, amplify and modulate electrical signals between a neuron and another cell.
Sleep deprivation	Sleep deprivation is an overall lack of the necessary amount of sleep. A person can be deprived of sleep by their own body and mind, insomnia, or actively deprived by another individual.
Complaint	Complaint refers to report made by the police or some other agency to the court that initiates the intake process.
Insomnia	Insomnia is a sleep disorder characterized by an inability to sleep and/or to remain asleep for a reasonable period during the night.
Sleep apnea	Sleep apnea refers to a sleep disorder involving periods during sleep when breathing stops and the person must awaken briefly in order to breathe; major symptoms are excessive daytime sleepiness and loud snoring.
Muscle	Muscle is a contractile form of tissue. It is one of the four major tissue types, the other three being epithelium, connective tissue and nervous tissue. Muscle contraction is used to move parts of the body, as well as to move substances within the body.

Oxygen	Oxygen is a chemical element in the periodic table. It has the symbol O and atomic number 8. Oxygen is the second most common element on Earth, composing around 46% of the mass of Earth's crust and 28% of the mass of Earth as a whole, and is the third most common element in the universe.
Apnea	Apnea is the absence of external breathing. During apnea there is no movement of the muscles of respiration and the volume of the lungs initially remains unchanged. .
Respiratory tract	In humans the respiratory tract is the part of the anatomy that has to do with the process of respiration or breathing.
Melatonin	Melatonin, 5-methoxy-N-acetyltryptamine, is a hormone produced by pinealocytes in the pineal gland (located in the brain) and also by the retina and GI tract. Production of melatonin by the pineal gland is stimulated by darkness and inhibited by light.
Hormone	A hormone is a chemical messenger from one cell to another. All multicellular organisms produce hormones. The best known hormones are those produced by endocrine glands of vertebrate animals, but hormones are produced by nearly every organ system and tissue type in a human or animal body. Hormone molecules are secreted directly into the bloodstream, they move by circulation or diffusion to their target cells, which may be nearby cells in the same tissue or cells of a distant organ of the body.
Circadian rhythm	Circadian rhythm is the name given to the roughly 24 hour cycles shown by physiological processes in plants, animals, fungi and cyanobacteria.
Sleep patterns	The order and timing of daily sleep and waking periods are called sleep patterns.
Light sleep	Stage 1 sleep, marked by small irregular brain waves and some alpha waves, is called light sleep.
Eye	An eye is an organ that detects light. Different kinds of light-sensitive organs are found in a variety of creatures. The simplest eyes do nothing but detect whether the surroundings are light or dark, while more complex eyes can distinguish shapes and colors.
Rapid eye movement	Rapid eye movement is the stage of sleep during which the most vivid dreams occur. During this stage, the eyes move rapidly, and the activity of the brain's neurons is quite similar to that during waking hours. It is the lightest form of sleep in that people awakened during this time usually feel alert and refreshed.
Heart rate	Heart rate is a term used to describe the frequency of the cardiac cycle. It is considered one of the four vital signs. Usually it is calculated as the number of contractions of the heart in one minute and expressed as "beats per minute".
Alcohol	Alcohol is a general term, applied to any organic compound in which a hydroxyl group (-OH) is bound to a carbon atom, which in turn is bound to other hydrogen and/or carbon atoms. The general formula for a simple acyclic alcohol is $C_nH_{2n+1}OH$.
Ritual	Formalized ceremonial behavior in which the members of a group or community regularly engage, is referred to as a ritual. In childbirth it is a repeated series of actions used by women as a way of dealing with the discomfort of labor.
Adrenal glands	The adrenal glands are the triangle-shaped endocrine glands that sit atop the kidneys; their name indicates that position. They are chiefly responsible for regulating the stress response through the synthesis of corticosteroids and catecholamines, including cortisol and adrenaline.
Adrenal gland	In mammals, the adrenal gland (also known as suprarenal glands or colloquially as kidney hats) are the triangle-shaped endocrine glands that sit atop the kidneys; their name indicates that position.

Go to **Cram101.com** for the Practice Tests for this Chapter.

Epinephrine	Epinephrine is a hormone and a neurotransmitter. Epinephrine plays a central role in the short-term stress reaction the physiological response to threatening or exciting conditions (fight-or-flight response). It is secreted by the adrenal medulla.
Adrenaline	Adrenaline is a hormone released by chromaffin cells and by some neurons in response to stress. Produces 'fight or flight' responses, including increased heart rate and blood sugar levels.
Adrenal	In mammals, the adrenal glands are the triangle-shaped endocrine glands that sit atop the kidneys. They are chiefly responsible for regulating the stress response through the synthesis of corticosteroids and catecholamines, including cortisol and adrenaline.
Gland	A gland is an organ in an animal's body that synthesizes a substance for release such as hormones, often into the bloodstream or into cavities inside the body or its outer surface.
Alcoholism	A disorder that involves long-term, repeated, uncontrolled, compulsive, and excessive use of alcoholic beverages and that impairs the drinker's health and work and social relationships is called alcoholism.
Personality disorder	A mental disorder characterized by a set of inflexible, maladaptive personality traits that keep a person from functioning properly in society is referred to as a personality disorder.
Minority group	A group of people who are defined on the basis of their ethnicity or race, is referred to as a minority group.
Crisis	A crisis is a temporary state of high anxiety where the persons usual coping mechanisims cease to work. This may have a result of disorganization or possibly personality growth.
Shock	Circulatory shock, a state of cardiac output that is insufficient to meet the body's physiological needs, with consequences ranging from fainting to death is referred to as shock. Insulin shock, a state of severe hypoglycemia caused by administration of insulin.
Humor	In traditional medicine practiced before the advent of modern technology, the four humours (or four humors) were four fluids that were thought to permeate the body and influence its health. A humor is any fluid substance in the body.
Coping mechanism	Coping mechanism is a pattern of behavior used to neutralize, deny, or counteract anxiety, a way to adapt to environmental stress.
Cohesion	The tendency of the molecules of a substance to stick together is referred to as cohesion.
Gender role	A cluster of behaviors that characterizes traditional female or male behaviors within a cultural setting is a gender role.
Consensus	General agreement is a consensus.
Conflict resolution	A concerted effort by all parties to resolve points in contention in a constructive manner is called conflict resolution.
Insight	Insight refers to a sudden awareness of the relationships among various elements that had previously appeared to be independent of one another.
Interferon	Interferon is a natural protein produced by the cells of the immune systems of most animals in response to challenges by foreign agents such as viruses, bacteria, parasites and tumor cells. They belong to the large class of glycoproteins known as cytokines.
Immunity	Resistance to the effects of specific disease-causing agents is called immunity.
Baseline	Measure of a particular behavior or process taken before the introduction of the independent variable or treatment is called the baseline.
Common traits	Common traits refer to personality traits that are shared by most members of a particular

28

	culture.
Melanoma	Melanoma is a malignant tumor of melanocytes. Melanocytes predominantly occur in the skin but can be found elsewhere, especially the eye. The vast majority of melanomas originate in the skin.
Skin	Skin is an organ of the integumentary system composed of a layer of tissues that protect underlying muscles and organs.
Gauge	The diameter of the needle is indicated by the needle gauge.
Drug interaction	A combined effect of two drugs that exceeds the addition of one drug's effects to the other is a drug interaction.
Mental illness	Mental illness is the term formerly used to mean psychological disorder but less preferred because it implies that the causes of the disorder can be found in a medical disease process.
Cardiovascular disease	Cardiovascular disease refers to afflictions in the mechanisms, including the heart, blood vessels, and their controllers, that are responsible for transporting blood to the body's tissues and organs. Psychological factors may play important roles in such diseases and their treatments.
World Health Organization	The World Health Organization (WHO) is a specialized agency of the United Nations, acting as a coordinating authority on international public health, headquartered in Geneva, Switzerland.
Substance abuse	Substance abuse refers to the overindulgence in and dependence on a stimulant, depressant, or other chemical substance, leading to effects that are detrimental to the individual's physical or mental health, or the welfare of others.
Panic disorder	A panic attack is a period of intense fear or discomfort, typically with an abrupt onset and usually lasting no more than thirty minutes. The disorder is strikingly different from other types of anxiety, in that panic attacks are very sudden, appear to be unprovoked, and are often disabling. People who have repeated attacks, or feel severe anxiety about having another attack are said to have panic disorder.
Social phobia	An irrational, excessive fear of public scrutiny is referred to as social phobia.
Phobia	A persistent, irrational fear of an object, situation, or activity that the person feels compelled to avoid is referred to as a phobia.
Anxiety disorder	Anxiety disorder is a blanket term covering several different forms of abnormal anxiety, fear, phobia and nervous condition, that come on suddenly and prevent pursuing normal daily routines.
Mood disorder	A mood disorder is a condition where the prevailing emotional mood is distorted or inappropriate to the circumstances.
Addiction	Addiction is an uncontrollable compulsion to repeat a behavior regardless of its consequences. Many drugs or behaviors can precipitate a pattern of conditions recognized as addiction, which include a craving for more of the drug or behavior, increased physiological tolerance to exposure, and withdrawal symptoms in the absence of the stimulus.
Bipolar disorder	Bipolar Disorder is a mood disorder typically characterized by fluctuations between manic and depressive states; and, more generally, atypical mood regulation and mood instability.
Common cold	An acute, self-limiting, and highly contagious virus infection of the upper respiratory tract that produces inflammation, profuse discharge, and other symptoms is referred to as the common cold.
Major	The diagnosis of a major depressive disorder occurs when an individual experiences a major

depressive disorder	depressive episode and depressed characteristics, such as lethargy and depression, last for 2 weeks or longer and daily functioning becomes impaired.
Catalyst	A chemical that speeds up a reaction but is not used up in the reaction is a catalyst.
Mental disorder	Mental disorder refers to a disturbance in a person's emotions, drives, thought processes, or behavior that involves serious and relatively prolonged distress and/or impairment in ability to function, is not simply a normal response to some event or set of events in the person's environment.
Insulin	Insulin is a polypeptide hormone that regulates carbohydrate metabolism. Apart from being the primary effector in carbohydrate homeostasis, it also has a substantial effect on small vessel muscle tone, controls storage and release of fat (triglycerides) and cellular uptake of both amino acids and some electrolytes.
Antidepressant	An antidepressant is a medication used primarily in the treatment of clinical depression. They are not thought to produce tolerance, although sudden withdrawal may produce adverse effects. They create little if any immediate change in mood and require between several days and several weeks to take effect.
Medical intervention	Medical intervention refers to the use of medications to treat a substance-related or mental disorder. This is usually done in combination with group/individual therapy or other treatment techniques.
Syndrome	Syndrome is the association of several clinically recognizable features, signs, symptoms, phenomena or characteristics which often occur together, so that the presence of one feature alerts the physician to the presence of the others
Thyroid	The thyroid is one of the larger endocrine glands in the body. It is located in the neck and produces hormones, principally thyroxine and triiodothyronine, that regulate the rate of metabolism and affect the growth and rate of function of many other systems in the body.
Chronic fatigue syndrome	Chronic fatigue syndrome is incapacitating exhaustion following only minimal exertion, accompanied by fever, headaches, muscle and joint pain, depression, and anxiety.
Multiple sclerosis	Multiple sclerosis affects neurons, the cells of the brain and spinal cord that carry information, create thought and perception, and allow the brain to control the body. Surrounding and protecting these neurons is a layer of fat, called myelin, which helps neurons carry electrical signals. MS causes gradual destruction of myelin (demyelination) in patches throughout the brain and/or spinal cord, causing various symptoms depending upon which signals are interrupted.
Psychotherapy	Psychotherapy is a set of techniques based on psychological principles intended to improve mental health, emotional or behavioral issues.
Clinical depression	Although nearly any mood with some element of sadness may colloquially be termed a depression, clinical depression is more than just a temporary state of sadness. Symptoms lasting two weeks or longer in duration, and of a severity that they begin to interfere with daily living.
Miscarriage	Miscarriage or spontaneous abortion is the natural or accidental termination of a pregnancy at a stage where the embryo or the fetus is incapable of surviving, generally defined at a gestation of prior to 20 weeks.
Menopause	Menopause is the physiological cessation of menstrual cycles associated with advancing age in species that experience such cycles. Menopause is sometimes referred to as change of life or climacteric.
Menstrual cycle	The menstrual cycle is the set of recurring physiological changes in a female's body that are under the control of the reproductive hormone system and necessary for reproduction. Besides

humans, only other great apes exhibit menstrual cycles, in contrast to the estrus cycle of most mammalian species.

Coronary	Referring to the heart or the blood vessels of the heart is referred to as coronary.
Coronary heart disease	Coronary heart disease is the end result of the accumulation of atheromatous plaques within the walls of the arteries that supply the myocardium (the muscle of the heart).
Mood disorders	Mood disorders refers to psychological disorders in which there is a primary disturbance in mood. Two main types are the depressive disorders and bipolar disorder.
Serotonin	Serotonin is a monoamine neurotransmitter synthesized in serotonergic neurons in the central nervous system and enterochromaffin cells in the gastrointestinal tract. It is believed to play an important part of the biochemistry of depression, migraine, bipolar disorder and anxiety.
Withdrawal symptoms	Withdrawal symptoms are physiological changes that occur when the use of a drug is stopped or dosage decreased.
Norepinephrine	Norepinephrine is a catecholamine and a phenethylamine with chemical formula $C_8H_{11}NO_3$. It is released from the adrenal glands as a hormone into the blood, but it is also a neurotransmitter in the nervous system where it is released from noradrenergic neurons during synaptic transmission.
Inhibitor	An inhibitor is a type of effector (biology) that decreases or prevents the rate of a chemical reaction. They are often called negative catalysts.
Reuptake	Reuptake is the reabsorption of a neurotransmitter by the molecular transporter of a pre-synaptic neuron after it has performed its function of transmitting a neural impulse.
Selective serotonin reuptake inhibitors	Selective serotonin reuptake inhibitors are a class of antidepressants. They act within the brain to increase the amount of the neurotransmitter, serotonin (5-hydroxytryptamine or 5-HT), in the synaptic gap by inhibiting its reuptake. It is often prescribed for depression.
Selective serotonin reuptake inhibitor	Selective serotonin reuptake inhibitor is a class of antidepressants for treating depression, anxiety disorders and some personality disorders. These drugs are designed to elevate the level of the neurotransmitter serotonin.
Older adult	Older adult is an adult over the age of 65.
Homosexual	Homosexual refers to referring to people who are sexually aroused by and interested in forming romantic relationships with people of the same gender.
Major depressive episode	A major depressive episode is a common and severe experience of depression. It includes feelings of worthlessness, disturbances in bodily activities such as sleep, loss of interest, and the inability to experience pleasure. It lasts for at least two weeks.
Major depression	Major depression is characterized by a severely depressed mood that persists for at least two weeks. Episodes of depression may start suddenly or slowly and can occur several times through a person's life. The disorder may be categorized as "single episode" or "recurrent" depending on whether previous episodes have been experienced before.
Interpersonal therapy	A brief psychotherapy designed to help depressed people better understand and cope with problems relating to their interpersonal relationships is referred to as interpersonal therapy.
Cognitive therapy	Cognitive therapy is a kind of psychotherapy used to treat depression, anxiety disorders, phobias, and other forms of mental disorder. It involves recognizing distorted thinking and learning how to replace it with more realistic thoughts and actions.

Go to **Cram101.com** for the Practice Tests for this Chapter.

Absorption	Absorption is a physical or chemical phenomenon or a process in which atoms, molecules, or ions enter some bulk phase - gas, liquid or solid material. In nutrition, amino acids are broken down through digestion, which begins in the stomach.
Tricyclic antidepressant	A tricyclic antidepressant is of a class of antidepressant drugs first used in the 1950s. They are named after the drugs' molecular structure, which contains three rings of atoms.
Antidepressants	Antidepressants are medications used primarily in the treatment of clinical depression. Antidepressants create little if any immediate change in mood and require between several days and several weeks to take effect.
Anesthesia	Anesthesia is the process of blocking the perception of pain and other sensations. This allows patients to undergo surgery and other procedures without the distress and pain they would otherwise experience.
General anesthesia	General anesthesia refers to the process of eliminating pain by putting the person to sleep.
Mania	Mania is a medical condition characterized by severely elevated mood. Mania is most usually associated with bipolar disorder, where episodes of mania may cyclically alternate with episodes of depression.
Adolescence	Adolescence is the period of psychological and social transition between childhood and adulthood (gender-specific manhood, or womanhood). As a transitional stage of human development it represents the period of time during which a juvenile matures into adulthood.
Irritability	Irritability is an excessive response to stimuli. Irritability takes many forms, from the contraction of a unicellular organism when touched to complex reactions involving all the senses of higher animals.
Euphoria	A feeling of well-being, extreme satiation, and satisfaction caused by many psychoactive drugs and certain behaviors, such as gambling and sex is referred to as euphoria.
Generalized anxiety disorder	Generalized anxiety disorder is an anxiety disorder that is characterized by uncontrollable worry about everyday things. The frequency, intensity, and duration of the worry are disproportionate to the actual source of worry, and such worry often interferes with daily functioning.
Specific phobia	A specific phobia is a generic term for anxiety disorders that amount to unreasonable or irrational fear or anxiety related with exposure to specific objects or situations. As a result, the affected persons tend to actively avoid these objects or situations.
Panic attack	An attack of overwhelming anxiety, fear, or terror is called panic attack.
Acute anxiety	Acute anxiety is a result of an imminent change or loss that disrupts one's since of security.
Acute	In medicine, an acute disease is a disease with either or both of: a rapid onset; and a short course (as opposed to a chronic course).
Incidence	In epidemiological studies of a particular disorder, the rate at which new cases occur in a given place at a given time is called incidence.
Hot flash	A hot flash is a symptom of menopause and changing hormone levels which typically expresses itself at night as periods of intense heat with sweating and rapid heartbeat and may typically last from two to thirty minutes on each occasion.
Stomach	The stomach is an organ in the alimentary canal used to digest food. It's primary function is not the absorption of nutrients from digested food; rather, the main job of the stomach is to break down large food molecules into smaller ones, so that they can be absorbed into the blood more easily.

Go to **Cram101.com** for the Practice Tests for this Chapter.

Cramp	A cramp is an unpleasant sensation caused by contraction, usually of a muscle. It can be caused by cold or overexertion.
Causation	The act of causing some effect is causation. Damage or harn that is caused by a breach of duty.
Heredity	Heredity refers to the transmission of genetic information from parent to offspring.
Behavioral therapy	The treatment of a mental disorder through the application of basic principles of conditioning and learning is called behavioral therapy.
Constant	A behavior or characteristic that does not vary from one observation to another is referred to as a constant.
Positron emission tomography	Positron Emission Tomography measures emissions from radioactively labeled chemicals that have been injected into the bloodstream. The greatest benefit is that different compounds can show blood flow and oxygen and glucose metabolism in the tissues of the working brain.
Psychological disorder	Mental processes and/or behavior patterns that cause emotional distress and/or substantial impairment in functioning is a psychological disorder.
Seasonal affective disorder	Seasonal affective disorder is an affective, or mood disorder. Most sufferers experience normal mental health throughout most of the year, but experience depressive symptoms in the winter.
Affective disorder	Affective disorder refers to any mood or emotional disorder, e.g., depression, bipolar affective disorder.
Carbohydrate	Carbohydrate is a chemical compound that contains oxygen, hydrogen, and carbon atoms. They consist of monosaccharide sugars of varying chain lengths and that have the general chemical formula $C_n(H_2O)_n$ or are derivatives of such.
Craving	Craving refers to the powerful desire to use a psychoactive drug or engage in a compulsive behavior. It is manifested in physiological changes, such as raised heart rate, sweating, anxiety, drop in body temperature, pupil dilation, and stomach muscle movements.
Apathy	Apathy is the lack of emotion, motivation, or enthusiasm. Apathy is a psychological term for a state of indifference where an individual is unresponsive or "indifferent" to aspects of emotional, social, or physical life.
Hypothalamus	Located below the thalamus, the hypothalamus links the nervous system to the endocrine system by synthesizing and secreting neurohormones often called releasing hormones because they function by stimulating the secretion of hormones from the anterior pituitary gland.
Light therapy	Light therapy consists of exposure to specific wavelengths of light using lasers, LEDs, fluorescent lamps, dichroic lamps or very bright, full-spectrum light, for a prescribed amount of time. It has proven effective in treating Acne vulgaris, seasonal affective disorder (SAD), and for some people it has ameliorated delayed sleep phase syndrome. It has recently been shown effective in non-seasonal depression.
Schizophrenia	Schizophrenia is characterized by persistent defects in the perception or expression of reality. A person suffering from untreated schizophrenia typically demonstrates grossly disorganized thinking, and may also experience delusions or auditory hallucinations
Hallucination	Hallucination refers to a perception in the absence of sensory stimulation that is confused with reality.
Auditory	Pertaining to the ear or to the sense of hearing is called auditory.
Scar	A scar results from the biologic process of wound repair in the skin and other tissues of the body. It is a connective tissue that fills the wound.

Go to **Cram101.com** for the Practice Tests for this Chapter.

Wound	A wound is type of physical trauma wherein the skin is torn, cut or punctured, or where blunt force trauma causes a contusion.
Dissociation	Dissociation is a general process in which complexes, molecules, or salts separate or split into smaller molecules, ions, or radicals, usually in a reversible manner.
Channel	Channel, in communications (sometimes called communications channel), refers to the medium used to convey information from a sender (or transmitter) to a receiver.
Puberty	A time in the life of a developing individual characterized by the increasing production of sex hormones, which cause it to reach sexual maturity is called puberty.
Magnetic resonance imaging	Magnetic resonance imaging refers to imaging technology that uses magnetism and radio waves to induce hydrogen nuclei in water molecules to emit faint radio signals. A computer creates images of the body from the radio signals.
Trimester	In human development, one of three 3-mnonth-long periods of pregnancy is called trimester.
Second trimester	The second trimester is the period of time extending from the 13th to the 27th week of gestation. During this period the embryo, now known as a fetus, is recognizable as human in form, but is not developed enough to be viable if born.
Psychoanalysis	Psychoanalysis refers to the school of psychology that emphasizes the importance of unconscious motives and conflicts as determinants of human behavior. It was Freud's method of exploring human personality.
Stigma	Stigma refers to a personal characteristic that at least some other individuals perceive negatively because that characteristic is different than those of the general population.
Diagnosis	In medicine, diagnosis is the process of identifying a medical condition or disease by its signs, symptoms, and from the results of various diagnostic procedures.
Clinician	A health professional authorized to provide services to people suffering from one or more pathologies is a clinician.
Antisocial	A person that cannot relate to others is said to be antisocial. They do not appear to experience a full range of human emotions.
Menstruation	Loss of blood and tissue from the uterine lining at the end of a female reproductive cycle are referred to as menstruation.
Risk factor	A risk factor is a variable associated with an increased risk of disease or infection but risk factors are not necessarily causal.
Rejection	Rejection is a response by caregivers where they distance themselves emotionally from a chronically ill patient. Although they provide physical care they tend to scold and and correct the patient continuously.
Mortality	The incidence of death in a population is mortality.
Counselor	A counselor is a mental health professional who specializes in helping people with problems not involving serious mental disorders.
Criterion	Criterion refers to a standard of comparison. For performance appraisal, it is the definition of good performance.
Psychiatrist	A psychiatrist is a physician who specializes in the diagnosis and treatment of psychological disorders.
Humanistic	Humanistic refers to any system of thought focused on subjective experience and human problems and potentials.
Contingency	Contingency refers to a close relationship, especially of a causal nature, between two

events, one of which regularly follows the other.

Gestalt therapy	Gestalt therapy is a form of psychotherapy, based on the experiential ideal of "here and now," and relationships with others and the world. By focusing the individual on their self-awareness as part of present reality, new insights can be made into their behavior, and they can engage in self-healing.
Maladaptive	In psychology, a behavior or trait is adaptive when it helps an individual adjust and function well within their social environment. A maladaptive behavior or trait is counterproductive to the individual.
Variable	A characteristic or aspect in which people, objects, events, or conditions vary is called variable.
Maladaptive behavior	Behavior that makes it difficult to adapt to the environment and meet the demands of day-to-day life is called maladaptive behavior.
Irrational beliefs	Self-defeating assumptions that are assumed by rational-emotive therapists to underlie psychological distress are referred to as irrational beliefs.
Clinical psychology	Clinical psychology is involved in the diagnosis, assessment, and treatment of patients with mental or behavioral disorders, and conducts research in these various areas.
Insight therapy	Insight therapy encourages self-awareness. They include the psychodynamic and humanistic therapies.
Psychoanalyst	A psychoanalyst is a specially trained therapist who attempts to treat the individual by uncovering and revealing to the individual otherwise subconscious factors that are contributing to some undesirable behavor.
Accreditation	Accreditation is the certification by a duly recognized body of the facilities, capability, objectivity, competence, and integrity of an agency, service or operational group or individual to provide the specific service(s) or operation(s) needed.
Group therapy	Group therapy is a form of psychotherapy during which one or several therapists treat a small group of clients together as a group. This may be more cost effective than individual therapy, and possibly even more effective.
Registered Nurse	A Registered Nurse is a professional nurse who often supervises the tasks performed by Licensed Practical Nurses, orderlies, medical assistants and nursing assistants. They provide direct care and make decisions regarding plans of care for individuals and groups of healthy, ill and injured people.
Assessment	In clinical practice, the process by which a mental health professional gathers and compiles information about a client for the purpose of describing the person's problems or disorder and developing a plan of treatment is an assessment.
Trial	In classical conditioning, any presentation of a stimulus or pair of stimuli is called a trial.

Stress	Stress refers to a condition that is a response to factors that change the human systems normal state.
Tissue	A collection of interconnected cells that perform a similar function within an organism is called tissue.
Stressor	A factor capable of stimulating a stress response is a stressor.
Adjustment	Adjustment is an attempt to cope with a given situation.
Adrenaline	Adrenaline is a hormone released by chromaffin cells and by some neurons in response to stress. Produces 'fight or flight' responses, including increased heart rate and blood sugar levels.
Hormone	A hormone is a chemical messenger from one cell to another. All multicellular organisms produce hormones. The best known hormones are those produced by endocrine glands of vertebrate animals, but hormones are produced by nearly every organ system and tissue type in a human or animal body. Hormone molecules are secreted directly into the bloodstream, they move by circulation or diffusion to their target cells, which may be nearby cells in the same tissue or cells of a distant organ of the body.
Gland	A gland is an organ in an animal's body that synthesizes a substance for release such as hormones, often into the bloodstream or into cavities inside the body or its outer surface.
Instincts	Inborn patterns of behavior that are biologically determined rather than learned are referred to as instincts.
Instinct	An inherited disposition to activate specific behavior patterns that are designed to reach certain goals is called instinct.
Course	Pattern of development and change of a disorder over time is a course.
Eye	An eye is an organ that detects light. Different kinds of light-sensitive organs are found in a variety of creatures. The simplest eyes do nothing but detect whether the surroundings are light or dark, while more complex eyes can distinguish shapes and colors.
Health	Health is a term that refers to a combination of the absence of illness, the ability to cope with everyday activities, physical fitness, and high quality of life.
Affect	Affect is the scientific term used to describe a subject's externally displayed mood. This can be assesed by the nurse by observing facial expression, tone of voice, and body language.
Irritability	Irritability is an excessive response to stimuli. Irritability takes many forms, from the contraction of a unicellular organism when touched to complex reactions involving all the senses of higher animals.
Depression	In everyday language depression refers to any downturn in mood, which may be relatively transitory and perhaps due to something trivial. This is differentiated from Clinical depression which is marked by symptoms that last two weeks or more and are so severe that they interfere with daily living.
Anxiety	Anxiety is a complex combination of the feeling of fear, apprehension and worry often accompanied by physical sensations such as palpitations, chest pain and/or shortness of breath.
Anger	Anger is an emotional response often based on a sensation or perception of threat to one's needs.
Arousal	Arousal is a physiological and psychological state involving the activation of the reticular activating system in the brain stem, the autonomic nervous system and the endocrine system, leading to increased heart rate and blood pressure and a condition of alertness and readiness

Go to **Cram101.com** for the Practice Tests for this Chapter.

	to respond.
Stress hormones	Group of hormones including cortico steroids, that are involved in the body's physiological stress response are referred to as stress hormones.
Brain	The part of the central nervous system involved in regulating and controlling body activity and interpreting information from the senses transmitted through the nervous system is referred to as the brain.
Nervous system	The nervous system of an animal coordinates the activity of the muscles, monitors the organs, constructs and processes input from the senses, and initiates actions.
Cortex	In anatomy and zoology the cortex is the outermost or superficial layer of an organ or the outer portion of the stem or root of a plant.
Autonomic nervous system	The autonomic nervous system is the part of the nervous system that is not consciously controlled. It is commonly divided into two usually antagonistic subsystems: the sympathetic and parasympathetic nervous system.
Cerebral cortex	The cerebral cortex is a brain structure in vertebrates. It is the outermost layer of the cerebrum and has a grey color. In the "higher" animals, the surface becomes folded. The cerebral cortex, made up of four lobes, is involved in many complex brain functions including memory, attention, perceptual awareness, "thinking", language and consciousness.
Central nervous system	The central nervous system comprized of the brain and spinal cord, represents the largest part of the nervous system. Together with the peripheral nervous system, it has a fundamental role in the control of behavior.
Sympathetic	The sympathetic nervous system activates what is often termed the "fight or flight response". It is an automatic regulation system, that is, one that operates without the intervention of conscious thought.
Sympathetic nervous system	The sympathetic nervous system activates what is often termed the "fight or flight response". Messages travel through in a bidirectional flow. Efferent messages can trigger changes in different parts of the body simultaneously.
Heart rate	Heart rate is a term used to describe the frequency of the cardiac cycle. It is considered one of the four vital signs. Usually it is calculated as the number of contractions of the heart in one minute and expressed as "beats per minute".
Parasympathetic nervous system	The parasympathetic nervous system is one of two divisions of the autonomic nervous system. It conserves energy as it slows the heart rate, increases intestinal and gland activity, and relaxes sphincter muscles in the gastro-intestinal tract. In other words, it acts to reverse the effects of the sympathetic nervous system.
Homeostasis	Homeostasis is the property of an open system, especially living organisms, to regulate its internal environment to maintain a stable, constant condition, by means of multiple dynamic equilibrium adjustments, controlled by interrelated regulation mechanisms.
Adaptation	A biological adaptation is an anatomical structure, physiological process or behavioral trait of an organism that has evolved over a period of time by the process of natural selection such that it increases the expected long-term reproductive success of the organism.
Resistance	Resistance refers to a nonspecific ability to ward off infection or disease regardless of whether the body has been previously exposed to it. A force that opposes the flow of a fluid such as air or blood. Compare with immunity.
Syndrome	Syndrome is the association of several clinically recognizable features, signs, symptoms, phenomena or characteristics which often occur together, so that the presence of one feature alerts the physician to the presence of the others

General adaptation syndrome	The predictable sequence of reactions that organisms show in response to stressors is called the general adaptation syndrome.
Digestive system	The organ system that ingests food, breaks it down into smaller chemical units, and absorbs the nutrient molecules is referred to as the digestive system.
Blood	Blood is a circulating tissue composed of fluid plasma and cells. The main function of blood is to supply nutrients (oxygen, glucose) and constitutional elements to tissues and to remove waste products.
Hypothalamus	Located below the thalamus, the hypothalamus links the nervous system to the endocrine system by synthesizing and secreting neurohormones often called releasing hormones because they function by stimulating the secretion of hormones from the anterior pituitary gland.
Epinephrine	Epinephrine is a hormone and a neurotransmitter. Epinephrine plays a central role in the short-term stress reaction the physiological response to threatening or exciting conditions (fight-or-flight response). It is secreted by the adrenal medulla.
Adrenal glands	The adrenal glands are the triangle-shaped endocrine glands that sit atop the kidneys; their name indicates that position. They are chiefly responsible for regulating the stress response through the synthesis of corticosteroids and catecholamines, including cortisol and adrenaline.
Adrenal gland	In mammals, the adrenal gland (also known as suprarenal glands or colloquially as kidney hats) are the triangle-shaped endocrine glands that sit atop the kidneys; their name indicates that position.
Cortisol	Cortisol is a corticosteroid hormone that is involved in the response to stress; it increases blood pressure and blood sugar levels and suppresses the immune system.
Adrenal	In mammals, the adrenal glands are the triangle-shaped endocrine glands that sit atop the kidneys. They are chiefly responsible for regulating the stress response through the synthesis of corticosteroids and catecholamines, including cortisol and adrenaline.
Adrenocortic-tropic hormone	Adrenocorticotropic hormone is a polypeptide hormone synthesised and secreted from corticotropes in the anterior lobe of the pituitary gland in response to the hormone corticotropin-releasing factor released by the hypothalamus. It stimulates the cortex of the adrenal gland and boosts the synthesis of corticosteroids, mainly glucocorticoids but also mineralcorticoids and sex steroids.
Control center	Control center refers to one of three interdependent components of homeostatic control mechanisms; determines the set point.
Bronchioles	The bronchioles are the first airway branches that no longer contain cartilage. They are branches of the bronchi, and are smaller than one millimetre in diameter.
Bronchiole	The bronchiole is the first airway branch that no longer contains cartilage. They are branches of the bronchi, and are smaller than one millimetre in diameter.
Glucose	Glucose, a simple monosaccharide sugar, is one of the most important carbohydrates and is used as a source of energy in animals and plants. Glucose is one of the main products of photosynthesis and starts respiration.
Air sac	Air sac is an anatomical structure unique to the dinosaur and bird respiratory system that allows unidirectional flow of air into the lungs and through the body
Oxygen	Oxygen is a chemical element in the periodic table. It has the symbol O and atomic number 8. Oxygen is the second most common element on Earth, composing around 46% of the mass of Earth's crust and 28% of the mass of Earth as a whole, and is the third most common element

in the universe.

Pupil	Pupil refers to the opening in the iris that admits light into the interior of the vertebrate eye. Muscles in the iris regulate its size.
Lungs	Lungs are the essential organs of respiration in air-breathing vertebrates. Their principal function is to transport oxygen from the atmosphere into the bloodstream, and to excrete carbon dioxide from the bloodstream into the atmosphere.
Liver	The liver is an organ in vertebrates, including humans. It plays a major role in metabolism and has a number of functions in the body including drug detoxification, glycogen storage, and plasma protein synthesis. It also produces bile, which is important for digestion.
Pituitary gland	The pituitary gland or hypophysis is an endocrine gland about the size of a pea that sits in the small, bony cavity (sella turcica) at the base of the brain. Its posterior lobe is connected to a part of the brain called the hypothalamus via the infundibulum (or stalk), giving rise to the tuberoinfundibular pathway.
Norepinephrine	Norepinephrine is a catecholamine and a phenethylamine with chemical formula $C_8H_{11}NO_3$. It is released from the adrenal glands as a hormone into the blood, but it is also a neurotransmitter in the nervous system where it is released from noradrenergic neurons during synaptic transmission.
Lead	Lead is a chemical element in the periodic table that has the symbol Pb and atomic number 82. A soft, heavy, toxic and malleable poor metal, lead is bluish white when freshly cut but tarnishes to dull gray when exposed to air. Lead is used in building construction, lead-acid batteries, bullets and shot, and is part of solder, pewter, and fusible alloys.
Immune system	The immune system is the system of specialized cells and organs that protect an organism from outside biological influences. When the immune system is functioning properly, it protects the body against bacteria and viral infections, destroying cancer cells and foreign substances.
Blood pressure	Blood pressure is the pressure exerted by the blood on the walls of the blood vessels.
Stress management	Stress management encompasses techniques intended to equip a person with effective coping mechanisms for dealing with psychological stress.
Aerobic	An aerobic organism is an organism that has an oxygen based metabolism. Aerobes, in a process known as cellular respiration, use oxygen to oxidize substrates (for example sugars and fats) in order to obtain energy.
Aerobic exercise	Exercise in which oxygen is used to produce ATP is aerobic exercise.
Cardiovascular disease	Cardiovascular disease refers to afflictions in the mechanisms, including the heart, blood vessels, and their controllers, that are responsible for transporting blood to the body's tissues and organs. Psychological factors may play important roles in such diseases and their treatments.
Hypertension	Hypertension is a medical condition where the blood pressure in the arteries is chronically elevated. Persistent hypertension is one of the risk factors for strokes, heart attacks, heart failure and arterial aneurysm, and is a leading cause of chronic renal failure.
Activation	As reflected by facial expressions, the degree of arousal a person is experiencing is referred to as activation.
Mortality	The incidence of death in a population is mortality.
Asthma	Asthma is a complex disease characterized by bronchial hyperresponsiveness (BHR), inflammation, mucus production and intermittent airway obstruction.

Ulcer	An ulcer is an open sore of the skin, eyes or mucous membrane, often caused by an initial abrasion and generally maintained by an inflammation and/or an infection.
Pain	Pain is an unpleasant sensation which may be associated with actual or potential tissue damage and which may have physical and emotional components.
Susceptibility	The degree of resistance of a host to a pathogen is susceptibility.
Mental health	Mental health refers to the 'thinking' part of psychosocial health; includes your values, attitudes, and beliefs.
Legitimacy	The generally held belief that a particular social institution is just and valid is legitimacy.
Theory	Theory refers to an explanatory statement, or set of statements, that concisely summarizes the state of knowledge on a phenomenon and provides direction for further study.
Assault	Assault is a crime of violence against another person that intentionally instills fear and creates a reasonable aprehension of harm.
Host	Host is an organism that harbors a parasite, mutual partner, or commensal partner; or a cell infected by a virus.
Assessment	In clinical practice, the process by which a mental health professional gathers and compiles information about a client for the purpose of describing the person's problems or disorder and developing a plan of treatment is an assessment.
Survey	A method of scientific investigation in which a large sample of people answer questions about their attitudes or behavior is referred to as a survey.
Conscious	Conscious refers to the thoughts, feelings, sensations, or memories of which a person is aware at any given moment.
Muscle	Muscle is a contractile form of tissue. It is one of the four major tissue types, the other three being epithelium, connective tissue and nervous tissue. Muscle contraction is used to move parts of the body, as well as to move substances within the body.
Blood vessel	A blood vessel is a part of the circulatory system and function to transport blood throughout the body. The most important types, arteries and veins, are so termed because they carry blood away from or towards the heart, respectively.
Inflammation	Inflammation is the first response of the immune system to infection or irritation and may be referred to as the innate cascade.
Viral	Viral phenomena are objects or patterns able to replicate themselves or convert other objects into copies of themselves when these objects are exposed to them.
Immune response	The body's defensive reaction to invasion by bacteria, viral agents, or other foreign substances is called immune response.
White blood cell	The white blood cell is a a component of blood. They help to defend the body against infectious disease and foreign materials as part of the immune system.
Older adult	Older adult is an adult over the age of 65.
Protein	A protein is a complex, high-molecular-weight organic compound that consists of amino acids joined by peptide bonds. They are essential to the structure and function of all living cells and viruses. Many are enzymes or subunits of enzymes.
Osteoporosis	Osteoporosis is a disease of bone in which bone mineral density (BMD) is reduced, bone microarchitecture is disrupted, the amount and variety of non-collagenous proteins in bone is changed, and a concomitantly fracture risk is increased.

Diabetes	Diabetes is a medical disorder characterized by varying or persistent elevated blood sugar levels, especially after eating. All types of diabetes share similar symptoms and complications at advanced stages: dehydration and ketoacidosis, cardiovascular disease, chronic renal failure, retinal damage which can lead to blindness, nerve damage which can lead to erectile dysfunction, gangrene with risk of amputation of toes, feet, and even legs.
Cancer	Cancer is a class of diseases or disorders characterized by uncontrolled division of cells and the ability of these cells to invade other tissues, either by direct growth into adjacent tissue through invasion or by implantation into distant sites by metastasis.
Control group	A group that does not receive the treatment effect in an experiment is referred to as the control group or sometimes as the comparison group.
Dementia	Dementia is progressive decline in cognitive function due to damage or disease in the brain beyond what might be expected from normal aging.
Isolation	Isolation refers to the degree to which groups do not live in the same communities.
Vaccine	A harmless variant or derivative of a pathogen used to stimulate a host organism's immune system to mount a long-term defense against the pathogen is referred to as vaccine.
Wound	A wound is type of physical trauma wherein the skin is torn, cut or punctured, or where blunt force trauma causes a contusion.
Infection	The invasion and multiplication of microorganisms in body tissues is called an infection.
Lifestyle	The culturally, socially, economically, and environmentally conditioned complex of actions characteristic of an individual, group, or community as a pattern of habituated behavior over time that is health related but not necessarily health directed is a lifestyle.
Infectious disease	In medicine, infectious disease or communicable disease is disease caused by a biological agent such as by a virus, bacterium or parasite. This is contrasted to physical causes, such as burns or chemical ones such as through intoxication.
Virus	Obligate intracellular parasite of living cells consisting of an outer capsid and an inner core of nucleic acid is referred to as virus. The term virus usually refers to those particles that infect eukaryotes whilst the term bacteriophage or phage is used to describe those infecting prokaryotes.
Hypothesis	A specific statement about behavior or mental processes that is testable through research is a hypothesis.
Sugar	A sugar is the simplest molecule that can be identified as a carbohydrate. These include monosaccharides and disaccharides, trisaccharides and the oligosaccharides. The term "glyco-" indicates the presence of a sugar in an otherwise non-carbohydrate substance.
Counselor	A counselor is a mental health professional who specializes in helping people with problems not involving serious mental disorders.
Life stages	Widely recognized periods of life corresponding to broad phases of development is referred to as life stages.
Pancreas	The pancreas is a retroperitoneal organ that serves two functions: exocrine - it produces pancreatic juice containing digestive enzymes, and endocrine - it produces several important hormones, namely insulin.
Insulin	Insulin is a polypeptide hormone that regulates carbohydrate metabolism. Apart from being the primary effector in carbohydrate homeostasis, it also has a substantial effect on small vessel muscle tone, controls storage and release of fat (triglycerides) and cellular uptake of both amino acids and some electrolytes.

Organ	Organ refers to a structure consisting of several tissues adapted as a group to perform specific functions.
Drug abuse	Drug abuse has a wide range of definitions, all of them relating either to the misuse or overuse of a psychoactive drug or performance enhancing drug for a non-therapeutic or non-medical effect, or referring to any use of illegal drug in the absence of a required, yet practically impossible to get, license from a government authority.
Addiction	Addiction is an uncontrollable compulsion to repeat a behavior regardless of its consequences. Many drugs or behaviors can precipitate a pattern of conditions recognized as addiction, which include a craving for more of the drug or behavior, increased physiological tolerance to exposure, and withdrawal symptoms in the absence of the stimulus.
Mental illness	Mental illness is the term formerly used to mean psychological disorder but less preferred because it implies that the causes of the disorder can be found in a medical disease process.
Coronary	Referring to the heart or the blood vessels of the heart is referred to as coronary.
Coronary heart disease	Coronary heart disease is the end result of the accumulation of atheromatous plaques within the walls of the arteries that supply the myocardium (the muscle of the heart).
Cumulative effect	cumulative effect is a condition that occurs when the body cannot metabolize a drug before additional doses are administered.
Adolescence	Adolescence is the period of psychological and social transition between childhood and adulthood (gender-specific manhood, or womanhood). As a transitional stage of human development it represents the period of time during which a juvenile matures into adulthood.
Value	Value is worth in general, and it is thought to be connected to reasons for certain practices, policies, actions, beliefs or emotions. Value is "that which one acts to gain and/or keep."
Solution	Solution refers to homogenous mixture formed when a solute is dissolved in a solvent.
Substance abuse	Substance abuse refers to the overindulgence in and dependence on a stimulant, depressant, or other chemical substance, leading to effects that are detrimental to the individual's physical or mental health, or the welfare of others.
Stomach	The stomach is an organ in the alimentary canal used to digest food. It's primary function is not the absorption of nutrients from digested food; rather, the main job of the stomach is to break down large food molecules into smaller ones, so that they can be absorbed into the blood more easily.
Skin	Skin is an organ of the integumentary system composed of a layer of tissues that protect underlying muscles and organs.
Abdomen	The abdomen is a part of the body. In humans, and in many other vertebrates, it is the region between the thorax and the pelvis. In fully developed insects, the abdomen is the third (or posterior) segment, after the head and thorax.
Trial	In classical conditioning, any presentation of a stimulus or pair of stimuli is called a trial.
Population	Population refers to all members of a well-defined group of organisms, events, or things.
Ethnicity	While ethnicity and race are related concepts, the concept of ethnicity is rooted in the idea of social groups, marked especially by shared nationality, tribal affiliation, religious faith, shared language, or cultural and traditional origins and backgrounds, whereas race is rooted in the idea of biological classification of Homo sapiens to subspecies according to chosen genotypic and/or phenotypic traits.

Constant	A behavior or characteristic that does not vary from one observation to another is referred to as a constant.
Channel	Channel, in communications (sometimes called communications channel), refers to the medium used to convey information from a sender (or transmitter) to a receiver.
Neuron	The neuron is a major class of cells in the nervous system. In vertebrates, they are found in the brain, the spinal cord and in the nerves and ganglia of the peripheral nervous system, and their primary role is to process and transmit neural information.
Acquired immunodeficiency syndrome	Acquired Immunodeficiency Syndrome is defined as a collection of symptoms and infections resulting from the depletion of the immune system caused by infection with the human immunodeficiency virus, commonly called HIV.
Multiple sclerosis	Multiple sclerosis affects neurons, the cells of the brain and spinal cord that carry information, create thought and perception, and allow the brain to control the body. Surrounding and protecting these neurons is a layer of fat, called myelin, which helps neurons carry electrical signals. MS causes gradual destruction of myelin (demyelination) in patches throughout the brain and/or spinal cord, causing various symptoms depending upon which signals are interrupted.
Immunodeficiency	Immunodeficiency is a state in which the immune system's ability to fight infectious disease is compromized or entirely absent. Most cases of immunodeficiency are either congenital or acquired.
Hardiness	A personality characteristic associated with a lower rate of stress-related illness, consisting of three components: commitment, challenge, and control is a hardiness.
Heart attack	A heart attack, is a serious, sudden heart condition usually characterized by varying degrees of chest pain or discomfort, weakness, sweating, nausea, vomiting, and arrhythmias, sometimes causing loss of consciousness. It occurs when the blood supply to a part of the heart is interrupted, causing death and scarring of the local heart tissue.
Base	The common definition of a base is a chemical compound that absorbs hydronium ions when dissolved in water (a proton acceptor). An alkali is a special example of a base, where in an aqueous environment, hydroxide ions are donated.
Locus of control	The place to which an individual attributes control over the receiving of reinforcers -either inside or outside the self is referred to as locus of control.
Outcome	Outcome is the impact of care provided to a patient. They can be positive, such as the ability to walk freely as a result of rehabilitation, or negative, such as the occurrence of bedsores as a result of lack of mobility of a patient.
Young adult	An young adult is someone between the ages of 20 and 40 years old.
Acute	In medicine, an acute disease is a disease with either or both of: a rapid onset; and a short course (as opposed to a chronic course).
Rape	Forcible sexual intercourse with a person who does not consent to it is rape.
Acute stress disorder	Acute stress disorder is a psychological condition arising in response to a terrifying event.
Stress disorder	A significant emotional disturbance caused by stresses outside the range of normal human experience is referred to as stress disorder.
Trauma	Trauma refers to a severe physical injury or wound to the body caused by an external force, or a psychological shock having a lasting effect on mental life.
Dissociation	Dissociation is a general process in which complexes, molecules, or salts separate or split

into smaller molecules, ions, or radicals, usually in a reversible manner.

Amnesia	Amnesia is a condition in which memory is disturbed. The causes of amnesia are organic or functional. Organic causes include damage to the brain, through trauma or disease, or use of certain (generally sedative) drugs.
Dissociative amnesia	Dissociative amnesia is marked by loss of memory or self-identity, thought to stem from psychological conflict or trauma; skills and general knowledge are usually retained. Previously termed psychogenic amnesia.
Acute anxiety	Acute anxiety is a result of an imminent change or loss that disrupts one's since of security.
Crisis	A crisis is a temporary state of high anxiety where the persons usual coping mechanisims cease to work. This may have a result of disorganization or possibly personality growth.
Antianxiety drugs	Drugs that can reduce a person's level of excitability while increasing feelings of well-being are called antianxiety drugs.
Alcohol	Alcohol is a general term, applied to any organic compound in which a hydroxyl group (-OH) is bound to a carbon atom, which in turn is bound to other hydrogen and/or carbon atoms. The general formula for a simple acyclic alcohol is $C_nH_{2n+1}OH$.
Independence	The condition in which one variable has no effect on another is referred to as independence.
Developmental task	Developmental task refers to any personal change that must take place for optimal development.
Anxiety disorder	Anxiety disorder is a blanket term covering several different forms of abnormal anxiety, fear, phobia and nervous condition, that come on suddenly and prevent pursuing normal daily routines.
Eating disorders	Psychological disorders characterized by distortion of the body image and gross disturbances in eating patterns are called eating disorders.
Centers for Disease Control and Prevention	The Centers for Disease Control and Prevention in Atlanta, Georgia, is recognized as the lead United States agency for protecting the public health and safety of people by providing credible information to enhance health decisions, and promoting health through strong partnerships with state health departments and other organizations.
Chronic disease	Disease of long duration often not detected in its early stages and from which the patient will not recover is referred to as a chronic disease.
Stress inoculation	Use of positive coping statements to control fear and anxiety is a form of stress inoculation.
Freezing	Freezing is the process in which blood is frozen and all of the plasma and 99% of the WBCs are eliminated when thawing takes place and the nontransferable cryoprotectant is removed.
Introspection	Deliberate looking into one's own mind to examine one's own thoughts and feelings is called introspection.
Irrational beliefs	Self-defeating assumptions that are assumed by rational-emotive therapists to underlie psychological distress are referred to as irrational beliefs.
Risk factor	A risk factor is a variable associated with an increased risk of disease or infection but risk factors are not necessarily causal.
Cholesterol	Cholesterol is a steroid, a lipid, and an alcohol, found in the cell membranes of all body tissues, and transported in the blood plasma of all animals. It is an important component of the membranes of cells, providing stability; it makes the membrane's fluidity stable over a bigger temperature interval.

Atherosclerosis	Process by which a fatty substance or plaque builds up inside arteries to form obstructions is called atherosclerosis.
Autonomy	Self-direction is referred to as autonomy. The ability to function in an independent manner.
Management techniques	Combining praise, recognition, approval, rules, and reasoning to enforce child discipline are referred to as management techniques.
Identity	The distinguishing character of the individual: who each of us is, what our roles are, and what we are capable of is called identity.
Alcoholic	An alcoholic is dependent on alcohol as characterized by craving, loss of control, physical dependence and withdrawal symptoms, and tolerance.
Dehydration	Dehydration is the removal of water from an object. Medically, dehydration is a serious and potentially life-threatening condition in which the body contains an insufficient volume of water for normal functioning.
Mantra	A mantra is a religious syllable or poem, typically from the Sanskrit language. Their use varies according to the school and philosophy associated with the mantra. They are primarily used as spiritual conduits, words and vibrations that instill one-pointed concentration in the devotee..
Chronic pain	Chronic pain is defined as pain that has lasted 6 months or longer.
Acupuncture	Acupuncture is a technique of inserting and manipulating needles into specific points on the body. Accordingly this will restore health and well-being.
Meridians	The concept of meridians arises from the techniques and doctrines of traditional Chinese medicine including acupuncture and acupressure. According to these practices, the body's vital energy, "qi", circulates through the body along specific interconnected channels called meridians.
Medicine	Medicine is the branch of health science and the sector of public life concerned with maintaining or restoring human health through the study, diagnosis and treatment of disease and injury.
Complement	Complement is a group of proteins of the complement system, found in blood serum which act in concert with antibodies to achieve the destruction of non-self particles such as foreign blood cells or bacteria.
Endorphins	Endorphins refer to neurotransmitters that are composed of amino acids and that are functionally similar to morphine.
Endorphin	Endorphin is an endogenous opioid biochemical compound. They are peptides produced by the pituitary gland and the hypothalamus in vertebrates, and they resemble the opiates in their abilities to produce analgesia and a sense of well-being.
Metabolic rate	Energy expended by the body per unit time is called metabolic rate.
Hyperactivity	Hyperactivity can be described as a state in which a individual is abnormally easily excitable and exuberant. Strong emotional reactions and a very short span of attention is also typical for the individual.
Megadose	Generally an intake of a nutrient in excess of 10 times human need is called megadose.
Vitamin	An organic compound other than a carbohydrate, lipid, or protein that is needed for normal metabolism but that the body cannot synthesize in adequate amounts is called a vitamin.
Assess	Assess is to systematically and continuously collect, validate, and communicate patient data.
Terminal illness	Terminal illness is a medical term popularized in the 20th century for an active and

Go to **Cram101.com** for the Practice Tests for this Chapter.

	progressive disease which cannot be cured and is expected to lead to death. Palliative care is often prescribed to manage symptoms and improve quality of life.
Biofeedback	Biofeedback is the process of measuring and quantifying an aspect of a subject's physiology, analyzing the data, and then feeding back the information to the subject in a form that allows the subject to enact physiological change.
Hypnosis	Hypnosis is a psychological state whose existence and effects are strongly debated. Some believe that it is a state under which the subject's mind becomes so suggestible that the hypnotist, the one who induces the state, can establish communication with the subconscious mind of the subject and command behavior that the subject would not choose to perform in a conscious state.
Right hemisphere	The brain is divided into left and right cerebral hemispheres. Popular psychology has suggested that the right hemisphere is responsible for creativity and emotion.
Acupressure	Acupressure involves placing physical pressure by hand, elbow, or with the aid of various devices on different acupuncture points on the surface of the body.
Buffer	A chemical substance that resists changes in pH by accepting H^+ ions from or donating H^+ ions to solutions is called a buffer.
Serum	Serum is the same as blood plasma except that clotting factors (such as fibrin) have been removed. Blood plasma contains fibrinogen.
Ambivalence	The simultaneous holding of strong positive and negative emotional attitudes toward the same situation or person is called ambivalence.
Lymphoma	Lymphoma is any of a variety of cancer that begins in the lymphatic system. In technical terms, lymphoma denotes malignancies of lymphocytes or, more rarely, of histiocytes.
Melanoma	Melanoma is a malignant tumor of melanocytes. Melanocytes predominantly occur in the skin but can be found elsewhere, especially the eye. The vast majority of melanomas originate in the skin.
Connectedness	Connectedness refers to according to Cooper and her colleagues, connectedness consists of two dimensions: mutuality and permeability.
Activities of daily living	Activities of daily living is a way to describe the functional status of a person.
Confidentiality	Confidentiality refers to an ethical principle associated with several professions (eg, medicine, law, religion, journalism,). In ethics, and in law, some types of communication between a person and one of these professionals are "privileged" and may not be discussed or divulged to third parties. In those jurisdictions in which the law makes provision for such confidentiality, there are usually penalties for its violation.
Mindfulness	Awareness and acceptance of the reality of the present moment are referred to as mindfulness.
Concept	A mental category used to class together objects, relations, events, abstractions, or qualities that have common properties is called concept.
Wellness	A dimension of health beyond the absence of disease or infirmity, including social, emotional, and spiritual aspects of health is called wellness.
Cardiovascular system	The circulatory system or cardiovascular system is the organ system which circulates blood around the body of most animals.
Blocking	A sudden break or interuption in the flow of thinking or speech that is seen as an absence in thought is refered to as blocking.
Insight	Insight refers to a sudden awareness of the relationships among various elements that had

	previously appeared to be independent of one another.
Intuition	Quick, impulsive thought that does not make use of formal logic or clear reasoning is referred to as intuition.
Psychoneuroi-munology	Psychoneuroimmunology is a specialist field of research that studies the connection between the brain, or mental states, and the immunal and hormonal systems of the human body.
Coping mechanism	Coping mechanism is a pattern of behavior used to neutralize, deny, or counteract anxiety, a way to adapt to environmental stress.
Intentional injuries	Injuries done on purpose with intent to harm are intentional injuries.

Course	Pattern of development and change of a disorder over time is a course.
Homicide	Death that results from intent to injure or kill is referred to as homicide.
Assault	Assault is a crime of violence against another person that intentionally instills fear and creates a reasonable aprehension of harm.
Concept	A mental category used to class together objects, relations, events, abstractions, or qualities that have common properties is called concept.
Outcome	Outcome is the impact of care provided to a patient. They can be positive, such as the ability to walk freely as a result of rehabilitation, or negative, such as the occurrence of bedsores as a result of lack of mobility of a patient.
Intentional injuries	Injuries done on purpose with intent to harm are intentional injuries.
Hate crimes	Violence committed against people because of their race, ethnicity, disability, religion, or sexual orientation are hate crimes.
Rape	Forcible sexual intercourse with a person who does not consent to it is rape.
Public health	Public health is concerned with threats to the overall health of a community based on population health analysis.
Health	Health is a term that refers to a combination of the absence of illness, the ability to cope with everyday activities, physical fitness, and high quality of life.
Survey	A method of scientific investigation in which a large sample of people answer questions about their attitudes or behavior is referred to as a survey.
Centers for Disease Control and Prevention	The Centers for Disease Control and Prevention in Atlanta, Georgia, is recognized as the lead United States agency for protecting the public health and safety of people by providing credible information to enhance health decisions, and promoting health through strong partnerships with state health departments and other organizations.
Chronic disease	Disease of long duration often not detected in its early stages and from which the patient will not recover is referred to as a chronic disease.
Population	Population refers to all members of a well-defined group of organisms, events, or things.
Elderly	Old age consists of ages nearing the average life span of human beings, and thus the end of the human life cycle. Euphemisms for older people include advanced adult, elderly, and senior or senior citizen.
Statistics	Statistics is a type of data analysis which practice includes the planning, summarizing, and interpreting of observations of a system possibly followed by predicting or forecasting of future events based on a mathematical model of the system being observed.
Statistic	A statistic is an observable random variable of a sample.
Affect	Affect is the scientific term used to describe a subject's externally displayed mood. This can be assesed by the nurse by observing facial expression, tone of voice, and body language.
World Health Organization	The World Health Organization (WHO) is a specialized agency of the United Nations, acting as a coordinating authority on international public health, headquartered in Geneva, Switzerland.
Child abuse	Child abuse is the physical or psychological maltreatment of a child.
Intervention	Intervention refers to a planned attempt to break through addicts' or abusers' denial and get them into treatment. Interventions most often occur when legal, workplace, health, relationship, or financial problems have become intolerable.

69

Culture	Culture, generally refers to patterns of human activity and the symbolic structures that give such activity significance.
Rehabilitation	Rehabilitation is the restoration of lost capabilities, or the treatment aimed at producing it. Also refers to treatment for dependency on psychoactive substances such as alcohol, prescription drugs, and illicit drugs such as cocaine, heroin or amphetamines.
Helplessness	A maladaptive pattern of achievement behavior in which children avoid challenge, do not persist in the face of difficulty, and tend to attribute their failure on tasks to a lack of ability rather than a lack of effort or an inappropriate strategy is referred to as helplessness.
Ethnicity	While ethnicity and race are related concepts, the concept of ethnicity is rooted in the idea of social groups, marked especially by shared nationality, tribal affiliation, religious faith, shared language, or cultural and traditional origins and backgrounds, whereas race is rooted in the idea of biological classification of Homo sapiens to subspecies according to chosen genotypic and/or phenotypic traits.
Alcohol	Alcohol is a general term, applied to any organic compound in which a hydroxyl group (-OH) is bound to a carbon atom, which in turn is bound to other hydrogen and/or carbon atoms. The general formula for a simple acyclic alcohol is $C_nH_{2n+1}OH$.
Stress	Stress refers to a condition that is a response to factors that change the human systems normal state.
Lead	Lead is a chemical element in the periodic table that has the symbol Pb and atomic number 82. A soft, heavy, toxic and malleable poor metal, lead is bluish white when freshly cut but tarnishes to dull gray when exposed to air. Lead is used in building construction, lead-acid batteries, bullets and shot, and is part of solder, pewter, and fusible alloys.
Trial	In classical conditioning, any presentation of a stimulus or pair of stimuli is called a trial.
Crisis	A crisis is a temporary state of high anxiety where the persons usual coping mechanisims cease to work. This may have a result of disorganization or possibly personality growth.
Aggression	The intentional verbal or non verbal infliction of injury or harm on another person is called aggression.
Anger	Anger is an emotional response often based on a sensation or perception of threat to one's needs.
Substance abuse	Substance abuse refers to the overindulgence in and dependence on a stimulant, depressant, or other chemical substance, leading to effects that are detrimental to the individual's physical or mental health, or the welfare of others.
Tolerance	Drug tolerance occurs when a subject's reaction to a drug decreases so that larger doses are required to achieve the same effect.
Acute	In medicine, an acute disease is a disease with either or both of: a rapid onset; and a short course (as opposed to a chronic course).
Anxiety	Anxiety is a complex combination of the feeling of fear, apprehension and worry often accompanied by physical sensations such as palpitations, chest pain and/or shortness of breath.
Psychoactive substance	A psychoactive substance is a chemical that alters brain function, resulting in temporary changes in perception, mood, consciousness, or behavior. Such drugs are often used for recreational and spiritual purposes, as well as in medicine, especially for treating neurological and psychological illnesses.

Cocaine	Cocaine is a crystalline tropane alkaloid that is obtained from the leaves of the coca plant. It is a stimulant of the central nervous system and an appetite suppressant, creating what has been described as a euphoric sense of happiness and increased energy.
Illicit drugs	Illicit drugs refers to drugs whose use, possession, cultivation, manufacture, and/or sale are against the law because they are generally recognized as harmful.
Depression	In everyday language depression refers to any downturn in mood, which may be relatively transitory and perhaps due to something trivial. This is differentiated from Clinical depression which is marked by symptoms that last two weeks or more and are so severe that they interfere with daily living.
Pain	Pain is an unpleasant sensation which may be associated with actual or potential tissue damage and which may have physical and emotional components.
Intolerance	Intolerance refers to a type of interaction in which two or more drugs produce extremely uncomfortable symptoms.
Value	Value is worth in general, and it is thought to be connected to reasons for certain practices, policies, actions, beliefs or emotions. Value is "that which one acts to gain and/or keep."
Thrill	Thrill is a vibration felt when the hand is placed flat on the chest; caused by abnormal blood flow through the heart as a result of disease.
Base	The common definition of a base is a chemical compound that absorbs hydronium ions when dissolved in water (a proton acceptor). An alkali is a special example of a base, where in an aqueous environment, hydroxide ions are donated.
Drug abuse	Drug abuse has a wide range of definitions, all of them relating either to the misuse or overuse of a psychoactive drug or performance enhancing drug for a non-therapeutic or non-medical effect, or referring to any use of illegal drug in the absence of a required, yet practically impossible to get, license from a government authority.
Evaluation	The fifth step of the nursing process where nursing care and the patient's goal achievement are measured is the evaluation.
Subculture	A subculture is a set of people with a distinct set of behavior and beliefs that differentiate them from a larger culture of which they are a part.
Risk factor	A risk factor is a variable associated with an increased risk of disease or infection but risk factors are not necessarily causal.
Learning disabilities	General term for learning disorders, communication disorders, and motor skills disorder is referred to as learning disabilities.
Learning disability	A learning disability exists when there is a significant discrepancy between one's ability and achievement.
Bioterrorism	Bioterrorism is terrorism using germ warfare, an intentional human release of a naturally-occurring or human-modified toxin or biological agent.
Assess	Assess is to systematically and continuously collect, validate, and communicate patient data.
Stressor	A factor capable of stimulating a stress response is a stressor.
Anthrax	Anthrax refers to an infectious disease of animals caused by ingesting Bacillus anthracis spores. Can also occur in humans and is sometimes called woolsorter's disease.
Agent	Agent refers to an epidemiological term referring to the organism or object that transmits a disease from the environment to the host.

Mortality	The incidence of death in a population is mortality.
Pathogen	A pathogen or infectious agent is a biological agent that causes disease or illness to its host. The term is most often used for agents that disrupt the normal physiology of a multicellular animal or plant.
Bacillus	Bacillus is a genus of rod-shaped bacteria.
Host	Host is an organism that harbors a parasite, mutual partner, or commensal partner; or a cell infected by a virus.
Infectious disease	In medicine, infectious disease or communicable disease is disease caused by a biological agent such as by a virus, bacterium or parasite. This is contrasted to physical causes, such as burns or chemical ones such as through intoxication.
Inhalation	Inhalation is the movement of air from the external environment, through the airways, into the alveoli during breathing.
Infection	The invasion and multiplication of microorganisms in body tissues is called an infection.
Skin	Skin is an organ of the integumentary system composed of a layer of tissues that protect underlying muscles and organs.
Common cold	An acute, self-limiting, and highly contagious virus infection of the upper respiratory tract that produces inflammation, profuse discharge, and other symptoms is referred to as the common cold.
Shock	Circulatory shock, a state of cardiac output that is insufficient to meet the body's physiological needs, with consequences ranging from fainting to death is referred to as shock. Insulin shock, a state of severe hypoglycemia caused by administration of insulin.
Diarrhea	Diarrhea or diarrhoea is a condition in which the sufferer has frequent and watery, chunky, or loose bowel movements.
Fever	Fever (also known as pyrexia, or a febrile response, and archaically known as ague) is a medical symptom that describes an increase in internal body temperature to levels that are above normal (37°C, 98.6°F).
Immunization	Use of a vaccine to protect the body against specific disease-causing agents is called immunization.
Antibiotic	Antibiotic refers to substance such as penicillin or streptomycin that is toxic to microorganisms. Usually a product of a particular microorvanism or plant.
Botulism	Botulism is a rare but serious paralytic illness caused by a nerve toxin, botulin, that is produced by the bacterium Clostridium botulinum.
Muscle	Muscle is a contractile form of tissue. It is one of the four major tissue types, the other three being epithelium, connective tissue and nervous tissue. Muscle contraction is used to move parts of the body, as well as to move substances within the body.
Toxin	Toxin refers to a microbial product or component that can injure another cell or organism at low concentrations. Often the term refers to a poisonous protein, but toxins may be lipids and other substances.
Intestine	The intestine is the portion of the alimentary canal extending from the stomach to the anus and, in humans and mammals, consists of two segments, the small intestine and the large intestine. The intestine is the part of the body responsible for extracting nutrition from food.
Double vision	Diplopia, colloquially known as double vision, is the perception of two images from a single object. The images may be horizontal, vertical, or diagonal.

Blood	Blood is a circulating tissue composed of fluid plasma and cells. The main function of blood is to supply nutrients (oxygen, glucose) and constitutional elements to tissues and to remove waste products.
Septic shock	Septic shock is a serious medical condition causing such effects as multiple organ failure and death in response to infection and sepsis.
Pneumonia	Pneumonia is an illness of the lungs and respiratory system in which the microscopic, air-filled sacs (alveoli) responsible for absorbing oxygen from the atmosphere become inflamed and flooded with fluid.
Epidemic	An epidemic is a disease that appears as new cases in a given human population, during a given period, at a rate that substantially exceeds what is "expected", based on recent experience.
Vaccine	A harmless variant or derivative of a pathogen used to stimulate a host organism's immune system to mount a long-term defense against the pathogen is referred to as vaccine.
Smallpox	Once a highly contagious, often fatal disease caused by a poxvirus. Its most noticeable symptom was the appearance of blisters and pustules on the skin. Vaccination has eradicated smallpox throughout the world.
Virus	Obligate intracellular parasite of living cells consisting of an outer capsid and an inner core of nucleic acid is referred to as virus. The term virus usually refers to those particles that infect eukaryotes whilst the term bacteriophage or phage is used to describe those infecting prokaryotes.
Saliva	Saliva is the moist, clear, and usually somewhat frothy substance produced in the mouths of some animals, including humans.
Lesion	A lesion is a non-specific term referring to abnormal tissue in the body. It can be caused by any disease process including trauma (physical, chemical, electrical), infection, neoplasm, metabolic and autoimmune.
Immunity	Resistance to the effects of specific disease-causing agents is called immunity.
Panic attack	An attack of overwhelming anxiety, fear, or terror is called panic attack.
Isolation	Isolation refers to the degree to which groups do not live in the same communities.
Migraine	Migraine is a neurologic disease, of which the most common symptom is an intense and disabling headache. Migraine is the most common type of vascular headache.
Ulcer	An ulcer is an open sore of the skin, eyes or mucous membrane, often caused by an initial abrasion and generally maintained by an inflammation and/or an infection.
Social isolation	Social isolation refers to a type of loneliness that occurs when a person lacks a sense of integrated involvement. Being deprived of participation in a group or community involving companionship, shared interests, organized activities, and meaningful roles causes a person to feel isolated.
Denial	Denial is a psychological defense mechanism in which a person faced with a fact that is uncomfortable or painful to accept rejects it instead, insisting that it is not true despite what may be overwhelming evidence.
Testosterone	Testosterone is a steroid hormone from the androgen group. Testosterone is secreted in the testes of men and the ovaries of women. It is the principal male sex hormone and the "original" anabolic steroid. In both males and females, it plays key roles in health and well-being.
Hormone	A hormone is a chemical messenger from one cell to another. All multicellular organisms

produce hormones. The best known hormones are those produced by endocrine glands of vertebrate animals, but hormones are produced by nearly every organ system and tissue type in a human or animal body. Hormone molecules are secreted directly into the bloodstream, they move by circulation or diffusion to their target cells, which may be nearby cells in the same tissue or cells of a distant organ of the body.

Personality disorder	A mental disorder characterized by a set of inflexible, maladaptive personality traits that keep a person from functioning properly in society is referred to as a personality disorder.
Sexual abuse	Sexual abuse is a relative cultural term used to describe sexual relations and behavior between two or more parties which are considered criminally and/or morally offensive.
Mental illness	Mental illness is the term formerly used to mean psychological disorder but less preferred because it implies that the causes of the disorder can be found in a medical disease process.
Incest	Incest refers to sexual relations between close relatives, most often between daughter and father or between brother and sister.
Clinical psychologist	A psychologist, usually with a Ph.D, whose training is in the diagnosis, treatment, or research of psychological and behavioral disorders is a clinical psychologist.
Genitals	Genitals refers to the internal and external reproductive organs.
Independence	The condition in which one variable has no effect on another is referred to as independence.
Character	Character is a constellation of enduring motivational and other traits that are manifested in the characteristic ways that an individual reacts to various kinds of challenges.
Assessment	In clinical practice, the process by which a mental health professional gathers and compiles information about a client for the purpose of describing the person's problems or disorder and developing a plan of treatment is an assessment.
Sexual assault	Sexual assault refers to any act in which one person is sexually intimate with another person without that other person's consent.
Community services	Community services refers to local delinquency prevention services such as recreational programs and drug and alcohol information programs in schools that help meet the community's needs for youths.
Conviction	Beliefs that are important to a person and that evoke strong emotion are a conviction.
Courtship	A process of acquaintance, selection, and attachment between potential mates that leads to the formation of strong sexual ties and possibly marriage is a courtship.
Ritual	Formalized ceremonial behavior in which the members of a group or community regularly engage, is referred to as a ritual. In childbirth it is a repeated series of actions used by women as a way of dealing with the discomfort of labor.
Resistance	Resistance refers to a nonspecific ability to ward off infection or disease regardless of whether the body has been previously exposed to it. A force that opposes the flow of a fluid such as air or blood. Compare with immunity.
Marriage	A socially approved sexual and economic relationship between two or more individuals is a marriage.
Sexual harassment	Deliberate or repeated verbal comments, gestures, or physical contact of a sexual nature that is unwanted by the recipient is called sexual harassment.
Alcoholism	A disorder that involves long-term, repeated, uncontrolled, compulsive, and excessive use of alcoholic beverages and that impairs the drinker's health and work and social relationships is called alcoholism.

Sexually transmitted disease	Infection transmitted from one individual to another by direct contact during sexual activity is referred to as a sexually transmitted disease.
Wound	A wound is type of physical trauma wherein the skin is torn, cut or punctured, or where blunt force trauma causes a contusion.
Scar	A scar results from the biologic process of wound repair in the skin and other tissues of the body. It is a connective tissue that fills the wound.
Consciousness	Consciousness refers to the ability to perceive, communicate, remember, understand, appreciate, and initiate voluntary movements; a functioning sensorium.
Humor	In traditional medicine practiced before the advent of modern technology, the four humours (or four humors) were four fluids that were thought to permeate the body and influence its health. A humor is any fluid substance in the body.
Malaria	Malaria refers to potentially fatal human disease caused by the protozoan parasite Plasmodium, which is transmitted by the bite of an infected mosquito.
Cancer	Cancer is a class of diseases or disorders characterized by uncontrolled division of cells and the ability of these cells to invade other tissues, either by direct growth into adjacent tissue through invasion or by implantation into distant sites by metastasis.
HIV	The virus that causes AIDS is HIV (human immunodeficiency virus).
Theory	Theory refers to an explanatory statement, or set of statements, that concisely summarizes the state of knowledge on a phenomenon and provides direction for further study.
Socialization	Socialization refers to guidance of people into socially desirable behavior by means of verbal messages, the systematic use of rewards and punishments, and other methods of teaching.
Stereotyping	Stereotyping refers to a process whereby a trait, usually negative, is generalized to all members of a particular group.
Representative sample	Representative sample refers to a sample of participants selected from the larger population in such a way that important subgroups within the population are included in the sample in the same proportions as they are found in the larger population.
Incidence	In epidemiological studies of a particular disorder, the rate at which new cases occur in a given place at a given time is called incidence.
Intuition	Quick, impulsive thought that does not make use of formal logic or clear reasoning is referred to as intuition.
Eye	An eye is an organ that detects light. Different kinds of light-sensitive organs are found in a variety of creatures. The simplest eyes do nothing but detect whether the surroundings are light or dark, while more complex eyes can distinguish shapes and colors.
Ecstasy	Ecstasy as an emotion is to be outside oneself, in a trancelike state in which an individual transcends ordinary consciousness and as a result has a heightened capacity for exceptional thought or experience. Ecstasy also refers to a relatively new hallucinogen that is chemically similar to mescaline and the amphetamines.
Sedative	A sedative is a drug that depresses the central nervous system (CNS), which causes calmness, relaxation, reduction of anxiety, sleepiness, slowed breathing, slurred speech, staggering gait, poor judgment, and slow, uncertain reflexes.
Amnesia	Amnesia is a condition in which memory is disturbed. The causes of amnesia are organic or functional. Organic causes include damage to the brain, through trauma or disease, or use of

certain (generally sedative) drugs.

Anesthetic	Anesthetic refers to a substance that causes the loss of the ability to feel pain or other sensory input, e.g., ether or halothane.
Heart rate	Heart rate is a term used to describe the frequency of the cardiac cycle. It is considered one of the four vital signs. Usually it is calculated as the number of contractions of the heart in one minute and expressed as "beats per minute".
Seizure	A seizure is a temporary alteration in brain function expressed as a changed mental state, tonic or clonic movements and various other symptoms. They are due to temporary abnormal electrical activity of a group of brain cells.
Advocate	An advocate is one who speaks on behalf of another, especially in a legal context. Implicit in the concept is the notion that the represented lacks the knowledge, skill, ability, or standing to speak for themselves.
Mental health	Mental health refers to the 'thinking' part of psychosocial health; includes your values, attitudes, and beliefs.
Marital status	Marital status refers to those who are reported as being married and where both are usual residents of the household at the time of the census. A de facto marriage is regarded as one where the relationship of two people of the same or opposite sex is reported.
Planning	In agreement with the patient, the nurse addresses each of the problems identified in the planning phase. For each problem a measurable goal is set. For example, for the patient discussed above, the goal would be for the patient's skin to remain intact. The result is a nursing care plan. This is the third step.
Halogen	Halogen is a chemical series. They are the elements in Group 17 (old-style: VII or VIIA) of the periodic table: fluorine (F), chlorine (Cl), bromine (Br), iodine (I), astatine (At) and the as yet undiscovered ununseptium (Uus). The term halogen was coined to mean elements which produce salt in union with a metal.
Compensation	Compensation refers to according to Adler, efforts to overcome imagined or real inferiorities by developing one's abilities.
Syndrome	Syndrome is the association of several clinically recognizable features, signs, symptoms, phenomena or characteristics which often occur together, so that the presence of one feature alerts the physician to the presence of the others
Carpal	In human anatomy, the carpal bones are the bones of the human wrist.There are eight of them altogether, and they can be thought of as forming two rows of four.
Hernia	Hernia refers to abnormal protrusion of an organ or a body part through the containing wall of its cavity. Commonly referred to as a rupture, a hernia often involves protrusion of the intestine through a break in the peritoneum.
Carpal tunnel syndrome	Carpal tunnel syndrome (CTS) is a medical condition in which the median nerve is compressed at the wrist causing symptoms like tingling, pain, coldness, and sometimes weakness in parts of the hand.
Identity	The distinguishing character of the individual: who each of us is, what our roles are, and what we are capable of is called identity.
Inventory	A paper-and-pencil test with questions about a person's thoughts, feelings, and behaviors, which can be scored according to a standard procedure is referred to as inventory.

Affect	Affect is the scientific term used to describe a subject's externally displayed mood. This can be assesed by the nurse by observing facial expression, tone of voice, and body language.
Health	Health is a term that refers to a combination of the absence of illness, the ability to cope with everyday activities, physical fitness, and high quality of life.
Eye	An eye is an organ that detects light. Different kinds of light-sensitive organs are found in a variety of creatures. The simplest eyes do nothing but detect whether the surroundings are light or dark, while more complex eyes can distinguish shapes and colors.
Culture	Culture, generally refers to patterns of human activity and the symbolic structures that give such activity significance.
Positive relationship	Statistically, a positive relationship refers to a mathematical relationship in which increases in one measure are matched by increases in the other.
Theory	Theory refers to an explanatory statement, or set of statements, that concisely summarizes the state of knowledge on a phenomenon and provides direction for further study.
Psychopathology	Psychopathology refers to the field concerned with the nature and development of mental disorders.
Marriage	A socially approved sexual and economic relationship between two or more individuals is a marriage.
Stress	Stress refers to a condition that is a response to factors that change the human systems normal state.
Mortality	The incidence of death in a population is mortality.
Lead	Lead is a chemical element in the periodic table that has the symbol Pb and atomic number 82. A soft, heavy, toxic and malleable poor metal, lead is bluish white when freshly cut but tarnishes to dull gray when exposed to air. Lead is used in building construction, lead-acid batteries, bullets and shot, and is part of solder, pewter, and fusible alloys.
Seizure	A seizure is a temporary alteration in brain function expressed as a changed mental state, tonic or clonic movements and various other symptoms. They are due to temporary abnormal electrical activity of a group of brain cells.
Host	Host is an organism that harbors a parasite, mutual partner, or commensal partner; or a cell infected by a virus.
Value	Value is worth in general, and it is thought to be connected to reasons for certain practices, policies, actions, beliefs or emotions. Value is "that which one acts to gain and/or keep."
Communicator	In persuasion, the person presenting arguments or information is referred to as communicator.
Insight	Insight refers to a sudden awareness of the relationships among various elements that had previously appeared to be independent of one another.
Confidentiality	Confidentiality refers to an ethical principle associated with several professions (eg, medicine, law, religion, journalism,). In ethics, and in law, some types of communication between a person and one of these professionals are "privileged" and may not be discussed or divulged to third parties. In those jurisdictions in which the law makes provision for such confidentiality, there are usually penalties for its violation.
Carl Rogers	Carl Rogers was instrumental in the development of non-directive psychotherapy, also known as "client-centered" psychotherapy. Rogers' basic tenets were unconditional positive regard, genuineness, and empathic understanding, with each demonstrated by the counselor.
Infection	The invasion and multiplication of microorganisms in body tissues is called an infection.

Virus	Obligate intracellular parasite of living cells consisting of an outer capsid and an inner core of nucleic acid is referred to as virus. The term virus usually refers to those particles that infect eukaryotes whilst the term bacteriophage or phage is used to describe those infecting prokaryotes.
HIV	The virus that causes AIDS is HIV (human immunodeficiency virus).
Interpersonal communication	Interpersonal communication refers to communication with another person. This kind of communication is subdivided into dyadic communication, public communication, and small-group or communication.
Stomach	The stomach is an organ in the alimentary canal used to digest food. It's primary function is not the absorption of nutrients from digested food; rather, the main job of the stomach is to break down large food molecules into smaller ones, so that they can be absorbed into the blood more easily.
Outcome	Outcome is the impact of care provided to a patient. They can be positive, such as the ability to walk freely as a result of rehabilitation, or negative, such as the occurrence of bedsores as a result of lack of mobility of a patient.
Anger	Anger is an emotional response often based on a sensation or perception of threat to one's needs.
I messages	Messages in which a person takes responsibility for communicating his or her own feelings, thoughts, and beliefs by using statements that begin with 'I,' not 'you' are I messages.
Assertiveness	Asking for what one wants while demonstrating respect for others is refered to as assertiveness.
Evaluation	The fifth step of the nursing process where nursing care and the patient's goal achievement are measured is the evaluation.
Intonation	The use of pitches of varying levels to help communicate meaning is called intonation.
Negative feedback	Negative feedback refers to a control mechanism in which a chemical reaction, metabolic pathway, or hormonesecreting gland is inhibited by the products of the reaction, pathway, or gland.
Motives	Needs or desires that energize and direct behavior toward a goal are motives.
Motive	Motive refers to a hypothetical state within an organism that propels the organism toward a goal.
Conflict resolution	A concerted effort by all parties to resolve points in contention in a constructive manner is called conflict resolution.
Solution	Solution refers to homogenous mixture formed when a solute is dissolved in a solvent.
Complaint	Complaint refers to report made by the police or some other agency to the court that initiates the intake process.
Intimate relationships	Relationships with family members, friends, and romantic partners, characterized by closeness and understanding are intimate relationships.
Cathartic	Cathartic is a medication that strongly increases gastrointestinal motility and promotes defecation.
Connectedness	Connectedness refers to according to Cooper and her colleagues, connectedness consists of two dimensions: mutuality and permeability.
Attachment	Attachment refers to the psychological tendency to seek closeness to another person, to feel secure when that person is present, and to feel anxious when that person is absent.

Introspection	Deliberate looking into one's own mind to examine one's own thoughts and feelings is called introspection.
Nuclear family	A nuclear family is a household consisting of two married, heterosexual parents and their legal children
Immune system	The immune system is the system of specialized cells and organs that protect an organism from outside biological influences. When the immune system is functioning properly, it protects the body against bacteria and viral infections, destroying cancer cells and foreign substances.
Consensus	General agreement is a consensus.
Heterosexual	Referring to people who are sexually aroused by and interested in forming romantic relationships with people of the other gender is referred to as heterosexual.
Sexuality	Sexuality refers to the expression of sexual sensation and related intimacy between human beings, as well as the expression of identity through sex and as influenced by or based on
Cultural values	The importance and desirability of various objects and activities as defined by people in a given culture is referred to as cultural values.
Companionate love	The strong affection we have for those with whom our lives are deeply involved is a companionate love.
Liking	A relationship based on intimacy, but lacking passion and commitment is a liking.
Ecstasy	Ecstasy as an emotion is to be outside oneself, in a trancelike state in which an individual transcends ordinary consciousness and as a result has a heightened capacity for exceptional thought or experience. Ecstasy also refers to a relatively new hallucinogen that is chemically similar to mescaline and the amphetamines.
Arousal	Arousal is a physiological and psychological state involving the activation of the reticular activating system in the brain stem, the autonomic nervous system and the endocrine system, leading to increased heart rate and blood pressure and a condition of alertness and readiness to respond.
Concept	A mental category used to class together objects, relations, events, abstractions, or qualities that have common properties is called concept.
Predisposition	Predisposition refers to an inclination or diathesis to respond in a certain way, either inborn or acquired. In abnormal psychology, it is a factor that lowers the ability to withstand stress and inclines the individual toward pathology.
Endorphins	Endorphins refer to neurotransmitters that are composed of amino acids and that are functionally similar to morphine.
Imprinting	A process occurring during a critical period in the development of an organism, in which that organism responds to a stimulus in a manner that will afterward be difficult to modify is referred to as imprinting.
Endorphin	Endorphin is an endogenous opioid biochemical compound. They are peptides produced by the pituitary gland and the hypothalamus in vertebrates, and they resemble the opiates in their abilities to produce analgesia and a sense of well-being.
Euphoria	A feeling of well-being, extreme satiation, and satisfaction caused by many psychoactive drugs and certain behaviors, such as gambling and sex is referred to as euphoria.
Oxytocin	Oxytocin is a hormone, found in humans and other mammals, which is involved in the facilitation of birth and breastfeeding as well as in bonding and the formation of trust between people.

Opiate	The term opiate refers to the alkaloids found in opium, an extract from the seed pods of the opium poppy (Papaver somniferum L.). It has also traditionally referred to natural and semi-synthetic derivatives of morphine.
Brain	The part of the central nervous system involved in regulating and controlling body activity and interpreting information from the senses transmitted through the nervous system is referred to as the brain.
Nerve	A nerve is an enclosed, cable-like bundle of nerve fibers or axons, which includes the glia that ensheath the axons in myelin.
Blood	Blood is a circulating tissue composed of fluid plasma and cells. The main function of blood is to supply nutrients (oxygen, glucose) and constitutional elements to tissues and to remove waste products.
Skin	Skin is an organ of the integumentary system composed of a layer of tissues that protect underlying muscles and organs.
Norepinephrine	Norepinephrine is a catecholamine and a phenethylamine with chemical formula $C_8H_{11}NO_3$. It is released from the adrenal glands as a hormone into the blood, but it is also a neurotransmitter in the nervous system where it is released from noradrenergic neurons during synaptic transmission.
Amphetamine	Amphetamine is a synthetic stimulant used to suppress the appetite, control weight, and treat disorders including narcolepsy and ADHD. It is also used recreationally and for performance enhancement.
Tolerance	Drug tolerance occurs when a subject's reaction to a drug decreases so that larger doses are required to achieve the same effect.
Dopamine	Dopamine is a chemical naturally produced in the body. In the brain, dopamine functions as a neurotransmitter, activating dopamine receptors. Dopamine is also a neurohormone released by the hypothalamus. Its main function as a hormone is to inhibit the release of prolactin from the anterior lobe of the pituitary.
Intoxication	Condition in which a substance affecting the central nervous system has been ingested and certain maladaptive behaviors or psychological changes, such as belligerence and impaired function, are evident is called intoxication.
Pheromone	Chemical signal that works at a distance and alters the behavior of another member of the same species is called a pheromone.
Vasopressin	Vasopressin is a human hormone that is mainly released when the body is low on water; it causes the kidneys to conserve water by concentrating the urine. It has also various functions in the brain.
Hormone	A hormone is a chemical messenger from one cell to another. All multicellular organisms produce hormones. The best known hormones are those produced by endocrine glands of vertebrate animals, but hormones are produced by nearly every organ system and tissue type in a human or animal body. Hormone molecules are secreted directly into the bloodstream, they move by circulation or diffusion to their target cells, which may be nearby cells in the same tissue or cells of a distant organ of the body.
Childbirth	Childbirth (also called labour, birth, partus or parturition) is the culmination of a human pregnancy with the emergence of a newborn infant from its mother's uterus.
Orgasm	Orgasm refers to rhythmic contractions of the reproductive structures, accompanied by extreme pleasure, at the peak of sexual excitement in both sexes; includes ejaculation by the male.
Monogamy	A mating system in which one male and one female mate exclusively, or almost exclusively,

with each other is referred to as monogamy.

Laboratory setting	Research setting in which the behavior of interest does not naturally occur is called a laboratory setting.
Rapport	Rapport is one of the most important features or characteristics of unconscious human interaction. It is commonality of perspective, being in "sync", being on the same wavelength as the person you are talking to.
Leveling	The communication of a clear, simple, and honest message is a leveling.
Pain	Pain is an unpleasant sensation which may be associated with actual or potential tissue damage and which may have physical and emotional components.
Identity	The distinguishing character of the individual: who each of us is, what our roles are, and what we are capable of is called identity.
Variable	A characteristic or aspect in which people, objects, events, or conditions vary is called variable.
Jealousy	An aversive reaction evoked by a real or imagined relationship involving a person's partner and a third person is a jealousy.
Alcohol	Alcohol is a general term, applied to any organic compound in which a hydroxyl group (-OH) is bound to a carbon atom, which in turn is bound to other hydrogen and/or carbon atoms. The general formula for a simple acyclic alcohol is $C_nH_{2n+1}OH$.
Rape	Forcible sexual intercourse with a person who does not consent to it is rape.
Microscope	A microscope is an instrument for viewing objects that are too small to be seen by the naked or unaided eye.
Alcoholic	An alcoholic is dependent on alcohol as characterized by craving, loss of control, physical dependence and withdrawal symptoms, and tolerance.
Adult Children of Alcoholics	Adult Children of Alcoholics is a support group that helps deal with similiar experiences and problems that the people have in there adult lives.
Sexual abuse	Sexual abuse is a relative cultural term used to describe sexual relations and behavior between two or more parties which are considered criminally and/or morally offensive.
Median	The median is a number that separates the higher half of a sample, a population, or a probability distribution from the lower half. It is the middle value in a distribution, above and below which lie an equal number of values.
Incentive	Incentive refers to an object, person, or situation perceived as being capable of satisfying a need.
Mental health	Mental health refers to the 'thinking' part of psychosocial health; includes your values, attitudes, and beliefs.
Older adult	Older adult is an adult over the age of 65.
Lifestyle	The culturally, socially, economically, and environmentally conditioned complex of actions characteristic of an individual, group, or community as a pattern of habituated behavior over time that is health related but not necessarily health directed is a lifestyle.
Independence	The condition in which one variable has no effect on another is referred to as independence.
Autonomy	Self-direction is referred to as autonomy. The ability to function in an independent manner.
Homosexual	Homosexual refers to referring to people who are sexually aroused by and interested in forming romantic relationships with people of the same gender.

Go to **Cram101.com** for the Practice Tests for this Chapter.

Validity	The extent to which a test measures what it is intended to measure is called validity.
Confounding	A state that occurs when two or more variable are tangled up such that conclusions about either one alone cannot be made is referred to as confounding.
Confounding variables	Confounding variables refers to any factors or conditions other than the independent variable that could cause observed changes in the dependent variable.
Confounding variable	A confounding variable is a variable which is the common cause of two things that may falsely appear to be in a causal relationship. It is the cause of a spurious relationship.
Adolescence	Adolescence is the period of psychological and social transition between childhood and adulthood (gender-specific manhood, or womanhood). As a transitional stage of human development it represents the period of time during which a juvenile matures into adulthood.
Constant	A behavior or characteristic that does not vary from one observation to another is referred to as a constant.
Accountability	Accepting responsibility for personal decisions, choices, and actions is referred to as accountability.
Course	Pattern of development and change of a disorder over time is a course.
Gender role	A cluster of behaviors that characterizes traditional female or male behaviors within a cultural setting is a gender role.
Blended family	A family formed when a widowed or divorced person, with or without children, marries another person who may or may not have been married before and who may or may not have children is referred to as a blended family.
Consistency	The extent to which an individual responds to a given stimulus or situation in the same way on different occasions is a consistency.
Survey	A method of scientific investigation in which a large sample of people answer questions about their attitudes or behavior is referred to as a survey.
Counselor	A counselor is a mental health professional who specializes in helping people with problems not involving serious mental disorders.
Trial	In classical conditioning, any presentation of a stimulus or pair of stimuli is called a trial.
Statistics	Statistics is a type of data analysis which practice includes the planning, summarizing, and interpreting of observations of a system possibly followed by predicting or forecasting of future events based on a mathematical model of the system being observed.
Statistic	A statistic is an observable random variable of a sample.
Rejection	Rejection is a response by caregivers where they distance themselves emotionally from a chronically ill patient. Although they provide physical care they tend to scold and and correct the patient continuously.
Friction	Friction is the force that opposes the relative motion or tendency of such motion of two surfaces in contact. The resulting injury to skin resembles an abrasion and can also damage superficial blood vessels directly under the skin.
Ritual	Formalized ceremonial behavior in which the members of a group or community regularly engage, is referred to as a ritual. In childbirth it is a repeated series of actions used by women as a way of dealing with the discomfort of labor.
Clinical psychologist	A psychologist, usually with a Ph.D, whose training is in the diagnosis, treatment, or research of psychological and behavioral disorders is a clinical psychologist.

Medicine	Medicine is the branch of health science and the sector of public life concerned with maintaining or restoring human health through the study, diagnosis and treatment of disease and injury.
Inventory	A paper-and-pencil test with questions about a person's thoughts, feelings, and behaviors, which can be scored according to a standard procedure is referred to as inventory.
Physiology	The study of the function of cells, tissues, and organs is referred to as physiology.
Anatomy	Anatomy is the branch of biology that deals with the structure and organization of living things. It can be divided into animal anatomy (zootomy) and plant anatomy (phytonomy).
Sexual dysfunction	Sexual dysfunction or sexual malfunction is difficulty during any stage of the sexual act (which includes desire, arousal, orgasm, and resolution) that prevents the individual or couple from enjoying sexual activity.
Gender identity	Gender identity refers to one's psychological sense of being female or male.

Testosterone	Testosterone is a steroid hormone from the androgen group. Testosterone is secreted in the testes of men and the ovaries of women. It is the principal male sex hormone and the "original" anabolic steroid. In both males and females, it plays key roles in health and well-being.
Hormone	A hormone is a chemical messenger from one cell to another. All multicellular organisms produce hormones. The best known hormones are those produced by endocrine glands of vertebrate animals, but hormones are produced by nearly every organ system and tissue type in a human or animal body. Hormone molecules are secreted directly into the bloodstream, they move by circulation or diffusion to their target cells, which may be nearby cells in the same tissue or cells of a distant organ of the body.
Stroke	A stroke or cerebrovascular accident (CVA) occurs when the blood supply to a part of the brain is suddenly interrupted.
Heart attack	A heart attack, is a serious, sudden heart condition usually characterized by varying degrees of chest pain or discomfort, weakness, sweating, nausea, vomiting, and arrhythmias, sometimes causing loss of consciousness. It occurs when the blood supply to a part of the heart is interrupted, causing death and scarring of the local heart tissue.
Sexuality	Sexuality refers to the expression of sexual sensation and related intimacy between human beings, as well as the expression of identity through sex and as influenced by or based on
Theory	Theory refers to an explanatory statement, or set of statements, that concisely summarizes the state of knowledge on a phenomenon and provides direction for further study.
Value	Value is worth in general, and it is thought to be connected to reasons for certain practices, policies, actions, beliefs or emotions. Value is "that which one acts to gain and/or keep."
Assessment	In clinical practice, the process by which a mental health professional gathers and compiles information about a client for the purpose of describing the person's problems or disorder and developing a plan of treatment is an assessment.
Health	Health is a term that refers to a combination of the absence of illness, the ability to cope with everyday activities, physical fitness, and high quality of life.
Contraception	A behavior or device that prevents fertilization is called contraception.
Condom	Sheath used to cover the penis during sexual intercourse is referred to as condom.
Identity	The distinguishing character of the individual: who each of us is, what our roles are, and what we are capable of is called identity.
Intersexuality	Not exhibiting exclusively female or male primary and secondary sex characteristics is referred to as intersexuality.
Secondary sex characteristics	Secondary sex characteristics are traits that distinguish the two sexes of a species, but that are not directly part of the reproductive system.
Puberty	A time in the life of a developing individual characterized by the increasing production of sex hormones, which cause it to reach sexual maturity is called puberty.
Ovaries	Ovaries are egg-producing reproductive organs found in female organisms.
Testes	The testes are the male generative glands in animals. Male mammals have two testes, which are often contained within an extension of the abdomen called the scrotum.
Ovary	The primary reproductive organ of a female is called an ovary.
Organ	Organ refers to a structure consisting of several tissues adapted as a group to perform specific functions.

Gonad	Gonad refers to a sex organ in an animal; an ovary or a testis. It is the organ that makes gametes.
Reproduction	Biological reproduction is the biological process by which new individual organisms are produced. Reproduction is a fundamental feature of all known life; each individual organism exists as the result of reproduction by an antecedent.
Socialization	Socialization refers to guidance of people into socially desirable behavior by means of verbal messages, the systematic use of rewards and punishments, and other methods of teaching.
Chromosomes	Physical structures in the cell's nucleus that house the genes. Each human cell has 23 pairs of chromosomes.
Conception	Conception is fusion of gametes to form a new organism. In animals, the process involves a sperm fusing with an ovum, which eventually leads to the development of an embryo.
Y chromosome	Male sex chromosome that carries genes involved in sex determination is referred to as the Y chromosome. It contains the genes that cause testis development, thus determining maleness.
Sperm	Sperm refers to the male sex cell with three distinct parts at maturity: head, middle piece, and tail.
Egg	An egg is the zygote, resulting from fertilization of the ovum. It nourishes and protects the embryo.
Lead	Lead is a chemical element in the periodic table that has the symbol Pb and atomic number 82. A soft, heavy, toxic and malleable poor metal, lead is bluish white when freshly cut but tarnishes to dull gray when exposed to air. Lead is used in building construction, lead-acid batteries, bullets and shot, and is part of solder, pewter, and fusible alloys.
Progesterone	Progesterone is a C-21 steroid hormone involved in the female menstrual cycle, pregnancy (supports gestation) and embryogenesis of humans and other species.
Estrogen	Estrogen is a steroid that functions as the primary female sex hormone. While present in both men and women, they are found in women in significantly higher quantities.
Adrenal glands	The adrenal glands are the triangle-shaped endocrine glands that sit atop the kidneys; their name indicates that position. They are chiefly responsible for regulating the stress response through the synthesis of corticosteroids and catecholamines, including cortisol and adrenaline.
Adrenal gland	In mammals, the adrenal gland (also known as suprarenal glands or colloquially as kidney hats) are the triangle-shaped endocrine glands that sit atop the kidneys; their name indicates that position.
Androgen	Androgen is the generic term for any natural or synthetic compound, usually a steroid hormone, that stimulates or controls the development and maintenance of masculine characteristics in vertebrates by binding to androgen receptors.
Adrenal	In mammals, the adrenal glands are the triangle-shaped endocrine glands that sit atop the kidneys. They are chiefly responsible for regulating the stress response through the synthesis of corticosteroids and catecholamines, including cortisol and adrenaline.
Gland	A gland is an organ in an animal's body that synthesizes a substance for release such as hormones, often into the bloodstream or into cavities inside the body or its outer surface.
Genitals	Genitals refers to the internal and external reproductive organs.
Penis	The penis is the male reproductive organ and for mammals additionally serves as the external male organ of urination.

Fetus	Fetus refers to a developing human from the ninth week of gestation until birth; has all the major structures of an adult.
Gonadotropin	A hormone that stimulates the gonads is gonadotropin. They are protein hormones secreted by gonadotrope cells of the pituitary gland of vertebrates.
Pituitary gland	The pituitary gland or hypophysis is an endocrine gland about the size of a pea that sits in the small, bony cavity (sella turcica) at the base of the brain. Its posterior lobe is connected to a part of the brain called the hypothalamus via the infundibulum (or stalk), giving rise to the tuberoinfundibular pathway.
Skeleton	In biology, the skeleton or skeletal system is the biological system providing physical support in living organisms.
Hip	In anatomy, the hip is the bony projection of the femur, known as the greater trochanter, and the overlying muscle and fat.
Culture	Culture, generally refers to patterns of human activity and the symbolic structures that give such activity significance.
Genitalia	The Latin term genitalia is used to describe the sex organs, and in the English language this term and genital area are most often used to describe the externally visible sex organs or external genitalia: in males the penis and scrotum, in females the vulva.
Syndrome	Syndrome is the association of several clinically recognizable features, signs, symptoms, phenomena or characteristics which often occur together, so that the presence of one feature alerts the physician to the presence of the others
Androgen insensitivity syndrome	Androgen insensitivity syndrome is a set of disorders of sexual differentiation that results from mutations of the gene encoding the androgen receptor.
Androgen insensitivity	Androgen insensitivity syndrome is a set of disorders of sexual differentiation that results from mutations of the gene encoding the androgen receptor. If androgen insensitivity is total, XY males develop as females in the sense that their bodies look completely female and they develop a female gender identity.
Adolescence	Adolescence is the period of psychological and social transition between childhood and adulthood (gender-specific manhood, or womanhood). As a transitional stage of human development it represents the period of time during which a juvenile matures into adulthood.
Gonadal dysgenesis	Gonadal dysgenesis, a type of intersexuality formerly known as "True Hermaphroditism", occurs in about one percent of mammals (including humans), but it is extremely rare for both sets of sexual organs to be functional, usually neither set is functional.
Ambiguous genitalia	The phrase "ambiguous genitalia " refers specifically to genital appearance, but not all intersex conditions result in atypical genital appearance.
Infection	The invasion and multiplication of microorganisms in body tissues is called an infection.
Salt	Salt is a term used for ionic compounds composed of positively charged cations and negatively charged anions, so that the product is neutral and without a net charge.
Menstruation	Loss of blood and tissue from the uterine lining at the end of a female reproductive cycle are referred to as menstruation.
Intersex	An intersex person (or organism of any unisexual species) is one who is born with genitalia and/or secondary sex characteristics determined as neither exclusively male nor female, or which combine features of the male and female sexes.
Gender role	A cluster of behaviors that characterizes traditional female or male behaviors within a

	cultural setting is a gender role.
Gender identity	Gender identity refers to one's psychological sense of being female or male.
Heterosexual	Referring to people who are sexually aroused by and interested in forming romantic relationships with people of the other gender is referred to as heterosexual.
Homosexual	Homosexual refers to referring to people who are sexually aroused by and interested in forming romantic relationships with people of the same gender.
Transsexual	A transsexual person establishes a permanent identity with the opposite gender to their assigned sex. They make or desire to make a transition from their birth sex to that of the opposite sex, with some type of medical alteration to their body.
Mental health	Mental health refers to the 'thinking' part of psychosocial health; includes your values, attitudes, and beliefs.
Mental illness	Mental illness is the term formerly used to mean psychological disorder but less preferred because it implies that the causes of the disorder can be found in a medical disease process.
Homosexuality	Sexual desire or activity directed toward a member of one's own sex is homosexuality.
Conversion	Conversion syndrome describes a condition in which physical symptoms arise for which there is no clear explanation.
Perinatal	Pertaining to the time five months before, during, and one month after birth is perinatal.
Anatomy	Anatomy is the branch of biology that deals with the structure and organization of living things. It can be divided into animal anatomy (zootomy) and plant anatomy (phytonomy).
Brain	The part of the central nervous system involved in regulating and controlling body activity and interpreting information from the senses transmitted through the nervous system is referred to as the brain.
Heterosexuality	Sexual attraction and behavior directed to the opposite sex is heterosexuality.
Homosexuals	Persons who are sexually attracted to people of their own sex are called homosexuals.
Homophobia	An intense, irrational hostility toward or fear of homosexuals is referred to as homophobia.
Physiology	The study of the function of cells, tissues, and organs is referred to as physiology.
Labia majora	A pair of outer thickened folds of skin that protect the female genital region is the labia majora.
Mons pubis	In human anatomy or in mammals in general, the mons pubis is the soft mound of flesh present in both genders just above the genitals, raised above the surrounding area due to a pad of fat lying just beneath it which protects the pubic bone.
Vestibule	Vestibule refers to the cavity enclosed by the labia minora, it is the space into which the vagina and urethral opening empty.
Clitoris	The clitoris is a sexual organ in the body of female mammals. The visible knob-like portion is located near the anterior junction of the labia minora, above the opening of the vagina. Unlike its male counterpart, the penis,the clitoris has no urethra, is not involved in urination, and its sole function is to induce sexual pleasure.
Vagina	The vagina is the tubular tract leading from the uterus to the exterior of the body in female placental mammals and marsupials, or to the cloaca in female birds, monotremes, and some reptiles. Female insects and other invertebrates also have a vagina, which is the terminal part of the oviduct.
Pubis	The pubis, the anterior part of the hip bone, is divisible into a body, a superior and an

	inferior ramus.
Tissue	A collection of interconnected cells that perform a similar function within an organism is called tissue.
Labia minora	The labia minora are two soft folds of skin within the labia majora and to either side of the opening of the vagina.
Skin	Skin is an organ of the integumentary system composed of a layer of tissues that protect underlying muscles and organs.
Urine	Concentrated filtrate produced by the kidneys and excreted via the bladder is called urine.
Hymen	The hymen is a ring of tissue around the vaginal opening. Although many people believe that the hymen completely occludes the vaginal opening in human females, this is quite rare. The hymen has great symbolic significance as an indicator of a woman's virginity.
Perineum	The perineum is the region between the genital area and the anus in both sexes.
Nerve	A nerve is an enclosed, cable-like bundle of nerve fibers or axons, which includes the glia that ensheath the axons in myelin.
Fallopian tube	The Fallopian tube is one of two very fine tubes leading from the ovaries of female mammals into the uterus. They deliver the ovum to the uterus.
Uterus	The uterus is the major female reproductive organ of most mammals. One end, the cervix, opens into the vagina; the other is connected on both sides to the fallopian tubes. The main function is to accept a fertilized ovum which becomes implanted into the endometrium, and derives nourishment from blood vessels which develop exclusively for this purpose.
Reproductive system	A reproductive system is the ensembles and interactions of organs and or substances within an organism that stricly pertain to reproduction. As an example, this would include in the case of female mammals, the hormone estrogen, the womb and eggs but not the breast.
Anus	In anatomy, the anus is the external opening of the rectum. Closure is controlled by sphincter muscles. Feces are expelled from the body through the anus during the act of defecation, which is the primary function of the anus.
Vulva	The outer features of the female reproductive anatomy is referred to as vulva.
Uterine tube	Also called the oviduct, the tube leading out of the ovary to the uterus, into which the secondary oocyte is released is referred to as uterine tube.
Endometrium	The endometrium is the inner uterine membrane in mammals which is developed in preparation for the implantation of a fertilized egg upon its arrival into the uterus.
Bladder	A hollow muscular storage organ for storing urine is a bladder.
Cervix	The cervix is actually the lower, narrow portion of the uterus where it joins with the top end of the vagina. It is cylindrical or conical in shape and protrudes through the upper anterior vaginal wall.
Fertilization	Fertilization is fusion of gametes to form a new organism. In animals, the process involves a sperm fusing with an ovum, which eventually leads to the development of an embryo.
Implantation	Implantation refers to attachment and penetration of the embryo into the lining of the uterus.
Blood	Blood is a circulating tissue composed of fluid plasma and cells. The main function of blood is to supply nutrients (oxygen, glucose) and constitutional elements to tissues and to remove waste products.
Reservoir	Reservoir is the source of infection. It is the environment in which microorganisms are able

	to live and grow.
Ovulation	Ovulation is the process in the menstrual cycle by which a mature ovarian follicle ruptures and discharges an ovum (also known as an oocyte, female gamete, or casually, an egg) that participates in reproduction.
Menstrual cycle	The menstrual cycle is the set of recurring physiological changes in a female's body that are under the control of the reproductive hormone system and necessary for reproduction. Besides humans, only other great apes exhibit menstrual cycles, in contrast to the estrus cycle of most mammalian species.
Endocrine gland	An endocrine gland is one of a set of internal organs involved in the secretion of hormones into the blood. These glands are known as ductless, which means they do not have tubes inside them.
Hypothalamus	Located below the thalamus, the hypothalamus links the nervous system to the endocrine system by synthesizing and secreting neurohormones often called releasing hormones because they function by stimulating the secretion of hormones from the anterior pituitary gland.
Follicle	Follicle refers to a cluster of cells surrounding, protecting, and nourishing a developing egg cell in the ovary; also secretes estrogen. In botany, a follicle is a type of simple dry fruit produced by certain flowering plants. It is regarded as one the most primitive types of fruits, and derives from a simple pistil or carpel.
Luteinizing hormone	Luteinizing hormone is a hormone synthesized and secreted by gonadotropes in the anterior lobe of the pituitary gland. In both males and females, it stimulates the production of sex steroids from the gonads.
Ovarian follicle	Ovarian follicle is the roughly spherical cell aggregation in the ovary containing an ovum and from which the egg is released during ovulation.
Reproductive cycle	The cycle of physiologic changes occurring in the female reproductive organs, from the time of fertilization of the ovum through gestation and parturition is referred to as reproductive cycle.
Menarche	Menarche is the first menstrual period as a girl's body progresses through the changes of puberty. Menarche usually occurs about two years after the first changes of breast development.
Obesity	The state of being more than 20 percent above the average weight for a person of one's height is called obesity.
Proliferative phase	About two or three days after a wound occurs, fibroblasts begin to enter the wound site, marking the onset of the proliferative phase even before the inflammatory phase has ended. As in the other phases of wound healing, steps in the proliferative phase do not occur in a series but rather partially overlap in time.
Secretory phase	The phase of development of the endometrium during which, after the proliferative phase, the endometrium stops growing but starts producing secretions under the influence of progesterone, so it corresponds with the luteal phase in the ovarian cycle is called the secretory phase.
Mucus	Mucus is a slippery secretion of the lining of various membranes in the body (mucous membranes). Mucus aids in the protection of the lungs by trapping foreign particles that enter the nose during normal breathing. Additionally, it prevents tissues from drying out.
Embryo	A prenatal stage of development after germ layers form but before the rudiments of all organs are present is referred to as an embryo.
Ovum	An ovum is a female sex cell or gamete. It is a mature egg cell released during ovulation

	from an ovary.
Corpus luteum	The corpus luteum is a small, temporary endocrine structure in animals. It develops from an ovarian follicle during the luteal phase of the estrous cycle, following the release of a mature egg from the follicle during ovulation. While the egg traverses the Fallopian tube into the uterus, the corpus luteum remains in the ovary.
Human chorionic gonadotropin	Human chorionic gonadotropin is a peptide hormone produced in pregnancy, that is made by the embryo soon after conception and later by the trophoblast. Its role is to prevent the disintegration of the corpus luteum of the ovary and thereby maintain progesterone production that is critical for a pregnancy in humans.
Chorionic gonadotropin	A hormone, secreted by the chorion, that maintains the integrity of the corpus luteum during early pregnancy is called chorionic gonadotropin.
Premenstrual syndrome	Premenstrual Syndrome is stress which is a physical symptom prior to the onset of menstruation. It is not dysmenorrhea (increasingly painful periods), in spite of the two conditions being commonly confused in usage. It occurs prior to the onset of menstrual bleeding, while dysmenorrha occurs during the period of bleeding.
Irritability	Irritability is an excessive response to stimuli. Irritability takes many forms, from the contraction of a unicellular organism when touched to complex reactions involving all the senses of higher animals.
Anxiety	Anxiety is a complex combination of the feeling of fear, apprehension and worry often accompanied by physical sensations such as palpitations, chest pain and/or shortness of breath.
Insomnia	Insomnia is a sleep disorder characterized by an inability to sleep and/or to remain asleep for a reasonable period during the night.
Carbohydrate	Carbohydrate is a chemical compound that contains oxygen, hydrogen, and carbon atoms. They consist of monosaccharide sugars of varying chain lengths and that have the general chemical formula $C_n(H_2O)_n$ or are derivatives of such.
Menopause	Menopause is the physiological cessation of menstrual cycles associated with advancing age in species that experience such cycles. Menopause is sometimes referred to as change of life or climacteric.
Stress	Stress refers to a condition that is a response to factors that change the human systems normal state.
Antidepressant	An antidepressant is a medication used primarily in the treatment of clinical depression. They are not thought to produce tolerance, although sudden withdrawal may produce adverse effects. They create little if any immediate change in mood and require between several days and several weeks to take effect.
Serotonin	Serotonin is a monoamine neurotransmitter synthesized in serotonergic neurons in the central nervous system and enterochromaffin cells in the gastrointestinal tract. It is believed to play an important part of the biochemistry of depression, migraine, bipolar disorder and anxiety.
Inhibitor	An inhibitor is a type of effector (biology) that decreases or prevents the rate of a chemical reaction. They are often called negative catalysts.
Reuptake	Reuptake is the reabsorption of a neurotransmitter by the molecular transporter of a pre-synaptic neuron after it has performed its function of transmitting a neural impulse.
Selective serotonin	Selective serotonin reuptake inhibitors are a class of antidepressants. They act within the brain to increase the amount of the neurotransmitter, serotonin (5-hydroxytryptamine or 5-

reuptake inhibitors	HT), in the synaptic gap by inhibiting its reuptake. It is often prescribed for depression.
Selective serotonin reuptake inhibitor	Selective serotonin reuptake inhibitor is a class of antidepressants for treating depression, anxiety disorders and some personality disorders. These drugs are designed to elevate the level of the neurotransmitter serotonin.
Shock	Circulatory shock, a state of cardiac output that is insufficient to meet the body's physiological needs, with consequences ranging from fainting to death is referred to as shock. Insulin shock, a state of severe hypoglycemia caused by administration of insulin.
Toxic shock syndrome	Toxic shock syndrome (TSS) is a rare but potentially fatal disease caused by a bacterial toxin. Different bacterial toxins may cause toxic shock syndrome, depending on the situation. The causative agent is Staphylococcus aureus.
Diaphragm	The diaphragm is a shelf of muscle extending across the bottom of the ribcage. It is critically important in respiration: in order to draw air into the lungs, the diaphragm contracts, thus enlarging the thoracic cavity and reducing intra-thoracic pressure.
Toxin	Toxin refers to a microbial product or component that can injure another cell or organism at low concentrations. Often the term refers to a poisonous protein, but toxins may be lipids and other substances.
Wound	A wound is type of physical trauma wherein the skin is torn, cut or punctured, or where blunt force trauma causes a contusion.
Dysmenorrhea	Dysmenorrhea, cramps or painful menstruation, involves menstrual periods that are accompanied by either sharp, intermittent pain or dull, aching pain, usually in the pelvis or lower abdomen.
Ibuprofen	A nonopiate pain reliever that controls pain, fever, and inflammation is referred to as ibuprofen.
Abdomen	The abdomen is a part of the body. In humans, and in many other vertebrates, it is the region between the thorax and the pelvis. In fully developed insects, the abdomen is the third (or posterior) segment, after the head and thorax.
Hormone replacement therapy	Hormone replacement therapy is a system of medical treatment for perimenopausal and postmenopausal women, based on the assumption that it may prevent discomfort and health problems caused by diminished circulating estrogen hormones.
Hot flash	A hot flash is a symptom of menopause and changing hormone levels which typically expresses itself at night as periods of intense heat with sweating and rapid heartbeat and may typically last from two to thirty minutes on each occasion.
Joint	A joint (articulation) is the location at which two bones make contact (articulate). They are constructed to both allow movement and provide mechanical support.
Pain	Pain is an unpleasant sensation which may be associated with actual or potential tissue damage and which may have physical and emotional components.
Osteoporosis	Osteoporosis is a disease of bone in which bone mineral density (BMD) is reduced, bone microarchitecture is disrupted, the amount and variety of non-collagenous proteins in bone is changed, and a concomitantly fracture risk is increased.
Circumcision	Circumcision is the removal of some or all of the foreskin (prepuce) from the penis.
Foreskin	The foreskin or prepuce is a retractable double-layered fold of skin and mucous membrane that covers the glans penis and protects the urinary meatus when the penis is not erect. Almost all mammals including marsupials and marine mammals have foreskin.

Prepuce	The prepuce is a retractable piece of skin which covers part of the genitals of primates and other mammals. On a male, this covers the head of the penis (the glans penis). On a female, it surrounds and protects the clitoris.
Glan	A glan is a structure internally composed of corpus spongiosum in males or of corpus cavernosa and vestibular tissue in females that is located at the tip of homologous genital structures involved in sexual arousal.
Gonorrhea	Gonorrhea refers to an acute infectious sexually transmitted disease of the mucous membranes of the genitourinary tract, eye, rectum, and throat. It is caused by Neisseria gonorrhoeae.
Syphilis	Syphilis is a sexually transmitted disease that is caused by a spirochaete bacterium, Treponema pallidum. If not treated, syphilis can cause serious effects such as damage to the nervous system, heart, or brain. Untreated syphilis can be ultimately fatal.
Cancer	Cancer is a class of diseases or disorders characterized by uncontrolled division of cells and the ability of these cells to invade other tissues, either by direct growth into adjacent tissue through invasion or by implantation into distant sites by metastasis.
HIV	The virus that causes AIDS is HIV (human immunodeficiency virus).
Lifestyle	The culturally, socially, economically, and environmentally conditioned complex of actions characteristic of an individual, group, or community as a pattern of habituated behavior over time that is health related but not necessarily health directed is a lifestyle.
Calcium	Calcium is the chemical element in the periodic table that has the symbol Ca and atomic number 20. Calcium is a soft grey alkaline earth metal that is used as a reducing agent in the extraction of thorium, zirconium and uranium. Calcium is also the fifth most abundant element in the Earth's crust.
Scrotum	In some male mammals the scrotum is an external bag of skin and muscle containing the testicles. It is an extension of the abdomen, and is located between the penis and anus.
Prostate	The prostate is a gland that is part of male mammalian sex organs. Its main function is to secrete and store a clear, slightly basic fluid that is part of semen. The prostate differs considerably between species anatomically, chemically and physiologically.
Urethra	In anatomy, the urethra is a tube which connects the urinary bladder to the outside of the body. The urethra has an excretory function in both sexes, to pass urine to the outside, and also a reproductive function in the male, as a passage for sperm.
Vesicle	Membranous, cytoplasmic sac formed by an infolding of the cell membrane is called a vesicle.
Semen	Semen is a fluid that contains spermatozoa. It is secreted by the gonads (sexual glands) of male or hermaphroditic animals including humans for fertilization of female ova. Semen discharged by an animal or human is known as ejaculate, and the process of discharge is called ejaculation.
Seminal vesicles	The seminal vesicles are a pair of glands on the posterior surface of the urinary bladder of males. They secrete a significant proportion of the fluid that ultimately becomes semen.
Arousal	Arousal is a physiological and psychological state involving the activation of the reticular activating system in the brain stem, the autonomic nervous system and the endocrine system, leading to increased heart rate and blood pressure and a condition of alertness and readiness to respond.
Spermatogenesis	Spermatogenesis refers to the creation, or genesis, of spermatozoa, which occurs in the male gonads.
Ejaculatory duct	The Ejaculatory duct is a part of the human male anatomy, which causes the reflex action of ejaculation. Each male has two of them. They begin at the vas deferens, pass through the

prostate, and empty into the urethra at the Colliculus seminalis.

Epididymis	The epididymis is part of the human male reproductive system and is present in all male mammals. It is a narrow, tightly-coiled tube connecting the efferent ducts from the rear of each testicle to its vas deferens.
Motility	Motility is the ability to move spontaneously and independently. The term can apply to single cells, or to multicellular organisms.
Urination	Urination is the process of disposing urine from the urinary bladder through the urethra to the outside of the body. The process of urination is usually under voluntary control.
Acid	An acid is a water-soluble, sour-tasting chemical compound that when dissolved in water, gives a solution with a pH of less than 7.
Bulbourethral gland	The bulbourethral gland is a small, rounded, and somewhat lobulated body, of a yellow color, about the size of a pea, placed behind and lateral to the membranous portion of the urethra, between the two layers of the fascia of the urogenital diaphragm. They secrete a clear fluid known as pre-ejaculate.
Urinary bladder	In the anatomy of mammals, the urinary bladder is the organ that collects urine excreted by the kidneys prior to disposal by urination. Urine enters the bladder via the ureters and exits via the urethra.
Viability	Viability means in general "capacity for survival" and is more specifically used to mean a capacity for living, developing, or germinating under favorable conditions. In the context of pregnancy, viability refers to either an early stage pregnancy that has a chance of reaching full-term and a live birth; or the shortest length of pregnancy after which a child born prematurely has a chance of survival. Generally, this ranges from 20-27 weeks.
Vasocongestion	The filling of a tissue with blood caused by increased blood flow through the arteries of that tissue is vasocongestion.
Engorgement	Breast engorgement occurs in the mammary glands when too much breast milk is contained within them. It is caused by insufficient breastfeeding and/or blocked milk ducts.
Orgasm	Orgasm refers to rhythmic contractions of the reproductive structures, accompanied by extreme pleasure, at the peak of sexual excitement in both sexes; includes ejaculation by the male.
Muscle	Muscle is a contractile form of tissue. It is one of the four major tissue types, the other three being epithelium, connective tissue and nervous tissue. Muscle contraction is used to move parts of the body, as well as to move substances within the body.
Sphincter	Muscle that surrounds a tube and closes or opens the tube by contracting and relaxing is referred to as sphincter.
Resolution phase	The resolution phase occurs after orgasm and allows the muscles to relax, blood pressure to drop and the body to slow down from its excited state.
Sexual response cycle	Masters and Johnson's model of the sexual response cycle consists of four stages or phases: excitement, plateau, orgasmic, resolution.
Elevation	Elevation refers to upward movement of a part of the body.
Coronal	A coronal (also known as frontal) plane is an Y-Z plane, perpendicular to the ground, which (in humans) separates the anterior from the posterior, the front from the back, the ventral from the dorsal.
Ductus deferens	The ductus deferens is part of the human male anatomy. There are two of them; they are muscular tubes (surrounded by smooth muscle) connecting the left and right epididymis to the ejaculatory ducts in order to move sperm.

Older adult	Older adult is an adult over the age of 65.
Friction	Friction is the force that opposes the relative motion or tendency of such motion of two surfaces in contact. The resulting injury to skin resembles an abrasion and can also damage superficial blood vessels directly under the skin.
Coitus	Sexual intercourse, specifically coitus, is the human form of copulation.
Assess	Assess is to systematically and continuously collect, validate, and communicate patient data.
Marriage	A socially approved sexual and economic relationship between two or more individuals is a marriage.
Moral	A "moral" may refer to a particular principle, usually as an informal and general summary with respect to a moral principle, as it is applied in a given human situation.
Masturbation	Sexual self-stimulation is called masturbation.
Life span	Life span refers to the upper boundary of life, the maximum number of years an individual can live. The maximum life span of human beings is about 120 years of age.
Erogenous zone	An erogenous zone is an area of the human body that has heightened sensitivity and stimulation normally results in sexual response.
Cunnilingus	Cunnilingus is the act of using the mouth and tongue to stimulate the female genitals, especially the clitoris.
Transvestite	A male who lives as a woman or a female who lives as a man but does not alter the genitalia, is referred to as a transvestite.
Voyeurism	Voyeurism is a practice in which an individual derives sexual pleasure from observing other people. Such people may be engaged in sexual acts, or be nude or in underwear, or dressed in whatever other way the "voyeur" finds appealing.
Oxygen	Oxygen is a chemical element in the periodic table. It has the symbol O and atomic number 8. Oxygen is the second most common element on Earth, composing around 46% of the mass of Earth's crust and 28% of the mass of Earth as a whole, and is the third most common element in the universe.
Asphyxiation	Asphyxia or asphyxiation is a condition of severely deficient supply of oxygen to the body. In the absence of remedial action it will very rapidly lead to unconsciousness and death.
Sexual dysfunction	Sexual dysfunction or sexual malfunction is difficulty during any stage of the sexual act (which includes desire, arousal, orgasm, and resolution) that prevents the individual or couple from enjoying sexual activity.
Sexual desire disorders	Sexual dysfunctions that are related to the appetite phase and are characterized by a lack of sexual desire are sexual desire disorders.
Inhibited sexual desire	Lack of sexual appetite or simply a lack of interest and pleasure in sexual activity is referred to as inhibited sexual desire.
Phobia	A persistent, irrational fear of an object, situation, or activity that the person feels compelled to avoid is referred to as a phobia.
Sexual aversion disorder	A sexual desire disorder characterized by an aversion to or a desire to avoid genital contact with a sexual partner is referred to as a sexual aversion disorder.
Impotence	Erectile dysfunction, also known as impotence, is a sexual dysfunction characterized by the inability to develop or maintain an erection of the penis for satisfactory sexual intercourse regardless of the capability of ejaculation.
Sexual arousal	Problems occurring during the excitement phase and relating to difficulties with feelings of

disorders	sexual pleasure or with the physiological changes associated with sexual excitement are called sexual arousal disorders.
Erectile dysfunction	Erectile dysfunction is the inability to develop or maintain an erection of the penis for satisfactory sexual intercourse regardless of the capability of ejaculation. There are various underlying causes, many of which are medically reversible.
Blood pressure	Blood pressure is the pressure exerted by the blood on the walls of the blood vessels.
Depression	In everyday language depression refers to any downturn in mood, which may be relatively transitory and perhaps due to something trivial. This is differentiated from Clinical depression which is marked by symptoms that last two weeks or more and are so severe that they interfere with daily living.
Diabetes	Diabetes is a medical disorder characterized by varying or persistent elevated blood sugar levels, especially after eating. All types of diabetes share similar symptoms and complications at advanced stages: dehydration and ketoacidosis, cardiovascular disease, chronic renal failure, retinal damage which can lead to blindness, nerve damage which can lead to erectile dysfunction, gangrene with risk of amputation of toes, feet, and even legs.
Alcohol	Alcohol is a general term, applied to any organic compound in which a hydroxyl group (-OH) is bound to a carbon atom, which in turn is bound to other hydrogen and/or carbon atoms. The general formula for a simple acyclic alcohol is $C_nH_{2n+1}OH$.
Performance anxiety	Anxiety concerning one's ability to perform, especially when performance may be evaluated by other people is performance anxiety.
Premature ejaculation	Premature ejaculation is the most common sexual problem in men, characterized by a lack of voluntary control over ejaculation
Diarrhea	Diarrhea or diarrhoea is a condition in which the sufferer has frequent and watery, chunky, or loose bowel movements.
Flushing	For a person to flush is to become markedly red in the face and often other areas of the skin, from various physiological conditions. Flushing is generally distingushed, despite a close physiological relation between them, from blushing, which is milder, generally restricted to the face or cheeks, and generally assumed to reflect embarrassment.
Urinary tract infection	A urinary tract infection is an infection anywhere from the kidneys to the ureters to the bladder to the urethra.
Cardiovascular disease	Cardiovascular disease refers to afflictions in the mechanisms, including the heart, blood vessels, and their controllers, that are responsible for transporting blood to the body's tissues and organs. Psychological factors may play important roles in such diseases and their treatments.
Nitrate	Nitrate refers to a salt of nitric acid; a compound containing the radical NO_3; biologically, the final form of nitrogen from the oxidation of organic nitrogen compounds.
Suppository	A suppository is a medicine that is inserted either into the rectum (rectal suppository) or into the vagina (vaginal suppository) where it melts.
Injection	A method of rapid drug delivery that puts the substance directly in the bloodstream, in a muscle, or under the skin is called injection.
Population	Population refers to all members of a well-defined group of organisms, events, or things.
Affect	Affect is the scientific term used to describe a subject's externally displayed mood. This can be assesed by the nurse by observing facial expression, tone of voice, and body language.
Addiction	Addiction is an uncontrollable compulsion to repeat a behavior regardless of its

consequences. Many drugs or behaviors can precipitate a pattern of conditions recognized as addiction, which include a craving for more of the drug or behavior, increased physiological tolerance to exposure, and withdrawal symptoms in the absence of the stimulus.

Addict	A person with an overpowering physical or psychological need to continue taking a particular substance or drug is referred to as an addict.
Orgasmic disorder	A sexual dysfunction in which people have persistent or recurrent problems in reaching orgasm is an orgasmic disorder.
Female orgasmic disorder	The persistent inability of a woman to reach orgasm, or a delay in reaching orgasm despite adequate sexual stimulation is called the female orgasmic disorder.
Ego	Ego refers to the second psychic structure to develop, characterized by self-awareness, planning, and delay of gratification.
Pain disorder	Pain disorder is when a patient experiences chronic and constant pain in one or more areas, and is thought to be caused by psychological stress. The pain is often so severe that it disables the patient from proper functioning. It can last as short as a few days, to as long as many years.
Dyspareunia	Dyspareunia is painful sexual intercourse, due to medical or psychological causes. The term is used almost exclusively in women, although the problem may occur in men.
Childbirth	Childbirth (also called labour, birth, partus or parturition) is the culmination of a human pregnancy with the emergence of a newborn infant from its mother's uterus.
Counselor	A counselor is a mental health professional who specializes in helping people with problems not involving serious mental disorders.
Inhibition	The ability to prevent from making some cognitive or behavioral response is called inhibition.
Rape	Forcible sexual intercourse with a person who does not consent to it is rape.
Ketamine	Ketamine refers to used as a recreational club drug, it is an anesthetic that produces catatonia and deep analgesia; side effects include excess saliva, dysphoria, and hallucinations. Its chemistry and effects are very similar to pcp.
Nervous system	The nervous system of an animal coordinates the activity of the muscles, monitors the organs, constructs and processes input from the senses, and initiates actions.
Central nervous system	The central nervous system comprized of the brain and spinal cord, represents the largest part of the nervous system. Together with the peripheral nervous system, it has a fundamental role in the control of behavior.
Hallucination	Hallucination refers to a perception in the absence of sensory stimulation that is confused with reality.
Delirium	Delirium is a medical term used to describe an acute decline in attention and cognition. Delirium is probably the single most common acute disorder affecting adults in general hospitals. It affects 10-20% of all adults in hospital, and 30-40% of older patients.
Amnesia	Amnesia is a condition in which memory is disturbed. The causes of amnesia are organic or functional. Organic causes include damage to the brain, through trauma or disease, or use of certain (generally sedative) drugs.
Transgender	Transgender is generally used as an overarching term for a variety of individuals, behaviors, and groups involving tendencies along the gender continuum that are opposite to or in divergence from the gender role (woman or man) commonly, but not always, assigned for life at birth.

Young adult	An young adult is someone between the ages of 20 and 40 years old.

Infection	The invasion and multiplication of microorganisms in body tissues is called an infection.
Abortion	An abortion is the termination of a pregnancy associated with the death of an embryo or a fetus.
Advocate	An advocate is one who speaks on behalf of another, especially in a legal context. Implicit in the concept is the notion that the represented lacks the knowledge, skill, ability, or standing to speak for themselves.
Outcome	Outcome is the impact of care provided to a patient. They can be positive, such as the ability to walk freely as a result of rehabilitation, or negative, such as the occurrence of bedsores as a result of lack of mobility of a patient.
Methotrexate	Methotrexate (abbreviated MTX; formerly known as amethopterin) is an antimetabolite drug used in treatment of cancer and autoimmune diseases. It acts by inhibiting the metabolism of folic acid.
Cancer	Cancer is a class of diseases or disorders characterized by uncontrolled division of cells and the ability of these cells to invade other tissues, either by direct growth into adjacent tissue through invasion or by implantation into distant sites by metastasis.
Reproduction	Biological reproduction is the biological process by which new individual organisms are produced. Reproduction is a fundamental feature of all known life; each individual organism exists as the result of reproduction by an antecedent.
Fertilization	Fertilization is fusion of gametes to form a new organism. In animals, the process involves a sperm fusing with an ovum, which eventually leads to the development of an embryo.
Contraception	A behavior or device that prevents fertilization is called contraception.
Conception	Conception is fusion of gametes to form a new organism. In animals, the process involves a sperm fusing with an ovum, which eventually leads to the development of an embryo.
Sperm	Sperm refers to the male sex cell with three distinct parts at maturity: head, middle piece, and tail.
Ovum	An ovum is a female sex cell or gamete. It is a mature egg cell released during ovulation from an ovary.
Barrier method	A barrier method refers to methods of preventing pregnancy by forming an impenetrable barrier between sexual partners.
Cervical cap	A birth control device consisting of a rubber cap that fits over the cervix, preventing sperm form entering the uterus is called cervical cap.
Spermicide	Spermicide refers to a sperm-killing chemical; used for contraceptive purposes.
Diaphragm	The diaphragm is a shelf of muscle extending across the bottom of the ribcage. It is critically important in respiration: in order to draw air into the lungs, the diaphragm contracts, thus enlarging the thoracic cavity and reducing intra-thoracic pressure.
Condom	Sheath used to cover the penis during sexual intercourse is referred to as condom.
Egg	An egg is the zygote, resulting from fertilization of the ovum. It nourishes and protects the embryo.
Penis	The penis is the male reproductive organ and for mammals additionally serves as the external male organ of urination.
Semen	Semen is a fluid that contains spermatozoa. It is secreted by the gonads (sexual glands) of male or hermaphroditic animals including humans for fertilization of female ova. Semen discharged by an animal or human is known as ejaculate, and the process of discharge is

called ejaculation.

Concept	A mental category used to class together objects, relations, events, abstractions, or qualities that have common properties is called concept.
Ovulation	Ovulation is the process in the menstrual cycle by which a mature ovarian follicle ruptures and discharges an ovum (also known as an oocyte, female gamete, or casually, an egg) that participates in reproduction.
Hormone	A hormone is a chemical messenger from one cell to another. All multicellular organisms produce hormones. The best known hormones are those produced by endocrine glands of vertebrate animals, but hormones are produced by nearly every organ system and tissue type in a human or animal body. Hormone molecules are secreted directly into the bloodstream, they move by circulation or diffusion to their target cells, which may be nearby cells in the same tissue or cells of a distant organ of the body.
Mucus	Mucus is a slippery secretion of the lining of various membranes in the body (mucous membranes). Mucus aids in the protection of the lungs by trapping foreign particles that enter the nose during normal breathing. Additionally, it prevents tissues from drying out.
Vagina	The vagina is the tubular tract leading from the uterus to the exterior of the body in female placental mammals and marsupials, or to the cloaca in female birds, monotremes, and some reptiles. Female insects and other invertebrates also have a vagina, which is the terminal part of the oviduct.
Reservoir	Reservoir is the source of infection. It is the environment in which microorganisms are able to live and grow.
Health	Health is a term that refers to a combination of the absence of illness, the ability to cope with everyday activities, physical fitness, and high quality of life.
Silicon	Silicon is the chemical element in the periodic table that has the symbol Si and atomic number 14. It is the second most abundant element in the Earth's crust, making up 25.7% of it by weight.
Cervix	The cervix is actually the lower, narrow portion of the uterus where it joins with the top end of the vagina. It is cylindrical or conical in shape and protrudes through the upper anterior vaginal wall.
Antibody	An antibody is a protein used by the immune system to identify and neutralize foreign objects like bacteria and viruses. Each antibody recognizes a specific antigen unique to its target.
Testosterone	Testosterone is a steroid hormone from the androgen group. Testosterone is secreted in the testes of men and the ovaries of women. It is the principal male sex hormone and the "original" anabolic steroid. In both males and females, it plays key roles in health and well-being.
Population	Population refers to all members of a well-defined group of organisms, events, or things.
Skin	Skin is an organ of the integumentary system composed of a layer of tissues that protect underlying muscles and organs.
Progestin	A progestin is a synthetic progestagen. These particular synthetic hormones are most often used in the production of contraceptives.
Gonadotropin	A hormone that stimulates the gonads is gonadotropin. They are protein hormones secreted by gonadotrope cells of the pituitary gland of vertebrates.
Agonist	Agonist refers to a drug that mimics or increases a neurotransmitter's effects.
Gland	A gland is an organ in an animal's body that synthesizes a substance for release such as

hormones, often into the bloodstream or into cavities inside the body or its outer surface.

Pituitary gland	The pituitary gland or hypophysis is an endocrine gland about the size of a pea that sits in the small, bony cavity (sella turcica) at the base of the brain. Its posterior lobe is connected to a part of the brain called the hypothalamus via the infundibulum (or stalk), giving rise to the tuberoinfundibular pathway.
Blocking	A sudden break or interuption in the flow of thinking or speech that is seen as an absence in thought is refered to as blocking.
Lead	Lead is a chemical element in the periodic table that has the symbol Pb and atomic number 82. A soft, heavy, toxic and malleable poor metal, lead is bluish white when freshly cut but tarnishes to dull gray when exposed to air. Lead is used in building construction, lead-acid batteries, bullets and shot, and is part of solder, pewter, and fusible alloys.
Hip	In anatomy, the hip is the bony projection of the femur, known as the greater trochanter, and the overlying muscle and fat.
Suppository	A suppository is a medicine that is inserted either into the rectum (rectal suppository) or into the vagina (vaginal suppository) where it melts.
Gonorrhea	Gonorrhea refers to an acute infectious sexually transmitted disease of the mucous membranes of the genitourinary tract, eye, rectum, and throat. It is caused by Neisseria gonorrhoeae.
Counselor	A counselor is a mental health professional who specializes in helping people with problems not involving serious mental disorders.
Base	The common definition of a base is a chemical compound that absorbs hydronium ions when dissolved in water (a proton acceptor). An alkali is a special example of a base, where in an aqueous environment, hydroxide ions are donated.
Chlamydia	A sexually transmitted disease, caused by a bacterium, that causes inflammation of the urethra in males and of the urethra and cervix in females is referred to as chlamydia.
Bacteria	The domain that contains procaryotic cells with primarily diacyl glycerol diesters in their membranes and with bacterial rRNA. Bacteria also is a general term for organisms that are composed of procaryotic cells and are not multicellular.
HIV	The virus that causes AIDS is HIV (human immunodeficiency virus).
Aerosol	Liquid that is dispersed in the form of a fine mist is called aerosol.
Uterus	The uterus is the major female reproductive organ of most mammals. One end, the cervix, opens into the vagina; the other is connected on both sides to the fallopian tubes. The main function is to accept a fertilized ovum which becomes implanted into the endometrium, and derives nourishment from blood vessels which develop exclusively for this purpose.
Blood pressure	Blood pressure is the pressure exerted by the blood on the walls of the blood vessels.
Diarrhea	Diarrhea or diarrhoea is a condition in which the sufferer has frequent and watery, chunky, or loose bowel movements.
Syndrome	Syndrome is the association of several clinically recognizable features, signs, symptoms, phenomena or characteristics which often occur together, so that the presence of one feature alerts the physician to the presence of the others
Virus	Obligate intracellular parasite of living cells consisting of an outer capsid and an inner core of nucleic acid is referred to as virus. The term virus usually refers to those particles that infect eukaryotes whilst the term bacteriophage or phage is used to describe those infecting prokaryotes.
Shock	Circulatory shock, a state of cardiac output that is insufficient to meet the body's

	physiological needs, with consequences ranging from fainting to death is referred to as shock. Insulin shock, a state of severe hypoglycemia caused by administration of insulin.
Fever	Fever (also known as pyrexia, or a febrile response, and archaically known as ague) is a medical symptom that describes an increase in internal body temperature to levels that are above normal (37°C, 98.6°F).
Blood	Blood is a circulating tissue composed of fluid plasma and cells. The main function of blood is to supply nutrients (oxygen, glucose) and constitutional elements to tissues and to remove waste products.
Human papilloma virus	Human papilloma virus is a member of a group of viruses in the genus Papillomavirus that can infect humans and cause changes in cells leading to abnormal tissue growth.
Toxic shock syndrome	Toxic shock syndrome (TSS) is a rare but potentially fatal disease caused by a bacterial toxin. Different bacterial toxins may cause toxic shock syndrome, depending on the situation. The causative agent is Staphylococcus aureus.
Urethra	In anatomy, the urethra is a tube which connects the urinary bladder to the outside of the body. The urethra has an excretory function in both sexes, to pass urine to the outside, and also a reproductive function in the male, as a passage for sperm.
Bladder	A hollow muscular storage organ for storing urine is a bladder.
Copper	Copper is a chemical element in the periodic table that has the symbol Cu (L.: Cuprum) and atomic number 29. It is a ductile metal with excellent electrical conductivity, and finds extensive use as a building material, as an electrical conductor, and as a component of various alloys.
Silver	Silver is a chemical element with the symbol Ag. A soft white lustrous transition metal, it has the highest electrical and thermal conductivity of any metal and occurs in minerals and in free form.
Toxin	Toxin refers to a microbial product or component that can injure another cell or organism at low concentrations. Often the term refers to a poisonous protein, but toxins may be lipids and other substances.
Wound	A wound is type of physical trauma wherein the skin is torn, cut or punctured, or where blunt force trauma causes a contusion.
Progesterone	Progesterone is a C-21 steroid hormone involved in the female menstrual cycle, pregnancy (supports gestation) and embryogenesis of humans and other species.
Estrogen	Estrogen is a steroid that functions as the primary female sex hormone. While present in both men and women, they are found in women in significantly higher quantities.
Follicle	Follicle refers to a cluster of cells surrounding, protecting, and nourishing a developing egg cell in the ovary; also secretes estrogen. In botany, a follicle is a type of simple dry fruit produced by certain flowering plants. It is regarded as one the most primitive types of fruits, and derives from a simple pistil or carpel.
Ovaries	Ovaries are egg-producing reproductive organs found in female organisms.
Ovary	The primary reproductive organ of a female is called an ovary.
Placebo	A placebo is an inactive substance (pill, liquid, etc.), which is administered as if it were a therapy, but which has no therapeutic value other than the placebo effect.
Vitamin	An organic compound other than a carbohydrate, lipid, or protein that is needed for normal metabolism but that the body cannot synthesize in adequate amounts is called a vitamin.
Pain	Pain is an unpleasant sensation which may be associated with actual or potential tissue

Go to **Cram101.com** for the Practice Tests for this Chapter.

damage and which may have physical and emotional components.

Eye	An eye is an organ that detects light. Different kinds of light-sensitive organs are found in a variety of creatures. The simplest eyes do nothing but detect whether the surroundings are light or dark, while more complex eyes can distinguish shapes and colors.
Riboflavin	Riboflavin is an easily absorbed, water-soluble micronutrient with a key role in maintaining human health. Like the other B vitamins, it supports energy production by aiding in the metabolising of fats, carbohydrates, and proteins.
Tetracycline	Tetracycline is an antibiotic produced by the streptomyces bacterium, indicated for use against many bacterial infections. It is commonly used to treat acne.
Pharmacist	A pharmacist takes requests for medicines from a physician in the form of a medical prescription and dispense the medication to the patient and counsel them on the proper use and adverse effects of that medication.
Infertility	The inability to conceive after one year of regular, unprotected intercourse is infertility.
Menstrual cycle	The menstrual cycle is the set of recurring physiological changes in a female's body that are under the control of the reproductive hormone system and necessary for reproduction. Besides humans, only other great apes exhibit menstrual cycles, in contrast to the estrus cycle of most mammalian species.
Stroke	A stroke or cerebrovascular accident (CVA) occurs when the blood supply to a part of the brain is suddenly interrupted.
Endometriosis	Endometriosis is a common medical condition where the tissue lining the uterus is found outside of the uterus, typically affecting other organs in the pelvis.
Heart attack	A heart attack, is a serious, sudden heart condition usually characterized by varying degrees of chest pain or discomfort, weakness, sweating, nausea, vomiting, and arrhythmias, sometimes causing loss of consciousness. It occurs when the blood supply to a part of the heart is interrupted, causing death and scarring of the local heart tissue.
Blood clot	A blood clot is the final product of the blood coagulation step in hemostasis. It is achieved via the aggregation of platelets that form a platelet plug, and the activation of the humoral coagulation system
Anemia	Anemia is a deficiency of red blood cells and/or hemoglobin. This results in a reduced ability of blood to transfer oxygen to the tissues, and this causes hypoxia; since all human cells depend on oxygen for survival, varying degrees of anemia can have a wide range of clinical consequences.
Pelvic inflammatory disease	Pelvic inflammatory disease is a generic term for infection of the female uterus, fallopian tubes, and/or ovaries as it progresses to scar formation with adhesions to nearby tissues and organs.
Cramp	A cramp is an unpleasant sensation caused by contraction, usually of a muscle. It can be caused by cold or overexertion.
Cyst	A cyst is a closed sac having a distinct membrane and developing abnormally in a cavity or structure of the body. They may occur as a result of a developmental error in the embryo during pregnancy or they may be caused by infections.
Iron	Iron is essential to all organisms, except for a few bacteria. It is mostly stably incorporated in the inside of metalloproteins, because in exposed or in free form it causes production of free radicals that are generally toxic to cells.
Ectopic pregnancy	An ectopic pregnancy is one in which the fertilized ovum is implanted in any tissue other than the uterine wall.

Go to **Cram101.com** for the Practice Tests for this Chapter.

Risk factor	A risk factor is a variable associated with an increased risk of disease or infection but risk factors are not necessarily causal.
Anxiety	Anxiety is a complex combination of the feeling of fear, apprehension and worry often accompanied by physical sensations such as palpitations, chest pain and/or shortness of breath.
Abdomen	The abdomen is a part of the body. In humans, and in many other vertebrates, it is the region between the thorax and the pelvis. In fully developed insects, the abdomen is the third (or posterior) segment, after the head and thorax.
Birth control pill	The birth control pill is a chemical taken by mouth to inhibit normal fertility. All act on the hormonal system.
Clinician	A health professional authorized to provide services to people suffering from one or more pathologies is a clinician.
Medicine	Medicine is the branch of health science and the sector of public life concerned with maintaining or restoring human health through the study, diagnosis and treatment of disease and injury.
Injection	A method of rapid drug delivery that puts the substance directly in the bloodstream, in a muscle, or under the skin is called injection.
Tubal ligation	Tubal ligation refers to a means of sterilization in which a woman's two oviducts are tied closed to prevent eggs from reaching the uterus. A segment of each oviduct is removed.
Ligation	Ligation refers to enzymatically catalyzed formation of a phosphodiester bond that links two DNA molecules.
Hysterectomy	A hysterectomy is the surgical removal of the uterus, usually done by a gynecologist. Hysterectomy may be total (removing the body and cervix of the uterus) or partial. In many cases, surgical removal of the ovaries (oophorectomy) is performed concurrent with a hysterectomy.
Sterilization	The process of rendering a person infertile, by performing either a vasectomy in the male or tubal ligation in the female, is referred to as sterilization. Also the process by which all microorganisms are destroyed.
Anesthetic	Anesthetic refers to a substance that causes the loss of the ability to feel pain or other sensory input, e.g., ether or halothane.
Outpatient	Outpatient refers to a patient who requires treatment but does not need to be admitted into the institution for those sevices.
Vasectomy	Vasectomy refers to surgical removal of a section of the two sperm ducts to prevent sperm from reaching the urethra; a means of sterilization in the male.
Local anesthetic	Local anesthetic drugs act mainly by inhibiting sodium influx through sodium-specific ion channels in the neuronal cell membrane, in particular the so-called voltage-gated sodium channels. When the influx of sodium is interrupted, an action potential cannot arise and signal conduction is thus inhibited.
Scrotum	In some male mammals the scrotum is an external bag of skin and muscle containing the testicles. It is an extension of the abdomen, and is located between the penis and anus.
Ductus deferens	The ductus deferens is part of the human male anatomy. There are two of them; they are muscular tubes (surrounded by smooth muscle) connecting the left and right epididymis to the ejaculatory ducts in order to move sperm.
Reproductive	A reproductive system is the ensembles and interactions of organs and or substances within an

system	organism that stricly pertain to reproduction. As an example, this would include in the case of female mammals, the hormone estrogen, the womb and eggs but not the breast.
Testes	The testes are the male generative glands in animals. Male mammals have two testes, which are often contained within an extension of the abdomen called the scrotum.
Ejaculatory duct	The Ejaculatory duct is a part of the human male anatomy, which causes the reflex action of ejaculation. Each male has two of them. They begin at the vas deferens, pass through the prostate, and empty into the urethra at the Colliculus seminalis.
Lymphatic system	Lymph originates as blood plasma lost from the circulatory system, which leaks out into the surrounding tissues. The lymphatic system collects this fluid by diffusion into lymph capillaries, and returns it to the circulatory system.
Syringe	A device for injecting drugs directly into the body is a syringe.
Laparoscope	A laparoscope consists of a Hopkins rod lens system , that is usually connected to a videocamera- single chip or three chip, a fibre optic cable system connected to a 'cold' light source, halogen or xenon, to illuminate the operative field, inserted through a 5 mm or 10 mm canula to view the operative field.
Affect	Affect is the scientific term used to describe a subject's externally displayed mood. This can be assesed by the nurse by observing facial expression, tone of voice, and body language.
Hemorrhage	Loss of blood from the circulatory system is referred to as a hemorrhage.
Embolism	An embolism occurs when an object (the embolus) migrates from one part of the body and causes a blockage of a blood vessel in another part of the body.
Pulmonary embolism	A pulmonary embolism occurs when a blood clot, generally a venous thrombus, becomes dislodged from its site of formation and embolizes to the arterial blood supply of one of the lungs.
Anesthesia	Anesthesia is the process of blocking the perception of pain and other sensations. This allows patients to undergo surgery and other procedures without the distress and pain they would otherwise experience.
General anesthesia	General anesthesia refers to the process of eliminating pain by putting the person to sleep.
Uterine tube	Also called the oviduct, the tube leading out of the ovary to the uterus, into which the secondary oocyte is released is referred to as uterine tube.
Planned parenthood	Planned Parenthood began as the National Birth Control League, which was founded in 1916 under the leadership of Mary Ware Dennett. The organization was later renamed the American Birth Control League under the direction of Margaret Sanger. The League was influential in liberalizing laws against birth control throughout the 1920s and 1930s before changing its name to Planned Parenthood Federation of America, Inc. in 1942.
Implantation	Implantation refers to attachment and penetration of the embryo into the lining of the uterus.
Miscarriage	Miscarriage or spontaneous abortion is the natural or accidental termination of a pregnancy at a stage where the embryo or the fetus is incapable of surviving, generally defined at a gestation of prior to 20 weeks.
Therapeutic abortion	A therapeutic abortion is the termination of a pregnancy because the pregnancy poses physical or mental health risk to the pregnant woman.
Intrauterine device	Intrauterine device refers to birth-control device consisting of a small piece of molded plastic inserted into the uterus, and believed to alter the uterine environment so that fertilization does not occur.

Go to **Cram101.com** for the Practice Tests for this Chapter.

Abstinence	Abstinence has diverse forms. In its oldest sense it is sexual, as in the practice of continence, chastity, and celibacy.
Rhythm method	Rhythm method refers to a form of contraception that relies on refraining from sexual intercourse when conception is most likely to occur; also called natural family planning.
Physiology	The study of the function of cells, tissues, and organs is referred to as physiology.
Centers for Disease Control and Prevention	The Centers for Disease Control and Prevention in Atlanta, Georgia, is recognized as the lead United States agency for protecting the public health and safety of people by providing credible information to enhance health decisions, and promoting health through strong partnerships with state health departments and other organizations.
Sexual assault	Sexual assault refers to any act in which one person is sexually intimate with another person without that other person's consent.
Assault	Assault is a crime of violence against another person that intentionally instills fear and creates a reasonable aprehension of harm.
Intervention	Intervention refers to a planned attempt to break through addicts' or abusers' denial and get them into treatment. Interventions most often occur when legal, workplace, health, relationship, or financial problems have become intolerable.
Menstruation	Loss of blood and tissue from the uterine lining at the end of a female reproductive cycle are referred to as menstruation.
Trimester	In human development, one of three 3-mnonth-long periods of pregnancy is called trimester.
First trimester	The first trimester is the period of time from the first day of the last menstrual period through 12 weeks of gestation. It is during this period that the embryo undergoes most of its early structural development. Most miscarriages occur during this period.
Legalization	Complete removal of all criminal sanctions for certain behaviors without subsequent regulation, is referred to as a legalization.
Mortality	The incidence of death in a population is mortality.
National Cancer Institute	The National Cancer Institute (NCI) is the United States federal government's principal agency for cancer research and training, and the first institute of the present-day National Institutes of Health. The NCI is a federally funded research and development center, one of eight agencies that compose the Public Health Service in the United States Department of Health and Human Services. The Institute coordinates the National Cancer Program.
Induced abortion	An abortion is the termination of a pregnancy associated with the death of an embryo or a fetus. This can occur spontaneously, in the form of a miscarriage, or be intentionally induced through chemical, surgical, or other means which would cause a induced abortion.
Embryo	A prenatal stage of development after germ layers form but before the rudiments of all organs are present is referred to as an embryo.
Fetus	Fetus refers to a developing human from the ninth week of gestation until birth; has all the major structures of an adult.
Culture	Culture, generally refers to patterns of human activity and the symbolic structures that give such activity significance.
Aspiration	In medicine, aspiration is the entry of secretions or foreign material into the trachea and lungs.
Tissue	A collection of interconnected cells that perform a similar function within an organism is called tissue.

Go to **Cram101.com** for the Practice Tests for this Chapter.

Second trimester	The second trimester is the period of time extending from the 13th to the 27th week of gestation. During this period the embryo, now known as a fetus, is recognizable as human in form, but is not developed enough to be viable if born.
Induction	A discipline technique in which a parent uses reason and explanation of the consequences for others of a child's actions is called induction.
Induction abortion	Induction abortion refers to a type of abortion in which chemicals are injected into the uterus through the uterine wall; labor begins and the woman delivers a dead fetus.
Tranquilizer	A sedative, or tranquilizer, is a drug that depresses the central nervous system (CNS), which causes calmness, relaxation, reduction of anxiety, sleepiness, slowed breathing, slurred speech, staggering gait, poor judgment, and slow, uncertain reflexes.
Prostaglandin	A prostaglandin is any member of a group of lipid compounds that are derived from fatty acids and have important functions in the animal body.
Solution	Solution refers to homogenous mixture formed when a solute is dissolved in a solvent.
Placenta	The placenta is an organ present only in female placental mammals during gestation. It is composed of two parts, one genetically and biologically part of the fetus, the other part of the mother. It is implanted in the wall of the uterus, where it receives nutrients and oxygen from the mother's blood and passes out waste.
Trauma	Trauma refers to a severe physical injury or wound to the body caused by an external force, or a psychological shock having a lasting effect on mental life.
Mortality rate	Mortality rate is the number of deaths (from a disease or in general) per 1000 people and typically reported on an annual basis.
Intact dilation and extraction	A late-term abortion procedure in which the body of the fetus is extracted up to the head and then the contents of the cranium are aspirated is called intact dilation and extraction.
Breech	A breech birth (also known as breech presentation) refers to the position of the baby in the uterus such that it will be delivered buttocks first as opposed to the normal head first position.
Cranium	A cranium is a bony structure of Craniates which serves as the general framework for a head. It supports the structures of the face and protects the brain against injury.
Medical abortion	Medical abortion refers to termination of pregnancy by nonsurgical means, such as by taking RU-486.
Steroid	A steroid is a lipid characterized by a carbon skeleton with four fused rings. Different steroids vary in the functional groups attached to these rings. Hundreds of distinct steroids have been identified in plants and animals. Their most important role in most living systems is as hormones.
Receptor	A receptor is a protein on the cell membrane or within the cytoplasm or cell nucleus that binds to a specific molecule (a ligand), such as a neurotransmitter, hormone, or other substance, and initiates the cellular response to the ligand. Receptor, in immunology, the region of an antibody which shows recognition of an antigen.
Trade name	A drug company's name for their patented medication is called a trade name.
Longitudinal study	Longitudinal study refers to a type of developmental study in which the same group of participants is followed and measured at different ages.
Marital status	Marital status refers to those who are reported as being married and where both are usual residents of the household at the time of the census. A de facto marriage is regarded as one where the relationship of two people of the same or opposite sex is reported.

Mental health	Mental health refers to the 'thinking' part of psychosocial health; includes your values, attitudes, and beliefs.
Assessment	In clinical practice, the process by which a mental health professional gathers and compiles information about a client for the purpose of describing the person's problems or disorder and developing a plan of treatment is an assessment.
Diabetes	Diabetes is a medical disorder characterized by varying or persistent elevated blood sugar levels, especially after eating. All types of diabetes share similar symptoms and complications at advanced stages: dehydration and ketoacidosis, cardiovascular disease, chronic renal failure, retinal damage which can lead to blindness, nerve damage which can lead to erectile dysfunction, gangrene with risk of amputation of toes, feet, and even legs.
Genetic disorder	A genetic disorder is a disease caused by abnormal expression of one or more genes in a person causing a clinical phenotype.
Alcohol	Alcohol is a general term, applied to any organic compound in which a hydroxyl group (-OH) is bound to a carbon atom, which in turn is bound to other hydrogen and/or carbon atoms. The general formula for a simple acyclic alcohol is $C_nH_{2n+1}OH$.
Folic acid	Folic acid and folate (the anion form) are forms of a water-soluble B vitamin. These occur naturally in food and can also be taken as supplements.
Acid	An acid is a water-soluble, sour-tasting chemical compound that when dissolved in water, gives a solution with a pH of less than 7.
Planning	In agreement with the patient, the nurse addresses each of the problems identified in the planning phase. For each problem a measurable goal is set. For example, for the patient discussed above, the goal would be for the patient's skin to remain intact. The result is a nursing care plan. This is the third step.
Chromosomes	Physical structures in the cell's nucleus that house the genes. Each human cell has 23 pairs of chromosomes.
DNA	Deoxyribonucleic acid (DNA) is a nucleic acid usually in the form of a double helix that contains the genetic instructions specifying the biological development of all cellular forms of life, and most viruses.
Obesity	The state of being more than 20 percent above the average weight for a person of one's height is called obesity.
Mental retardation	Mental retardation refers to having significantly below-average intellectual functioning and limitations in at least two areas of adaptive functioning. Many categorize retardation as mild, moderate, severe, or profound.
Evaluation	The fifth step of the nursing process where nursing care and the patient's goal achievement are measured is the evaluation.
Contingency	Contingency refers to a close relationship, especially of a causal nature, between two events, one of which regularly follows the other.
Fetal alcohol syndrome	A cluster of abnormalities that appears in the offspring of mothers who drink alcohol heavily during pregnancy is called fetal alcohol syndrome.
Nerve	A nerve is an enclosed, cable-like bundle of nerve fibers or axons, which includes the glia that ensheath the axons in myelin.
Stillbirth	A stillbirth occurs when a fetus, of mid-second trimester to full term gestational age, which has died in the womb or during labour or delivery, exits the maternal body.
Infant mortality	Infant mortality is the death of infants in the first year of life. The leading causes of

Go to Cram101.com for the Practice Tests for this Chapter.

infant mortality are dehydration and disease. Major causes of infant mortality in more developed countries include congenital malformation, infection and SIDS. Infant mortality rate is the number of newborns dying under a year of age divided by the number of live births during the year.

Low birth weight	Low birth weight is defined as a fetus that weighs less than 2500 g (5 lb 8 oz) regardless of gestational age.
Oxygen	Oxygen is a chemical element in the periodic table. It has the symbol O and atomic number 8. Oxygen is the second most common element on Earth, composing around 46% of the mass of Earth's crust and 28% of the mass of Earth as a whole, and is the third most common element in the universe.
Sudden infant death syndrome	Sudden Infant Death Syndrome is the term for the sudden and unexplained death of an apparently healthy infant aged one month to one year.
Cleft	Cleft is a congenital deformity caused by a failure in facial development during pregnancy.
Bronchitis	Bronchitis is an obstructive pulmonary disease characterized by inflammation of the bronchi of the lungs.
Pneumonia	Pneumonia is an illness of the lungs and respiratory system in which the microscopic, air-filled sacs (alveoli) responsible for absorbing oxygen from the atmosphere become inflamed and flooded with fluid.
Statistics	Statistics is a type of data analysis which practice includes the planning, summarizing, and interpreting of observations of a system possibly followed by predicting or forecasting of future events based on a mathematical model of the system being observed.
Statistic	A statistic is an observable random variable of a sample.
Radiation	The emission of electromagnetic waves by all objects warmer than absolute zero is referred to as radiation.
Minerals	Minerals refer to inorganic chemical compounds found in nature; salts.
Protein	A protein is a complex, high-molecular-weight organic compound that consists of amino acids joined by peptide bonds. They are essential to the structure and function of all living cells and viruses. Many are enzymes or subunits of enzymes.
Calorie	Calorie refers to a unit used to measure heat energy and the energy contents of foods.
Calcium	Calcium is the chemical element in the periodic table that has the symbol Ca and atomic number 20. Calcium is a soft grey alkaline earth metal that is used as a reducing agent in the extraction of thorium, zirconium and uranium. Calcium is also the fifth most abundant element in the Earth's crust.
Liver	The liver is an organ in vertebrates, including humans. It plays a major role in metabolism and has a number of functions in the body including drug detoxification, glycogen storage, and plasma protein synthesis. It also produces bile, which is important for digestion.
Yolk	Dense nutrient material that is present in the egg of a bird or reptile is referred to as yolk.
Spina bifida	Spina bifida are birth defects caused by an incomplete closure of one or more vertebral arches of the spine, resulting in malformations of the spinal cord. Spina bifida results in varying degrees of paralysis, absence of skin sensation, incontinence, and spine and limb problems depending on the severity and location of the lesion damage on the spine.
Neural tube	The neural tube is the embryonal structure that gives rise to the brain and spinal cord. The neural tube is derived from a thickened area of ectoderm, the neural plate. The process of

formation of the neural tube is called neurulation.

Neural tube defect	Normally the closure of the neural tube occurs around the 30th day after fertilization. However, if something interferes and the tube fails to close properly, a neural tube defect will occur.
Forceps	A curved instrument that fits around the head of the baby and permits it to be pulled through the birth canal is referred to as forceps.
Organ	Organ refers to a structure consisting of several tissues adapted as a group to perform specific functions.
Registered Nurse	A Registered Nurse is a professional nurse who often supervises the tasks performed by Licensed Practical Nurses, orderlies, medical assistants and nursing assistants. They provide direct care and make decisions regarding plans of care for individuals and groups of healthy, ill and injured people.
Teratogenic	Capacity for causing birth defects is referred to as teratogenic. It is the ability of a chemical to cause birth defects.
Tolerance	Drug tolerance occurs when a subject's reaction to a drug decreases so that larger doses are required to achieve the same effect.
Addiction	Addiction is an uncontrollable compulsion to repeat a behavior regardless of its consequences. Many drugs or behaviors can precipitate a pattern of conditions recognized as addiction, which include a craving for more of the drug or behavior, increased physiological tolerance to exposure, and withdrawal symptoms in the absence of the stimulus.
Hypertension	Hypertension is a medical condition where the blood pressure in the arteries is chronically elevated. Persistent hypertension is one of the risk factors for strokes, heart attacks, heart failure and arterial aneurysm, and is a leading cause of chronic renal failure.
Gestational diabetes	A form of diabetes that develops during pregnancy and typically disappears after the baby is delivered is gestational diabetes.
Measles	Measles refers to a highly contagious skin disease that is endemic throughout the world. It is caused by a morbilli virus in the family Paramyxoviridae, which enters the body through the respiratory tract or through the conjunctiva.
Rubella	An infectious disease that, if contracted by the mother during the first three months of pregnancy, has a high risk of causing mental retardation and physical deformity in the child is called rubella.
Genital herpes	Genital herpes refers to a sexually transmitted disease, caused by a virus, that can cause painful blisters on the genitals and surrounding skin.
Cesarean	A caesarean section (cesarean section AE), or C-section, is a form of childbirth in which a surgical incision is made through a mother's abdomen (laparotomy) and uterus (hysterotomy) to deliver one or more babies. It is usually performed when a vaginal delivery would lead to medical complications.
Lesion	A lesion is a non-specific term referring to abnormal tissue in the body. It can be caused by any disease process including trauma (physical, chemical, electrical), infection, neoplasm, metabolic and autoimmune.
Cesarean section	A cesarean section is a form of childbirth in which a surgical incision is made through a mother's abdomen and uterus to deliver one or more babies. It is usually performed when a vaginal delivery would lead to medical complications.
Menopause	Menopause is the physiological cessation of menstrual cycles associated with advancing age in species that experience such cycles. Menopause is sometimes referred to as change of life or

	climacteric.
Life span	Life span refers to the upper boundary of life, the maximum number of years an individual can live. The maximum life span of human beings is about 120 years of age.
Menarche	Menarche is the first menstrual period as a girl's body progresses through the changes of puberty. Menarche usually occurs about two years after the first changes of breast development.
Toxoplasmosis	A disease of animals and humans caused by the parasitic protozoan, Toxoplasma gondii is called toxoplasmosis.
Zona pellucida	The zona pellucida is a glycoprotein matrix surrounding the plasma membrane of an oocyte. This structure binds spermatozoa, and is required to initiate the acrosome reaction.
Endometrium	The endometrium is the inner uterine membrane in mammals which is developed in preparation for the implantation of a fertilized egg upon its arrival into the uterus.
Blastocyst	An early stage of prenatal development that consists of a hollow ball of cells is a blastocyst.
Corona radiata	The layer of cells surrounding an egg after ovulation is a corona radiata.
Zygote	A zygote is a cell that is the result of fertilization. That is, two haploid cells usually (but not always) an ovum from a female and a sperm cell from a male merge into a single diploid cell called the zygote.
Viability	Viability means in general "capacity for survival" and is more specifically used to mean a capacity for living, developing, or germinating under favorable conditions. In the context of pregnancy, viability refers to either an early stage pregnancy that has a chance of reaching full-term and a live birth; or the shortest length of pregnancy after which a child born prematurely has a chance of survival. Generally, this ranges from 20-27 weeks.
Severe mental retardation	A limitation in mental development as measured on the Wechsler Adult Intelligence Scale with scores between 20 -34 is called severe mental retardation.
Incidence	In epidemiological studies of a particular disorder, the rate at which new cases occur in a given place at a given time is called incidence.
Third trimester	The third trimester is the period of time extending from the 28th week of gestation to delivery. It is during this period that the fetus reaches viability, and may survive if born prematurely.
Stress	Stress refers to a condition that is a response to factors that change the human systems normal state.
Human chorionic gonadotropin	Human chorionic gonadotropin is a peptide hormone produced in pregnancy, that is made by the embryo soon after conception and later by the trophoblast. Its role is to prevent the disintegration of the corpus luteum of the ovary and thereby maintain progesterone production that is critical for a pregnancy in humans.
Urine	Concentrated filtrate produced by the kidneys and excreted via the bladder is called urine.
Chorionic gonadotropin	A hormone, secreted by the chorion, that maintains the integrity of the corpus luteum during early pregnancy is called chorionic gonadotropin.
Red blood cell	The red blood cell is the most common type of blood cell and is the vertebrate body's principal means of delivering oxygen from the lungs or gills to body tissues via the blood.
Red blood cells	Red blood cells are the most common type of blood cell and are the vertebrate body's principal means of delivering oxygen from the lungs or gills to body tissues via the blood.

False negative	A false negative, also called a Type II error or miss, exists when a test incorrectly reports that a result was not detected, when it was really present.
Circulatory system	The circulatory system or cardiovascular system is the organ system which circulates blood around the body of most animals.
Umbilical cord	A structure containing arteries and veins that connects a developing embryo to the placenta of the mother is an umbilical cord.
Blood vessel	A blood vessel is a part of the circulatory system and function to transport blood throughout the body. The most important types, arteries and veins, are so termed because they carry blood away from or towards the heart, respectively.
Course	Pattern of development and change of a disorder over time is a course.
Amniocentesis	Amniocentesis is a medical procedure used for prenatal diagnosis, in which a small amount of amniotic fluid is extracted from the amnion around a developing fetus. It is usually offered when there may be an increased risk for genetic conditions in the pregnancy.
Amniotic sac	A sac within the uterus that contains the embryo or fetus is an amniotic sac.
Sonography	Medical ultrasonography (sonography) is an ultrasound-based diagnostic imaging technique used to visualize muscles and internal organs, their size, structure and any pathological lesions, making them useful for scanning the organs. Obstetric sonography is commonly used during pregnancy.
Ultrasound	Ultrasound is sound with a frequency greater than the upper limit of human hearing, approximately 20 kilohertz. Medical use can visualise muscle and soft tissue, making them useful for scanning the organs, and obstetric ultrasonography is commonly used during pregnancy.
Nervous system	The nervous system of an animal coordinates the activity of the muscles, monitors the organs, constructs and processes input from the senses, and initiates actions.
Central nervous system	The central nervous system comprized of the brain and spinal cord, represents the largest part of the nervous system. Together with the peripheral nervous system, it has a fundamental role in the control of behavior.
Digestive system	The organ system that ingests food, breaks it down into smaller chemical units, and absorbs the nutrient molecules is referred to as the digestive system.
Fetoscopy	Fetoscopy is an endoscopic procedure during pregnancy to allow access to the fetus, the amniotic cavity, the umbilical cord, and the fetal side of the placenta.
Genetic counseling	Genetic counseling generally refers to prenatal counseling done when a genetic condition is suspected in a pregnancy. Genetic counseling is the process by which patients or relatives at risk of an inherited disorder are advised of the consequences and nature of the disorder, the probability of developing or transmitting it, and the options open to them in management and family planning in order to prevent, avoid or ameliorate it.
Trial	In classical conditioning, any presentation of a stimulus or pair of stimuli is called a trial.
Childbirth	Childbirth (also called labour, birth, partus or parturition) is the culmination of a human pregnancy with the emergence of a newborn infant from its mother's uterus.
Episiotomy	An episiotomy is a surgical incision through the perineum made to enlarge the vagina and assist childbirth.
Perineum	The perineum is the region between the genital area and the anus in both sexes.
Afterbirth	The placenta is connected to the fetus via the umbilical cord which is composed of blood

	vessels and connective tissue. When the fetus is delivered, the placenta is delivered afterwards, and for this reason is often called the afterbirth.
Vulva	The outer features of the female reproductive anatomy is referred to as vulva.
Anus	In anatomy, the anus is the external opening of the rectum. Closure is controlled by sphincter muscles. Feces are expelled from the body through the anus during the act of defecation, which is the primary function of the anus.
Lamaze method	Lamaze method refers to a childbirth method in which women are educated about childbirth, learn to relax and breathe in patterns that conserve energy and lessen pain, and have a coach present during childbirth. Also termed prepared childbirth.
Midwife	A midwife is an autonomous practitioner who specializes in normal pregnancy, childbirth and the postpartum. They generally strive to help women have a healthy pregnancy and natural birth experience.
Colostrum	Thin, milky fluid rich in proteins, including antibodies, that is secreted by the mammary glands a few days prior to or after delivery before true milk is secreted is called colostrum.
Immune system	The immune system is the system of specialized cells and organs that protect an organism from outside biological influences. When the immune system is functioning properly, it protects the body against bacteria and viral infections, destroying cancer cells and foreign substances.
Depression	In everyday language depression refers to any downturn in mood, which may be relatively transitory and perhaps due to something trivial. This is differentiated from Clinical depression which is marked by symptoms that last two weeks or more and are so severe that they interfere with daily living.
Brain	The part of the central nervous system involved in regulating and controlling body activity and interpreting information from the senses transmitted through the nervous system is referred to as the brain.
Postpartum depression	After giving birth, about 70-80% of women experience an episode of baby blues, feelings of depression, anger, anxiety and guilt lasting for several days. About 10% of new mothers develop the more severe postpartum depression, a form of major depression for which treatment is widely recommended.
Preeclampsia	A complication in pregnancy characterized by high blood pressure, protein in the urine, and edema is referred to as preeclampsia.
Edema	Edema is swelling of any organ or tissue due to accumulation of excess fluid. Edema has many root causes, but its common mechanism is accumulation of fluid into the tissues.
Stomach	The stomach is an organ in the alimentary canal used to digest food. It's primary function is not the absorption of nutrients from digested food; rather, the main job of the stomach is to break down large food molecules into smaller ones, so that they can be absorbed into the blood more easily.
Pulse	The rhythmic stretching of the arteries caused by the pressure of blood forced through the arteries by contractions of the ventricles during systole is a pulse.
Eclampsia	Eclampsia is a serious complication of pregnancy and is characterised by convulsions.
Seizure	A seizure is a temporary alteration in brain function expressed as a changed mental state, tonic or clonic movements and various other symptoms. They are due to temporary abnormal electrical activity of a group of brain cells.
Kidney	The kidney is a bean-shaped excretory organ in vertebrates. Part of the urinary system, the

Go to **Cram101.com** for the Practice Tests for this Chapter.

	kidneys filter wastes (especially urea) from the blood and excrete them, along with water, as urine.
Pelvis	The pelvis is the bony structure located at the base of the spine (properly known as the caudal end). The pelvis incorporates the socket portion of the hip joint for each leg (in bipeds) or hind leg (in quadrupeds). It forms the lower limb (or hind-limb) girdle of the skeleton.
Spontaneous abortion	Spontaneous abortion is the natural or accidental termination of a pregnancy at a stage where the embryo or the fetus is incapable of surviving, generally defined at a gestation less than 20 weeks.
Genetic abnormality	Any abnormality in the genes, including missing genes, extra genes, or defective genes is called genetic abnormality.
Rh factor	Rh factor refers to a protein on the red blood cells of some people but not others ; the exposure of Rh-negative individuals to Rh-positive blood triggers the production of antibodies to Rh-positive blood cells.
Grief	Grief is a multi-faceted response to loss. Although conventionally focused on the emotional response to loss, it also has a physical, cognitive, behavioral, social and philosophical dimensions.
Diagnosis	In medicine, diagnosis is the process of identifying a medical condition or disease by its signs, symptoms, and from the results of various diagnostic procedures.
Fallopian tube	The Fallopian tube is one of two very fine tubes leading from the ovaries of female mammals into the uterus. They deliver the ovum to the uterus.
Scar	A scar results from the biologic process of wound repair in the skin and other tissues of the body. It is a connective tissue that fills the wound.
Varicose veins	Varicose veins are veins on the leg which are large, twisted, and ropelike, and can cause pain, swelling, or itching. They are an extreme form of telangiectasia, or spider veins.
Veins	Blood vessels that return blood toward the heart from the circulation are referred to as veins.
Vein	Vein in animals, is a vessel that returns blood to the heart. In plants, a vascular bundle in a leaf, composed of xylem and phloem.
Motility	Motility is the ability to move spontaneously and independently. The term can apply to single cells, or to multicellular organisms.
Irritability	Irritability is an excessive response to stimuli. Irritability takes many forms, from the contraction of a unicellular organism when touched to complex reactions involving all the senses of higher animals.
Hot flash	A hot flash is a symptom of menopause and changing hormone levels which typically expresses itself at night as periods of intense heat with sweating and rapid heartbeat and may typically last from two to thirty minutes on each occasion.
Donor	Blood donation is a process by which a blood donor voluntarily has blood drawn for storage in a blood bank for subsequent use in a blood transfusion.
In vitro	In vitro is an experimental technique where the experiment is performed in a test tube, or generally outside a living organism or cell.
In vitro fertilization	In vitro fertilization is a technique in which egg cells are fertilized outside the woman's body. It is a major treatment in infertility where other methods of achieving conception have failed.

Go to **Cram101.com** for the Practice Tests for this Chapter.

Intracytoplamic sperm injection	Intracytoplasmic sperm injection is an in vitro fertilization procedure in which a single sperm is injected directly into an egg; this procedure is most commonly used to overcome male infertility problems.
Freezing	Freezing is the process in which blood is frozen and all of the plasma and 99% of the WBCs are eliminated when thawing takes place and the nontransferable cryoprotectant is removed.
Moral	A "moral" may refer to a particular principle, usually as an informal and general summary with respect to a moral principle, as it is applied in a given human situation.
Gamete	A gamete is a specialized germ cell that unites with another gamete during fertilization in organisms that reproduce sexually. They are haploid cells; that is, they contain one complete set of chromosomes. When they unite they form a zygote a cell having two complete sets of chromosomes and therefore diploid.
Gamete intrafallopian transfer	Gamete intrafallopian transfer refers to an infertility treatment in which sperm and oocytes are placed in a woman's fallopian tube, assisting fertilization in a natural setting.
Artificial insemination	Artificial insemination is when sperm is placed into a female's ovarian follicle (intrafollicular), uterus (intrauterine), cervix (intracervical), or fallopian tubes (intratubal) using artificial means rather than by sexual intercourse.
Stigma	Stigma refers to a personal characteristic that at least some other individuals perceive negatively because that characteristic is different than those of the general population.
Crisis	A crisis is a temporary state of high anxiety where the persons usual coping mechanisims cease to work. This may have a result of disorganization or possibly personality growth.
Sexuality	Sexuality refers to the expression of sexual sensation and related intimacy between human beings, as well as the expression of identity through sex and as influenced by or based on
Insight	Insight refers to a sudden awareness of the relationships among various elements that had previously appeared to be independent of one another.

159

Health	Health is a term that refers to a combination of the absence of illness, the ability to cope with everyday activities, physical fitness, and high quality of life.
Fiber	Fibers used by man come from a wide variety of sources: Natural fiber include those made out of plants, animal and mineral sources. Natural fibers can be classified according to their origin.
Advocate	An advocate is one who speaks on behalf of another, especially in a legal context. Implicit in the concept is the notion that the represented lacks the knowledge, skill, ability, or standing to speak for themselves.
Planning	In agreement with the patient, the nurse addresses each of the problems identified in the planning phase. For each problem a measurable goal is set. For example, for the patient discussed above, the goal would be for the patient's skin to remain intact. The result is a nursing care plan. This is the third step.
Hypothalamus	Located below the thalamus, the hypothalamus links the nervous system to the endocrine system by synthesizing and secreting neurohormones often called releasing hormones because they function by stimulating the secretion of hormones from the anterior pituitary gland.
Brain	The part of the central nervous system involved in regulating and controlling body activity and interpreting information from the senses transmitted through the nervous system is referred to as the brain.
Constant	A behavior or characteristic that does not vary from one observation to another is referred to as a constant.
Carbohydrate	Carbohydrate is a chemical compound that contains oxygen, hydrogen, and carbon atoms. They consist of monosaccharide sugars of varying chain lengths and that have the general chemical formula $C_n(H_2O)_n$ or are derivatives of such.
Minerals	Minerals refer to inorganic chemical compounds found in nature; salts.
Protein	A protein is a complex, high-molecular-weight organic compound that consists of amino acids joined by peptide bonds. They are essential to the structure and function of all living cells and viruses. Many are enzymes or subunits of enzymes.
Vitamin	An organic compound other than a carbohydrate, lipid, or protein that is needed for normal metabolism but that the body cannot synthesize in adequate amounts is called a vitamin.
Obesity	The state of being more than 20 percent above the average weight for a person of one's height is called obesity.
Calorie	Calorie refers to a unit used to measure heat energy and the energy contents of foods.
Alcoholic	An alcoholic is dependent on alcohol as characterized by craving, loss of control, physical dependence and withdrawal symptoms, and tolerance.
Lifestyle	The culturally, socially, economically, and environmentally conditioned complex of actions characteristic of an individual, group, or community as a pattern of habituated behavior over time that is health related but not necessarily health directed is a lifestyle.
Sugar	A sugar is the simplest molecule that can be identified as a carbohydrate. These include monosaccharides and disaccharides, trisaccharides and the oligosaccharides. The term "glyco-" indicates the presence of a sugar in an otherwise non-carbohydrate substance.
Dental caries	Dental caries, also known colloquially as tooth decay, is a disease of the teeth resulting in damage to tooth structure.
Medicine	Medicine is the branch of health science and the sector of public life concerned with maintaining or restoring human health through the study, diagnosis and treatment of disease

	and injury.
Caries	Caries is a progressive destruction of any kind of bone structure, including the skull, the ribs and other bones.
Assess	Assess is to systematically and continuously collect, validate, and communicate patient data.
Blood	Blood is a circulating tissue composed of fluid plasma and cells. The main function of blood is to supply nutrients (oxygen, glucose) and constitutional elements to tissues and to remove waste products.
Skin	Skin is an organ of the integumentary system composed of a layer of tissues that protect underlying muscles and organs.
Monounsaturated fats	In nutrition, monounsaturated fats are dietary fats with one double-bonded carbon in the molecule, with all of the others single-bonded carbons.
Affect	Affect is the scientific term used to describe a subject's externally displayed mood. This can be assesed by the nurse by observing facial expression, tone of voice, and body language.
Fructose	Fructose is a simple sugar (monosaccharide) found in many foods and one of the three most important blood sugars along with glucose and galactose.
Diabetes	Diabetes is a medical disorder characterized by varying or persistent elevated blood sugar levels, especially after eating. All types of diabetes share similar symptoms and complications at advanced stages: dehydration and ketoacidosis, cardiovascular disease, chronic renal failure, retinal damage which can lead to blindness, nerve damage which can lead to erectile dysfunction, gangrene with risk of amputation of toes, feet, and even legs.
Magnesium	Magnesium is the chemical element in the periodic table that has the symbol Mg and atomic number 12 and an atomic mass of 24.31.
Selenium	Selenium is a chemical element in the periodic table that has the symbol Se and atomic number 34. It is a toxic nonmetal that is chemically related to sulfur and tellurium. It occurs in several different forms but one of these is a stable gray metallike form that conducts electricity better in the light than in the dark and is used in photocells.
Unsaturated fat	An unsaturated fat is a fat or fatty acid in which there is one or more double bonds between carbon atoms of the fatty acid chain. Such fat molecules are monounsaturated if each contains one double bond, and polyunsaturated if each contain more than one.
Metabolism	Metabolism is the biochemical modification of chemical compounds in living organisms and cells. This includes the biosynthesis of complex organic molecules (anabolism) and their breakdown (catabolism).
Salmonella	Salmonella is a genus of rod-shaped Gram-negative enterobacteria that causes typhoid fever, paratyphoid and foodborne illness. It is motile in nature and produces hydrogen sulfide.
Bacteria	The domain that contains procaryotic cells with primarily diacyl glycerol diesters in their membranes and with bacterial rRNA. Bacteria also is a general term for organisms that are composed of procaryotic cells and are not multicellular.
Value	Value is worth in general, and it is thought to be connected to reasons for certain practices, policies, actions, beliefs or emotions. Value is "that which one acts to gain and/or keep."
Course	Pattern of development and change of a disorder over time is a course.
Cancer	Cancer is a class of diseases or disorders characterized by uncontrolled division of cells and the ability of these cells to invade other tissues, either by direct growth into adjacent tissue through invasion or by implantation into distant sites by metastasis.

Go to **Cram101.com** for the Practice Tests for this Chapter.

Survey	A method of scientific investigation in which a large sample of people answer questions about their attitudes or behavior is referred to as a survey.
Egg	An egg is the zygote, resulting from fertilization of the ovum. It nourishes and protects the embryo.
Gauge	The diameter of the needle is indicated by the needle gauge.
Epidemic	An epidemic is a disease that appears as new cases in a given human population, during a given period, at a rate that substantially exceeds what is "expected", based on recent experience.
Base	The common definition of a base is a chemical compound that absorbs hydronium ions when dissolved in water (a proton acceptor). An alkali is a special example of a base, where in an aqueous environment, hydroxide ions are donated.
Saturated fat	Saturated fat is fat that consists of triglycerides containing only fatty acids that have no double bonds between the carbon atoms of the fatty acid chain (hence, they are fully saturated with hydrogen atoms).
Cholesterol	Cholesterol is a steroid, a lipid, and an alcohol, found in the cell membranes of all body tissues, and transported in the blood plasma of all animals. It is an important component of the membranes of cells, providing stability; it makes the membrane's fluidity stable over a bigger temperature interval.
Alcohol	Alcohol is a general term, applied to any organic compound in which a hydroxyl group (-OH) is bound to a carbon atom, which in turn is bound to other hydrogen and/or carbon atoms. The general formula for a simple acyclic alcohol is $C_nH_{2n+1}OH$.
Salt	Salt is a term used for ionic compounds composed of positively charged cations and negatively charged anions, so that the product is neutral and without a net charge.
Essential nutrient	An essential nutrient is a nutrient required for normal body functioning that can not be synthesized by the body. Categories of essential nutrient include vitamins, dietary minerals, essential fatty acids and essential amino acids.
Digestive system	The organ system that ingests food, breaks it down into smaller chemical units, and absorbs the nutrient molecules is referred to as the digestive system.
Amylase	Amylase is a digestive enzyme classified as a saccharidase. It is mainly a constituent of pancreatic juice and saliva, needed for the breakdown of long-chain carbohydrates (such as starch) into smaller units.
Enzyme	An enzyme is a protein that catalyzes, or speeds up, a chemical reaction. They are essential to sustain life because most chemical reactions in biological cells would occur too slowly, or would lead to different products, without them.
Saliva	Saliva is the moist, clear, and usually somewhat frothy substance produced in the mouths of some animals, including humans.
Chemical reaction	Chemical reaction refers to a process leading to chemical changes in matter; involves the making and/or breaking of chemical bonds.
Esophagus	The esophagus, or gullet is the muscular tube in vertebrates through which ingested food passes from the mouth area to the stomach. Food is passed through the esophagus by using the process of peristalsis.
Stomach	The stomach is an organ in the alimentary canal used to digest food. It's primary function is not the absorption of nutrients from digested food; rather, the main job of the stomach is to break down large food molecules into smaller ones, so that they can be absorbed into the blood more easily.

Muscle	Muscle is a contractile form of tissue. It is one of the four major tissue types, the other three being epithelium, connective tissue and nervous tissue. Muscle contraction is used to move parts of the body, as well as to move substances within the body.
Organ	Organ refers to a structure consisting of several tissues adapted as a group to perform specific functions.
Pepsin	Pepsin is a digestive protease released by the chief cells in the stomach that functions to degrade food proteins into peptides. It was the first animal enzyme to be discovered.
Acid	An acid is a water-soluble, sour-tasting chemical compound that when dissolved in water, gives a solution with a pH of less than 7.
Hydrochloric acid	The chemical substance hydrochloric acid is the aqueous solution of hydrogen chloride gas. It is a strong acid, the major component of gastric acid.
Mucus	Mucus is a slippery secretion of the lining of various membranes in the body (mucous membranes). Mucus aids in the protection of the lungs by trapping foreign particles that enter the nose during normal breathing. Additionally, it prevents tissues from drying out.
Pancreas	The pancreas is a retroperitoneal organ that serves two functions: exocrine - it produces pancreatic juice containing digestive enzymes, and endocrine - it produces several important hormones, namely insulin.
Liver	The liver is an organ in vertebrates, including humans. It plays a major role in metabolism and has a number of functions in the body including drug detoxification, glycogen storage, and plasma protein synthesis. It also produces bile, which is important for digestion.
Salivary gland	The salivary gland produces saliva, which keeps the mouth and other parts of the digestive system moist. It also helps break down carbohydrates and lubricates the passage of food down from the oro-pharynx to the esophagus to the stomach.
Digestion	Digestion refers to the mechanical and chemical breakdown of food into molecules small enough for the body to absorb; the second main stage of food processing, following ingestion.
Gland	A gland is an organ in an animal's body that synthesizes a substance for release such as hormones, often into the bloodstream or into cavities inside the body or its outer surface.
Intestine	The intestine is the portion of the alimentary canal extending from the stomach to the anus and, in humans and mammals, consists of two segments, the small intestine and the large intestine. The intestine is the part of the body responsible for extracting nutrition from food.
Duodenum	The duodenum is a hollow jointed tube connecting the stomach to the jejunum. It is the first part of the small intestine. Two very important ducts open into the duodenum, namely the bile duct and the pancreatic duct. The duodenum is largely responsible for the breakdown of food in the small intestine.
Jejunum	The jejunum is the central of the three divisions of the small intestine. The inner surface of the jejunum, its mucous membrane, is covered in projections called villi, which increase the surface area of tissue available to absorb nutrients from the gut contents.
Ileum	The ileum is the final section of the small intestine. Its function is to absorb vitamin B12 and bile salts. The wall itself made up of folds, each of which has many tiny finger-like projections known as villi, on its surface.
Small intestine	The small intestine is the part of the gastrointestinal tract between the stomach and the large intestine (colon). In humans over 5 years old it is about 7m long. It is divided into three structural parts: duodenum, jejunum and ileum.
Dehydration	Dehydration is the removal of water from an object. Medically, dehydration is a serious and

Go to **Cram101.com** for the Practice Tests for this Chapter.

	potentially life-threatening condition in which the body contains an insufficient volume of water for normal functioning.
Anus	In anatomy, the anus is the external opening of the rectum. Closure is controlled by sphincter muscles. Feces are expelled from the body through the anus during the act of defecation, which is the primary function of the anus.
Large intestine	In anatomy of the digestive system, the colon, also called the large intestine or large bowel, is the part of the intestine from the cecum ('caecum' in British English) to the rectum. Its primary purpose is to extract water from feces.
Electrolyte	An electrolyte is a substance that dissociates into free ions when dissolved (or molten), to produce an electrically conductive medium. Because they generally consist of ions in solution, they are also known as ionic solutions.
Tissue	A collection of interconnected cells that perform a similar function within an organism is called tissue.
Oxygen	Oxygen is a chemical element in the periodic table. It has the symbol O and atomic number 8. Oxygen is the second most common element on Earth, composing around 46% of the mass of Earth's crust and 28% of the mass of Earth as a whole, and is the third most common element in the universe.
Fibrosis	Replacement of damaged tissue with fibrous scar tissue rather than by the original tissue type is called fibrosis.
Cystic fibrosis	Cystic fibrosis is an autosomal recessive hereditary disease of the exocrine glands. It affects the lungs, sweat glands and the digestive system. It causes chronic respiratory and digestive problems.
Bladder	A hollow muscular storage organ for storing urine is a bladder.
Stress	Stress refers to a condition that is a response to factors that change the human systems normal state.
Intoxication	Condition in which a substance affecting the central nervous system has been ingested and certain maladaptive behaviors or psychological changes, such as belligerence and impaired function, are evident is called intoxication.
Arrhythmias	Arrhythmias refers to abnormal heart rhythms which may be too slow, too early, too rapid, or irregular.
Arrhythmia	Cardiac arrhythmia is a group of conditions in which muscle contraction of the heart is irregular for any reason.
Ecstasy	Ecstasy as an emotion is to be outside oneself, in a trancelike state in which an individual transcends ordinary consciousness and as a result has a heightened capacity for exceptional thought or experience. Ecstasy also refers to a relatively new hallucinogen that is chemically similar to mescaline and the amphetamines.
Sodium	Sodium is the chemical element in the periodic table that has the symbol Na (Natrium in Latin) and atomic number 11. Sodium is a soft, waxy, silvery reactive metal belonging to the alkali metals that is abundant in natural compounds (especially halite). It is highly reactive.
Lead	Lead is a chemical element in the periodic table that has the symbol Pb and atomic number 82. A soft, heavy, toxic and malleable poor metal, lead is bluish white when freshly cut but tarnishes to dull gray when exposed to air. Lead is used in building construction, lead-acid batteries, bullets and shot, and is part of solder, pewter, and fusible alloys.
Diuretic	A diuretic is any drug that elevates the rate of bodily urine excretion.

Go to **Cram101.com** for the Practice Tests for this Chapter.

Physiology	The study of the function of cells, tissues, and organs is referred to as physiology.
Antibody	An antibody is a protein used by the immune system to identify and neutralize foreign objects like bacteria and viruses. Each antibody recognizes a specific antigen unique to its target.
Hormone	A hormone is a chemical messenger from one cell to another. All multicellular organisms produce hormones. The best known hormones are those produced by endocrine glands of vertebrate animals, but hormones are produced by nearly every organ system and tissue type in a human or animal body. Hormone molecules are secreted directly into the bloodstream, they move by circulation or diffusion to their target cells, which may be nearby cells in the same tissue or cells of a distant organ of the body.
Amino acid	An amino acid is any molecule that contains both amino and carboxylic acid functional groups. They are the basic structural building units of proteins. They form short polymer chains called peptides or polypeptides which in turn form structures called proteins.
Essential amino acid	An essential amino acid for an organism is an amino acid that cannot be synthesized by the organism from other available resources, and therefore must be supplied as part of its diet.
Prostate	The prostate is a gland that is part of male mammalian sex organs. Its main function is to secrete and store a clear, slightly basic fluid that is part of semen. The prostate differs considerably between species anatomically, chemically and physiologically.
Tumor	An abnormal mass of cells that forms within otherwise normal tissue is a tumor. This growth can be either malignant or benign
Calcium	Calcium is the chemical element in the periodic table that has the symbol Ca and atomic number 20. Calcium is a soft grey alkaline earth metal that is used as a reducing agent in the extraction of thorium, zirconium and uranium. Calcium is also the fifth most abundant element in the Earth's crust.
Incomplete protein	A protein that lacks adequate amounts of essential amino acids is an incomplete protein.
Osteoporosis	Osteoporosis is a disease of bone in which bone mineral density (BMD) is reduced, bone microarchitecture is disrupted, the amount and variety of non-collagenous proteins in bone is changed, and a concomitantly fracture risk is increased.
Excretion	Excretion is the biological process by which an organism chemically separates waste products from its body. The waste products are then usually expelled from the body by elimination.
Urine	Concentrated filtrate produced by the kidneys and excreted via the bladder is called urine.
Infection	The invasion and multiplication of microorganisms in body tissues is called an infection.
Muscle fiber	Cell with myofibrils containing actin and myosin filaments arranged within sarcomeres is a muscle fiber.
Population	Population refers to all members of a well-defined group of organisms, events, or things.
Recommended dietary allowance	A recommendation for daily nutrient intake established by nutritionists is referred to as recommended dietary Allowance.
Glucose	Glucose, a simple monosaccharide sugar, is one of the most important carbohydrates and is used as a source of energy in animals and plants. Glucose is one of the main products of photosynthesis and starts respiration.
Monosaccharide	A monosaccharide is simplest form of a carbohydrate. They consist of one sugar and are usually colorless, water-soluble, crystalline solids. Some monosaccharides have a sweet taste. They are the building blocks of disaccharides like sucrose and polysaccharides.

Disaccharide	A disaccharide is a sugar (a carbohydrate) composed of two monosaccharides. The two monosaccharides are bonded via a condensation reaction.
Polysaccharide	A carbohydrate composed of many joined monosaccharides is called a polysaccharide.
Glycogen	Glycogen refers to a complex, extensively branched polysaccharide of many glucose monomers; serves as an energy-storage molecule in liver and muscle cells.
Galactose	Galactose is a type of sugar found in dairy products, in sugar beets and other gums and mucilages. It is also synthesized by the body, where it forms part of glycolipids and glycoproteins in several tissues.
Lactose	Lactose is a disaccharide that makes up around 2-8% of the solids in milk. Lactose is a disaccharide consisting of two subunits, a galactose and a glucose linked together.
Starch	Biochemically, starch is a combination of two polymeric carbohydrates (polysaccharides) called amylose and amylopectin.
Gastrointest-nal tract	The gastrointestinal tract is the system of organs within multicellular animals which takes in food, digests it to extract energy and nutrients, and expels the remaining waste.
Diarrhea	Diarrhea or diarrhoea is a condition in which the sufferer has frequent and watery, chunky, or loose bowel movements.
Colon	The colon is the part of the intestine from the cecum to the rectum. Its primary purpose is to extract water from feces.
Hydration	Hydration can create a hydrate from which water can be reextracted. When hydration occurs in a chemical reaction it is called a hydration reaction, in which water is permanently and chemically combined with a reactant in a way that it can no longer be reextracted.
Absorption	Absorption is a physical or chemical phenomenon or a process in which atoms, molecules, or ions enter some bulk phase - gas, liquid or solid material. In nutrition, amino acids are broken down through digestion, which begins in the stomach.
Carbohydrate loading	Carbohydrate loading refers to a week-long program of diet and exercise that results in an increase in muscle glycogen stores.
Hyperactivity	Hyperactivity can be described as a state in which a individual is abnormally easily excitable and exuberant. Strong emotional reactions and a very short span of attention is also typical for the individual.
Psychological test	Psychological test refers to a standardized measure of a sample of a person's behavior.
Addiction	Addiction is an uncontrollable compulsion to repeat a behavior regardless of its consequences. Many drugs or behaviors can precipitate a pattern of conditions recognized as addiction, which include a craving for more of the drug or behavior, increased physiological tolerance to exposure, and withdrawal symptoms in the absence of the stimulus.
Taste bud	A taste bud is a small structure on the upper surface of the tongue, soft palate, and epiglottis that provides information about the taste of food being eaten. The majority on the tongue sit on raized protrusions of the tongue surface called papillae.
Culture	Culture, generally refers to patterns of human activity and the symbolic structures that give such activity significance.
Carcinogen	A carcinogen is any substance or agent that promotes cancer. A carcinogen is often, but not necessarily, a mutagen or teratogen.
World Health Organization	The World Health Organization (WHO) is a specialized agency of the United Nations, acting as a coordinating authority on international public health, headquartered in Geneva,

	Switzerland.
Stool	Stool is the waste matter discharged in a bowel movement.
Cardiovascular disease	Cardiovascular disease refers to afflictions in the mechanisms, including the heart, blood vessels, and their controllers, that are responsible for transporting blood to the body's tissues and organs. Psychological factors may play important roles in such diseases and their treatments.
Kidney	The kidney is a bean-shaped excretory organ in vertebrates. Part of the urinary system, the kidneys filter wastes (especially urea) from the blood and excrete them, along with water, as urine.
Lysine	Lysine is one of the 20 amino acids normally found in proteins. With its 4-aminobutyl side-chain, it is classified as a basic amino acid, along with arginine and histidine.
Copper	Copper is a chemical element in the periodic table that has the symbol Cu (L.: Cuprum) and atomic number 29. It is a ductile metal with excellent electrical conductivity, and finds extensive use as a building material, as an electrical conductor, and as a component of various alloys.
Consistency	The extent to which an individual responds to a given stimulus or situation in the same way on different occasions is a consistency.
Dietary fiber	Dietary fiber is the indigestible portion of plant foods that move food through the digestive system and absorb water.
Flatulence	Flatulence is the presence of a mixture of gases known as flatus produced by symbiotic bacteria and yeasts living in the gastrointestinal tract of mammals.
Colorectal cancer	Colorectal cancer includes cancerous growths in the colon, rectum and appendix. It is the third most common form of cancer and the second leading cause of death among cancers in the Western world.
Theory	Theory refers to an explanatory statement, or set of statements, that concisely summarizes the state of knowledge on a phenomenon and provides direction for further study.
Bile acid	A bile acid is a steroid acid found predominantly in bile of mammals. They are produced in liver by oxidation of cholesterol, in the form of their salts are stored in gallbladder and secreted into the intestine. They act as surfactants, emulsifying lipids and assisting with their digestion and absorption.
Bile	Bile is a bitter, greenish-yellow alkaline fluid secreted by the liver of most vertebrates. In many species, it is stored in the gallbladder between meals and upon eating is discharged into the duodenum where it aids the process of digestion.
Iron	Iron is essential to all organisms, except for a few bacteria. It is mostly stably incorporated in the inside of metalloproteins, because in exposed or in free form it causes production of free radicals that are generally toxic to cells.
Complete protein	Complete protein refers to a protein that contains adequate amounts of the essential amino acids to maintain body tissues and to promote normal growth and development.
Constipation	Constipation is a condition of the digestive system where a person (or other animal) experiences hard feces that are difficult to eliminate; it may be extremely painful, and in severe cases (fecal impaction) lead to symptoms of bowel obstruction.
Displacement	An unconscious defense mechanism in which the individual directs aggressive or sexual feelings away from the primary object to someone or something safe is referred to as displacement. Displacement in linguistics is simply the ability to talk about things not present.

Go to **Cram101.com** for the Practice Tests for this Chapter.

Insulin	Insulin is a polypeptide hormone that regulates carbohydrate metabolism. Apart from being the primary effector in carbohydrate homeostasis, it also has a substantial effect on small vessel muscle tone, controls storage and release of fat (triglycerides) and cellular uptake of both amino acids and some electrolytes.
Icon	A mental representation of a visual stimulus that is held briefly in sensory memory is called an icon.
Blood clotting	A complex process by which platelets, the protein fibrin, and red blood cells block an irregular surface in or on the body, such as a damaged blood vessel, sealing the wound is referred to as blood clotting.
Fatty acid	A fatty acid is a carboxylic acid (or organic acid), often with a long aliphatic tail (long chains), either saturated or unsaturated.
Lipid	Lipid is one class of aliphatic hydrocarbon-containing organic compounds essential for the structure and function of living cells. They are characterized by being water-insoluble but soluble in nonpolar organic solvents.
Shock	Circulatory shock, a state of cardiac output that is insufficient to meet the body's physiological needs, with consequences ranging from fainting to death is referred to as shock. Insulin shock, a state of severe hypoglycemia caused by administration of insulin.
Triglycerides	Triglycerides refer to fats and oils composed of fatty acids and glycerol; are the body's most concentrated source of energy fuel; also known as neutral fats.
Triglyceride	Triglyceride is a glyceride in which the glycerol is esterified with three fatty acids. They are the main constituent of vegetable oil and animal fats and play an important role in metabolism as energy sources. They contain a bit more than twice as much energy as carbohydrates and proteins.
Channel	Channel, in communications (sometimes called communications channel), refers to the medium used to convey information from a sender (or transmitter) to a receiver.
Artery	Vessel that takes blood away from the heart to the tissues and organs of the body is called an artery.
Lipoprotein	A lipoprotein is a biochemical assembly that contains both proteins and lipids and may be structural or catalytic in function. They may be enzymes, proton pumps, ion pumps, or some combination of these functions.
Ratio	In number and more generally in algebra, a ratio is the linear relationship between two quantities.
Elimination	Elimination refers to the physiologic excretion of drugs and other substances from the body.
Hydrogen	Hydrogen is a chemical element in the periodic table that has the symbol H and atomic number 1. At standard temperature and pressure it is a colorless, odorless, nonmetallic, univalent, tasteless, highly flammable diatomic gas.
Carbon	Carbon is a chemical element in the periodic table that has the symbol C and atomic number 6. An abundant nonmetallic, tetravalent element, carbon has several allotropic forms.
Atom	An atom is the smallest possible particle of a chemical element that retains its chemical properties.
Atherosclerosis	Process by which a fatty substance or plaque builds up inside arteries to form obstructions is called atherosclerosis.
Trans fat	Trans fat is an unsaturated fatty acid whose molecules contain trans double bonds between carbon atoms, which makes the molecules less kinked compared with those of 'cis fat'.

Blood vessel	A blood vessel is a part of the circulatory system and function to transport blood throughout the body. The most important types, arteries and veins, are so termed because they carry blood away from or towards the heart, respectively.
Inflammation	Inflammation is the first response of the immune system to infection or irritation and may be referred to as the innate cascade.
Blood clot	A blood clot is the final product of the blood coagulation step in hemostasis. It is achieved via the aggregation of platelets that form a platelet plug, and the activation of the humoral coagulation system
Organic compound	An organic compound is any member of a large class of chemical compounds whose molecules contain carbon, with the exception of carbides, carbonates, carbon oxides and gases containing carbon.
Nerve	A nerve is an enclosed, cable-like bundle of nerve fibers or axons, which includes the glia that ensheath the axons in myelin.
Wound	A wound is type of physical trauma wherein the skin is torn, cut or punctured, or where blunt force trauma causes a contusion.
Cirrhosis	Cirrhosis is a chronic disease of the liver in which liver tissue is replaced by connective tissue, resulting in the loss of liver function. Cirrhosis is caused by damage from toxins (including alcohol), metabolic problems, chronic viral hepatitis or other causes
Macromineral	An inorganic substance that is necessary for metabolism and is one of a group that accounts for 75% of the mineral elements within the body is called a macromineral.
Phosphorus	Phosphorus is the chemical element in the periodic table that has the symbol P and atomic number 15.
Potassium	Potassium is a chemical element in the periodic table. It has the symbol K (L. kalium) and atomic number 19. Potassium is a soft silvery-white metallic alkali metal that occurs naturally bound to other elements in seawater and many minerals.
Sulfur	Sulfur is the chemical element in the periodic table that has the symbol S and atomic number 16. It is an abundant, tasteless, odorless, multivalent non-metal. Sulfur, in its native form, is a yellow crystaline solid. In nature, it can be found as the pure element or as sulfide and sulfate minerals.
Manganese	Manganese is a chemical element in the periodic table that has the symbol Mn and atomic number 25.
Iodine	Iodine is a chemical element in the periodic table that has the symbol I and atomic number 53. It is required as a trace element for most living organisms. Chemically, iodine is the least reactive of the halogens, and the most electropositive halogen. Iodine is primarily used in medicine, photography and in dyes.
Zinc	Zinc is a chemical element in the periodic table that has the symbol Zn and atomic number 30.
Blood pressure	Blood pressure is the pressure exerted by the blood on the walls of the blood vessels.
Hypertension	Hypertension is a medical condition where the blood pressure in the arteries is chronically elevated. Persistent hypertension is one of the risk factors for strokes, heart attacks, heart failure and arterial aneurysm, and is a leading cause of chronic renal failure.
Older adult	Older adult is an adult over the age of 65.
Incidence	In epidemiological studies of a particular disorder, the rate at which new cases occur in a given place at a given time is called incidence.
Inhibition	The ability to prevent from making some cognitive or behavioral response is called

inhibition.

Nervous system	The nervous system of an animal coordinates the activity of the muscles, monitors the organs, constructs and processes input from the senses, and initiates actions.
Tremor	Tremor is the rhythmic, oscillating shaking movement of the whole body or just a certain part of it, caused by problems of the neurons responsible from muscle action.
Contamination	The introduction of microorganisms or particulate matter into a normally sterile environment is called contamination.
Phosphate	A phosphate is a polyatomic ion or radical consisting of one phosphorus atom and four oxygen. In the ionic form, it carries a -3 formal charge, and is denoted PO_4^{3-}.
Iron deficiency	Iron deficiency (or "sideropenia") is the most common known form of nutritional deficiency.
Hemoglobin	Hemoglobin is the iron-containing oxygen-transport metalloprotein in the red cells of the blood in mammals and other animals. Hemoglobin transports oxygen from the lungs to the rest of the body, such as to the muscles, where it releases the oxygen load.
Toddler	Toddler refers to a child who walks with short, uncertain steps. Toddlerhood lasts from about 18 to 30 months of age, thereby bridging infancy and early childhood.
Anemia	Anemia is a deficiency of red blood cells and/or hemoglobin. This results in a reduced ability of blood to transfer oxygen to the tissues, and this causes hypoxia; since all human cells depend on oxygen for survival, varying degrees of anemia can have a wide range of clinical consequences.
Craving	Craving refers to the powerful desire to use a psychoactive drug or engage in a compulsive behavior. It is manifested in physiological changes, such as raised heart rate, sweating, anxiety, drop in body temperature, pupil dilation, and stomach muscle movements.
Pica	Pica is an appetite for non-foods or an abnormal appetite for some things that may be considered foods, such as food ingredients (e.g. flour, raw potato, starch).
Carbon dioxide	Carbon dioxide is an atmospheric gas comprized of one carbon and two oxygen atoms. A very widely known chemical compound, it is frequently called by its formula CO_2. In its solid state, it is commonly known as dry ice.
Ulcer	An ulcer is an open sore of the skin, eyes or mucous membrane, often caused by an initial abrasion and generally maintained by an inflammation and/or an infection.
Host	Host is an organism that harbors a parasite, mutual partner, or commensal partner; or a cell infected by a virus.
Immune system	The immune system is the system of specialized cells and organs that protect an organism from outside biological influences. When the immune system is functioning properly, it protects the body against bacteria and viral infections, destroying cancer cells and foreign substances.
Pulse	The rhythmic stretching of the arteries caused by the pressure of blood forced through the arteries by contractions of the ventricles during systole is a pulse.
Trial	In classical conditioning, any presentation of a stimulus or pair of stimuli is called a trial.
Control group	A group that does not receive the treatment effect in an experiment is referred to as the control group or sometimes as the comparison group.
Intervention	Intervention refers to a planned attempt to break through addicts' or abusers' denial and get them into treatment. Interventions most often occur when legal, workplace, health, relationship, or financial problems have become intolerable.

Go to **Cram101.com** for the Practice Tests for this Chapter.

Tetracycline	Tetracycline is an antibiotic produced by the streptomyces bacterium, indicated for use against many bacterial infections. It is commonly used to treat acne.
Antibiotic	Antibiotic refers to substance such as penicillin or streptomycin that is toxic to microorganisms. Usually a product of a particular microorvanism or plant.
Penicillin	Penicillin refers to a group of β-lactam antibiotics used in the treatment of bacterial infections caused by susceptible, usually Gram-positive, organisms.
Inhibitor	An inhibitor is a type of effector (biology) that decreases or prevents the rate of a chemical reaction. They are often called negative catalysts.
Hyperkalemia	Hyperkalemia is an elevated blood level (above 5.0 mmol/L) of the electrolyte potassium.
Anticoagulant	A biochemical that inhibits blood clotting is referred to as an anticoagulant.
Reabsorption	In physiology, reabsorption or tubular reabsorption is the flow of glomerular filtrate from the proximal tubule of the nephron into the peritubular capillaries. This happens as a result of sodium transport from the lumen into the blood by the Na+/K+ ATPase in the basolateral membrane of the epithelial cells.
Heart attack	A heart attack, is a serious, sudden heart condition usually characterized by varying degrees of chest pain or discomfort, weakness, sweating, nausea, vomiting, and arrhythmias, sometimes causing loss of consciousness. It occurs when the blood supply to a part of the heart is interrupted, causing death and scarring of the local heart tissue.
Theophylline	Theophylline is a methylxanthine drug and is used in therapy for respiratory diseases, under a variety of brand names. As a member of the xanthine family, it bears structural and pharmacological similarity to caffeine. It is naturally found in black tea and green tea.
Convulsions	Involuntary muscle spasms, often severe, that can be caused by stimulant overdose or by depressant withdrawal are called convulsions.
Stroke	A stroke or cerebrovascular accident (CVA) occurs when the blood supply to a part of the brain is suddenly interrupted.
Angina	Angina pectoris is chest pain due to ischemia (a lack of blood and hence oxygen supply) to the heart muscle, generally due to obstruction or spasm of the coronary arteries (the heart's blood vessels). Coronary artery disease, the main cause of angina, is due to atherosclerosis of the cardiac arteries.
Unstable angina	Worsening angina attacks, sudden-onset angina at rest, and angina lasting more than 15 minutes are symptoms of unstable angina or acute coronary syndrome. As these may herald myocardial infarction (a heart attack), they require urgent medical attention and are generally treated quite similarly
Evaluation	The fifth step of the nursing process where nursing care and the patient's goal achievement are measured is the evaluation.
Outcome	Outcome is the impact of care provided to a patient. They can be positive, such as the ability to walk freely as a result of rehabilitation, or negative, such as the occurrence of bedsores as a result of lack of mobility of a patient.
Mortality	The incidence of death in a population is mortality.
Internal medicine	Doctors of internal medicine ("internists") focus on adult medicine and have had special study and training focusing on the prevention and treatment of adult diseases. At least three of their seven or more years of medical school and postgraduate training are dedicated to learning how to prevent, diagnose, and treat diseases that affect adults.
Free radicals	Free radicals are atomic or molecular species with unpaired electrons on an otherwise open

shell configuration.

Arthritis	Arthritis is a group of conditions that affect the health of the bone joints in the body. Arthritis can be caused from strains and injuries caused by repetitive motion, sports, overexertion, and falls. Unlike the autoimmune diseases, it largely affects older people and results from the degeneration of joint cartilage.
Consensus	General agreement is a consensus.
DNA	Deoxyribonucleic acid (DNA) is a nucleic acid usually in the form of a double helix that contains the genetic instructions specifying the biological development of all cellular forms of life, and most viruses.
National Cancer Institute	The National Cancer Institute (NCI) is the United States federal government's principal agency for cancer research and training, and the first institute of the present-day National Institutes of Health. The NCI is a federally funded research and development center, one of eight agencies that compose the Public Health Service in the United States Department of Health and Human Services. The Institute coordinates the National Cancer Program.
Eye	An eye is an organ that detects light. Different kinds of light-sensitive organs are found in a variety of creatures. The simplest eyes do nothing but detect whether the surroundings are light or dark, while more complex eyes can distinguish shapes and colors.
Cataract	Opaqueness of the lens of the eye, making the lens incapable of transmitting light is called a cataract.
Folate	Folic acid and folate (the anion form) are forms of a water-soluble B vitamin. These occur naturally in food and can also be taken as supplements.
Autoimmune	Autoimmune refers to immune reactions against normal body cells; self against self.
Asthma	Asthma is a complex disease characterized by bronchial hyperresponsiveness (BHR), inflammation, mucus production and intermittent airway obstruction.
Rheumatoid arthritis	Rheumatoid arthritis is a chronic, inflammatory autoimmune disorder that causes the immune system to attack the joints. It is a disabling and painful inflammatory condition, which can lead to substantial loss of mobility due to pain and joint destruction.
Autoimmune disease	Disease that results when the immune system mistakenly attacks the body's own tissues is referred to as autoimmune disease.
Methionine	Methionine and cysteine are the only sulfur-containing proteinogenic amino acids. The methionine derivative S-adenosyl methionine (SAM) serves as a methyl donor.
International unit	International unit refers to a crude measure of vitamin activity, often based on the growth rate of animals. Today these units have generally been replaced by precise measurement of actual quantities in milligrams or micrograms.
Riboflavin	Riboflavin is an easily absorbed, water-soluble micronutrient with a key role in maintaining human health. Like the other B vitamins, it supports energy production by aiding in the metabolising of fats, carbohydrates, and proteins.
Niacin	Niacin, also known as vitamin B3, is a water-soluble vitamin whose derivatives such as NADH play essential roles in energy metabolism in the living cell and DNA repair. The designation vitamin B3 also includes the amide form, nicotinamide or niacinamide.
Folic acid	Folic acid and folate (the anion form) are forms of a water-soluble B vitamin. These occur naturally in food and can also be taken as supplements.
Metabolic rate	Energy expended by the body per unit time is called metabolic rate.
Immunodeficiency	Immunodeficiency is a state in which the immune system's ability to fight infectious disease

is compromized or entirely absent. Most cases of immunodeficiency are either congenital or acquired.

Menopause	Menopause is the physiological cessation of menstrual cycles associated with advancing age in species that experience such cycles. Menopause is sometimes referred to as change of life or climacteric.
Menarche	Menarche is the first menstrual period as a girl's body progresses through the changes of puberty. Menarche usually occurs about two years after the first changes of breast development.
Physiological changes	Alterations in heart rate, blood pressure, perspiration, and other involuntary responses are physiological changes.
Menstrual cycle	The menstrual cycle is the set of recurring physiological changes in a female's body that are under the control of the reproductive hormone system and necessary for reproduction. Besides humans, only other great apes exhibit menstrual cycles, in contrast to the estrus cycle of most mammalian species.
Estrogen	Estrogen is a steroid that functions as the primary female sex hormone. While present in both men and women, they are found in women in significantly higher quantities.
Lung cancer	Lung cancer is a malignant tumour of the lungs. Most commonly it is bronchogenic carcinoma (about 90%).
Adequate intake	Adequate intake are recommendations for nutrient intake when not enough information is available to establish an RDA.
Micronutrients	Micronutrients are essential elements only needed by life in small quantities. Vitamins and trace minerals are sometimes included in the term.
Micronutrient	Micronutrient refers to an element that an organism needs in very small amounts and that functions as a component or cofactor of enzymes.
Daily reference values	Recommended amounts for micronutrients such as total fat, saturated fat, and cholesterol are called daily reference values.
Daily values	A set of standard nutrient-intake values developed by FDA and used as a reference for expressing nutrient content on nutrition labels are called daily values.
Daily value	Daily value refers to dietary reference values useful for planning a healthy diet. The daily values are taken from the Reference Daily Intakes and the Daily Reference Values.
Macronutrients	Macrominerals are macronutrients that are chemical elements. They include calcium, magnesium, sodium, potassium, phosphorus and chlorine. They are dietary minerals needed by the human body in high quantities (generally more than 100 mg/day) as opposed to microminerals (trace elements) which are only required in very small amounts.
Macronutrient	A chemical substance that an organism must obtain in relatively large amounts is referred to as macronutrient.
Variable	A characteristic or aspect in which people, objects, events, or conditions vary is called variable.
Elderly	Old age consists of ages nearing the average life span of human beings, and thus the end of the human life cycle. Euphemisms for older people include advanced adult, elderly, and senior or senior citizen.
Aerobic	An aerobic organism is an organism that has an oxygen based metabolism. Aerobes, in a process known as cellular respiration, use oxygen to oxidize substrates (for example sugars and fats) in order to obtain energy.

Go to **Cram101.com** for the Practice Tests for this Chapter.

Aerobic exercise	Exercise in which oxygen is used to produce ATP is aerobic exercise.
Freezing	Freezing is the process in which blood is frozen and all of the plasma and 99% of the WBCs are eliminated when thawing takes place and the nontransferable cryoprotectant is removed.
Coronary	Referring to the heart or the blood vessels of the heart is referred to as coronary.
Coronary heart disease	Coronary heart disease is the end result of the accumulation of atheromatous plaques within the walls of the arteries that supply the myocardium (the muscle of the heart).
Chronic disease	Disease of long duration often not detected in its early stages and from which the patient will not recover is referred to as a chronic disease.
Stressor	A factor capable of stimulating a stress response is a stressor.
Megadose	Generally an intake of a nutrient in excess of 10 times human need is called megadose.
Virulence	The degree or intensity of pathogenicity of an organism as indicated by case fatality rates and/or ability to invade host tissues and cause disease is referred to as the virulence.
Pathogen	A pathogen or infectious agent is a biological agent that causes disease or illness to its host. The term is most often used for agents that disrupt the normal physiology of a multicellular animal or plant.
Epidemiologist	A epidemiologist specializes in the scientific study of factors affecting the health and illness of individuals and populations, and serves as the foundation and logic of interventions made in the interest of public health and preventive medicine.
Crop	An organ, found in both earthworms and birds, in which ingested food is temporarily stored before being passed to the gizzard, where it is pulverized is the crop.
Escherichia coli	Escherichia coli is one of the main species of bacteria that live in the lower intestines of warm-blooded animals, including birds and mammals. They are necessary for the proper digestion of food and are part of the intestinal flora. Its presence in groundwater is a common indicator of fecal contamination.
Cholera	Cholera is a water-borne disease caused by the bacterium Vibrio cholerae, which are typically ingested by drinking contaminated water, or by eating improperly cooked fish, especially shellfish.
Susceptibility	The degree of resistance of a host to a pathogen is susceptibility.
Malnutrition	Malnutrition is a general term for the medical condition in a person or animal caused by an unbalanced diet either too little or too much food, or a diet missing one or more important nutrients.
HIV	The virus that causes AIDS is HIV (human immunodeficiency virus).
Immunosuppre-sive drug	A immunosuppressive drug is a drug that is used in immunosuppressive therapy to inhibit or prevent activity of the immune system.
Longevity	A long duration of life is referred to as longevity.
Expiration	In respiration, expiration is initiated by a decrease in volume and positive pressure exerted upon the intrapleural space upon diaphragm relaxation.
Fever	Fever (also known as pyrexia, or a febrile response, and archaically known as ague) is a medical symptom that describes an increase in internal body temperature to levels that are above normal (37°C, 98.6°F).
Pain	Pain is an unpleasant sensation which may be associated with actual or potential tissue damage and which may have physical and emotional components.

189

Incubation	In problem solving, a hypothetical process that sometimes occurs when we stand back from a frustrating problem for a while and the solution 'suddenly' appears is an incubation.
Incubation period	The period after pathogen entry into a host and before signs and symptoms appear is called the incubation period.
Cramp	A cramp is an unpleasant sensation caused by contraction, usually of a muscle. It can be caused by cold or overexertion.
Red blood cell	The red blood cell is the most common type of blood cell and is the vertebrate body's principal means of delivering oxygen from the lungs or gills to body tissues via the blood.
Syndrome	Syndrome is the association of several clinically recognizable features, signs, symptoms, phenomena or characteristics which often occur together, so that the presence of one feature alerts the physician to the presence of the others
Seizure	A seizure is a temporary alteration in brain function expressed as a changed mental state, tonic or clonic movements and various other symptoms. They are due to temporary abnormal electrical activity of a group of brain cells.
Hemolytic uremic syndrome	Hemolytic uremic syndrome refers to a kidney disease characterized by blood in the urine and often by kidney failure.
Red blood cells	Red blood cells are the most common type of blood cell and are the vertebrate body's principal means of delivering oxygen from the lungs or gills to body tissues via the blood.
Stillbirth	A stillbirth occurs when a fetus, of mid-second trimester to full term gestational age, which has died in the womb or during labour or delivery, exits the maternal body.
Fetus	Fetus refers to a developing human from the ninth week of gestation until birth; has all the major structures of an adult.
Mental retardation	Mental retardation refers to having significantly below-average intellectual functioning and limitations in at least two areas of adaptive functioning. Many categorize retardation as mild, moderate, severe, or profound.
Staphylococcus	Staphylococcus is a genus of gram-positive bacteria. Under the microscope they appear round (cocci), and form in grape-like clusters.
Toxin	Toxin refers to a microbial product or component that can injure another cell or organism at low concentrations. Often the term refers to a poisonous protein, but toxins may be lipids and other substances.
Staphylococcus aureus	Staphylococcus aureus (which is occasionally given the nickname golden staph) is a bacterium, frequently living on the skin or in the nose of a healthy person, that can cause illnesses ranging from minor skin infections (such as pimples, boils, and cellulitis) and abscesses, to life-threatening diseases such as pneumonia, meningitis, endocarditis and septicemia.
Toxoplasmosis	A disease of animals and humans caused by the parasitic protozoan, Toxoplasma gondii is called toxoplasmosis.
Irradiation	A process in which radiation energy is applied to foods, creating compounds within the food that destroy cell membranes, break down DNA, link proteins together, limit enzyme activity, and alter a variety of other proteins and cell functions is referred to as irradiation.
Radiation	The emission of electromagnetic waves by all objects warmer than absolute zero is referred to as radiation.
Cesium	Cesium is a chemical element in the periodic table that has the symbol Cs and atomic number 55. It is a soft silvery-gold alkali metal which is one of at least three metals that are liquid at or near room temperature. This element is most notably used in atomic clocks.

Cobalt	Cobalt is a chemical element in the periodic table that has the symbol Co and atomic number 27. Cobalt is a hard ferromagnetic silver-white element.
Chemical bond	Chemical bond refers to an attraction between two atoms resulting from a sharing of outer-shell electrons or the presence of opposite charges on the atoms. The bonded atoms gain complete outer electron shells.
Residue	A residue refers to a portion of a larger molecule, a specific monomer of a polysaccharide, protein or nucleic acid.
Nitrate	Nitrate refers to a salt of nitric acid; a compound containing the radical NO_3; biologically, the final form of nitrogen from the oxidation of organic nitrogen compounds.
Public health	Public health is concerned with threats to the overall health of a community based on population health analysis.
Solution	Solution refers to homogenous mixture formed when a solute is dissolved in a solvent.
Growth hormone	Growth hormone is a polypeptide hormone synthesised and secreted by the anterior pituitary gland which stimulates growth and cell reproduction in humans and other vertebrate animals.
Intolerance	Intolerance refers to a type of interaction in which two or more drugs produce extremely uncomfortable symptoms.
Allergy	An allergy or Type I hypersensitivity is an immune malfunction whereby a person's body is hypersensitized to react immunologically to typically nonimmunogenic substances. When a person is hypersensitized, these substances are known as allergens.
Hypersensitivity	Hypersensitivity is an immune response that damages the body's own tissues. Four or five types of hypersensitivity are often described; immediate, antibody-dependent, immune complex, cell-mediated, and stimulatory.
Anaphylaxis	Anaphylaxis refers to an immediate hypersensitivity reaction following exposure of a sensitized individual to the appropriate antigen.
Allergen	An allergen is any substance (antigen), most often eaten or inhaled, that is recognized by the immune system and causes an allergic reaction.
Lactose intolerance	Lactose intolerance is the condition in which lactase, an enzyme needed for proper metabolization of lactose (a constituent of milk and other dairy products), is not produced in adulthood.
Lactase	Lactase (LCT), a member of the β-galactosidase family of enzyme, is involved in the hydrolysis of lactose into constituent galactose and glucose monomers. In humans, lactase is present predominantly along the brush border membrane of the differentiated enterocytes lining the villi of the small intestine.
Health outcome	Any medically or epidemiologically defined characteristic of a patient or population that results from health promotion or care provided or required, as measured at one point in time is a health outcome.
Hypothesis	A specific statement about behavior or mental processes that is testable through research is a hypothesis.
Eating disorders	Psychological disorders characterized by distortion of the body image and gross disturbances in eating patterns are called eating disorders.

Epidemic	An epidemic is a disease that appears as new cases in a given human population, during a given period, at a rate that substantially exceeds what is "expected", based on recent experience.
Obesity	The state of being more than 20 percent above the average weight for a person of one's height is called obesity.
Joint	A joint (articulation) is the location at which two bones make contact (articulate). They are constructed to both allow movement and provide mechanical support.
Hypertension	Hypertension is a medical condition where the blood pressure in the arteries is chronically elevated. Persistent hypertension is one of the risk factors for strokes, heart attacks, heart failure and arterial aneurysm, and is a leading cause of chronic renal failure.
Diabetes	Diabetes is a medical disorder characterized by varying or persistent elevated blood sugar levels, especially after eating. All types of diabetes share similar symptoms and complications at advanced stages: dehydration and ketoacidosis, cardiovascular disease, chronic renal failure, retinal damage which can lead to blindness, nerve damage which can lead to erectile dysfunction, gangrene with risk of amputation of toes, feet, and even legs.
Health	Health is a term that refers to a combination of the absence of illness, the ability to cope with everyday activities, physical fitness, and high quality of life.
Risk factor	A risk factor is a variable associated with an increased risk of disease or infection but risk factors are not necessarily causal.
Survey	A method of scientific investigation in which a large sample of people answer questions about their attitudes or behavior is referred to as a survey.
Assessment	In clinical practice, the process by which a mental health professional gathers and compiles information about a client for the purpose of describing the person's problems or disorder and developing a plan of treatment is an assessment.
Statistics	Statistics is a type of data analysis which practice includes the planning, summarizing, and interpreting of observations of a system possibly followed by predicting or forecasting of future events based on a mathematical model of the system being observed.
Statistic	A statistic is an observable random variable of a sample.
Stroke	A stroke or cerebrovascular accident (CVA) occurs when the blood supply to a part of the brain is suddenly interrupted.
Cancer	Cancer is a class of diseases or disorders characterized by uncontrolled division of cells and the ability of these cells to invade other tissues, either by direct growth into adjacent tissue through invasion or by implantation into distant sites by metastasis.
Population	Population refers to all members of a well-defined group of organisms, events, or things.
Medicaid	Medicaid in the United States is a program managed by the states and funded jointly by the states and federal government to provide health insurance for individuals and families with low incomes and resources. Medicaid is the largest source of funding for medical and health-related services for people with limited income.
Medicare	Medicare refers to government health insurance for those over sixty-five.
Cardiovascular disease	Cardiovascular disease refers to afflictions in the mechanisms, including the heart, blood vessels, and their controllers, that are responsible for transporting blood to the body's tissues and organs. Psychological factors may play important roles in such diseases and their treatments.
Blood pressure	Blood pressure is the pressure exerted by the blood on the walls of the blood vessels.

Blood	Blood is a circulating tissue composed of fluid plasma and cells. The main function of blood is to supply nutrients (oxygen, glucose) and constitutional elements to tissues and to remove waste products.
Incidence	In epidemiological studies of a particular disorder, the rate at which new cases occur in a given place at a given time is called incidence.
Triglycerides	Triglycerides refer to fats and oils composed of fatty acids and glycerol; are the body's most concentrated source of energy fuel; also known as neutral fats.
Triglyceride	Triglyceride is a glyceride in which the glycerol is esterified with three fatty acids. They are the main constituent of vegetable oil and animal fats and play an important role in metabolism as energy sources. They contain a bit more than twice as much energy as carbohydrates and proteins.
Cholesterol	Cholesterol is a steroid, a lipid, and an alcohol, found in the cell membranes of all body tissues, and transported in the blood plasma of all animals. It is an important component of the membranes of cells, providing stability; it makes the membrane's fluidity stable over a bigger temperature interval.
Gallbladder	The gallbladder is a pear-shaped organ that stores bile until the body needs it for digestion. It is connected to the liver and the duodenum by the biliary tract.
Prostate	The prostate is a gland that is part of male mammalian sex organs. Its main function is to secrete and store a clear, slightly basic fluid that is part of semen. The prostate differs considerably between species anatomically, chemically and physiologically.
Kidney	The kidney is a bean-shaped excretory organ in vertebrates. Part of the urinary system, the kidneys filter wastes (especially urea) from the blood and excrete them, along with water, as urine.
Colon	The colon is the part of the intestine from the cecum to the rectum. Its primary purpose is to extract water from feces.
Sleep apnea	Sleep apnea refers to a sleep disorder involving periods during sleep when breathing stops and the person must awaken briefly in order to breathe; major symptoms are excessive daytime sleepiness and loud snoring.
Asthma	Asthma is a complex disease characterized by bronchial hyperresponsiveness (BHR), inflammation, mucus production and intermittent airway obstruction.
Apnea	Apnea is the absence of external breathing. During apnea there is no movement of the muscles of respiration and the volume of the lungs initially remains unchanged. .
Arthritis	Arthritis is a group of conditions that affect the health of the bone joints in the body. Arthritis can be caused from strains and injuries caused by repetitive motion, sports, overexertion, and falls. Unlike the autoimmune diseases, it largely affects older people and results from the degeneration of joint cartilage.
Heart attack	A heart attack, is a serious, sudden heart condition usually characterized by varying degrees of chest pain or discomfort, weakness, sweating, nausea, vomiting, and arrhythmias, sometimes causing loss of consciousness. It occurs when the blood supply to a part of the heart is interrupted, causing death and scarring of the local heart tissue.
Isolation	Isolation refers to the degree to which groups do not live in the same communities.
Course	Pattern of development and change of a disorder over time is a course.
Assess	Assess is to systematically and continuously collect, validate, and communicate patient data.
Value	Value is worth in general, and it is thought to be connected to reasons for certain

Go to **Cram101.com** for the Practice Tests for this Chapter.

	practices, policies, actions, beliefs or emotions. Value is "that which one acts to gain and/or keep."
Social isolation	Social isolation refers to a type of loneliness that occurs when a person lacks a sense of integrated involvement. Being deprived of participation in a group or community involving companionship, shared interests, organized activities, and meaningful roles causes a person to feel isolated.
Activities of daily living	Activities of daily living is a way to describe the functional status of a person.
Lifestyle	The culturally, socially, economically, and environmentally conditioned complex of actions characteristic of an individual, group, or community as a pattern of habituated behavior over time that is health related but not necessarily health directed is a lifestyle.
Counselor	A counselor is a mental health professional who specializes in helping people with problems not involving serious mental disorders.
Eating disorders	Psychological disorders characterized by distortion of the body image and gross disturbances in eating patterns are called eating disorders.
Distribution	Distribution in pharmacology is a branch of pharmacokinetics describing reversible transfer of drug from one location to another within the body.
Variable	A characteristic or aspect in which people, objects, events, or conditions vary is called variable.
Tissue	A collection of interconnected cells that perform a similar function within an organism is called tissue.
Ratio	In number and more generally in algebra, a ratio is the linear relationship between two quantities.
Muscle	Muscle is a contractile form of tissue. It is one of the four major tissue types, the other three being epithelium, connective tissue and nervous tissue. Muscle contraction is used to move parts of the body, as well as to move substances within the body.
Older adult	Older adult is an adult over the age of 65.
Anorexia	Anorexia nervosa is an eating disorder characterized by voluntary starvation and exercise stress.
Adipose tissue	Adipose tissue is an anatomical term for loose connective tissue composed of adipocytes. Its main role is to store energy in the form of fat, although it also cushions and insulates the body. It has an important endocrine function in producing recently-discovered hormones such as leptin, resistin and TNFalpha.
Ultrasound	Ultrasound is sound with a frequency greater than the upper limit of human hearing, approximately 20 kilohertz. Medical use can visualise muscle and soft tissue, making them useful for scanning the organs, and obstetric ultrasonography is commonly used during pregnancy.
Magnetic resonance imaging	Magnetic resonance imaging refers to imaging technology that uses magnetism and radio waves to induce hydrogen nuclei in water molecules to emit faint radio signals. A computer creates images of the body from the radio signals.
Computed tomography	Computed tomography is an imaging method employing tomography where digital processing is used to generate a three-dimensional image of the internals of an object from a large series of two-dimensional X-ray images taken around a single axis of rotation.
Body mass index	Body mass index refers to a number derived from an individual's weight and height used to

	estimate body fat. The formula is- weight /height' .
Hormone	A hormone is a chemical messenger from one cell to another. All multicellular organisms produce hormones. The best known hormones are those produced by endocrine glands of vertebrate animals, but hormones are produced by nearly every organ system and tissue type in a human or animal body. Hormone molecules are secreted directly into the bloodstream, they move by circulation or diffusion to their target cells, which may be nearby cells in the same tissue or cells of a distant organ of the body.
Organ	Organ refers to a structure consisting of several tissues adapted as a group to perform specific functions.
Liver	The liver is an organ in vertebrates, including humans. It plays a major role in metabolism and has a number of functions in the body including drug detoxification, glycogen storage, and plasma protein synthesis. It also produces bile, which is important for digestion.
Nerve	A nerve is an enclosed, cable-like bundle of nerve fibers or axons, which includes the glia that ensheath the axons in myelin.
Amenorrhea	Amenorrhea is the absence of a menstrual period in a woman of reproductive age. Physiologic states of amenorrhea are seen during pregnancy and lactation (breastfeeding).
Lead	Lead is a chemical element in the periodic table that has the symbol Pb and atomic number 82. A soft, heavy, toxic and malleable poor metal, lead is bluish white when freshly cut but tarnishes to dull gray when exposed to air. Lead is used in building construction, lead-acid batteries, bullets and shot, and is part of solder, pewter, and fusible alloys.
Menstrual cycle	The menstrual cycle is the set of recurring physiological changes in a female's body that are under the control of the reproductive hormone system and necessary for reproduction. Besides humans, only other great apes exhibit menstrual cycles, in contrast to the estrus cycle of most mammalian species.
Affect	Affect is the scientific term used to describe a subject's externally displayed mood. This can be assesed by the nurse by observing facial expression, tone of voice, and body language.
Calorie	Calorie refers to a unit used to measure heat energy and the energy contents of foods.
Artery	Vessel that takes blood away from the heart to the tissues and organs of the body is called an artery.
Extension	Movement increasing the angle between parts at a joint is referred to as extension.
Theory	Theory refers to an explanatory statement, or set of statements, that concisely summarizes the state of knowledge on a phenomenon and provides direction for further study.
Osteoporosis	Osteoporosis is a disease of bone in which bone mineral density (BMD) is reduced, bone microarchitecture is disrupted, the amount and variety of non-collagenous proteins in bone is changed, and a concomitantly fracture risk is increased.
Lungs	Lungs are the essential organs of respiration in air-breathing vertebrates. Their principal function is to transport oxygen from the atmosphere into the bloodstream, and to excrete carbon dioxide from the bloodstream into the atmosphere.
Gold	Gold is a chemical element in the periodic table that has the symbol Au and atomic number 79. A soft, shiny, yellow, dense, malleable, ductile (trivalent and univalent) transition metal, gold does not react with most chemicals but is attacked by chlorine, fluorine and aqua regia.
Skin	Skin is an organ of the integumentary system composed of a layer of tissues that protect underlying muscles and organs.
Physiology	The study of the function of cells, tissues, and organs is referred to as physiology.

Fiber	Fibers used by man come from a wide variety of sources: Natural fiber include those made out of plants, animal and mineral sources. Natural fibers can be classified according to their origin.
Electromagnetic force	The force that the electromagnetic field exerts on electrically charged particles, called the electromagnetic force, is one of the four fundamental forces. The other fundamental forces are the strong nuclear force, the weak nuclear force, and the gravitational force.
Diagnosis	In medicine, diagnosis is the process of identifying a medical condition or disease by its signs, symptoms, and from the results of various diagnostic procedures.
Radiation	The emission of electromagnetic waves by all objects warmer than absolute zero is referred to as radiation.
Abdomen	The abdomen is a part of the body. In humans, and in many other vertebrates, it is the region between the thorax and the pelvis. In fully developed insects, the abdomen is the third (or posterior) segment, after the head and thorax.
Hip	In anatomy, the hip is the bony projection of the femur, known as the greater trochanter, and the overlying muscle and fat.
Heredity	Heredity refers to the transmission of genetic information from parent to offspring.
Conscious	Conscious refers to the thoughts, feelings, sensations, or memories of which a person is aware at any given moment.
Crisis	A crisis is a temporary state of high anxiety where the persons usual coping mechanisims cease to work. This may have a result of disorganization or possibly personality growth.
Genes	Genes are the units of heredity in living organisms. They are encoded in the organism's genetic material (usually DNA or RNA), and control the development and behavior of the organism.
Identical twins	Identical twins occur when a single egg is fertilized to form one zygote (monozygotic) but the zygote then divides into two separate embryos.
Metabolic rate	Energy expended by the body per unit time is called metabolic rate.
Basal metabolic rate	Basal metabolic rate, is the rate of metabolism that occurs when an individual is at rest in a warm environment and is in the post absorptive state, and has not eaten for at least 12 hours.
Construct	Generalized concept, such as anxiety or gravity, which is constructed in a theoretical manner is referred to as construct.
Adrenergic	Pertaining to epinephrine or norepinephrine, as in adrenergic neurons that secrete one of these chemicals or adrenergic effects on a target organ is called adrenegic.
Receptor	A receptor is a protein on the cell membrane or within the cytoplasm or cell nucleus that binds to a specific molecule (a ligand), such as a neurotransmitter, hormone, or other substance, and initiates the cellular response to the ligand. Receptor, in immunology, the region of an antibody which shows recognition of an antigen.
Adrenergic receptor	Receptor molecule that binds to adrenergic agents such as epinephrine and norepinephrine is called adrenergic receptor. They specifically bind their endogenous ligands, the catecholamines adrenaline and noradrenaline (also called epinephrine and norepinephrine) and are activated by these.
Protein	A protein is a complex, high-molecular-weight organic compound that consists of amino acids joined by peptide bonds. They are essential to the structure and function of all living cells and viruses. Many are enzymes or subunits of enzymes.

Go to **Cram101.com** for the Practice Tests for this Chapter.

Leptin	Leptin is a 16 kDa protein hormone that plays a key role in metabolism and regulation of adipose tissue. It is released by fat cells in amounts mirroring overall body fat stores. Thus, circulating leptin levels give the brain a reading of energy storage for the purposes of regulating appetite and metabolism.
Brain	The part of the central nervous system involved in regulating and controlling body activity and interpreting information from the senses transmitted through the nervous system is referred to as the brain.
Stomach	The stomach is an organ in the alimentary canal used to digest food. It's primary function is not the absorption of nutrients from digested food; rather, the main job of the stomach is to break down large food molecules into smaller ones, so that they can be absorbed into the blood more easily.
Ghrelin	Ghrelin is a hormone that is produced by cells lining the stomach and stimulates the appetite. Ghrelin levels are increased prior to a meal and decreased after a meal. It is considered the counterpart of the hormone leptin, produced by adipose tissue, which induces satiation when present at higher levels.
Control group	A group that does not receive the treatment effect in an experiment is referred to as the control group or sometimes as the comparison group.
Bypass	In medicine, a bypass generally means an alternate or additional route for blood flow, which is created in bypass surgery, e.g. coronary artery bypass surgery by moving blood vessels or implanting synthetic tubing.
Intervention	Intervention refers to a planned attempt to break through addicts' or abusers' denial and get them into treatment. Interventions most often occur when legal, workplace, health, relationship, or financial problems have become intolerable.
Insulin	Insulin is a polypeptide hormone that regulates carbohydrate metabolism. Apart from being the primary effector in carbohydrate homeostasis, it also has a substantial effect on small vessel muscle tone, controls storage and release of fat (triglycerides) and cellular uptake of both amino acids and some electrolytes.
Thyroid	The thyroid is one of the larger endocrine glands in the body. It is located in the neck and produces hormones, principally thyroxine and triiodothyronine, that regulate the rate of metabolism and affect the growth and rate of function of many other systems in the body.
Gland	A gland is an organ in an animal's body that synthesizes a substance for release such as hormones, often into the bloodstream or into cavities inside the body or its outer surface.
Hypothalamus	Located below the thalamus, the hypothalamus links the nervous system to the endocrine system by synthesizing and secreting neurohormones often called releasing hormones because they function by stimulating the secretion of hormones from the anterior pituitary gland.
Craving	Craving refers to the powerful desire to use a psychoactive drug or engage in a compulsive behavior. It is manifested in physiological changes, such as raised heart rate, sweating, anxiety, drop in body temperature, pupil dilation, and stomach muscle movements.
Hyperplasia	Hyperplasia is a general term for an increase in the number of the cells of an organ or tissue causing it to increase in size.
Causation	The act of causing some effect is causation. Damage or harn that is caused by a breach of duty.
Hypothesis	A specific statement about behavior or mental processes that is testable through research is a hypothesis.
Critical period	A period of time when an instinctive response can be elicited by a particular stimulus is

	referred to as critical period.
Binge	Binge refers to relatively brief episode of uncontrolled, excessive consumption.
Metabolism	Metabolism is the biochemical modification of chemical compounds in living organisms and cells. This includes the biosynthesis of complex organic molecules (anabolism) and their breakdown (catabolism).
Constant	A behavior or characteristic that does not vary from one observation to another is referred to as a constant.
Ritual	Formalized ceremonial behavior in which the members of a group or community regularly engage, is referred to as a ritual. In childbirth it is a repeated series of actions used by women as a way of dealing with the discomfort of labor.
Adolescence	Adolescence is the period of psychological and social transition between childhood and adulthood (gender-specific manhood, or womanhood). As a transitional stage of human development it represents the period of time during which a juvenile matures into adulthood.
Carbohydrate	Carbohydrate is a chemical compound that contains oxygen, hydrogen, and carbon atoms. They consist of monosaccharide sugars of varying chain lengths and that have the general chemical formula $C_n(H_2O)_n$ or are derivatives of such.
Sugar	A sugar is the simplest molecule that can be identified as a carbohydrate. These include monosaccharides and disaccharides, trisaccharides and the oligosaccharides. The term "glyco-" indicates the presence of a sugar in an otherwise non-carbohydrate substance.
Glucose	Glucose, a simple monosaccharide sugar, is one of the most important carbohydrates and is used as a source of energy in animals and plants. Glucose is one of the main products of photosynthesis and starts respiration.
Saturated fat	Saturated fat is fat that consists of triglycerides containing only fatty acids that have no double bonds between the carbon atoms of the fatty acid chain (hence, they are fully saturated with hydrogen atoms).
Starch	Biochemically, starch is a combination of two polymeric carbohydrates (polysaccharides) called amylose and amylopectin.
Absorption	Absorption is a physical or chemical phenomenon or a process in which atoms, molecules, or ions enter some bulk phase - gas, liquid or solid material. In nutrition, amino acids are broken down through digestion, which begins in the stomach.
Medicine	Medicine is the branch of health science and the sector of public life concerned with maintaining or restoring human health through the study, diagnosis and treatment of disease and injury.
Trial	In classical conditioning, any presentation of a stimulus or pair of stimuli is called a trial.
Puberty	A time in the life of a developing individual characterized by the increasing production of sex hormones, which cause it to reach sexual maturity is called puberty.
Housework	Unpaid work carried on in and around the home such as cooking, cleaning and shopping, is referred to as a housework.
Channel	Channel, in communications (sometimes called communications channel), refers to the medium used to convey information from a sender (or transmitter) to a receiver.
Enzyme	An enzyme is a protein that catalyzes, or speeds up, a chemical reaction. They are essential to sustain life because most chemical reactions in biological cells would occur too slowly, or would lead to different products, without them.

Blood vessel	A blood vessel is a part of the circulatory system and function to transport blood throughout the body. The most important types, arteries and veins, are so termed because they carry blood away from or towards the heart, respectively.
Oxygen	Oxygen is a chemical element in the periodic table. It has the symbol O and atomic number 8. Oxygen is the second most common element on Earth, composing around 46% of the mass of Earth's crust and 28% of the mass of Earth as a whole, and is the third most common element in the universe.
Nicotine	Nicotine is an organic compound, an alkaloid found naturally throughout the tobacco plant, with a high concentration in the leaves. It is a potent nerve poison and is included in many insecticides. In lower concentrations, the substance is a stimulant and is one of the main factors leading to the pleasure and habit-forming qualities of tobacco smoking.
Stigma	Stigma refers to a personal characteristic that at least some other individuals perceive negatively because that characteristic is different than those of the general population.
Anxiety	Anxiety is a complex combination of the feeling of fear, apprehension and worry often accompanied by physical sensations such as palpitations, chest pain and/or shortness of breath.
Ego	Ego refers to the second psychic structure to develop, characterized by self-awareness, planning, and delay of gratification.
Depression	In everyday language depression refers to any downturn in mood, which may be relatively transitory and perhaps due to something trivial. This is differentiated from Clinical depression which is marked by symptoms that last two weeks or more and are so severe that they interfere with daily living.
Culture	Culture, generally refers to patterns of human activity and the symbolic structures that give such activity significance.
Stress	Stress refers to a condition that is a response to factors that change the human systems normal state.
Cis	A double bond in which the greater radical on both ends is on the same side of the bond is called a cis.
Concept	A mental category used to class together objects, relations, events, abstractions, or qualities that have common properties is called concept.
Digestion	Digestion refers to the mechanical and chemical breakdown of food into molecules small enough for the body to absorb; the second main stage of food processing, following ingestion.
Planning	In agreement with the patient, the nurse addresses each of the problems identified in the planning phase. For each problem a measurable goal is set. For example, for the patient discussed above, the goal would be for the patient's skin to remain intact. The result is a nursing care plan. This is the third step.
Stress management	Stress management encompasses techniques intended to equip a person with effective coping mechanisms for dealing with psychological stress.
Adjustment	Adjustment is an attempt to cope with a given situation.
Constipation	Constipation is a condition of the digestive system where a person (or other animal) experiences hard feces that are difficult to eliminate; it may be extremely painful, and in severe cases (fecal impaction) lead to symptoms of bowel obstruction.
Intolerance	Intolerance refers to a type of interaction in which two or more drugs produce extremely uncomfortable symptoms.

Dehydration	Dehydration is the removal of water from an object. Medically, dehydration is a serious and potentially life-threatening condition in which the body contains an insufficient volume of water for normal functioning.
Infection	The invasion and multiplication of microorganisms in body tissues is called an infection.
Diarrhea	Diarrhea or diarrhoea is a condition in which the sufferer has frequent and watery, chunky, or loose bowel movements.
Ketosis	Ketosis refers to an abnormal elevation of ketone bodies in body fluids.
Chronic disease	Disease of long duration often not detected in its early stages and from which the patient will not recover is referred to as a chronic disease.
Chemical name	The primary function of chemical nomenclature is to ensure that the person who hears or reads a chemical name is under no ambiguity as to which chemical compound it refers: each name should refer to a single substance. It is considered less important to ensure that each substance should have a single name, although the number of acceptable names is limited.
Pulmonary hypertension	Pulmonary hypertension (PH) is an increase in blood pressure in the pulmonary artery or lung vasculature.
Lipase	A lipase is a water-soluble enzyme that catalyzes the hydrolysis of ester bonds in water insoluble, lipid substrates. Most lipases act at a specific position on the glycerol backbone of a lipid substrate (A1, A2 or A3).
Urgency	Urgency is an intense and sudden desire to urinate.
Vitamin	An organic compound other than a carbohydrate, lipid, or protein that is needed for normal metabolism but that the body cannot synthesize in adequate amounts is called a vitamin.
Stool	Stool is the waste matter discharged in a bowel movement.
Serotonin	Serotonin is a monoamine neurotransmitter synthesized in serotonergic neurons in the central nervous system and enterochromaffin cells in the gastrointestinal tract. It is believed to play an important part of the biochemistry of depression, migraine, bipolar disorder and anxiety.
Insomnia	Insomnia is a sleep disorder characterized by an inability to sleep and/or to remain asleep for a reasonable period during the night.
Pulse	The rhythmic stretching of the arteries caused by the pressure of blood forced through the arteries by contractions of the ventricles during systole is a pulse.
Stimulant	A stimulant is a drug which increases the activity of the sympathetic nervous system and produces a sense of euphoria or awakeness.
Ephedrine	Ephedrine (EPH) is a sympathomimetic amine commonly used as a decongestant and to treat hypotension associated with regional anaesthesia. Chemically, it is an alkaloid derived from various plants in the genus Ephedra (family Ephedraceae).
Solution	Solution refers to homogenous mixture formed when a solute is dissolved in a solvent.
Seizure	A seizure is a temporary alteration in brain function expressed as a changed mental state, tonic or clonic movements and various other symptoms. They are due to temporary abnormal electrical activity of a group of brain cells.
Allergy	An allergy or Type I hypersensitivity is an immune malfunction whereby a person's body is hypersensitized to react immunologically to typically nonimmunogenic substances. When a person is hypersensitized, these substances are known as allergens.
Egg	An egg is the zygote, resulting from fertilization of the ovum. It nourishes and protects the

Go to **Cram101.com** for the Practice Tests for this Chapter.

	embryo.
Carbon	Carbon is a chemical element in the periodic table that has the symbol C and atomic number 6. An abundant nonmetallic, tetravalent element, carbon has several allotropic forms.
Calcium	Calcium is the chemical element in the periodic table that has the symbol Ca and atomic number 20. Calcium is a soft grey alkaline earth metal that is used as a reducing agent in the extraction of thorium, zirconium and uranium. Calcium is also the fifth most abundant element in the Earth's crust.
Base	The common definition of a base is a chemical compound that absorbs hydronium ions when dissolved in water (a proton acceptor). An alkali is a special example of a base, where in an aqueous environment, hydroxide ions are donated.
Wellness	A dimension of health beyond the absence of disease or infirmity, including social, emotional, and spiritual aspects of health is called wellness.
Motives	Needs or desires that energize and direct behavior toward a goal are motives.
Motive	Motive refers to a hypothetical state within an organism that propels the organism toward a goal.
Immune system	The immune system is the system of specialized cells and organs that protect an organism from outside biological influences. When the immune system is functioning properly, it protects the body against bacteria and viral infections, destroying cancer cells and foreign substances.
Host	Host is an organism that harbors a parasite, mutual partner, or commensal partner; or a cell infected by a virus.
Laxatives	Medications used to soften stool and relieve constipation are referred to as laxatives.
Diuretic	A diuretic is any drug that elevates the rate of bodily urine excretion.
Laxative	Laxative refers to a medication or other substance that stimulates evacuation of the intestinal tract.
Body image	A person's body image is their perception of their physical appearance. It is more than what a person thinks they will see in a mirror, it is inextricably tied to their self-esteem and acceptance by peers.
Obsession	An obsession is a thought or idea that the sufferer cannot stop thinking about. Common examples include fears of acquiring disease, getting hurt, or causing harm to someone. They are typically automatic, frequent, distressing, and difficult to control or put an end to by themselves.
Public health	Public health is concerned with threats to the overall health of a community based on population health analysis.
Anorexia nervosa	Anorexia nervosa is an eating disorder characterized by voluntary starvation and exercise stress.
Bulimia	Bulimia refers to a disorder in which a person binges on incredibly large quantities of food, then purges by vomiting or by using laxatives. Bulimia is often less about food, and more to do with deep psychological issues and profound feelings of lack of control.
Bulimia nervosa	Bulimia nervosa is a psychological condition in which the subject engages in recurrent binge eating followed by intentionally; vomiting, misuse of laxatives or other medication, excessive exercising, and fasting, in order to compensate for the intake of the food and prevent weight gain:
Binge eating	Binge eating disorder is a syndrome in which people feel their eating is out of control; eat

disorder	what most would think is an unusually large amount of food; eat much more quickly than usual; eat until so full they are uncomfortable; eat large amounts of food, even when they are not really hungry; eat alone because they are embarrassed about the amount of food they eat; feel disgusted, depressed, or guilty after overeating.
Late adolescence	Late adolescence refers to approximately the latter half of the second decade of life. Career interests, dating, and identity exploration are often more pronounced in late adolescence than in early adolescence.
Eye	An eye is an organ that detects light. Different kinds of light-sensitive organs are found in a variety of creatures. The simplest eyes do nothing but detect whether the surroundings are light or dark, while more complex eyes can distinguish shapes and colors.
Mental health	Mental health refers to the 'thinking' part of psychosocial health; includes your values, attitudes, and beliefs.
Life span	Life span refers to the upper boundary of life, the maximum number of years an individual can live. The maximum life span of human beings is about 120 years of age.
Resistance	Resistance refers to a nonspecific ability to ward off infection or disease regardless of whether the body has been previously exposed to it. A force that opposes the flow of a fluid such as air or blood. Compare with immunity.

Go to **Cram101.com** for the Practice Tests for this Chapter.

Control group	A group that does not receive the treatment effect in an experiment is referred to as the control group or sometimes as the comparison group.
Obesity	The state of being more than 20 percent above the average weight for a person of one's height is called obesity.
Cardiovascular disease	Cardiovascular disease refers to afflictions in the mechanisms, including the heart, blood vessels, and their controllers, that are responsible for transporting blood to the body's tissues and organs. Psychological factors may play important roles in such diseases and their treatments.
Blood pressure	Blood pressure is the pressure exerted by the blood on the walls of the blood vessels.
Osteoporosis	Osteoporosis is a disease of bone in which bone mineral density (BMD) is reduced, bone microarchitecture is disrupted, the amount and variety of non-collagenous proteins in bone is changed, and a concomitantly fracture risk is increased.
Depression	In everyday language depression refers to any downturn in mood, which may be relatively transitory and perhaps due to something trivial. This is differentiated from Clinical depression which is marked by symptoms that last two weeks or more and are so severe that they interfere with daily living.
Mortality	The incidence of death in a population is mortality.
Diabetes	Diabetes is a medical disorder characterized by varying or persistent elevated blood sugar levels, especially after eating. All types of diabetes share similar symptoms and complications at advanced stages: dehydration and ketoacidosis, cardiovascular disease, chronic renal failure, retinal damage which can lead to blindness, nerve damage which can lead to erectile dysfunction, gangrene with risk of amputation of toes, feet, and even legs.
Anxiety	Anxiety is a complex combination of the feeling of fear, apprehension and worry often accompanied by physical sensations such as palpitations, chest pain and/or shortness of breath.
Cancer	Cancer is a class of diseases or disorders characterized by uncontrolled division of cells and the ability of these cells to invade other tissues, either by direct growth into adjacent tissue through invasion or by implantation into distant sites by metastasis.
Blood	Blood is a circulating tissue composed of fluid plasma and cells. The main function of blood is to supply nutrients (oxygen, glucose) and constitutional elements to tissues and to remove waste products.
Colon	The colon is the part of the intestine from the cecum to the rectum. Its primary purpose is to extract water from feces.
Statistics	Statistics is a type of data analysis which practice includes the planning, summarizing, and interpreting of observations of a system possibly followed by predicting or forecasting of future events based on a mathematical model of the system being observed.
Statistic	A statistic is an observable random variable of a sample.
Depressive disorders	Depressive disorders are mood disorders in which the individual suffers depression without ever experiencing mania.
Anxiety disorder	Anxiety disorder is a blanket term covering several different forms of abnormal anxiety, fear, phobia and nervous condition, that come on suddenly and prevent pursuing normal daily routines.
Health	Health is a term that refers to a combination of the absence of illness, the ability to cope with everyday activities, physical fitness, and high quality of life.

Go to **Cram101.com** for the Practice Tests for this Chapter.

Risk factor	A risk factor is a variable associated with an increased risk of disease or infection but risk factors are not necessarily causal.
Survey	A method of scientific investigation in which a large sample of people answer questions about their attitudes or behavior is referred to as a survey.
Centers for Disease Control and Prevention	The Centers for Disease Control and Prevention in Atlanta, Georgia, is recognized as the lead United States agency for protecting the public health and safety of people by providing credible information to enhance health decisions, and promoting health through strong partnerships with state health departments and other organizations.
Muscle	Muscle is a contractile form of tissue. It is one of the four major tissue types, the other three being epithelium, connective tissue and nervous tissue. Muscle contraction is used to move parts of the body, as well as to move substances within the body.
Skeletal muscle	Skeletal muscle is a type of striated muscle, attached to the skeleton. They are used to facilitate movement, by applying force to bones and joints; via contraction. They generally contract voluntarily (via nerve stimulation), although they can contract involuntarily.
Medicine	Medicine is the branch of health science and the sector of public life concerned with maintaining or restoring human health through the study, diagnosis and treatment of disease and injury.
Stress	Stress refers to a condition that is a response to factors that change the human systems normal state.
Joint	A joint (articulation) is the location at which two bones make contact (articulate). They are constructed to both allow movement and provide mechanical support.
Range of motion	Range of motion is a measurement of movement through a particular joint or muscle range.
Tissue	A collection of interconnected cells that perform a similar function within an organism is called tissue.
Oxygen	Oxygen is a chemical element in the periodic table. It has the symbol O and atomic number 8. Oxygen is the second most common element on Earth, composing around 46% of the mass of Earth's crust and 28% of the mass of Earth as a whole, and is the third most common element in the universe.
Organ	Organ refers to a structure consisting of several tissues adapted as a group to perform specific functions.
Respiratory system	The respiratory system is the biological system of any organism that engages in gas exchange.In humans and other mammals, the respiratory system consists of the airways, the lungs, and the respiratory muscles that mediate the movement of air into and out of the body.
Blood vessel	A blood vessel is a part of the circulatory system and function to transport blood throughout the body. The most important types, arteries and veins, are so termed because they carry blood away from or towards the heart, respectively.
Hypertension	Hypertension is a medical condition where the blood pressure in the arteries is chronically elevated. Persistent hypertension is one of the risk factors for strokes, heart attacks, heart failure and arterial aneurysm, and is a leading cause of chronic renal failure.
Stroke	A stroke or cerebrovascular accident (CVA) occurs when the blood supply to a part of the brain is suddenly interrupted.
Lipoprotein	A lipoprotein is a biochemical assembly that contains both proteins and lipids and may be structural or catalytic in function. They may be enzymes, proton pumps, ion pumps, or some combination of these functions.

Go to **Cram101.com** for the Practice Tests for this Chapter.

Lipid	Lipid is one class of aliphatic hydrocarbon-containing organic compounds essential for the structure and function of living cells. They are characterized by being water-insoluble but soluble in nonpolar organic solvents.
Cholesterol	Cholesterol is a steroid, a lipid, and an alcohol, found in the cell membranes of all body tissues, and transported in the blood plasma of all animals. It is an important component of the membranes of cells, providing stability; it makes the membrane's fluidity stable over a bigger temperature interval.
Carcinogen	A carcinogen is any substance or agent that promotes cancer. A carcinogen is often, but not necessarily, a mutagen or teratogen.
Digestive system	The organ system that ingests food, breaks it down into smaller chemical units, and absorbs the nutrient molecules is referred to as the digestive system.
Digestive tract	The digestive tract is the system of organs within multicellular animals which takes in food, digests it to extract energy and nutrients, and expels the remaining waste.
Prostaglandin	A prostaglandin is any member of a group of lipid compounds that are derived from fatty acids and have important functions in the animal body.
Intestine	The intestine is the portion of the alimentary canal extending from the stomach to the anus and, in humans and mammals, consists of two segments, the small intestine and the large intestine. The intestine is the part of the body responsible for extracting nutrition from food.
Large intestine	In anatomy of the digestive system, the colon, also called the large intestine or large bowel, is the part of the intestine from the cecum ('caecum' in British English) to the rectum. Its primary purpose is to extract water from feces.
Older adult	Older adult is an adult over the age of 65.
Affect	Affect is the scientific term used to describe a subject's externally displayed mood. This can be assesed by the nurse by observing facial expression, tone of voice, and body language.
Menopause	Menopause is the physiological cessation of menstrual cycles associated with advancing age in species that experience such cycles. Menopause is sometimes referred to as change of life or climacteric.
Estrogen	Estrogen is a steroid that functions as the primary female sex hormone. While present in both men and women, they are found in women in significantly higher quantities.
Lungs	Lungs are the essential organs of respiration in air-breathing vertebrates. Their principal function is to transport oxygen from the atmosphere into the bloodstream, and to excrete carbon dioxide from the bloodstream into the atmosphere.
Hip	In anatomy, the hip is the bony projection of the femur, known as the greater trochanter, and the overlying muscle and fat.
Population	Population refers to all members of a well-defined group of organisms, events, or things.
Calcium	Calcium is the chemical element in the periodic table that has the symbol Ca and atomic number 20. Calcium is a soft grey alkaline earth metal that is used as a reducing agent in the extraction of thorium, zirconium and uranium. Calcium is also the fifth most abundant element in the Earth's crust.
Metabolic rate	Energy expended by the body per unit time is called metabolic rate.
Calorie	Calorie refers to a unit used to measure heat energy and the energy contents of foods.
Life span	Life span refers to the upper boundary of life, the maximum number of years an individual can live. The maximum life span of human beings is about 120 years of age.

Incidence	In epidemiological studies of a particular disorder, the rate at which new cases occur in a given place at a given time is called incidence.
Immune system	The immune system is the system of specialized cells and organs that protect an organism from outside biological influences. When the immune system is functioning properly, it protects the body against bacteria and viral infections, destroying cancer cells and foreign substances.
Immunity	Resistance to the effects of specific disease-causing agents is called immunity.
Bacteria	The domain that contains procaryotic cells with primarily diacyl glycerol diesters in their membranes and with bacterial rRNA. Bacteria also is a general term for organisms that are composed of procaryotic cells and are not multicellular.
Lifestyle	The culturally, socially, economically, and environmentally conditioned complex of actions characteristic of an individual, group, or community as a pattern of habituated behavior over time that is health related but not necessarily health directed is a lifestyle.
Brain	The part of the central nervous system involved in regulating and controlling body activity and interpreting information from the senses transmitted through the nervous system is referred to as the brain.
Planning	In agreement with the patient, the nurse addresses each of the problems identified in the planning phase. For each problem a measurable goal is set. For example, for the patient discussed above, the goal would be for the patient's skin to remain intact. The result is a nursing care plan. This is the third step.
Mental processes	The thoughts, feelings, and motives that each of us experiences privately but that cannot be observed directly are called mental processes.
Aerobic	An aerobic organism is an organism that has an oxygen based metabolism. Aerobes, in a process known as cellular respiration, use oxygen to oxidize substrates (for example sugars and fats) in order to obtain energy.
Aerobic exercise	Exercise in which oxygen is used to produce ATP is aerobic exercise.
Theory	Theory refers to an explanatory statement, or set of statements, that concisely summarizes the state of knowledge on a phenomenon and provides direction for further study.
Correlation	A statistical technique for determining the degree of association between two or more variables is referred to as correlation.
Internal medicine	Doctors of internal medicine ("internists") focus on adult medicine and have had special study and training focusing on the prevention and treatment of adult diseases. At least three of their seven or more years of medical school and postgraduate training are dedicated to learning how to prevent, diagnose, and treat diseases that affect adults.
Major depression	Major depression is characterized by a severely depressed mood that persists for at least two weeks. Episodes of depression may start suddenly or slowly and can occur several times through a person's life. The disorder may be categorized as "single episode" or "recurrent" depending on whether previous episodes have been experienced before.
Resistance	Resistance refers to a nonspecific ability to ward off infection or disease regardless of whether the body has been previously exposed to it. A force that opposes the flow of a fluid such as air or blood. Compare with immunity.
Elderly	Old age consists of ages nearing the average life span of human beings, and thus the end of the human life cycle. Euphemisms for older people include advanced adult, elderly, and senior or senior citizen.
Animal model	An animal model usually refers to a non-human animal with a disease that is similar to a

223

human condition.

Prospective study	Prospective study is a long-term study of a group of people, beginning before the onset of a common disorder. It allows investigators to see how the disorder develops.
Nervous system	The nervous system of an animal coordinates the activity of the muscles, monitors the organs, constructs and processes input from the senses, and initiates actions.
Mental health	Mental health refers to the 'thinking' part of psychosocial health; includes your values, attitudes, and beliefs.
Stress management	Stress management encompasses techniques intended to equip a person with effective coping mechanisms for dealing with psychological stress.
Anorexia	Anorexia nervosa is an eating disorder characterized by voluntary starvation and exercise stress.
Bulimia	Bulimia refers to a disorder in which a person binges on incredibly large quantities of food, then purges by vomiting or by using laxatives. Bulimia is often less about food, and more to do with deep psychological issues and profound feelings of lack of control.
Intervention	Intervention refers to a planned attempt to break through addicts' or abusers' denial and get them into treatment. Interventions most often occur when legal, workplace, health, relationship, or financial problems have become intolerable.
Hormone	A hormone is a chemical messenger from one cell to another. All multicellular organisms produce hormones. The best known hormones are those produced by endocrine glands of vertebrate animals, but hormones are produced by nearly every organ system and tissue type in a human or animal body. Hormone molecules are secreted directly into the bloodstream, they move by circulation or diffusion to their target cells, which may be nearby cells in the same tissue or cells of a distant organ of the body.
Lead	Lead is a chemical element in the periodic table that has the symbol Pb and atomic number 82. A soft, heavy, toxic and malleable poor metal, lead is bluish white when freshly cut but tarnishes to dull gray when exposed to air. Lead is used in building construction, lead-acid batteries, bullets and shot, and is part of solder, pewter, and fusible alloys.
Value	Value is worth in general, and it is thought to be connected to reasons for certain practices, policies, actions, beliefs or emotions. Value is "that which one acts to gain and/or keep."
Constipation	Constipation is a condition of the digestive system where a person (or other animal) experiences hard feces that are difficult to eliminate; it may be extremely painful, and in severe cases (fecal impaction) lead to symptoms of bowel obstruction.
Intolerance	Intolerance refers to a type of interaction in which two or more drugs produce extremely uncomfortable symptoms.
Laxatives	Medications used to soften stool and relieve constipation are referred to as laxatives.
Laxative	Laxative refers to a medication or other substance that stimulates evacuation of the intestinal tract.
Anemia	Anemia is a deficiency of red blood cells and/or hemoglobin. This results in a reduced ability of blood to transfer oxygen to the tissues, and this causes hypoxia; since all human cells depend on oxygen for survival, varying degrees of anemia can have a wide range of clinical consequences.
Lanugo	Lanugo are hairs that grow on the body to attempt to insulate it because of lack of fat. It is normal in fetuses, the unborn baby cosumes the hair, and this contribute to the newborn babies first feces.

Go to **Cram101.com** for the Practice Tests for this Chapter.

Skin	Skin is an organ of the integumentary system composed of a layer of tissues that protect underlying muscles and organs.
Pain	Pain is an unpleasant sensation which may be associated with actual or potential tissue damage and which may have physical and emotional components.
Heart rate	Heart rate is a term used to describe the frequency of the cardiac cycle. It is considered one of the four vital signs. Usually it is calculated as the number of contractions of the heart in one minute and expressed as "beats per minute".
Cardiovascular system	The circulatory system or cardiovascular system is the organ system which circulates blood around the body of most animals.
Assess	Assess is to systematically and continuously collect, validate, and communicate patient data.
Asthma	Asthma is a complex disease characterized by bronchial hyperresponsiveness (BHR), inflammation, mucus production and intermittent airway obstruction.
Pulse	The rhythmic stretching of the arteries caused by the pressure of blood forced through the arteries by contractions of the ventricles during systole is a pulse.
Radial artery	The radial artery is the main blood vessel, with oxygenated blood, of the lateral aspect of the forearm. It arises from the brachial artery and terminates in the deep palmar arch.
Artery	Vessel that takes blood away from the heart to the tissues and organs of the body is called an artery.
Scientific method	Psychologists gather data in order to describe, understand, predict, and control behavior. Scientific method refers to an approach that can be used to discover accurate information. It includes these steps: understand the problem, collect data, draw conclusions, and revise research conclusions.
Incentive	Incentive refers to an object, person, or situation perceived as being capable of satisfying a need.
Conditioning	Processes by which behaviors can be learned or modified through interaction with the environment are conditioning.
Tendon	A tendon or sinew is a tough band of fibrous connective tissue that connects muscle to bone. They are similar to ligaments except that ligaments join one bone to another.
Attachment	Attachment refers to the psychological tendency to seek closeness to another person, to feel secure when that person is present, and to feel anxious when that person is absent.
Skeleton	In biology, the skeleton or skeletal system is the biological system providing physical support in living organisms.
Physiology	The study of the function of cells, tissues, and organs is referred to as physiology.
Radius	The radius is the bone of the forearm that extends from the inside of the elbow to the thumb side of the wrist. The radius is situated on the lateral side of the ulna, which exceeds it in length and size.
Receptor	A receptor is a protein on the cell membrane or within the cytoplasm or cell nucleus that binds to a specific molecule (a ligand), such as a neurotransmitter, hormone, or other substance, and initiates the cellular response to the ligand. Receptor, in immunology, the region of an antibody which shows recognition of an antigen.
Muscle contraction	A muscle contraction occurs when a muscle cell (called a muscle fiber) shortens. There are three general types: skeletal, heart, and smooth.
Methodology	Techniques of measurement used to collect and manipulate empirical data refer to a

Go to **Cram101.com** for the Practice Tests for this Chapter.

227

	methodology.
Rehabilitation	Rehabilitation is the restoration of lost capabilities, or the treatment aimed at producing it. Also refers to treatment for dependency on psychoactive substances such as alcohol, prescription drugs, and illicit drugs such as cocaine, heroin or amphetamines.
Specificity	A medical diagnostic test for a certain disease, specificity is the proportion of true negatives of all the negative samples tested.
Hypertrophy	Hypertrophy is the increase of the size of an organ. It should be distinguished from hyperplasia which occurs due to cell division; hypertrophy occurs due to an increase in cell size rather than division. It is most commonly seen in muscle that has been actively stimulated, the most well-known method being exercise.
Testosterone	Testosterone is a steroid hormone from the androgen group. Testosterone is secreted in the testes of men and the ovaries of women. It is the principal male sex hormone and the "original" anabolic steroid. In both males and females, it plays key roles in health and well-being.
Puberty	A time in the life of a developing individual characterized by the increasing production of sex hormones, which cause it to reach sexual maturity is called puberty.
Adolescence	Adolescence is the period of psychological and social transition between childhood and adulthood (gender-specific manhood, or womanhood). As a transitional stage of human development it represents the period of time during which a juvenile matures into adulthood.
Steroid	A steroid is a lipid characterized by a carbon skeleton with four fused rings. Different steroids vary in the functional groups attached to these rings. Hundreds of distinct steroids have been identified in plants and animals. Their most important role in most living systems is as hormones.
Anabolic steroid	An anabolic steroid is a class of natural and synthetic steroid hormones that promote cell growth and division, resulting in growth of muscle tissue and sometimes bone size and strength. They act in different ways on the body to promote muscle growth, and each has androgenic and anabolic properties.
Variable	A characteristic or aspect in which people, objects, events, or conditions vary is called variable.
Isometric contraction	A muscle contraction in which there is no movement and the length of the muscle does not change is an isometric contraction.
Constant	A behavior or characteristic that does not vary from one observation to another is referred to as a constant.
Stimulus	Stimulus in a nervous system, a factor that triggers sensory transduction.
Syndrome	Syndrome is the association of several clinically recognizable features, signs, symptoms, phenomena or characteristics which often occur together, so that the presence of one feature alerts the physician to the presence of the others
Ligament	A ligament is a short band of tough fibrous connective tissue composed mainly of long, stringy collagen fibres. They connect bones to other bones to form a joint. (They do not connect muscles to bones.)
Contusion	Brain contusion, a form of traumatic brain injury, is a bruise of the brain tissue. Like bruises in other tissues, cerebral contusion can be caused by multiple microhemorrhages, small blood vessel leaks into brain tissue.
Anatomy	Anatomy is the branch of biology that deals with the structure and organization of living things. It can be divided into animal anatomy (zootomy) and plant anatomy (phytonomy).

Go to **Cram101.com** for the Practice Tests for this Chapter.

Eye	An eye is an organ that detects light. Different kinds of light-sensitive organs are found in a variety of creatures. The simplest eyes do nothing but detect whether the surroundings are light or dark, while more complex eyes can distinguish shapes and colors.
Inflammation	Inflammation is the first response of the immune system to infection or irritation and may be referred to as the innate cascade.
Fascia	Fascia is specialized connective tissue layer which surrounds muscles, bones, and joints, providing support and protection and giving structure to the body. It consists of three layers: the superficial fascia, the deep fascia and the subserous fascia. Fascia is one of the 3 types of dense connective tissue (the other two being ligaments and tendons).
Nerve	A nerve is an enclosed, cable-like bundle of nerve fibers or axons, which includes the glia that ensheath the axons in myelin.
Shock	Circulatory shock, a state of cardiac output that is insufficient to meet the body's physiological needs, with consequences ranging from fainting to death is referred to as shock. Insulin shock, a state of severe hypoglycemia caused by administration of insulin.
Tibia	The Tibia or shin bone, in human anatomy, is the larger of the two bones in the leg below the knee. It is found medial (towards the middle) and anterior (towards the front) to the other such bone, the fibula. It is the second-longest bone in the human body.
Certification	A professional certification, trade certification, or professional designation often called simply certification or qualification is a designation earned by a person to certify that he is qualified to perform a job. Certification indicates that the individual has a specific knowledge, skills, or abilities in the view of the certifying body.
Carrier	Person in apparent health whose chromosomes contain a pathologic mutant gene that may be transmitted to his or her children is a carrier.
Cartilage	Cartilage is a type of dense connective tissue. Cartilage is composed of cells called chondrocytes which are dispersed in a firm gel-like ground substance, called the matrix. Cartilage is avascular (contains no blood vessels) and nutrients are diffused through the matrix.
Elevation	Elevation refers to upward movement of a part of the body.
Acclimatization	The word acclimatization is used to describe the process of an organism adjusting to changes in its environment, often involving temperature or climate. Acclimatization usually occurs in a short time, and within one organism's lifetime.
Core temperature	Core temperature is the operating temperature of an organism, specifically in deep structures of the body such as the liver, in comparison to temperatures of peripheral tissues.
Dehydration	Dehydration is the removal of water from an object. Medically, dehydration is a serious and potentially life-threatening condition in which the body contains an insufficient volume of water for normal functioning.
Cramp	A cramp is an unpleasant sensation caused by contraction, usually of a muscle. It can be caused by cold or overexertion.
Carbohydrate	Carbohydrate is a chemical compound that contains oxygen, hydrogen, and carbon atoms. They consist of monosaccharide sugars of varying chain lengths and that have the general chemical formula $C_n(H_2O)_n$ or are derivatives of such.
Electrolytes	Electrolytes refers to compounds that separate into ions in water and, in turn, are able to conduct an electrical current. These include sodium, chloride, and potassium.
Hypothermia	Hypothermia is a low core body temperature, defined clinically as a temperature of less than 35 degrees celsius.

Electrolyte	An electrolyte is a substance that dissociates into free ions when dissolved (or molten), to produce an electrically conductive medium. Because they generally consist of ions in solution, they are also known as ionic solutions.
Sodium	Sodium is the chemical element in the periodic table that has the symbol Na (Natrium in Latin) and atomic number 11. Sodium is a soft, waxy, silvery reactive metal belonging to the alkali metals that is abundant in natural compounds (especially halite). It is highly reactive.
Hyponatremia	The electrolyte disturbance hyponatremia exists in humans when the sodium level in the plasma falls below 135 mmol/l. At lower levels water intoxication may result, an urgently dangerous condition.
Heart attack	A heart attack, is a serious, sudden heart condition usually characterized by varying degrees of chest pain or discomfort, weakness, sweating, nausea, vomiting, and arrhythmias, sometimes causing loss of consciousness. It occurs when the blood supply to a part of the heart is interrupted, causing death and scarring of the local heart tissue.
Solution	Solution refers to homogenous mixture formed when a solute is dissolved in a solvent.
Amnesia	Amnesia is a condition in which memory is disturbed. The causes of amnesia are organic or functional. Organic causes include damage to the brain, through trauma or disease, or use of certain (generally sedative) drugs.
Apathy	Apathy is the lack of emotion, motivation, or enthusiasm. Apathy is a psychological term for a state of indifference where an individual is unresponsive or "indifferent" to aspects of emotional, social, or physical life.
Muscle fiber	Cell with myofibrils containing actin and myosin filaments arranged within sarcomeres is a muscle fiber.
Fiber	Fibers used by man come from a wide variety of sources: Natural fiber include those made out of plants, animal and mineral sources. Natural fibers can be classified according to their origin.
Hyperkalemia	Hyperkalemia is an elevated blood level (above 5.0 mmol/L) of the electrolyte potassium.
Hypokalemia	Hypokalemia is a potentially fatal condition in which the body fails to retain sufficient potassium to maintain health.
Potassium	Potassium is a chemical element in the periodic table. It has the symbol K (L. kalium) and atomic number 19. Potassium is a soft silvery-white metallic alkali metal that occurs naturally bound to other elements in seawater and many minerals.
Paralysis	Paralysis is the complete loss of muscle function for one or more muscle groups. Paralysis may be localized, or generalized, or it may follow a certain pattern.
Urine	Concentrated filtrate produced by the kidneys and excreted via the bladder is called urine.
Cross training	Participation in one sport to improve performance in another, or use of several different types of training to achieve a goal is called cross training.
Trauma	Trauma refers to a severe physical injury or wound to the body caused by an external force, or a psychological shock having a lasting effect on mental life.
Insight	Insight refers to a sudden awareness of the relationships among various elements that had previously appeared to be independent of one another.
Assessment	In clinical practice, the process by which a mental health professional gathers and compiles information about a client for the purpose of describing the person's problems or disorder and developing a plan of treatment is an assessment.

Health promotion	Any planned combination of educational, political, regulatory, and organizational supports for actions and conditions of living conducive to the health of individuals, groups, or communities is called health promotion.
Chronic disease	Disease of long duration often not detected in its early stages and from which the patient will not recover is referred to as a chronic disease.
Addiction	Addiction is an uncontrollable compulsion to repeat a behavior regardless of its consequences. Many drugs or behaviors can precipitate a pattern of conditions recognized as addiction, which include a craving for more of the drug or behavior, increased physiological tolerance to exposure, and withdrawal symptoms in the absence of the stimulus.
Biopsychosocial	The biopsychosocial model is a way of looking at the mind and body of a patient as two important systems that are interlinked. The biopsychosocial model draws a distinction between the actual pathological processes that cause disease, and the patient's perception of their health and the effects on it, called the illness.
Internet addiction	Internet addiction disorder is a theorized disorder coined by Ivan Goldberg, M.D., in 1997. It is compared to pathological gambling as diagnosed by the DSM-IV.

Nicotine	Nicotine is an organic compound, an alkaloid found naturally throughout the tobacco plant, with a high concentration in the leaves. It is a potent nerve poison and is included in many insecticides. In lower concentrations, the substance is a stimulant and is one of the main factors leading to the pleasure and habit-forming qualities of tobacco smoking.
Stimulant	A stimulant is a drug which increases the activity of the sympathetic nervous system and produces a sense of euphoria or awakeness.
Addiction	Addiction is an uncontrollable compulsion to repeat a behavior regardless of its consequences. Many drugs or behaviors can precipitate a pattern of conditions recognized as addiction, which include a craving for more of the drug or behavior, increased physiological tolerance to exposure, and withdrawal symptoms in the absence of the stimulus.
Alcohol	Alcohol is a general term, applied to any organic compound in which a hydroxyl group (-OH) is bound to a carbon atom, which in turn is bound to other hydrogen and/or carbon atoms. The general formula for a simple acyclic alcohol is $C_nH_{2n+1}OH$.
Lead	Lead is a chemical element in the periodic table that has the symbol Pb and atomic number 82. A soft, heavy, toxic and malleable poor metal, lead is bluish white when freshly cut but tarnishes to dull gray when exposed to air. Lead is used in building construction, lead-acid batteries, bullets and shot, and is part of solder, pewter, and fusible alloys.
Dependence	Dependence refers to a mental or physical craving for a drug and withdrawal symptoms when use of the drug is stopped.
Metabolism	Metabolism is the biochemical modification of chemical compounds in living organisms and cells. This includes the biosynthesis of complex organic molecules (anabolism) and their breakdown (catabolism).
Addict	A person with an overpowering physical or psychological need to continue taking a particular substance or drug is referred to as an addict.
Psychological dependence	Psychological dependence may lead to psychological withdrawal symptoms. Addictions can theoretically form for any rewarding behavior, or as a habitual means to avoid undesired activity, but typically they only do so to a clinical level in individuals who have emotional, social, or psychological dysfunctions, taking the place of normal positive stimuli not otherwise attained
Biopsy	Removal of small tissue sample from the body for microscopic examination is called biopsy.
Abstinence	Abstinence has diverse forms. In its oldest sense it is sexual, as in the practice of continence, chastity, and celibacy.
Obsession	An obsession is a thought or idea that the sufferer cannot stop thinking about. Common examples include fears of acquiring disease, getting hurt, or causing harm to someone. They are typically automatic, frequent, distressing, and difficult to control or put an end to by themselves.
Brain	The part of the central nervous system involved in regulating and controlling body activity and interpreting information from the senses transmitted through the nervous system is referred to as the brain.
Epidemic	An epidemic is a disease that appears as new cases in a given human population, during a given period, at a rate that substantially exceeds what is "expected", based on recent experience.
Drug addiction	Drug addiction, or substance dependence is the compulsive use of drugs, to the point where the user has no effective choice but to continue use.
Health	Health is a term that refers to a combination of the absence of illness, the ability to cope

Go to **Cram101.com** for the Practice Tests for this Chapter.

	with everyday activities, physical fitness, and high quality of life.
Opiate	The term opiate refers to the alkaloids found in opium, an extract from the seed pods of the opium poppy (Papaver somniferum L.). It has also traditionally referred to natural and semi-synthetic derivatives of morphine.
Heroin	Heroin is widely and illegally used as a powerful and addictive drug producing intense euphoria, which often disappears with increasing tolerance. Heroin is a semi-synthetic opioid. It is the 3,6-diacetyl derivative of morphine and is synthesized from it by acetylation.
Cocaine	Cocaine is a crystalline tropane alkaloid that is obtained from the leaves of the coca plant. It is a stimulant of the central nervous system and an appetite suppressant, creating what has been described as a euphoric sense of happiness and increased energy.
Drug abuse	Drug abuse has a wide range of definitions, all of them relating either to the misuse or overuse of a psychoactive drug or performance enhancing drug for a non-therapeutic or non-medical effect, or referring to any use of illegal drug in the absence of a required, yet practically impossible to get, license from a government authority.
Amphetamine	Amphetamine is a synthetic stimulant used to suppress the appetite, control weight, and treat disorders including narcolepsy and ADHD. It is also used recreationally and for performance enhancement.
Marijuana	Marijuana refers to the dried vegetable matter of the Cannabis sativa plant.
Hashish	Hashish is a psychoactive drug derived from the Cannabis plant. It is used for its relaxing and mind-altering effects.
Culture	Culture, generally refers to patterns of human activity and the symbolic structures that give such activity significance.
Compulsion	An apparently irresistible urge to repeat an act or engage in ritualistic behavior such as hand washing is referred to as a compulsion.
Orgasm	Orgasm refers to rhythmic contractions of the reproductive structures, accompanied by extreme pleasure, at the peak of sexual excitement in both sexes; includes ejaculation by the male.
Loss of control	The point in drug use where the user becomes unable to limit or stop use is referred to as loss of control.
Denial	Denial is a psychological defense mechanism in which a person faced with a fact that is uncomfortable or painful to accept rejects it instead, insisting that it is not true despite what may be overwhelming evidence.
Maladaptive	In psychology, a behavior or trait is adaptive when it helps an individual adjust and function well within their social environment. A maladaptive behavior or trait is counterproductive to the individual.
Nerve cell	A cell specialized to originate or transmit nerve impulses is referred to as nerve cell.
Receptor	A receptor is a protein on the cell membrane or within the cytoplasm or cell nucleus that binds to a specific molecule (a ligand), such as a neurotransmitter, hormone, or other substance, and initiates the cellular response to the ligand. Receptor, in immunology, the region of an antibody which shows recognition of an antigen.
Nerve	A nerve is an enclosed, cable-like bundle of nerve fibers or axons, which includes the glia that ensheath the axons in myelin.
Neurotransmitter	A neurotransmitter is a chemical that is used to relay, amplify and modulate electrical signals between a neuron and another cell.

239

Tolerance	Drug tolerance occurs when a subject's reaction to a drug decreases so that larger doses are required to achieve the same effect.
Physiology	The study of the function of cells, tissues, and organs is referred to as physiology.
Stress	Stress refers to a condition that is a response to factors that change the human systems normal state.
Endorphins	Endorphins refer to neurotransmitters that are composed of amino acids and that are functionally similar to morphine.
Endorphin	Endorphin is an endogenous opioid biochemical compound. They are peptides produced by the pituitary gland and the hypothalamus in vertebrates, and they resemble the opiates in their abilities to produce analgesia and a sense of well-being.
Syndrome	Syndrome is the association of several clinically recognizable features, signs, symptoms, phenomena or characteristics which often occur together, so that the presence of one feature alerts the physician to the presence of the others
Withdrawal symptoms	Withdrawal symptoms are physiological changes that occur when the use of a drug is stopped or dosage decreased.
Delirium	Delirium is a medical term used to describe an acute decline in attention and cognition. Delirium is probably the single most common acute disorder affecting adults in general hospitals. It affects 10-20% of all adults in hospital, and 30-40% of older patients.
Delirium tremens	Delirium tremens refers to a condition characterized by sweating, restlessness, disorientation, and hallucinations. It occurs in some chronic alcohol users when there is a sudden decrease in usage.
Craving	Craving refers to the powerful desire to use a psychoactive drug or engage in a compulsive behavior. It is manifested in physiological changes, such as raised heart rate, sweating, anxiety, drop in body temperature, pupil dilation, and stomach muscle movements.
Pain	Pain is an unpleasant sensation which may be associated with actual or potential tissue damage and which may have physical and emotional components.
Psychological addiction	Psychological addiction is a person's need to use a drug out of desire for the effects it produces, rather than to relieve withdrawal symptoms.
Theory	Theory refers to an explanatory statement, or set of statements, that concisely summarizes the state of knowledge on a phenomenon and provides direction for further study.
Biopsychosocial	The biopsychosocial model is a way of looking at the mind and body of a patient as two important systems that are interlinked. The biopsychosocial model draws a distinction between the actual pathological processes that cause disease, and the patient's perception of their health and the effects on it, called the illness.
Solution	Solution refers to homogenous mixture formed when a solute is dissolved in a solvent.
Alcoholism	A disorder that involves long-term, repeated, uncontrolled, compulsive, and excessive use of alcoholic beverages and that impairs the drinker's health and work and social relationships is called alcoholism.
Intoxication	Condition in which a substance affecting the central nervous system has been ingested and certain maladaptive behaviors or psychological changes, such as belligerence and impaired function, are evident is called intoxication.
Incidence	In epidemiological studies of a particular disorder, the rate at which new cases occur in a given place at a given time is called incidence.
Value	Value is worth in general, and it is thought to be connected to reasons for certain

Go to **Cram101.com** for the Practice Tests for this Chapter.

	practices, policies, actions, beliefs or emotions. Value is "that which one acts to gain and/or keep."
Learning theory	Learning theory refers to posits that delinquency is learned through close relationships with others; asserts that children are born 'good' and learn to be 'bad' from others.
Imitation	An attempt to match one's own behavior to another person's behavior is called imitation.
Marriage	A socially approved sexual and economic relationship between two or more individuals is a marriage.
Elderly	Old age consists of ages nearing the average life span of human beings, and thus the end of the human life cycle. Euphemisms for older people include advanced adult, elderly, and senior or senior citizen.
Stressor	A factor capable of stimulating a stress response is a stressor.
Acute	In medicine, an acute disease is a disease with either or both of: a rapid onset; and a short course (as opposed to a chronic course).
Sexual abuse	Sexual abuse is a relative cultural term used to describe sexual relations and behavior between two or more parties which are considered criminally and/or morally offensive.
Locus of control	The place to which an individual attributes control over the receiving of reinforcers -either inside or outside the self is referred to as locus of control.
Course	Pattern of development and change of a disorder over time is a course.
Compulsive gambling	A progressive impulse control disorder characterized by a preoccupation with and a compulsion to bet increasing amounts of money on games of chance, continued gambling despite financial, work-related, and relationship problems, is compulsive gambling.
Elevation	Elevation refers to upward movement of a part of the body.
Depression	In everyday language depression refers to any downturn in mood, which may be relatively transitory and perhaps due to something trivial. This is differentiated from Clinical depression which is marked by symptoms that last two weeks or more and are so severe that they interfere with daily living.
Insomnia	Insomnia is a sleep disorder characterized by an inability to sleep and/or to remain asleep for a reasonable period during the night.
Anxiety	Anxiety is a complex combination of the feeling of fear, apprehension and worry often accompanied by physical sensations such as palpitations, chest pain and/or shortness of breath.
Anger	Anger is an emotional response often based on a sensation or perception of threat to one's needs.
Older adult	Older adult is an adult over the age of 65.
Population	Population refers to all members of a well-defined group of organisms, events, or things.
Affect	Affect is the scientific term used to describe a subject's externally displayed mood. This can be assesed by the nurse by observing facial expression, tone of voice, and body language.
Compulsive gambler	A person addicted to gambling is referred to as compulsive gambler.
Planning	In agreement with the patient, the nurse addresses each of the problems identified in the planning phase. For each problem a measurable goal is set. For example, for the patient discussed above, the goal would be for the patient's skin to remain intact. The result is a nursing care plan. This is the third step.

Concept	A mental category used to class together objects, relations, events, abstractions, or qualities that have common properties is called concept.
Identity	The distinguishing character of the individual: who each of us is, what our roles are, and what we are capable of is called identity.
Alcoholic	An alcoholic is dependent on alcohol as characterized by craving, loss of control, physical dependence and withdrawal symptoms, and tolerance.
Survey	A method of scientific investigation in which a large sample of people answer questions about their attitudes or behavior is referred to as a survey.
Cardiovascular disease	Cardiovascular disease refers to afflictions in the mechanisms, including the heart, blood vessels, and their controllers, that are responsible for transporting blood to the body's tissues and organs. Psychological factors may play important roles in such diseases and their treatments.
Hypertension	Hypertension is a medical condition where the blood pressure in the arteries is chronically elevated. Persistent hypertension is one of the risk factors for strokes, heart attacks, heart failure and arterial aneurysm, and is a leading cause of chronic renal failure.
Adrenaline	Adrenaline is a hormone released by chromaffin cells and by some neurons in response to stress. Produces 'fight or flight' responses, including increased heart rate and blood sugar levels.
Gastrointestnal tract	The gastrointestinal tract is the system of organs within multicellular animals which takes in food, digests it to extract energy and nutrients, and expels the remaining waste.
Advocate	An advocate is one who speaks on behalf of another, especially in a legal context. Implicit in the concept is the notion that the represented lacks the knowledge, skill, ability, or standing to speak for themselves.
Statistics	Statistics is a type of data analysis which practice includes the planning, summarizing, and interpreting of observations of a system possibly followed by predicting or forecasting of future events based on a mathematical model of the system being observed.
Statistic	A statistic is an observable random variable of a sample.
Anorexia	Anorexia nervosa is an eating disorder characterized by voluntary starvation and exercise stress.
Bulimia	Bulimia refers to a disorder in which a person binges on incredibly large quantities of food, then purges by vomiting or by using laxatives. Bulimia is often less about food, and more to do with deep psychological issues and profound feelings of lack of control.
Addictive exercisers	People who exercise compulsively to try to meet needs of nurturance, intimacy, self-esteem, and self-competency are addictive exercisers.
Muscle	Muscle is a contractile form of tissue. It is one of the four major tissue types, the other three being epithelium, connective tissue and nervous tissue. Muscle contraction is used to move parts of the body, as well as to move substances within the body.
Assess	Assess is to systematically and continuously collect, validate, and communicate patient data.
Steroid	A steroid is a lipid characterized by a carbon skeleton with four fused rings. Different steroids vary in the functional groups attached to these rings. Hundreds of distinct steroids have been identified in plants and animals. Their most important role in most living systems is as hormones.
Internet addiction	Internet addiction disorder is a theorized disorder coined by Ivan Goldberg, M.D., in 1997. It is compared to pathological gambling as diagnosed by the DSM-IV.

Compulsive behaviors	Compulsive behaviors refers to compulsive gambling, anorexia, bulimia, overeating, sexual addiction, compulsive shopping, codependency, etc. Drug addiction is a compulsive behavior.
Arousal	Arousal is a physiological and psychological state involving the activation of the reticular activating system in the brain stem, the autonomic nervous system and the endocrine system, leading to increased heart rate and blood pressure and a condition of alertness and readiness to respond.
Outcome	Outcome is the impact of care provided to a patient. They can be positive, such as the ability to walk freely as a result of rehabilitation, or negative, such as the occurrence of bedsores as a result of lack of mobility of a patient.
Codependent	Codependent is when a person exhibits too much, and often inappropriate, caring for other people's struggles.
Crisis	A crisis is a temporary state of high anxiety where the persons usual coping mechanisims cease to work. This may have a result of disorganization or possibly personality growth.
Intervention	Intervention refers to a planned attempt to break through addicts' or abusers' denial and get them into treatment. Interventions most often occur when legal, workplace, health, relationship, or financial problems have become intolerable.
Wound	A wound is type of physical trauma wherein the skin is torn, cut or punctured, or where blunt force trauma causes a contusion.
Accreditation	Accreditation is the certification by a duly recognized body of the facilities, capability, objectivity, competence, and integrity of an agency, service or operational group or individual to provide the specific service(s) or operation(s) needed.
Joint	A joint (articulation) is the location at which two bones make contact (articulate). They are constructed to both allow movement and provide mechanical support.
Alcoholics Anonymous	Alcoholics anonymous refers to the first 12-step, self-help, alcoholism recovery group; tens-of-thousands of chapters exist worldwide.
Matching	In connection with experiments, the procedure whereby pairs of subjects are matched on the basis of their similarities on one or more variables, and one member of the pair is assigned to the experimental group and the other to the control group, is referred to as matching.
Inpatient	Inpatient refers to a person who enters a healthcare setting for a stay ranging from 24 hours to many years.
Inpatient treatment	A 7-28 day program in a hospital or other residential facility that focuses on detoxification, therapy, and education is an inpatient treatment.
Substance abuse	Substance abuse refers to the overindulgence in and dependence on a stimulant, depressant, or other chemical substance, leading to effects that are detrimental to the individual's physical or mental health, or the welfare of others.
Relapse prevention	Extending therapeutic progress by teaching the client how to cope with future troubling situations is a relapse prevention technique.
Counselor	A counselor is a mental health professional who specializes in helping people with problems not involving serious mental disorders.
Community services	Community services refers to local delinquency prevention services such as recreational programs and drug and alcohol information programs in schools that help meet the community's needs for youths.
Family therapy	Family therapy is a branch of psychotherapy that treats family problems. Family therapists consider the family as a system of interacting members; as such, the problems in the family

Go to **Cram101.com** for the Practice Tests for this Chapter.

	are seen to arise as an emergent property of the interactions in the system, rather than ascribed exclusively to the "faults" or psychological problems of individual members.
Risk factor	A risk factor is a variable associated with an increased risk of disease or infection but risk factors are not necessarily causal.
Absorption	Absorption is a physical or chemical phenomenon or a process in which atoms, molecules, or ions enter some bulk phase - gas, liquid or solid material. In nutrition, amino acids are broken down through digestion, which begins in the stomach.
Blood	Blood is a circulating tissue composed of fluid plasma and cells. The main function of blood is to supply nutrients (oxygen, glucose) and constitutional elements to tissues and to remove waste products.

Go to **Cram101.com** for the Practice Tests for this Chapter.
And, **NEVER** highlight a book again!

Alcohol	Alcohol is a general term, applied to any organic compound in which a hydroxyl group (-OH) is bound to a carbon atom, which in turn is bound to other hydrogen and/or carbon atoms. The general formula for a simple acyclic alcohol is $C_nH_{2n+1}OH$.
Binge drinking	Binge drinking refers to consuming 5 or more drinks in a short time or drinking alchohol for the sole purpose of intoxication.
Health	Health is a term that refers to a combination of the absence of illness, the ability to cope with everyday activities, physical fitness, and high quality of life.
Binge	Binge refers to relatively brief episode of uncontrolled, excessive consumption.
Reid	Reid was the founder of the Scottish School of Common Sense, and played an integral role in the Scottish Enlightenment. He advocated direct realism, or common sense realism, and argued strongly against the Theory of Ideas advocated by John Locke and René Descartes.
Alcoholic	An alcoholic is dependent on alcohol as characterized by craving, loss of control, physical dependence and withdrawal symptoms, and tolerance.
Denial	Denial is a psychological defense mechanism in which a person faced with a fact that is uncomfortable or painful to accept rejects it instead, insisting that it is not true despite what may be overwhelming evidence.
Dependence	Dependence refers to a mental or physical craving for a drug and withdrawal symptoms when use of the drug is stopped.
Alcoholism	A disorder that involves long-term, repeated, uncontrolled, compulsive, and excessive use of alcoholic beverages and that impairs the drinker's health and work and social relationships is called alcoholism.
Diagnosis	In medicine, diagnosis is the process of identifying a medical condition or disease by its signs, symptoms, and from the results of various diagnostic procedures.
Consciousness	Consciousness refers to the ability to perceive, communicate, remember, understand, appreciate, and initiate voluntary movements; a functioning sensorium.
Carbohydrate	Carbohydrate is a chemical compound that contains oxygen, hydrogen, and carbon atoms. They consist of monosaccharide sugars of varying chain lengths and that have the general chemical formula $C_n(H_2O)_n$ or are derivatives of such.
Calorie	Calorie refers to a unit used to measure heat energy and the energy contents of foods.
Ethanol	Ethanol is a flammable, colorless chemical compound, one of the alcohols that is most often found in alcoholic beverages. In common parlance, it is often referred to simply as alcohol. Its chemical formula is C_2H_5OH, also written as C_2H_6O.
Ethyl	In chemistry, an ethyl group is an alkyl functional group derived from ethane (C_2H_6). It has the formula $-C_2H_5$ and is very often abbreviated -Et.
Fermentation	Fermentation is the anaerobic metabolic breakdown of a nutrient molecule, such as glucose, without net oxidation. Fermentation does not release all the available energy in a molecule; it merely allows glycolysis to continue by replenishing reduced coenzymes.
Carbon	Carbon is a chemical element in the periodic table that has the symbol C and atomic number 6. An abundant nonmetallic, tetravalent element, carbon has several allotropic forms.
Sugar	A sugar is the simplest molecule that can be identified as a carbohydrate. These include monosaccharides and disaccharides, trisaccharides and the oligosaccharides. The term "glyco-" indicates the presence of a sugar in an otherwise non-carbohydrate substance.
Carbon dioxide	Carbon dioxide is an atmospheric gas comprized of one carbon and two oxygen atoms. A very widely known chemical compound, it is frequently called by its formula CO_2. In its solid

	state, it is commonly known as dry ice.
Solution	Solution refers to homogenous mixture formed when a solute is dissolved in a solvent.
Chemical reaction	Chemical reaction refers to a process leading to chemical changes in matter; involves the making and/or breaking of chemical bonds.
Addictive drug	An addictive drug produces a biological or psychological dependence in the user; withdrawal from them leads to a craving for the drug that in some cases can be nearly irresistible.
Ratio	In number and more generally in algebra, a ratio is the linear relationship between two quantities.
Blood	Blood is a circulating tissue composed of fluid plasma and cells. The main function of blood is to supply nutrients (oxygen, glucose) and constitutional elements to tissues and to remove waste products.
Tolerance	Drug tolerance occurs when a subject's reaction to a drug decreases so that larger doses are required to achieve the same effect.
Learned behavioral tolerance	The ability of heavy drinkers to modify behavior so that they appear to be sober even when they have high BAC levels is called learned behavioral tolerance.
Behavioral Tolerance	Behavioral tolerance is a form of tolerance influenced by learning and conditioning; through experience an organism can learn to decrease the effect that a stimulus such as a drug is having on them.
Nervous system	The nervous system of an animal coordinates the activity of the muscles, monitors the organs, constructs and processes input from the senses, and initiates actions.
Absorption	Absorption is a physical or chemical phenomenon or a process in which atoms, molecules, or ions enter some bulk phase - gas, liquid or solid material. In nutrition, amino acids are broken down through digestion, which begins in the stomach.
Metabolism	Metabolism is the biochemical modification of chemical compounds in living organisms and cells. This includes the biosynthesis of complex organic molecules (anabolism) and their breakdown (catabolism).
Gastrointest-nal system	The gastrointestinal system is the system of organs within multicellular animals which takes in food, digests it to extract energy and nutrients, and expels the remaining waste.
Intestine	The intestine is the portion of the alimentary canal extending from the stomach to the anus and, in humans and mammals, consists of two segments, the small intestine and the large intestine. The intestine is the part of the body responsible for extracting nutrition from food.
Stomach	The stomach is an organ in the alimentary canal used to digest food. It's primary function is not the absorption of nutrients from digested food; rather, the main job of the stomach is to break down large food molecules into smaller ones, so that they can be absorbed into the blood more easily.
Small intestine	The small intestine is the part of the gastrointestinal tract between the stomach and the large intestine (colon). In humans over 5 years old it is about 7m long. It is divided into three structural parts: duodenum, jejunum and ileum.
Pyloric valve	The pyloric valve, is a strong ring of smooth muscle at the end of the pyloric canal and lets food pass from the stomach to the duodenum.
Digestive system	The organ system that ingests food, breaks it down into smaller chemical units, and absorbs the nutrient molecules is referred to as the digestive system.

Go to **Cram101.com** for the Practice Tests for this Chapter.

Body mass index	Body mass index refers to a number derived from an individual's weight and height used to estimate body fat. The formula is- weight /height' .
Digestive tract	The digestive tract is the system of organs within multicellular animals which takes in food, digests it to extract energy and nutrients, and expels the remaining waste.
Affect	Affect is the scientific term used to describe a subject's externally displayed mood. This can be assesed by the nurse by observing facial expression, tone of voice, and body language.
Stress	Stress refers to a condition that is a response to factors that change the human systems normal state.
Enzyme	An enzyme is a protein that catalyzes, or speeds up, a chemical reaction. They are essential to sustain life because most chemical reactions in biological cells would occur too slowly, or would lead to different products, without them.
Liver	The liver is an organ in vertebrates, including humans. It plays a major role in metabolism and has a number of functions in the body including drug detoxification, glycogen storage, and plasma protein synthesis. It also produces bile, which is important for digestion.
Alcohol dehydrogenase	Alcohol dehydrogenase is a group of dehydrogenase enzymes that occur in many organisms and facilitate the conversion between alcohols and aldehydes or ketones. In humans and many other animals, they serve to break down alcohols which could otherwise be toxic; in yeast and many bacteria they catalyze the opposite reaction as part of fermentation.
Acetate	Acetate is the anion of a salt or ester of acetic acid.
Lungs	Lungs are the essential organs of respiration in air-breathing vertebrates. Their principal function is to transport oxygen from the atmosphere into the bloodstream, and to excrete carbon dioxide from the bloodstream into the atmosphere.
Skin	Skin is an organ of the integumentary system composed of a layer of tissues that protect underlying muscles and organs.
Protein	A protein is a complex, high-molecular-weight organic compound that consists of amino acids joined by peptide bonds. They are essential to the structure and function of all living cells and viruses. Many are enzymes or subunits of enzymes.
Starch	Biochemically, starch is a combination of two polymeric carbohydrates (polysaccharides) called amylose and amylopectin.
Constant	A behavior or characteristic that does not vary from one observation to another is referred to as a constant.
Variable	A characteristic or aspect in which people, objects, events, or conditions vary is called variable.
Tissue	A collection of interconnected cells that perform a similar function within an organism is called tissue.
Depression	In everyday language depression refers to any downturn in mood, which may be relatively transitory and perhaps due to something trivial. This is differentiated from Clinical depression which is marked by symptoms that last two weeks or more and are so severe that they interfere with daily living.
Inhalation	Inhalation is the movement of air from the external environment, through the airways, into the alveoli during breathing.
Central nervous system	The central nervous system comprized of the brain and spinal cord, represents the largest part of the nervous system. Together with the peripheral nervous system, it has a fundamental role in the control of behavior.

Go to **Cram101.com** for the Practice Tests for this Chapter.

Lethal dose	Lethal dose refers to the amount of a drug that will kill the user. It can vary radically depending on purity, sensitivity of the user, tolerance, etc.
Brain	The part of the central nervous system involved in regulating and controlling body activity and interpreting information from the senses transmitted through the nervous system is referred to as the brain.
Intoxication	Condition in which a substance affecting the central nervous system has been ingested and certain maladaptive behaviors or psychological changes, such as belligerence and impaired function, are evident is called intoxication.
Dehydration	Dehydration is the removal of water from an object. Medically, dehydration is a serious and potentially life-threatening condition in which the body contains an insufficient volume of water for normal functioning.
Spinal cord	The spinal cord is a part of the vertebrate nervous system that is enclosed in and protected by the vertebral column (it passes through the spinal canal). It consists of nerve cells. The spinal cord carries sensory signals and motor innervation to most of the skeletal muscles in the body.
Cerebrospinal fluid	Cerebrospinal fluid is a clear bodily fluid that occupies the subarachnoid space in the brain (the space between the skull and the cerebral cortex). It is basically a saline solution and acts as a "cushion" or buffer for the cortex.
Matching	In connection with experiments, the procedure whereby pairs of subjects are matched on the basis of their similarities on one or more variables, and one member of the pair is assigned to the experimental group and the other to the control group, is referred to as matching.
Urinalysis	A urinalysis (or "UA") is an array of tests performed on urine and one of the most common methods of medical diagnosis. A part of a urinalysis can be performed by using urine dipsticks, in which the test results can be read as color changes.
Urine	Concentrated filtrate produced by the kidneys and excreted via the bladder is called urine.
Nerve	A nerve is an enclosed, cable-like bundle of nerve fibers or axons, which includes the glia that ensheath the axons in myelin.
Diuretic	A diuretic is any drug that elevates the rate of bodily urine excretion.
Muscle	Muscle is a contractile form of tissue. It is one of the four major tissue types, the other three being epithelium, connective tissue and nervous tissue. Muscle contraction is used to move parts of the body, as well as to move substances within the body.
Lead	Lead is a chemical element in the periodic table that has the symbol Pb and atomic number 82. A soft, heavy, toxic and malleable poor metal, lead is bluish white when freshly cut but tarnishes to dull gray when exposed to air. Lead is used in building construction, lead-acid batteries, bullets and shot, and is part of solder, pewter, and fusible alloys.
Fluid balance	Fluid balance refers to equilibrium between fluid intake and output or between the amounts of fluid contained in the body's different fluid compartments.
Mitochondria	Cytoplasmic organelles responsible for ATP generation for cellular activities are referred to as mitochondria.
Organ	Organ refers to a structure consisting of several tissues adapted as a group to perform specific functions.
Heartburn	A pain emanating from the esophagus, caused by stomach acid backing up into the esophagus and irritating the esophageal tissue is heartburn.
Esophagus	The esophagus, or gullet is the muscular tube in vertebrates through which ingested food

	passes from the mouth area to the stomach. Food is passed through the esophagus by using the process of peristalsis.
Cancer	Cancer is a class of diseases or disorders characterized by uncontrolled division of cells and the ability of these cells to invade other tissues, either by direct growth into adjacent tissue through invasion or by implantation into distant sites by metastasis.
Hangover	Hangover refers to alcohol withdrawal symptoms that occur 8-12 hours after stopping drinking. They include headache, dizziness, nausea, thirst, and dry mouth. The causes are the direct effects of alcohol and its additives.
Diarrhea	Diarrhea or diarrhoea is a condition in which the sufferer has frequent and watery, chunky, or loose bowel movements.
Anxiety	Anxiety is a complex combination of the feeling of fear, apprehension and worry often accompanied by physical sensations such as palpitations, chest pain and/or shortness of breath.
Congeners	Congeners refers to a chemical relative of another drug.
Urination	Urination is the process of disposing urine from the urinary bladder through the urethra to the outside of the body. The process of urination is usually under voluntary control.
Acid	An acid is a water-soluble, sour-tasting chemical compound that when dissolved in water, gives a solution with a pH of less than 7.
Hydrochloric acid	The chemical substance hydrochloric acid is the aqueous solution of hydrogen chloride gas. It is a strong acid, the major component of gastric acid.
Drug interaction	A combined effect of two drugs that exceeds the addition of one drug's effects to the other is a drug interaction.
Cardiovascular system	The circulatory system or cardiovascular system is the organ system which circulates blood around the body of most animals.
Antibiotic	Antibiotic refers to substance such as penicillin or streptomycin that is toxic to microorganisms. Usually a product of a particular microorvanism or plant.
Penicillin	Penicillin refers to a group of β-lactam antibiotics used in the treatment of bacterial infections caused by susceptible, usually Gram-positive, organisms.
Antidepressant	An antidepressant is a medication used primarily in the treatment of clinical depression. They are not thought to produce tolerance, although sudden withdrawal may produce adverse effects. They create little if any immediate change in mood and require between several days and several weeks to take effect.
Blood pressure	Blood pressure is the pressure exerted by the blood on the walls of the blood vessels.
Antidepressants	Antidepressants are medications used primarily in the treatment of clinical depression. Antidepressants create little if any immediate change in mood and require between several days and several weeks to take effect.
Hemorrhage	Loss of blood from the circulatory system is referred to as a hemorrhage.
Antihistamine	An antihistamine is a drug which serves to reduce or eliminate effects mediated by histamine, an endogenous chemical mediator released during allergic reactions, through action at the histamine receptor.
Narcotic	The term narcotic originally referred to a variety of substances that induced sleep (such state is narcosis). In legal context, narcotic refers to opium, opium derivatives, and their semisynthetic or totally synthetic substitutes.

Go to **Cram101.com** for the Practice Tests for this Chapter.

Go to **Cram101.com** for the Practice Tests for this Chapter.
And, **NEVER** highlight a book again!

Codeine	Codeine is an opioid used for its analgesic, antitussive and antidiarrheal properties
Heroin	Heroin is widely and illegally used as a powerful and addictive drug producing intense euphoria, which often disappears with increasing tolerance. Heroin is a semi-synthetic opioid. It is the 3,6-diacetyl derivative of morphine and is synthesized from it by acetylation.
Stimulant	A stimulant is a drug which increases the activity of the sympathetic nervous system and produces a sense of euphoria or awakeness.
Coronary	Referring to the heart or the blood vessels of the heart is referred to as coronary.
Artery	Vessel that takes blood away from the heart to the tissues and organs of the body is called an artery.
Coronary artery disease	Coronary artery disease (CAD) is the end result of the accumulation of atheromatous plaques within the walls of the arteries that supply the myocardium (the muscle of the heart).
Coronary artery	An artery that supplies blood to the wall of the heart is called a coronary artery.
Cirrhosis	Cirrhosis is a chronic disease of the liver in which liver tissue is replaced by connective tissue, resulting in the loss of liver function. Cirrhosis is caused by damage from toxins (including alcohol), metabolic problems, chronic viral hepatitis or other causes
Hepatitis	Hepatitis is a gastroenterological disease, featuring inflammation of the liver. The clinical signs and prognosis, as well as the therapy, depend on the cause.
Lipoprotein	A lipoprotein is a biochemical assembly that contains both proteins and lipids and may be structural or catalytic in function. They may be enzymes, proton pumps, ion pumps, or some combination of these functions.
Cholesterol	Cholesterol is a steroid, a lipid, and an alcohol, found in the cell membranes of all body tissues, and transported in the blood plasma of all animals. It is an important component of the membranes of cells, providing stability; it makes the membrane's fluidity stable over a bigger temperature interval.
Atherosclerosis	Process by which a fatty substance or plaque builds up inside arteries to form obstructions is called atherosclerosis.
Heart rate	Heart rate is a term used to describe the frequency of the cardiac cycle. It is considered one of the four vital signs. Usually it is calculated as the number of contractions of the heart in one minute and expressed as "beats per minute".
Cardiac output	Cardiac output is the volume of blood being pumped by the heart in a minute. It is equal to the heart rate multiplied by the stroke volume.
Fatty liver	Fatty liver or steatorrhoeic hepatosis is a reversible condition seen in chronic alcoholism and many other conditions, where large vacuoles of lipid accumulate in hepatocytes.
Fibrosis	Replacement of damaged tissue with fibrous scar tissue rather than by the original tissue type is called fibrosis.
Scar	A scar results from the biologic process of wound repair in the skin and other tissues of the body. It is a connective tissue that fills the wound.
Abstinence	Abstinence has diverse forms. In its oldest sense it is sexual, as in the practice of continence, chastity, and celibacy.
Inflammation	Inflammation is the first response of the immune system to infection or irritation and may be referred to as the innate cascade.
Pancreas	The pancreas is a retroperitoneal organ that serves two functions: exocrine - it produces

Go to **Cram101.com** for the Practice Tests for this Chapter.

	pancreatic juice containing digestive enzymes, and endocrine - it produces several important hormones, namely insulin.
Insulin	Insulin is a polypeptide hormone that regulates carbohydrate metabolism. Apart from being the primary effector in carbohydrate homeostasis, it also has a substantial effect on small vessel muscle tone, controls storage and release of fat (triglycerides) and cellular uptake of both amino acids and some electrolytes.
Calcium	Calcium is the chemical element in the periodic table that has the symbol Ca and atomic number 20. Calcium is a soft grey alkaline earth metal that is used as a reducing agent in the extraction of thorium, zirconium and uranium. Calcium is also the fifth most abundant element in the Earth's crust.
Bacteria	The domain that contains procaryotic cells with primarily diacyl glycerol diesters in their membranes and with bacterial rRNA. Bacteria also is a general term for organisms that are composed of procaryotic cells and are not multicellular.
Population	Population refers to all members of a well-defined group of organisms, events, or things.
Teratogen	Teratogen refers to a substance that causes a birth defect.
Learning disabilities	General term for learning disorders, communication disorders, and motor skills disorder is referred to as learning disabilities.
Learning disability	A learning disability exists when there is a significant discrepancy between one's ability and achievement.
Syndrome	Syndrome is the association of several clinically recognizable features, signs, symptoms, phenomena or characteristics which often occur together, so that the presence of one feature alerts the physician to the presence of the others
Fetal alcohol syndrome	A cluster of abnormalities that appears in the offspring of mothers who drink alcohol heavily during pregnancy is called fetal alcohol syndrome.
Trimester	In human development, one of three 3-mnonth-long periods of pregnancy is called trimester.
First trimester	The first trimester is the period of time from the first day of the last menstrual period through 12 weeks of gestation. It is during this period that the embryo undergoes most of its early structural development. Most miscarriages occur during this period.
Mental retardation	Mental retardation refers to having significantly below-average intellectual functioning and limitations in at least two areas of adaptive functioning. Many categorize retardation as mild, moderate, severe, or profound.
Incidence	In epidemiological studies of a particular disorder, the rate at which new cases occur in a given place at a given time is called incidence.
Placenta	The placenta is an organ present only in female placental mammals during gestation. It is composed of two parts, one genetically and biologically part of the fetus, the other part of the mother. It is implanted in the wall of the uterus, where it receives nutrients and oxygen from the mother's blood and passes out waste.
Fetus	Fetus refers to a developing human from the ninth week of gestation until birth; has all the major structures of an adult.
Tremor	Tremor is the rhythmic, oscillating shaking movement of the whole body or just a certain part of it, caused by problems of the neurons responsible from muscle action.
Irritability	Irritability is an excessive response to stimuli. Irritability takes many forms, from the contraction of a unicellular organism when touched to complex reactions involving all the senses of higher animals.

Go to **Cram101.com** for the Practice Tests for this Chapter.

263

Withdrawal symptoms	Withdrawal symptoms are physiological changes that occur when the use of a drug is stopped or dosage decreased.
Drug addiction	Drug addiction, or substance dependence is the compulsive use of drugs, to the point where the user has no effective choice but to continue use.
Addiction	Addiction is an uncontrollable compulsion to repeat a behavior regardless of its consequences. Many drugs or behaviors can precipitate a pattern of conditions recognized as addiction, which include a craving for more of the drug or behavior, increased physiological tolerance to exposure, and withdrawal symptoms in the absence of the stimulus.
Addict	A person with an overpowering physical or psychological need to continue taking a particular substance or drug is referred to as an addict.
Psychological dependence	Psychological dependence may lead to psychological withdrawal symptoms. Addictions can theoretically form for any rewarding behavior, or as a habitual means to avoid undesired activity, but typically they only do so to a clinical level in individuals who have emotional, social, or psychological dysfunctions, taking the place of normal positive stimuli not otherwise attained
Survey	A method of scientific investigation in which a large sample of people answer questions about their attitudes or behavior is referred to as a survey.
Assess	Assess is to systematically and continuously collect, validate, and communicate patient data.
Young adult	An young adult is someone between the ages of 20 and 40 years old.
Craving	Craving refers to the powerful desire to use a psychoactive drug or engage in a compulsive behavior. It is manifested in physiological changes, such as raised heart rate, sweating, anxiety, drop in body temperature, pupil dilation, and stomach muscle movements.
Loss of control	The point in drug use where the user becomes unable to limit or stop use is referred to as loss of control.
Physical dependence	Physical dependence describes increased tolerance of a drug combined with a physical need of the drug to function. Abrupt cessation of the drug is typically associated with negative physical withdrawal symptoms. Physical dependence is distinguished from addiction. While addiction tends to describe psychological and behavioral attributes, physical dependence is defined primarily using physical and biological concepts.
Intervention	Intervention refers to a planned attempt to break through addicts' or abusers' denial and get them into treatment. Interventions most often occur when legal, workplace, health, relationship, or financial problems have become intolerable.
Harm reduction	Harm reduction refers to a tertiary prevention and treatment technique that tries to minimize the medical and social problems associated with drug use rather than making abstinence the primary goal, e.g., needle exchange and methadone maintenance.
Adoption study	A study in which investigators seek to discover whether, in behavior and psychological characteristics, adopted children are more like their adoptive parents, who provided a home environment, or more like their biological parents, who contributed their genetic code is called adoption study.
Heredity	Heredity refers to the transmission of genetic information from parent to offspring.
Adoption studies	Research studies that assess hereditary influence by examining the resemblance between adopted children and both their biological and their adoptive parents are referred to as adoption studies. The studies have been inconclusive about the relative importance of heredity in intelligence.
Identical twins	Identical twins occur when a single egg is fertilized to form one zygote (monozygotic) but

Go to **Cram101.com** for the Practice Tests for this Chapter.

265

	the zygote then divides into two separate embryos.
Acute	In medicine, an acute disease is a disease with either or both of: a rapid onset; and a short course (as opposed to a chronic course).
Pain	Pain is an unpleasant sensation which may be associated with actual or potential tissue damage and which may have physical and emotional components.
Anesthetic	Anesthetic refers to a substance that causes the loss of the ability to feel pain or other sensory input, e.g., ether or halothane.
Culture	Culture, generally refers to patterns of human activity and the symbolic structures that give such activity significance.
Incest	Incest refers to sexual relations between close relatives, most often between daughter and father or between brother and sister.
Adult Children of Alcoholics	Adult Children of Alcoholics is a support group that helps deal with similiar experiences and problems that the people have in there adult lives.
Attachment	Attachment refers to the psychological tendency to seek closeness to another person, to feel secure when that person is present, and to feel anxious when that person is absent.
Child abuse	Child abuse is the physical or psychological maltreatment of a child.
Stroke	A stroke or cerebrovascular accident (CVA) occurs when the blood supply to a part of the brain is suddenly interrupted.
Risk factor	A risk factor is a variable associated with an increased risk of disease or infection but risk factors are not necessarily causal.
Assault	Assault is a crime of violence against another person that intentionally instills fear and creates a reasonable aprehension of harm.
Rehabilitation	Rehabilitation is the restoration of lost capabilities, or the treatment aimed at producing it. Also refers to treatment for dependency on psychoactive substances such as alcohol, prescription drugs, and illicit drugs such as cocaine, heroin or amphetamines.
Stigma	Stigma refers to a personal characteristic that at least some other individuals perceive negatively because that characteristic is different than those of the general population.
Hallucination	Hallucination refers to a perception in the absence of sensory stimulation that is confused with reality.
Mental health	Mental health refers to the 'thinking' part of psychosocial health; includes your values, attitudes, and beliefs.
Psychiatrist	A psychiatrist is a physician who specializes in the diagnosis and treatment of psychological disorders.
Community mental health	Community mental health refers to the delivery of services to needy, underserved groups through centers that offer outpatient therapy, short-term inpatient care, day hospitalization, twenty-four-horn- emergency services, and consultation and education to other community agencies.
Alcoholics Anonymous	Alcoholics anonymous refers to the first 12-step, self-help, alcoholism recovery group; tens-of-thousands of chapters exist worldwide.
Convulsions	Involuntary muscle spasms, often severe, that can be caused by stimulant overdose or by depressant withdrawal are called convulsions.
Seizure	A seizure is a temporary alteration in brain function expressed as a changed mental state, tonic or clonic movements and various other symptoms. They are due to temporary abnormal

Go to **Cram101.com** for the Practice Tests for this Chapter.

	electrical activity of a group of brain cells.
Psychological addiction	Psychological addiction is a person's need to use a drug out of desire for the effects it produces, rather than to relieve withdrawal symptoms.
Family therapy	Family therapy is a branch of psychotherapy that treats family problems. Family therapists consider the family as a system of interacting members; as such, the problems in the family are seen to arise as an emergent property of the interactions in the system, rather than ascribed exclusively to the "faults" or psychological problems of individual members.
Group therapy	Group therapy is a form of psychotherapy during which one or several therapists treat a small group of clients together as a group. This may be more cost effective than individual therapy, and possibly even more effective.
Disulfiram	Disulfiram is a drug used to support the treatment of chronic alcoholism by producing an acute sensitivity to alcohol.
Trade name	A drug company's name for their patented medication is called a trade name.
Antabuse	A drug that makes the drinking of alcohol produce nausea and other unpleasant effects is an antabuse.
Atheist	An atheist who advocates his atheist views may be considered anti-theist, so some atheists call themselves agnostics even if they don't believe in deities, in order to not seem in opposition to other people's faith.
HIV	The virus that causes AIDS is HIV (human immunodeficiency virus).
Alateen	Alateen refers to a 12-step organization for teenagers affected by an alcoholic parent or friend. It helps them deal with the pain and disruption in their lives.
Lifestyle	The culturally, socially, economically, and environmentally conditioned complex of actions characteristic of an individual, group, or community as a pattern of habituated behavior over time that is health related but not necessarily health directed is a lifestyle.
Course	Pattern of development and change of a disorder over time is a course.
Life crisis	Life crisis refers to an internal conflict that attends each stage of psychosocial development. Positive resolution of early life crises sets the stage for positive resolution of subsequent life crises.
Crisis	A crisis is a temporary state of high anxiety where the persons usual coping mechanisims cease to work. This may have a result of disorganization or possibly personality growth.
Kuhn	Kuhn is most famous for his book The Structure of Scientific Revolutions in which he presented the idea that science does not evolve gradually toward truth, but instead undergoes periodic revolutions which he calls "paradigm shifts."
Older adult	Older adult is an adult over the age of 65.
Cardiovascular disease	Cardiovascular disease refers to afflictions in the mechanisms, including the heart, blood vessels, and their controllers, that are responsible for transporting blood to the body's tissues and organs. Psychological factors may play important roles in such diseases and their treatments.
Nicotine	Nicotine is an organic compound, an alkaloid found naturally throughout the tobacco plant, with a high concentration in the leaves. It is a potent nerve poison and is included in many insecticides. In lower concentrations, the substance is a stimulant and is one of the main factors leading to the pleasure and habit-forming qualities of tobacco smoking.

Go to **Cram101.com** for the Practice Tests for this Chapter.

Morphine	Morphine, the principal active agent in opium, is a powerful opioid analgesic drug. According to recent research, it may also be produced naturally by the human brain. Morphine is usually highly addictive, and tolerance and physical and psychological dependence develop quickly.
Heroin	Heroin is widely and illegally used as a powerful and addictive drug producing intense euphoria, which often disappears with increasing tolerance. Heroin is a semi-synthetic opioid. It is the 3,6-diacetyl derivative of morphine and is synthesized from it by acetylation.
Brain	The part of the central nervous system involved in regulating and controlling body activity and interpreting information from the senses transmitted through the nervous system is referred to as the brain.
Opioid	An opioid is any agent that binds to opioid receptors, found principally in the central nervous system and gastrointestinal tract. There are four broad classes of opioids: endogenous opioid peptides, produced in the body; opium alkaloids, such as morphine and codeine; semi-synthetic opioids such as heroin and oxycodone.
Pain	Pain is an unpleasant sensation which may be associated with actual or potential tissue damage and which may have physical and emotional components.
Positron emission tomography	Positron Emission Tomography measures emissions from radioactively labeled chemicals that have been injected into the bloodstream. The greatest benefit is that different compounds can show blood flow and oxygen and glucose metabolism in the tissues of the working brain.
Survey	A method of scientific investigation in which a large sample of people answer questions about their attitudes or behavior is referred to as a survey.
Morbidity	Morbidity refers to any condition that causes illness.
Mortality	The incidence of death in a population is mortality.
Centers for Disease Control and Prevention	The Centers for Disease Control and Prevention in Atlanta, Georgia, is recognized as the lead United States agency for protecting the public health and safety of people by providing credible information to enhance health decisions, and promoting health through strong partnerships with state health departments and other organizations.
Distribution	Distribution in pharmacology is a branch of pharmacokinetics describing reversible transfer of drug from one location to another within the body.
Health	Health is a term that refers to a combination of the absence of illness, the ability to cope with everyday activities, physical fitness, and high quality of life.
Young adult	An young adult is someone between the ages of 20 and 40 years old.
Independence	The condition in which one variable has no effect on another is referred to as independence.
Addiction	Addiction is an uncontrollable compulsion to repeat a behavior regardless of its consequences. Many drugs or behaviors can precipitate a pattern of conditions recognized as addiction, which include a craving for more of the drug or behavior, increased physiological tolerance to exposure, and withdrawal symptoms in the absence of the stimulus.
Lung cancer	Lung cancer is a malignant tumour of the lungs. Most commonly it is bronchogenic carcinoma (about 90%).
Cancer	Cancer is a class of diseases or disorders characterized by uncontrolled division of cells and the ability of these cells to invade other tissues, either by direct growth into adjacent tissue through invasion or by implantation into distant sites by metastasis.
Conscious	Conscious refers to the thoughts, feelings, sensations, or memories of which a person is aware at any given moment.

Go to **Cram101.com** for the Practice Tests for this Chapter.

Oxygen	Oxygen is a chemical element in the periodic table. It has the symbol O and atomic number 8. Oxygen is the second most common element on Earth, composing around 46% of the mass of Earth's crust and 28% of the mass of Earth as a whole, and is the third most common element in the universe.
Lungs	Lungs are the essential organs of respiration in air-breathing vertebrates. Their principal function is to transport oxygen from the atmosphere into the bloodstream, and to excrete carbon dioxide from the bloodstream into the atmosphere.
Dependence	Dependence refers to a mental or physical craving for a drug and withdrawal symptoms when use of the drug is stopped.
Tolerance	Drug tolerance occurs when a subject's reaction to a drug decreases so that larger doses are required to achieve the same effect.
Oxidation	Oxidation refers to the loss of electrons from a substance involved in a redox reaction; always accompanies reduction.
Saliva	Saliva is the moist, clear, and usually somewhat frothy substance produced in the mouths of some animals, including humans.
Phenol	Phenol, also known under the old name carbolic acid, is a colorless crystalline solid with a typical sweet tarry odor. Its chemical formula is C_6H_5OH and its structure is that of a hydroxyl group (-OH) bonded to a phenyl ring; it is thus an aromatic compound.
Agent	Agent refers to an epidemiological term referring to the organism or object that transmits a disease from the environment to the host.
Tissue	A collection of interconnected cells that perform a similar function within an organism is called tissue.
Cilia	Microscopic, hairlike processes on the exposed surfaces of certain epithelial cells are cilia.
Carbon	Carbon is a chemical element in the periodic table that has the symbol C and atomic number 6. An abundant nonmetallic, tetravalent element, carbon has several allotropic forms.
Red blood cell	The red blood cell is the most common type of blood cell and is the vertebrate body's principal means of delivering oxygen from the lungs or gills to body tissues via the blood.
Receptor	A receptor is a protein on the cell membrane or within the cytoplasm or cell nucleus that binds to a specific molecule (a ligand), such as a neurotransmitter, hormone, or other substance, and initiates the cellular response to the ligand. Receptor, in immunology, the region of an antibody which shows recognition of an antigen.
Blood	Blood is a circulating tissue composed of fluid plasma and cells. The main function of blood is to supply nutrients (oxygen, glucose) and constitutional elements to tissues and to remove waste products.
Red blood cells	Red blood cells are the most common type of blood cell and are the vertebrate body's principal means of delivering oxygen from the lungs or gills to body tissues via the blood.
Larynx	The larynx is an organ in the neck of mammals involved in protection of the trachea and sound production. The larynx houses the vocal cords, and is situated at the point where the upper tract splits into the trachea and the esophagus.
Hydrocarbon	A chemical compound composed only of the elements carbon and hydrogen is called hydrocarbon.
Hydrogen	Hydrogen is a chemical element in the periodic table that has the symbol H and atomic number 1. At standard temperature and pressure it is a colorless, odorless, nonmetallic, univalent, tasteless, highly flammable diatomic gas.

Go to **Cram101.com** for the Practice Tests for this Chapter.

Stimulant	A stimulant is a drug which increases the activity of the sympathetic nervous system and produces a sense of euphoria or awakeness.
Naphthalene	Naphthalene is a crystalline, aromatic, white, solid hydrocarbon, best known as the primary ingredient of mothballs.
Aromatic	In chemistry, an aromatic molecule is one in which a conjugated ring of unsaturated bonds, lone pairs, or empty orbitals exhibit a stabilization stronger than would be expected by the stabilization of conjugation alone.
Methanol	Methanol refers to wood alcohol; used a toxic industrial solvent; it can be synthesized.
Polonium	Polonium is a chemical element in the periodic table that has the symbol Po and atomic number 84. A rare radioactive metalloid, polonium is chemically similar to tellurium and bismuth and occurs in uranium ores. Polonium had been studied for possible use in heating spacecraft.
Solvent	A solvent is a liquid that dissolves a solid, liquid, or gaseous solute, resulting in a solution. The most common solvent in everyday life is water.
Cadmium	Cadmium is a chemical element in the periodic table that has the symbol Cd and atomic number 48. A relatively rare, soft, bluish-white, toxic transition metal, cadmium occurs with zinc ores and is used largely in batteries.
Alcohol	Alcohol is a general term, applied to any organic compound in which a hydroxyl group (-OH) is bound to a carbon atom, which in turn is bound to other hydrogen and/or carbon atoms. The general formula for a simple acyclic alcohol is $C_nH_{2n+1}OH$.
Nickel	Nickel is a metallic chemical element in the periodic table that has the symbol Ni and atomic number 28. Notable characteristicsNickel is a silvery white metal that takes on a high polish. It belongs to the iron group, and is hard, malleable, and ductile. It occurs combined with sulfur in millerite, with arsenic in the mineral niccolite, and with arsenic and sulfur in nickel glance.
Acid	An acid is a water-soluble, sour-tasting chemical compound that when dissolved in water, gives a solution with a pH of less than 7.
Aromatic hydrocarbon	An aromatic hydrocarbon, or arene is a hydrocarbon, the molecular structure of which incorporates one or more planar sets of six carbon atoms that are connected by delocalized electrons numbering the same as if they consisted of alternating single and double covalent bonds.
Carcinogen	A carcinogen is any substance or agent that promotes cancer. A carcinogen is often, but not necessarily, a mutagen or teratogen.
Oral cavity	The mouth, also known as the buccal cavity or the oral cavity, is the opening through which an animal or human takes in food and water. It is usually located in the head, but not always; the mouth of a planarium is in the middle of its belly.
Esophagus	The esophagus, or gullet is the muscular tube in vertebrates through which ingested food passes from the mouth area to the stomach. Food is passed through the esophagus by using the process of peristalsis.
Stroke	A stroke or cerebrovascular accident (CVA) occurs when the blood supply to a part of the brain is suddenly interrupted.
Heart attack	A heart attack, is a serious, sudden heart condition usually characterized by varying degrees of chest pain or discomfort, weakness, sweating, nausea, vomiting, and arrhythmias, sometimes causing loss of consciousness. It occurs when the blood supply to a part of the heart is interrupted, causing death and scarring of the local heart tissue.
Bypass	In medicine, a bypass generally means an alternate or additional route for blood flow, which

Go to **Cram101.com** for the Practice Tests for this Chapter.

	is created in bypass surgery, e.g. coronary artery bypass surgery by moving blood vessels or implanting synthetic tubing.
Chronic obstructive pulmonary disease	Chronic obstructive pulmonary disease is an umbrella term for a group of respiratory tract diseases that are characterized by airflow obstruction or limitation. It is usually caused by tobacco smoking.
Esophageal cancer	Esophageal cancer is malignancy of the esophagus. There are various subtypes. Esophageal tumors usually lead to dysphagia (difficulty swallowing), pain and other symptoms, and is diagnosed with biopsy.
Lymph node	A lymph node acts as a filter, with an internal honeycomb of connective tissue filled with lymphocytes that collect and destroy bacteria and viruses. When the body is fighting an infection, these lymphocytes multiply rapidly and produce a characteristic swelling of the lymph node.
Muscle	Muscle is a contractile form of tissue. It is one of the four major tissue types, the other three being epithelium, connective tissue and nervous tissue. Muscle contraction is used to move parts of the body, as well as to move substances within the body.
Lymph	Lymph originates as blood plasma lost from the circulatory system, which leaks out into the surrounding tissues. The lymphatic system collects this fluid by diffusion into lymph capillaries, and returns it to the circulatory system.
Coronary	Referring to the heart or the blood vessels of the heart is referred to as coronary.
Coronary heart disease	Coronary heart disease is the end result of the accumulation of atheromatous plaques within the walls of the arteries that supply the myocardium (the muscle of the heart).
Absorption	Absorption is a physical or chemical phenomenon or a process in which atoms, molecules, or ions enter some bulk phase - gas, liquid or solid material. In nutrition, amino acids are broken down through digestion, which begins in the stomach.
Nasal cavity	The nasal cavity is a large air-filled space above and behind the nose in the middle of the face. The nasal cavity is important in warming and cleaning the air as it is inhaled. The nasal cavity also contains organs involved in olfaction.
Pancreas	The pancreas is a retroperitoneal organ that serves two functions: exocrine - it produces pancreatic juice containing digestive enzymes, and endocrine - it produces several important hormones, namely insulin.
Bladder	A hollow muscular storage organ for storing urine is a bladder.
Kidney	The kidney is a bean-shaped excretory organ in vertebrates. Part of the urinary system, the kidneys filter wastes (especially urea) from the blood and excrete them, along with water, as urine.
Epidemic	An epidemic is a disease that appears as new cases in a given human population, during a given period, at a rate that substantially exceeds what is "expected", based on recent experience.
Oncology	Oncology is the medical subspecialty dealing with the study and treatment of cancer. A physician who practices oncology is an oncologist.
Lesion	A lesion is a non-specific term referring to abnormal tissue in the body. It can be caused by any disease process including trauma (physical, chemical, electrical), infection, neoplasm, metabolic and autoimmune.
Incidence	In epidemiological studies of a particular disorder, the rate at which new cases occur in a given place at a given time is called incidence.

Lead	Lead is a chemical element in the periodic table that has the symbol Pb and atomic number 82. A soft, heavy, toxic and malleable poor metal, lead is bluish white when freshly cut but tarnishes to dull gray when exposed to air. Lead is used in building construction, lead-acid batteries, bullets and shot, and is part of solder, pewter, and fusible alloys.
Toxin	Toxin refers to a microbial product or component that can injure another cell or organism at low concentrations. Often the term refers to a poisonous protein, but toxins may be lipids and other substances.
Stigma	Stigma refers to a personal characteristic that at least some other individuals perceive negatively because that characteristic is different than those of the general population.
Peptic ulcer	Peptic ulcer is an ulcer of one of those areas of the gastrointestinal tract that are usually acidic.
Ulcer	An ulcer is an open sore of the skin, eyes or mucous membrane, often caused by an initial abrasion and generally maintained by an inflammation and/or an infection.
Wound	A wound is type of physical trauma wherein the skin is torn, cut or punctured, or where blunt force trauma causes a contusion.
Blood pressure	Blood pressure is the pressure exerted by the blood on the walls of the blood vessels.
Obesity	The state of being more than 20 percent above the average weight for a person of one's height is called obesity.
Sugar	A sugar is the simplest molecule that can be identified as a carbohydrate. These include monosaccharides and disaccharides, trisaccharides and the oligosaccharides. The term "glyco-" indicates the presence of a sugar in an otherwise non-carbohydrate substance.
Salt	Salt is a term used for ionic compounds composed of positively charged cations and negatively charged anions, so that the product is neutral and without a net charge.
Sodium	Sodium is the chemical element in the periodic table that has the symbol Na (Natrium in Latin) and atomic number 11. Sodium is a soft, waxy, silvery reactive metal belonging to the alkali metals that is abundant in natural compounds (especially halite). It is highly reactive.
Vitamin	An organic compound other than a carbohydrate, lipid, or protein that is needed for normal metabolism but that the body cannot synthesize in adequate amounts is called a vitamin.
Nervous system	The nervous system of an animal coordinates the activity of the muscles, monitors the organs, constructs and processes input from the senses, and initiates actions.
Central nervous system	The central nervous system comprized of the brain and spinal cord, represents the largest part of the nervous system. Together with the peripheral nervous system, it has a fundamental role in the control of behavior.
Cortex	In anatomy and zoology the cortex is the outermost or superficial layer of an organ or the outer portion of the stem or root of a plant.
Cerebral cortex	The cerebral cortex is a brain structure in vertebrates. It is the outermost layer of the cerebrum and has a grey color. In the "higher" animals, the surface becomes folded. The cerebral cortex, made up of four lobes, is involved in many complex brain functions including memory, attention, perceptual awareness, "thinking", language and consciousness.
Adrenal glands	The adrenal glands are the triangle-shaped endocrine glands that sit atop the kidneys; their name indicates that position. They are chiefly responsible for regulating the stress response through the synthesis of corticosteroids and catecholamines, including cortisol and adrenaline.

279

Adrenal gland	In mammals, the adrenal gland (also known as suprarenal glands or colloquially as kidney hats) are the triangle-shaped endocrine glands that sit atop the kidneys; their name indicates that position.
Adrenaline	Adrenaline is a hormone released by chromaffin cells and by some neurons in response to stress. Produces 'fight or flight' responses, including increased heart rate and blood sugar levels.
Adrenal	In mammals, the adrenal glands are the triangle-shaped endocrine glands that sit atop the kidneys. They are chiefly responsible for regulating the stress response through the synthesis of corticosteroids and catecholamines, including cortisol and adrenaline.
Gland	A gland is an organ in an animal's body that synthesizes a substance for release such as hormones, often into the bloodstream or into cavities inside the body or its outer surface.
Blood vessel	A blood vessel is a part of the circulatory system and function to transport blood throughout the body. The most important types, arteries and veins, are so termed because they carry blood away from or towards the heart, respectively.
Stomach	The stomach is an organ in the alimentary canal used to digest food. It's primary function is not the absorption of nutrients from digested food; rather, the main job of the stomach is to break down large food molecules into smaller ones, so that they can be absorbed into the blood more easily.
Diarrhea	Diarrhea or diarrhoea is a condition in which the sufferer has frequent and watery, chunky, or loose bowel movements.
Pulse	The rhythmic stretching of the arteries caused by the pressure of blood forced through the arteries by contractions of the ventricles during systole is a pulse.
Skin	Skin is an organ of the integumentary system composed of a layer of tissues that protect underlying muscles and organs.
Craving	Craving refers to the powerful desire to use a psychoactive drug or engage in a compulsive behavior. It is manifested in physiological changes, such as raised heart rate, sweating, anxiety, drop in body temperature, pupil dilation, and stomach muscle movements.
Genes	Genes are the units of heredity in living organisms. They are encoded in the organism's genetic material (usually DNA or RNA), and control the development and behavior of the organism.
Dopamine	Dopamine is a chemical naturally produced in the body. In the brain, dopamine functions as a neurotransmitter, activating dopamine receptors. Dopamine is also a neurohormone released by the hypothalamus. Its main function as a hormone is to inhibit the release of prolactin from the anterior lobe of the pituitary.
Affect	Affect is the scientific term used to describe a subject's externally displayed mood. This can be assesed by the nurse by observing facial expression, tone of voice, and body language.
Cardiovascular disease	Cardiovascular disease refers to afflictions in the mechanisms, including the heart, blood vessels, and their controllers, that are responsible for transporting blood to the body's tissues and organs. Psychological factors may play important roles in such diseases and their treatments.
Bronchiole	The bronchiole is the first airway branch that no longer contains cartilage. They are branches of the bronchi, and are smaller than one millimetre in diameter.
Alveoli	Alveoli are anatomical structures that have the form of a hollow cavity. In the lung, the pulmonary alveoli are spherical outcroppings of the respiratory bronchioles and are the primary sites of gas exchange with the blood.

Mucus	Mucus is a slippery secretion of the lining of various membranes in the body (mucous membranes). Mucus aids in the protection of the lungs by trapping foreign particles that enter the nose during normal breathing. Additionally, it prevents tissues from drying out.
Radon	Radon refers to a radioactive gas that is formed by the disintegration of radium, radon is one of the heaviest gases and is considered to be a health hazard.
Diagnosis	In medicine, diagnosis is the process of identifying a medical condition or disease by its signs, symptoms, and from the results of various diagnostic procedures.
Salivary gland	The salivary gland produces saliva, which keeps the mouth and other parts of the digestive system moist. It also helps break down carbohydrates and lubricates the passage of food down from the oro-pharynx to the esophagus to the stomach.
Bronchitis	Bronchitis is an obstructive pulmonary disease characterized by inflammation of the bronchi of the lungs.
Chronic bronchitis	A persistent lung infection characterized by coughing, swelling of the lining of the respiratory tract, an increase in mucus production, a decrease in the number and activity of cilia, and produces sputum for at least three months in two consecutive years is called chronic bronchitis.
Productive cough	A cough in which phlegm or mucus is dislodged, enabling a person to clear mucus from the lungs is a productive cough.
Pneumonia	Pneumonia is an illness of the lungs and respiratory system in which the microscopic, air-filled sacs (alveoli) responsible for absorbing oxygen from the atmosphere become inflamed and flooded with fluid.
Influenza	Influenza or flu refers to an acute viral infection of the respiratory tract, occurring in isolated cases, epidemics, and pandemics. Influenza is caused by three strains of influenza virus, labeled types A, B, and C, based on the antigens of their protein coats.
Emphysema	Emphysema is a chronic lung disease. It is often caused by exposure to toxic chemicals or long-term exposure to tobacco smoke..
Air sac	Air sac is an anatomical structure unique to the dinosaur and bird respiratory system that allows unidirectional flow of air into the lungs and through the body
Chronic disease	Disease of long duration often not detected in its early stages and from which the patient will not recover is referred to as a chronic disease.
Carbon dioxide	Carbon dioxide is an atmospheric gas comprized of one carbon and two oxygen atoms. A very widely known chemical compound, it is frequently called by its formula CO_2. In its solid state, it is commonly known as dry ice.
Impotence	Erectile dysfunction, also known as impotence, is a sexual dysfunction characterized by the inability to develop or maintain an erection of the penis for satisfactory sexual intercourse regardless of the capability of ejaculation.
Sexual dysfunction	Sexual dysfunction or sexual malfunction is difficulty during any stage of the sexual act (which includes desire, arousal, orgasm, and resolution) that prevents the individual or couple from enjoying sexual activity.
Penis	The penis is the male reproductive organ and for mammals additionally serves as the external male organ of urination.
Metabolism	Metabolism is the biochemical modification of chemical compounds in living organisms and cells. This includes the biosynthesis of complex organic molecules (anabolism) and their breakdown (catabolism).

Go to **Cram101.com** for the Practice Tests for this Chapter.

Artery	Vessel that takes blood away from the heart to the tissues and organs of the body is called an artery.
Atherosclerosis	Process by which a fatty substance or plaque builds up inside arteries to form obstructions is called atherosclerosis.
Blood clot	A blood clot is the final product of the blood coagulation step in hemostasis. It is achieved via the aggregation of platelets that form a platelet plug, and the activation of the humoral coagulation system
Platelet	Cell fragment that is necessary to blood clotting is a platelet. They are the blood cell fragments that are involved in the cellular mechanisms that lead to the formation of blood clots.
Angina	Angina pectoris is chest pain due to ischemia (a lack of blood and hence oxygen supply) to the heart muscle, generally due to obstruction or spasm of the coronary arteries (the heart's blood vessels). Coronary artery disease, the main cause of angina, is due to atherosclerosis of the cardiac arteries.
Paralysis	Paralysis is the complete loss of muscle function for one or more muscle groups. Paralysis may be localized, or generalized, or it may follow a certain pattern.
Stress	Stress refers to a condition that is a response to factors that change the human systems normal state.
Respiratory system	The respiratory system is the biological system of any organism that engages in gas exchange.In humans and other mammals, the respiratory system consists of the airways, the lungs, and the respiratory muscles that mediate the movement of air into and out of the body.
Organ	Organ refers to a structure consisting of several tissues adapted as a group to perform specific functions.
Cervical cancer	Cervical cancer is a malignancy of the cervix. Worldwide, it is the second most common cancer of women.
Menopause	Menopause is the physiological cessation of menstrual cycles associated with advancing age in species that experience such cycles. Menopause is sometimes referred to as change of life or climacteric.
Osteoporosis	Osteoporosis is a disease of bone in which bone mineral density (BMD) is reduced, bone microarchitecture is disrupted, the amount and variety of non-collagenous proteins in bone is changed, and a concomitantly fracture risk is increased.
Birth control pill	The birth control pill is a chemical taken by mouth to inhibit normal fertility. All act on the hormonal system.
Miscarriage	Miscarriage or spontaneous abortion is the natural or accidental termination of a pregnancy at a stage where the embryo or the fetus is incapable of surviving, generally defined at a gestation of prior to 20 weeks.
Low birth weight	Low birth weight is defined as a fetus that weighs less than 2500 g (5 lb 8 oz) regardless of gestational age.
Cognition	The ability of an animal's nervous system to perceive, store, process, and use information obtained by its sensory receptors is referred to as cognition.
Mortality rate	Mortality rate is the number of deaths (from a disease or in general) per 1000 people and typically reported on an annual basis.
Infant mortality rate	Infant mortality rate refers to proportion of babies born alive who die within the first year.

Go to **Cram101.com** for the Practice Tests for this Chapter.

Infant mortality	Infant mortality is the death of infants in the first year of life. The leading causes of infant mortality are dehydration and disease. Major causes of infant mortality in more developed countries include congenital malformation, infection and SIDS. Infant mortality rate is the number of newborns dying under a year of age divided by the number of live births during the year.
Syndrome	Syndrome is the association of several clinically recognizable features, signs, symptoms, phenomena or characteristics which often occur together, so that the presence of one feature alerts the physician to the presence of the others
Sudden infant death syndrome	Sudden Infant Death Syndrome is the term for the sudden and unexplained death of an apparently healthy infant aged one month to one year.
Apnea	Apnea is the absence of external breathing. During apnea there is no movement of the muscles of respiration and the volume of the lungs initially remains unchanged. .
Adolescence	Adolescence is the period of psychological and social transition between childhood and adulthood (gender-specific manhood, or womanhood). As a transitional stage of human development it represents the period of time during which a juvenile matures into adulthood.
Fetus	Fetus refers to a developing human from the ninth week of gestation until birth; has all the major structures of an adult.
Placental barrier	The placental barrier between the fetus and the wall of the mother s uterus allows for the transfer of materials from mother, and eliminates waste products of fetus.
Mainstream smoke	Mainstream smoke refers to smoke that is drawn through tobacco while inhaling.
Ammonia	Ammonia is a compound of nitrogen and hydrogen with the formula NH_3. At standard temperature and pressure ammonia is a gas. It is toxic and corrosive to some materials, and has a characteristic pungent odor.
Benzene	Benzene is an organic chemical compound that is a colorless and flammable liquid with a pleasant, sweet smell. Benzene is a known carcinogen. It is a minor, or additive, component of gasoline. It is an important industrial solvent and precursor in the production of drugs, plastics, gasoline, synthetic rubber, and dyes.
Arsenic	Arsenic is a chemical element in the periodic table that has the symbol As and atomic number 33. This is a notoriously poisonous metalloid that has many allotropic forms; yellow, black and grey are a few that are regularly seen. Arsenic and its compounds are used as pesticides, herbicides, insecticides and various alloys.
Infection	The invasion and multiplication of microorganisms in body tissues is called an infection.
Respiratory tract	In humans the respiratory tract is the part of the anatomy that has to do with the process of respiration or breathing.
Wheezing	Wheezing is a continuous, coarse, whistling sound produced in the respiratory airways during breathing. For wheezing to occur, some part of the respiratory tree must be narrowed or obstructed, or airflow velocity within the respiratory tree must be heightened.
Asthma	Asthma is a complex disease characterized by bronchial hyperresponsiveness (BHR), inflammation, mucus production and intermittent airway obstruction.
Acute	In medicine, an acute disease is a disease with either or both of: a rapid onset; and a short course (as opposed to a chronic course).
Character	Character is a constellation of enduring motivational and other traits that are manifested in the characteristic ways that an individual reacts to various kinds of challenges.
Intervention	Intervention refers to a planned attempt to break through addicts' or abusers' denial and get

them into treatment. Interventions most often occur when legal, workplace, health, relationship, or financial problems have become intolerable.

Behavior modification	Behavior Modification is a technique of altering an individual's reactions to stimuli through positive reinforcement and the extinction of maladaptive behavior.
Withdrawal symptoms	Withdrawal symptoms are physiological changes that occur when the use of a drug is stopped or dosage decreased.
Seizure	A seizure is a temporary alteration in brain function expressed as a changed mental state, tonic or clonic movements and various other symptoms. They are due to temporary abnormal electrical activity of a group of brain cells.
Joint	A joint (articulation) is the location at which two bones make contact (articulate). They are constructed to both allow movement and provide mechanical support.
Temporomandi-ular joint	The temporomandibular joint is a diarthrosis joint that connects the mandible (lower jaw) to the temporal bone at the side of a skull. As a modified hinge joint, not only does the TMJ enable the jaw to open and close, it also enables the jaw to move forward and backward, as well as laterally.
Allergy	An allergy or Type I hypersensitivity is an immune malfunction whereby a person's body is hypersensitized to react immunologically to typically nonimmunogenic substances. When a person is hypersensitized, these substances are known as allergens.
Clinician	A health professional authorized to provide services to people suffering from one or more pathologies is a clinician.
Insomnia	Insomnia is a sleep disorder characterized by an inability to sleep and/or to remain asleep for a reasonable period during the night.
Sinus	A sinus is a pouch or cavity in any organ or tissue, or an abnormal cavity or passage caused by the destruction of tissue.
Norepinephrine	Norepinephrine is a catecholamine and a phenethylamine with chemical formula $C_8H_{11}NO_3$. It is released from the adrenal glands as a hormone into the blood, but it is also a neurotransmitter in the nervous system where it is released from noradrenergic neurons during synaptic transmission.
Planning	In agreement with the patient, the nurse addresses each of the problems identified in the planning phase. For each problem a measurable goal is set. For example, for the patient discussed above, the goal would be for the patient's skin to remain intact. The result is a nursing care plan. This is the third step.
Abstinence	Abstinence has diverse forms. In its oldest sense it is sexual, as in the practice of continence, chastity, and celibacy.
Conditioning	Processes by which behaviors can be learned or modified through interaction with the environment are conditioning.
Stimulus	Stimulus in a nervous system, a factor that triggers sensory transduction.
Congestion	In medicine and pathology the term congestion is used to describe excessive accumulation of blood or other fluid in a particular part of the body.
Cervix	The cervix is actually the lower, narrow portion of the uterus where it joins with the top end of the vagina. It is cylindrical or conical in shape and protrudes through the upper anterior vaginal wall.
Life span	Life span refers to the upper boundary of life, the maximum number of years an individual can live. The maximum life span of human beings is about 120 years of age.

Calorie	Calorie refers to a unit used to measure heat energy and the energy contents of foods.
Xanthine	A xanthine is a alkaloid that is commonly used for its effects as mild stimulants and as bronchodilators, notably in treating the symptoms of asthma.
Theophylline	Theophylline is a methylxanthine drug and is used in therapy for respiratory diseases, under a variety of brand names. As a member of the xanthine family, it bears structural and pharmacological similarity to caffeine. It is naturally found in black tea and green tea.
Delirium	Delirium is a medical term used to describe an acute decline in attention and cognition. Delirium is probably the single most common acute disorder affecting adults in general hospitals. It affects 10-20% of all adults in hospital, and 30-40% of older patients.
Nerve	A nerve is an enclosed, cable-like bundle of nerve fibers or axons, which includes the glia that ensheath the axons in myelin.
Irritability	Irritability is an excessive response to stimuli. Irritability takes many forms, from the contraction of a unicellular organism when touched to complex reactions involving all the senses of higher animals.
Caffeinism	Excessive consumption of caffeine, leading to dependence and a variety of physical and psychological complaints is called caffeinism.
Anxiety	Anxiety is a complex combination of the feeling of fear, apprehension and worry often accompanied by physical sensations such as palpitations, chest pain and/or shortness of breath.
Intoxication	Condition in which a substance affecting the central nervous system has been ingested and certain maladaptive behaviors or psychological changes, such as belligerence and impaired function, are evident is called intoxication.
Heart rate	Heart rate is a term used to describe the frequency of the cardiac cycle. It is considered one of the four vital signs. Usually it is calculated as the number of contractions of the heart in one minute and expressed as "beats per minute".
Cyst	A cyst is a closed sac having a distinct membrane and developing abnormally in a cavity or structure of the body. They may occur as a result of a developmental error in the embryo during pregnancy or they may be caused by infections.
Assess	Assess is to systematically and continuously collect, validate, and communicate patient data.
Advocate	An advocate is one who speaks on behalf of another, especially in a legal context. Implicit in the concept is the notion that the represented lacks the knowledge, skill, ability, or standing to speak for themselves.
Public health	Public health is concerned with threats to the overall health of a community based on population health analysis.
Hallucinogen	Hallucinogen refers to drugs that can affect the subjective qualities of perception, thought or emotion, resulting in altered interpretations of sensory input, alternate states of consciousness, or hallucinations.
Amphetamine	Amphetamine is a synthetic stimulant used to suppress the appetite, control weight, and treat disorders including narcolepsy and ADHD. It is also used recreationally and for performance enhancement.
Inhalant	Inhalant refers to any substance that is vaporized, misted, or gaseous that is inhaled and absorbed through the capillaries in the alveoli of the lungs.
Steroid	A steroid is a lipid characterized by a carbon skeleton with four fused rings. Different steroids vary in the functional groups attached to these rings. Hundreds of distinct steroids

Go to **Cram101.com** for the Practice Tests for this Chapter.

have been identified in plants and animals. Their most important role in most living systems is as hormones.

Cocaine

Cocaine is a crystalline tropane alkaloid that is obtained from the leaves of the coca plant. It is a stimulant of the central nervous system and an appetite suppressant, creating what has been described as a euphoric sense of happiness and increased energy.

Opiate

The term opiate refers to the alkaloids found in opium, an extract from the seed pods of the opium poppy (Papaver somniferum L.). It has also traditionally referred to natural and semi-synthetic derivatives of morphine.

Go to **Cram101.com** for the Practice Tests for this Chapter.

Craving	Craving refers to the powerful desire to use a psychoactive drug or engage in a compulsive behavior. It is manifested in physiological changes, such as raised heart rate, sweating, anxiety, drop in body temperature, pupil dilation, and stomach muscle movements.
Tissue	A collection of interconnected cells that perform a similar function within an organism is called tissue.
Addict	A person with an overpowering physical or psychological need to continue taking a particular substance or drug is referred to as an addict.
Brain	The part of the central nervous system involved in regulating and controlling body activity and interpreting information from the senses transmitted through the nervous system is referred to as the brain.
Methamphetamine	Methamphetamine is a synthetic stimulant drug used for both medicinal and illicit recreational purposes. Like most stimulants, methamphetamine may induce strong feelings of euphoria and can be addictive. Pure methamphetamine is prescribed by physicians in formulations such as Desoxyn.
Misuse	Misuse refers to an unusual or illegal use of a prescription, usually for drug diversion purposes.
Alcohol	Alcohol is a general term, applied to any organic compound in which a hydroxyl group (-OH) is bound to a carbon atom, which in turn is bound to other hydrogen and/or carbon atoms. The general formula for a simple acyclic alcohol is $C_nH_{2n+1}OH$.
Pain	Pain is an unpleasant sensation which may be associated with actual or potential tissue damage and which may have physical and emotional components.
Consciousness	Consciousness refers to the ability to perceive, communicate, remember, understand, appreciate, and initiate voluntary movements; a functioning sensorium.
Endorphins	Endorphins refer to neurotransmitters that are composed of amino acids and that are functionally similar to morphine.
Endorphin	Endorphin is an endogenous opioid biochemical compound. They are peptides produced by the pituitary gland and the hypothalamus in vertebrates, and they resemble the opiates in their abilities to produce analgesia and a sense of well-being.
Morphine	Morphine, the principal active agent in opium, is a powerful opioid analgesic drug. According to recent research, it may also be produced naturally by the human brain. Morphine is usually highly addictive, and tolerance and physical and psychological dependence develop quickly.
Chemical reaction	Chemical reaction refers to a process leading to chemical changes in matter; involves the making and/or breaking of chemical bonds.
Affect	Affect is the scientific term used to describe a subject's externally displayed mood. This can be assesed by the nurse by observing facial expression, tone of voice, and body language.
Drug action	The drugs that enter the human tend to stimulate certain receptors, ion channels, act on enzymes or transporter proteins. As a result, they cause the human body to reaction in a specific way which is the drug action.
Receptor	A receptor is a protein on the cell membrane or within the cytoplasm or cell nucleus that binds to a specific molecule (a ligand), such as a neurotransmitter, hormone, or other substance, and initiates the cellular response to the ligand. Receptor, in immunology, the region of an antibody which shows recognition of an antigen.
Theory	Theory refers to an explanatory statement, or set of statements, that concisely summarizes the state of knowledge on a phenomenon and provides direction for further study.

Go to **Cram101.com** for the Practice Tests for this Chapter.

Go to **Cram101.com** for the Practice Tests for this Chapter.
And, **NEVER** highlight a book again!

Ovaries	Ovaries are egg-producing reproductive organs found in female organisms.
Ovary	The primary reproductive organ of a female is called an ovary.
Lungs	Lungs are the essential organs of respiration in air-breathing vertebrates. Their principal function is to transport oxygen from the atmosphere into the bloodstream, and to excrete carbon dioxide from the bloodstream into the atmosphere.
Liver	The liver is an organ in vertebrates, including humans. It plays a major role in metabolism and has a number of functions in the body including drug detoxification, glycogen storage, and plasma protein synthesis. It also produces bile, which is important for digestion.
Gonad	Gonad refers to a sex organ in an animal; an ovary or a testis. It is the organ that makes gametes.
Blood	Blood is a circulating tissue composed of fluid plasma and cells. The main function of blood is to supply nutrients (oxygen, glucose) and constitutional elements to tissues and to remove waste products.
Skin	Skin is an organ of the integumentary system composed of a layer of tissues that protect underlying muscles and organs.
Hallucination	Hallucination refers to a perception in the absence of sensory stimulation that is confused with reality.
Auditory	Pertaining to the ear or to the sense of hearing is called auditory.
Herbal preparations	Substances of plant origin that are believed to have medicinal properties are called herbal preparations.
Illicit drugs	Illicit drugs refers to drugs whose use, possession, cultivation, manufacture, and/or sale are against the law because they are generally recognized as harmful.
Cultivation	The process by which the mass media is socialized through training and education is cultivation.
Commercial preparations	Commonly used chemical substances including cosmetics, household cleaning products, and industrial by-products are commercial preparations.
Suppository	A suppository is a medicine that is inserted either into the rectum (rectal suppository) or into the vagina (vaginal suppository) where it melts.
Inhalation	Inhalation is the movement of air from the external environment, through the airways, into the alveoli during breathing.
Injection	A method of rapid drug delivery that puts the substance directly in the bloodstream, in a muscle, or under the skin is called injection.
Inunction	The introduction of drugs through the skin is called inunction.
Absorption	Absorption is a physical or chemical phenomenon or a process in which atoms, molecules, or ions enter some bulk phase - gas, liquid or solid material. In nutrition, amino acids are broken down through digestion, which begins in the stomach.
Intestine	The intestine is the portion of the alimentary canal extending from the stomach to the anus and, in humans and mammals, consists of two segments, the small intestine and the large intestine. The intestine is the part of the body responsible for extracting nutrition from food.
Stomach	The stomach is an organ in the alimentary canal used to digest food. It's primary function is not the absorption of nutrients from digested food; rather, the main job of the stomach is to break down large food molecules into smaller ones, so that they can be absorbed into the

	blood more easily.
Small intestine	The small intestine is the part of the gastrointestinal tract between the stomach and the large intestine (colon). In humans over 5 years old it is about 7m long. It is divided into three structural parts: duodenum, jejunum and ileum.
Acid	An acid is a water-soluble, sour-tasting chemical compound that when dissolved in water, gives a solution with a pH of less than 7.
Syringe	A device for injecting drugs directly into the body is a syringe.
Intravenous	Present or occurring within a vein, such as an intravenous blood clot is referred to as intravenous. Introduced directly into a vein, such as an intravenous injection or I.V. drip.
Vein	Vein in animals, is a vessel that returns blood to the heart. In plants, a vascular bundle in a leaf, composed of xylem and phloem.
Intravenous injection	The introduction of drugs directly into a vein is an intravenous injection.
Hypodermic needle	A device for injecting a fluid into the body intramuscularly, intravenously, or subcutaneously is a hypodermic needle.
Intramuscular Injection	You have intramuscular injection when a needle is inserted in a muscle, usually a large muscle, and the drug is injected into that muscle.
Antibiotic	Antibiotic refers to substance such as penicillin or streptomycin that is toxic to microorganisms. Usually a product of a particular microorvanism or plant.
Subcutaneous	Subcutaneous injections are given by injecting a fluid into the subcutis. It is relatively painless and an effective way to administer particular types of medication.
Subcutaneous Injection	Subcutaneous injection is a type injection in which a drug is injected just under the skin.
Anesthetic	Anesthetic refers to a substance that causes the loss of the ability to feel pain or other sensory input, e.g., ether or halothane.
Insulin	Insulin is a polypeptide hormone that regulates carbohydrate metabolism. Apart from being the primary effector in carbohydrate homeostasis, it also has a substantial effect on small vessel muscle tone, controls storage and release of fat (triglycerides) and cellular uptake of both amino acids and some electrolytes.
Local anesthetic	Local anesthetic drugs act mainly by inhibiting sodium influx through sodium-specific ion channels in the neuronal cell membrane, in particular the so-called voltage-gated sodium channels. When the influx of sodium is interrupted, an action potential cannot arise and signal conduction is thus inhibited.
Sphincter	Muscle that surrounds a tube and closes or opens the tube by contracting and relaxing is referred to as sphincter.
Muscle	Muscle is a contractile form of tissue. It is one of the four major tissue types, the other three being epithelium, connective tissue and nervous tissue. Muscle contraction is used to move parts of the body, as well as to move substances within the body.
Anus	In anatomy, the anus is the external opening of the rectum. Closure is controlled by sphincter muscles. Feces are expelled from the body through the anus during the act of defecation, which is the primary function of the anus.
Vagina	The vagina is the tubular tract leading from the uterus to the exterior of the body in female placental mammals and marsupials, or to the cloaca in female birds, monotremes, and some reptiles. Female insects and other invertebrates also have a vagina, which is the terminal

Go to **Cram101.com** for the Practice Tests for this Chapter.

	part of the oviduct.
Blood vessel	A blood vessel is a part of the circulatory system and function to transport blood throughout the body. The most important types, arteries and veins, are so termed because they carry blood away from or towards the heart, respectively.
Agent	Agent refers to an epidemiological term referring to the organism or object that transmits a disease from the environment to the host.
Drug abuse	Drug abuse has a wide range of definitions, all of them relating either to the misuse or overuse of a psychoactive drug or performance enhancing drug for a non-therapeutic or non-medical effect, or referring to any use of illegal drug in the absence of a required, yet practically impossible to get, license from a government authority.
Addiction	Addiction is an uncontrollable compulsion to repeat a behavior regardless of its consequences. Many drugs or behaviors can precipitate a pattern of conditions recognized as addiction, which include a craving for more of the drug or behavior, increased physiological tolerance to exposure, and withdrawal symptoms in the absence of the stimulus.
Lead	Lead is a chemical element in the periodic table that has the symbol Pb and atomic number 82. A soft, heavy, toxic and malleable poor metal, lead is bluish white when freshly cut but tarnishes to dull gray when exposed to air. Lead is used in building construction, lead-acid batteries, bullets and shot, and is part of solder, pewter, and fusible alloys.
Evaluation	The fifth step of the nursing process where nursing care and the patient's goal achievement are measured is the evaluation.
Rehabilitation	Rehabilitation is the restoration of lost capabilities, or the treatment aimed at producing it. Also refers to treatment for dependency on psychoactive substances such as alcohol, prescription drugs, and illicit drugs such as cocaine, heroin or amphetamines.
Marijuana	Marijuana refers to the dried vegetable matter of the Cannabis sativa plant.
Cocaine	Cocaine is a crystalline tropane alkaloid that is obtained from the leaves of the coca plant. It is a stimulant of the central nervous system and an appetite suppressant, creating what has been described as a euphoric sense of happiness and increased energy.
Opiate	The term opiate refers to the alkaloids found in opium, an extract from the seed pods of the opium poppy (Papaver somniferum L.). It has also traditionally referred to natural and semi-synthetic derivatives of morphine.
Ethnicity	While ethnicity and race are related concepts, the concept of ethnicity is rooted in the idea of social groups, marked especially by shared nationality, tribal affiliation, religious faith, shared language, or cultural and traditional origins and backgrounds, whereas race is rooted in the idea of biological classification of Homo sapiens to subspecies according to chosen genotypic and/or phenotypic traits.
LSD	A powerful hallucinogen with unpredictable effects ranging from perceptual changes and vivid hallucinations to states of panic and terror is referred to as LSD.
Barbiturate	A barbiturate is a drug that acts as a central nervous system (CNS) depressant, and by virtue of this produces a wide spectrum of effects, from mild sedation to anesthesia.
Amphetamine	Amphetamine is a synthetic stimulant used to suppress the appetite, control weight, and treat disorders including narcolepsy and ADHD. It is also used recreationally and for performance enhancement.
Dependence	Dependence refers to a mental or physical craving for a drug and withdrawal symptoms when use of the drug is stopped.
Sedative	A sedative is a drug that depresses the central nervous system (CNS), which causes calmness,

Go to **Cram101.com** for the Practice Tests for this Chapter.

	relaxation, reduction of anxiety, sleepiness, slowed breathing, slurred speech, staggering gait, poor judgment, and slow, uncertain reflexes.
Ecstasy	Ecstasy as an emotion is to be outside oneself, in a trancelike state in which an individual transcends ordinary consciousness and as a result has a heightened capacity for exceptional thought or experience. Ecstasy also refers to a relatively new hallucinogen that is chemically similar to mescaline and the amphetamines.
MDMA	MDMA, most commonly known today by the street name ecstasy, is a synthetic entactogen of the phenethylamine family whose primary effect is to stimulate the secretion of large amounts of serotonin as well as dopamine and noradrenaline in the brain, causing a general sense of openness, empathy, energy, euphoria, and well-being.
Monitoring the Future	Monitoring the Future is an annual survey given to 50,000 8th, 10th and 12th graders in the United States to determine drug use trends and patterns. The survey started in 1975, with 12th graders. It was expanded in 1991 to include 8th and 10th graders as well.
Health	Health is a term that refers to a combination of the absence of illness, the ability to cope with everyday activities, physical fitness, and high quality of life.
Sinusitis	Sinusitis is inflammation, either bacterial, fungal, viral, allergic or autoimmune, of the paranasal sinuses.
Septum	A septum, in general, is a wall separating two cavities or two spaces containing a less dense material. The muscle wall that divides the heart chambers.
Hepatitis	Hepatitis is a gastroenterological disease, featuring inflammation of the liver. The clinical signs and prognosis, as well as the therapy, depend on the cause.
Veins	Blood vessels that return blood toward the heart from the circulation are referred to as veins.
Infection	The invasion and multiplication of microorganisms in body tissues is called an infection.
Artery	Vessel that takes blood away from the heart to the tissues and organs of the body is called an artery.
Nervous system	The nervous system of an animal coordinates the activity of the muscles, monitors the organs, constructs and processes input from the senses, and initiates actions.
Central nervous system	The central nervous system comprized of the brain and spinal cord, represents the largest part of the nervous system. Together with the peripheral nervous system, it has a fundamental role in the control of behavior.
Stimulant	A stimulant is a drug which increases the activity of the sympathetic nervous system and produces a sense of euphoria or awakeness.
Euphoria	A feeling of well-being, extreme satiation, and satisfaction caused by many psychoactive drugs and certain behaviors, such as gambling and sex is referred to as euphoria.
Course	Pattern of development and change of a disorder over time is a course.
Blood pressure	Blood pressure is the pressure exerted by the blood on the walls of the blood vessels.
Convulsions	Involuntary muscle spasms, often severe, that can be caused by stimulant overdose or by depressant withdrawal are called convulsions.
Heart rate	Heart rate is a term used to describe the frequency of the cardiac cycle. It is considered one of the four vital signs. Usually it is calculated as the number of contractions of the heart in one minute and expressed as "beats per minute".
Placenta	The placenta is an organ present only in female placental mammals during gestation. It is

composed of two parts, one genetically and biologically part of the fetus, the other part of the mother. It is implanted in the wall of the uterus, where it receives nutrients and oxygen from the mother's blood and passes out waste.

Fetus	Fetus refers to a developing human from the ninth week of gestation until birth; has all the major structures of an adult.
Gauge	The diameter of the needle is indicated by the needle gauge.
Miscarriage	Miscarriage or spontaneous abortion is the natural or accidental termination of a pregnancy at a stage where the embryo or the fetus is incapable of surviving, generally defined at a gestation of prior to 20 weeks.
Irritability	Irritability is an excessive response to stimuli. Irritability takes many forms, from the contraction of a unicellular organism when touched to complex reactions involving all the senses of higher animals.
Intervention	Intervention refers to a planned attempt to break through addicts' or abusers' denial and get them into treatment. Interventions most often occur when legal, workplace, health, relationship, or financial problems have become intolerable.
Base	The common definition of a base is a chemical compound that absorbs hydronium ions when dissolved in water (a proton acceptor). An alkali is a special example of a base, where in an aqueous environment, hydroxide ions are donated.
Salt	Salt is a term used for ionic compounds composed of positively charged cations and negatively charged anions, so that the product is neutral and without a net charge.
Freebase	Freebase refers to the standalone basic form of an alkaloid, as opposed to its salt form. The term freebase is also often used to refer solely to the freebase form of cocaine, known as crack.
Arsenic	Arsenic is a chemical element in the periodic table that has the symbol As and atomic number 33. This is a notoriously poisonous metalloid that has many allotropic forms; yellow, black and grey are a few that are regularly seen. Arsenic and its compounds are used as pesticides, herbicides, insecticides and various alloys.
Sugar	A sugar is the simplest molecule that can be identified as a carbohydrate. These include monosaccharides and disaccharides, trisaccharides and the oligosaccharides. The term "glyco-" indicates the presence of a sugar in an otherwise non-carbohydrate substance.
Psychological dependence	Psychological dependence may lead to psychological withdrawal symptoms. Addictions can theoretically form for any rewarding behavior, or as a habitual means to avoid undesired activity, but typically they only do so to a clinical level in individuals who have emotional, social, or psychological dysfunctions, taking the place of normal positive stimuli not otherwise attained
Sleep patterns	The order and timing of daily sleep and waking periods are called sleep patterns.
Insomnia	Insomnia is a sleep disorder characterized by an inability to sleep and/or to remain asleep for a reasonable period during the night.
Suppression	Suppression is the defense mechanism where a memory is deliberately forgotten.
Anxiety	Anxiety is a complex combination of the feeling of fear, apprehension and worry often accompanied by physical sensations such as palpitations, chest pain and/or shortness of breath.
Delusion	A false belief, not generally shared by others, and that cannot be changed despite strong evidence to the contrary is a delusion.

Paranoid	The term paranoid is typically used in a general sense to signify any self-referential delusion, or more specifically, to signify a delusion involving the fear of persecution.
Popper	Popper proposed a set of methodological rules called Falsificationism. Falsificationism is the idea that science advances by unjustified, exaggerated guesses followed by unstinting criticism. Only hypotheses capable of clashing with observation reports are allowed to count as scientific. Falsifiable theories enhance our control over error while expanding the richness of what we can say about the world.
Addictive drug	An addictive drug produces a biological or psychological dependence in the user; withdrawal from them leads to a craving for the drug that in some cases can be nearly irresistible.
Obesity	The state of being more than 20 percent above the average weight for a person of one's height is called obesity.
Ritalin	Ritalin, a methylphenidate, is a central nervous system stimulant. It has a "calming" effect on many children who have ADHD, reducing impulsive behavior and the tendency to "act out", and helps them concentrate on schoolwork and other tasks.
Attention deficit/hypeactivity disorder	Disorders of childhood and adolescence characterized by socially disruptive behaviors-either attentional problems or hyperactivity-that persist for at least six months are an attention deficit/hyperactivity disorder.
Depression	In everyday language depression refers to any downturn in mood, which may be relatively transitory and perhaps due to something trivial. This is differentiated from Clinical depression which is marked by symptoms that last two weeks or more and are so severe that they interfere with daily living.
Paranoia	In popular culture, the term paranoia is usually used to describe excessive concern about one's own well-being, sometimes suggesting a person holds persecutory beliefs concerning a threat to themselves or their property and is often linked to a belief in conspiracy theories.
Bicarbonate	A Bicarbonate or, more properly, a hydrogen carbonate is a polyatomic ion. It is the intermediate form in the deprotonation of carbonic acid: removing the first proton from carbonic acid forms bicarbonate; removing the second proton leads to the carbonate ion.
Ammonia	Ammonia is a compound of nitrogen and hydrogen with the formula NH_3. At standard temperature and pressure ammonia is a gas. It is toxic and corrosive to some materials, and has a characteristic pungent odor.
Sodium	Sodium is the chemical element in the periodic table that has the symbol Na (Natrium in Latin) and atomic number 11. Sodium is a soft, waxy, silvery reactive metal belonging to the alkali metals that is abundant in natural compounds (especially halite). It is highly reactive.
Vial	A glass bottle with a self-sealing stopper from which medication is removed is a vial.
Lifestyle	The culturally, socially, economically, and environmentally conditioned complex of actions characteristic of an individual, group, or community as a pattern of habituated behavior over time that is health related but not necessarily health directed is a lifestyle.
Methamphetamine A	Methamphetamine A refers to powerfully addictive drug that strongly activates certain areas of the brain and affects the central nervous system.
Ephedrine	Ephedrine (EPH) is a sympathomimetic amine commonly used as a decongestant and to treat hypotension associated with regional anaesthesia. Chemically, it is an alkaloid derived from various plants in the genus Ephedra (family Ephedraceae).

Go to **Cram101.com** for the Practice Tests for this Chapter.

307

Kidney	The kidney is a bean-shaped excretory organ in vertebrates. Part of the urinary system, the kidneys filter wastes (especially urea) from the blood and excrete them, along with water, as urine.
Hash oil	Hash oil refers to an extract of marijuana that is added to food or to marijuana cigarettes. Its thc content can be as high as 20% to 80%.
Solvent	A solvent is a liquid that dissolves a solid, liquid, or gaseous solute, resulting in a solution. The most common solvent in everyday life is water.
Hashish	Hashish is a psychoactive drug derived from the Cannabis plant. It is used for its relaxing and mind-altering effects.
Joint	A joint (articulation) is the location at which two bones make contact (articulate). They are constructed to both allow movement and provide mechanical support.
Eye	An eye is an organ that detects light. Different kinds of light-sensitive organs are found in a variety of creatures. The simplest eyes do nothing but detect whether the surroundings are light or dark, while more complex eyes can distinguish shapes and colors.
Psychosis	Psychosis is a generic term for mental states in which the components of rational thought and perception are severely impaired. Persons experiencing a psychosis may experience hallucinations, hold paranoid or delusional beliefs, demonstrate personality changes and exhibit disorganized thinking. This is usually accompanied by features such as a lack of insight into the unusual or bizarre nature of their behavior, difficulties with social interaction and impairments in carrying out the activities of daily living.
Chemical name	The primary function of chemical nomenclature is to ensure that the person who hears or reads a chemical name is under no ambiguity as to which chemical compound it refers: each name should refer to a single substance. It is considered less important to ensure that each substance should have a single name, although the number of acceptable names is limited.
Carbon	Carbon is a chemical element in the periodic table that has the symbol C and atomic number 6. An abundant nonmetallic, tetravalent element, carbon has several allotropic forms.
Affinity	Chemical affinity results from electronic properties by which dissimilar substances are capable of forming chemical compounds. Specifically, the term refers to the tendency of an atom or compound to combine by chemical reaction with atoms or compounds of unlike composition.
Oxygen	Oxygen is a chemical element in the periodic table. It has the symbol O and atomic number 8. Oxygen is the second most common element on Earth, composing around 46% of the mass of Earth's crust and 28% of the mass of Earth as a whole, and is the third most common element in the universe.
Respiratory tract	In humans the respiratory tract is the part of the anatomy that has to do with the process of respiration or breathing.
Stillbirth	A stillbirth occurs when a fetus, of mid-second trimester to full term gestational age, which has died in the womb or during labour or delivery, exits the maternal body.
Syndrome	Syndrome is the association of several clinically recognizable features, signs, symptoms, phenomena or characteristics which often occur together, so that the presence of one feature alerts the physician to the presence of the others
Fetal alcohol syndrome	A cluster of abnormalities that appears in the offspring of mothers who drink alcohol heavily during pregnancy is called fetal alcohol syndrome.
Value	Value is worth in general, and it is thought to be connected to reasons for certain practices, policies, actions, beliefs or emotions. Value is "that which one acts to gain

Go to **Cram101.com** for the Practice Tests for this Chapter.

309

	and/or keep."
Testosterone	Testosterone is a steroid hormone from the androgen group. Testosterone is secreted in the testes of men and the ovaries of women. It is the principal male sex hormone and the "original" anabolic steroid. In both males and females, it plays key roles in health and well-being.
Sperm	Sperm refers to the male sex cell with three distinct parts at maturity: head, middle piece, and tail.
Medicine	Medicine is the branch of health science and the sector of public life concerned with maintaining or restoring human health through the study, diagnosis and treatment of disease and injury.
Chemotherapy	Chemotherapy is the use of chemical substances to treat disease. In its modern-day use, it refers almost exclusively to cytostatic drugs used to treat cancer.In its non-oncological use, the term may also refer to antibiotics.
Spasticity	Spasticity is a disorder of the body's motor system in which certain muscles are continuously contracted. This contraction causes stiffness or tightness of the muscles and may interfere with gait, movement, and speech.
Cancer	Cancer is a class of diseases or disorders characterized by uncontrolled division of cells and the ability of these cells to invade other tissues, either by direct growth into adjacent tissue through invasion or by implantation into distant sites by metastasis.
Multiple sclerosis	Multiple sclerosis affects neurons, the cells of the brain and spinal cord that carry information, create thought and perception, and allow the brain to control the body. Surrounding and protecting these neurons is a layer of fat, called myelin, which helps neurons carry electrical signals. MS causes gradual destruction of myelin (demyelination) in patches throughout the brain and/or spinal cord, causing various symptoms depending upon which signals are interrupted.
Glaucoma	Glaucoma is a group of diseases of the optic nerve involving loss of retinal ganglion cells in a characteristic pattern of optic neuropathy.
Narcotic	The term narcotic originally referred to a variety of substances that induced sleep (such state is narcosis). In legal context, narcotic refers to opium, opium derivatives, and their semisynthetic or totally synthetic substitutes.
Opium	Opium is a narcotic analgesic drug which is obtained from the unripe seed pods of the opium poppy (Papaver somniferum L. or the synonym paeoniflorum).
Cramp	A cramp is an unpleasant sensation caused by contraction, usually of a muscle. It can be caused by cold or overexertion.
Analgesic	An analgesic is any member of the diverse group of drugs used to relieve pain and to achieve analgesia. Analgesic drugs act in various ways on the peripheral and central nervous system.
Codeine	Codeine is an opioid used for its analgesic, antitussive and antidiarrheal properties
Heroin	Heroin is widely and illegally used as a powerful and addictive drug producing intense euphoria, which often disappears with increasing tolerance. Heroin is a semi-synthetic opioid. It is the 3,6-diacetyl derivative of morphine and is synthesized from it by acetylation.
Epidemic	An epidemic is a disease that appears as new cases in a given human population, during a given period, at a rate that substantially exceeds what is "expected", based on recent experience.
Pupil	Pupil refers to the opening in the iris that admits light into the interior of the vertebrate

eye. Muscles in the iris regulate its size.

Tolerance	Drug tolerance occurs when a subject's reaction to a drug decreases so that larger doses are required to achieve the same effect.
Survey	A method of scientific investigation in which a large sample of people answer questions about their attitudes or behavior is referred to as a survey.
Chronic pain	Chronic pain is defined as pain that has lasted 6 months or longer.
Young adult	An young adult is someone between the ages of 20 and 40 years old.
Acute pain	Acute pain refers to pain that typically follows an injury and that disappears once the injury heals or is effectively treated.
Acute	In medicine, an acute disease is a disease with either or both of: a rapid onset; and a short course (as opposed to a chronic course).
Scar	A scar results from the biologic process of wound repair in the skin and other tissues of the body. It is a connective tissue that fills the wound.
Physiology	The study of the function of cells, tissues, and organs is referred to as physiology.
Hormone	A hormone is a chemical messenger from one cell to another. All multicellular organisms produce hormones. The best known hormones are those produced by endocrine glands of vertebrate animals, but hormones are produced by nearly every organ system and tissue type in a human or animal body. Hormone molecules are secreted directly into the bloodstream, they move by circulation or diffusion to their target cells, which may be nearby cells in the same tissue or cells of a distant organ of the body.
Tremor	Tremor is the rhythmic, oscillating shaking movement of the whole body or just a certain part of it, caused by problems of the neurons responsible from muscle action.
Diarrhea	Diarrhea or diarrhoea is a condition in which the sufferer has frequent and watery, chunky, or loose bowel movements.
Methadone	Methadone is a synthetic heroin substitute used for treating heroin addicts that acts as a substitute for heroin by eliminating its effects and the craving for it. Just like heroin, tolerance and dependence frequently develop.
Methadone maintenance	A treatment and harm reduction technique that keeps a heroin addict on methadone for long periods of time, even a lifetime is called methadone maintenance.
Hallucinogen	Hallucinogen refers to drugs that can affect the subjective qualities of perception, thought or emotion, resulting in altered interpretations of sensory input, alternate states of consciousness, or hallucinations.
Brain stem	The brain stem refers to a composite substructure of the brain. It includes the midbrain, the pons and the medulla oblongata. It is the major route for communication between the forebrain, the spinal cord, and peripheral nerves. It also controls various functions including respiration, regulation of heart rhythms, and primary aspects of sound localization.
Reticular formation	The reticular formation is a system of neurons containing over 90 separate nuclei, which is involved in stereotypical actions, such as walking, sleeping, and lying down.
Antagonist	A antagonist is a drug that interacts with the target cell of a receptor site to inhibit or prevent the action of an agonist.
Naltrexone	Naltrexone is an opioid receptor antagonist used primarily in the management of alcohol dependence and opioid dependence. It is marketed as its hydrochloride salt, naltrexone hydrochloride, under the trade name Revia.

313

Compulsion	An apparently irresistible urge to repeat an act or engage in ritualistic behavior such as hand washing is referred to as a compulsion.
Mescaline	Mescaline is a hallucinogenic drug derived from the mescal cactus. Users typically experience visual hallucinations and radically altered states of consciousness, often experienced as pleasurable and illuminating but occasionally as accompanied by feelings of anxiety or revulsion.
Psychiatrist	A psychiatrist is a physician who specializes in the diagnosis and treatment of psychological disorders.
Trauma	Trauma refers to a severe physical injury or wound to the body caused by an external force, or a psychological shock having a lasting effect on mental life.
Cerebellum	The cerebellum is a region of the brain that plays an important role in the integration of sensory perception and motor output. The cerebellum integrates these two functions, using the constant feedback on body position to fine-tune motor movements.
Spinal cord	The spinal cord is a part of the vertebrate nervous system that is enclosed in and protected by the vertebral column (it passes through the spinal canal). It consists of nerve cells. The spinal cord carries sensory signals and motor innervation to most of the skeletal muscles in the body.
Pons	The pons is a knob on the brain stem. It is part of the autonomic nervous system, and relays sensory information between the cerebellum and cerebrum. Some theories posit that it has a role in dreaming.
Solution	Solution refers to homogenous mixture formed when a solute is dissolved in a solvent.
Gelatin	Gelatin is a translucent brittle solid substance, colorless or slightly yellow, nearly tasteless and odorless, which is created by prolonged boiling of animal skin, connective tissue or bones. It has many uses in food, medicine, and manufacturing. Substances that contain or resemble gelatin are called gelatinous.
Muscle contraction	A muscle contraction occurs when a muscle cell (called a muscle fiber) shortens. There are three general types: skeletal, heart, and smooth.
Psychological addiction	Psychological addiction is a person's need to use a drug out of desire for the effects it produces, rather than to relieve withdrawal symptoms.
Peyote	Peyote is a hallucinogen obtained from the root of the peyote cactus. The active ingredient is mescaline, an alkaloid.
Hallucinogenic	Drugs that give rise to hallucinations are said to produce hallucinogenic effects.
Serotonin	Serotonin is a monoamine neurotransmitter synthesized in serotonergic neurons in the central nervous system and enterochromaffin cells in the gastrointestinal tract. It is believed to play an important part of the biochemistry of depression, migraine, bipolar disorder and anxiety.
Fever	Fever (also known as pyrexia, or a febrile response, and archaically known as ague) is a medical symptom that describes an increase in internal body temperature to levels that are above normal (37°C, 98.6°F).
Phencyclidine	Phencyclidine is a dissociative psychedelic drug formerly used as an anaesthetic agent. Although the primary psychoactive effects of the drug only last hours, total elimination from the body is prolonged, typically extending over weeks.
Conscious	Conscious refers to the thoughts, feelings, sensations, or memories of which a person is aware at any given moment.

Go to **Cram101.com** for the Practice Tests for this Chapter.

Amnesia	Amnesia is a condition in which memory is disturbed. The causes of amnesia are organic or functional. Organic causes include damage to the brain, through trauma or disease, or use of certain (generally sedative) drugs.
Tranquilizer	A sedative, or tranquilizer, is a drug that depresses the central nervous system (CNS), which causes calmness, relaxation, reduction of anxiety, sleepiness, slowed breathing, slurred speech, staggering gait, poor judgment, and slow, uncertain reflexes.
Delirium	Delirium is a medical term used to describe an acute decline in attention and cognition. Delirium is probably the single most common acute disorder affecting adults in general hospitals. It affects 10-20% of all adults in hospital, and 30-40% of older patients.
Ketamine	Ketamine refers to used as a recreational club drug, it is an anesthetic that produces catatonia and deep analgesia; side effects include excess saliva, dysphoria, and hallucinations. Its chemistry and effects are very similar to pcp.
Rape	Forcible sexual intercourse with a person who does not consent to it is rape.
Inhibition	The ability to prevent from making some cognitive or behavioral response is called inhibition.
Aphrodisiac	An aphrodisiac is an agent which causes the arousal of sexual desire.
Residue	A residue refers to a portion of a larger molecule, a specific monomer of a polysaccharide, protein or nucleic acid.
Sensory input	The conduction of signals from sensory receptors to processing centers in the central nervous system is sensory input.
Sexual assault	Sexual assault refers to any act in which one person is sexually intimate with another person without that other person's consent.
Assault	Assault is a crime of violence against another person that intentionally instills fear and creates a reasonable aprehension of harm.
Seizure	A seizure is a temporary alteration in brain function expressed as a changed mental state, tonic or clonic movements and various other symptoms. They are due to temporary abnormal electrical activity of a group of brain cells.
Icon	A mental representation of a visual stimulus that is held briefly in sensory memory is called an icon.
Inhalant	Inhalant refers to any substance that is vaporized, misted, or gaseous that is inhaled and absorbed through the capillaries in the alveoli of the lungs.
Disorientation	A state of mental confusion with respect to time, place, identity of self, other persons, and objects is disorientation.
Reaction time	The amount of time required to respond to a stimulus is referred to as reaction time.
Synergistic effect	Synergistic effect is when two or more substances cooperate to produce an effect that is greater than the effect that would have been produced had the substances acted independently of one another.
Orgasm	Orgasm refers to rhythmic contractions of the reproductive structures, accompanied by extreme pleasure, at the peak of sexual excitement in both sexes; includes ejaculation by the male.
Flushing	For a person to flush is to become markedly red in the face and often other areas of the skin, from various physiological conditions. Flushing is generally distingushed, despite a close physiological relation between them, from blushing, which is milder, generally restricted to the face or cheeks, and generally assumed to reflect embarrassment.

Go to **Cram101.com** for the Practice Tests for this Chapter.

Anesthesia	Anesthesia is the process of blocking the perception of pain and other sensations. This allows patients to undergo surgery and other procedures without the distress and pain they would otherwise experience.
Floating	Floating is a technique used to advance the IV catheter into the vein, whereby the catheter is inserted halfway into the vein and the tourniquet and needle are removed. The cannula hub is then attached to the infusion tubing and the control clamp on the tubing is slowly opened, floating the catheter into the vein with the infusate.
Laughing gas	Laughing gas refers to nitrous oxide; an anesthetic that was originally used and abused in the nineteenth century for its intoxicating effect.
Steroid	A steroid is a lipid characterized by a carbon skeleton with four fused rings. Different steroids vary in the functional groups attached to these rings. Hundreds of distinct steroids have been identified in plants and animals. Their most important role in most living systems is as hormones.
Anabolic steroid	An anabolic steroid is a class of natural and synthetic steroid hormones that promote cell growth and division, resulting in growth of muscle tissue and sometimes bone size and strength. They act in different ways on the body to promote muscle growth, and each has androgenic and anabolic properties.
Menstruation	Loss of blood and tissue from the uterine lining at the end of a female reproductive cycle are referred to as menstruation.
Clitoris	The clitoris is a sexual organ in the body of female mammals. The visible knob-like portion is located near the anterior junction of the labia minora, above the opening of the vagina. Unlike its male counterpart, the penis,the clitoris has no urethra, is not involved in urination, and its sole function is to induce sexual pleasure.
Atrophy	Atrophy is the partial or complete wasting away of a part of the body. Causes of atrophy include poor nourishment, poor circulation, loss of hormonal support, loss of nerve supply to the target organ, disuse or lack of exercise, or disease intrinsic to the tissue itself.
Adrenal	In mammals, the adrenal glands are the triangle-shaped endocrine glands that sit atop the kidneys. They are chiefly responsible for regulating the stress response through the synthesis of corticosteroids and catecholamines, including cortisol and adrenaline.
Androstenedione	Androstenedione is a 19-carbon steroid hormone produced in the adrenal glands and the gonads as an intermediate step in the biochemical pathway that produces the androgen testosterone and the estrogens estrone and estradiol. It is the common precursor of male and female sex hormones. Some androstenedione is also secreted into the plasma, and may be converted in peripheral tissues to testosterone and estrogens.
Estrogen	Estrogen is a steroid that functions as the primary female sex hormone. While present in both men and women, they are found in women in significantly higher quantities.
Prostate	The prostate is a gland that is part of male mammalian sex organs. Its main function is to secrete and store a clear, slightly basic fluid that is part of semen. The prostate differs considerably between species anatomically, chemically and physiologically.
Gland	A gland is an organ in an animal's body that synthesizes a substance for release such as hormones, often into the bloodstream or into cavities inside the body or its outer surface.
Substance abuse	Substance abuse refers to the overindulgence in and dependence on a stimulant, depressant, or other chemical substance, leading to effects that are detrimental to the individual's physical or mental health, or the welfare of others.
False negative	A false negative, also called a Type II error or miss, exists when a test incorrectly reports that a result was not detected, when it was really present.

Go to **Cram101.com** for the Practice Tests for this Chapter.

Resistance	Resistance refers to a nonspecific ability to ward off infection or disease regardless of whether the body has been previously exposed to it. A force that opposes the flow of a fluid such as air or blood. Compare with immunity.
Outcome	Outcome is the impact of care provided to a patient. They can be positive, such as the ability to walk freely as a result of rehabilitation, or negative, such as the occurrence of bedsores as a result of lack of mobility of a patient.
Population	Population refers to all members of a well-defined group of organisms, events, or things.
Mental health	Mental health refers to the 'thinking' part of psychosocial health; includes your values, attitudes, and beliefs.
Statistics	Statistics is a type of data analysis which practice includes the planning, summarizing, and interpreting of observations of a system possibly followed by predicting or forecasting of future events based on a mathematical model of the system being observed.
Statistic	A statistic is an observable random variable of a sample.
Cardiovascular disease	Cardiovascular disease refers to afflictions in the mechanisms, including the heart, blood vessels, and their controllers, that are responsible for transporting blood to the body's tissues and organs. Psychological factors may play important roles in such diseases and their treatments.
Triglycerides	Triglycerides refer to fats and oils composed of fatty acids and glycerol; are the body's most concentrated source of energy fuel; also known as neutral fats.
Hypertension	Hypertension is a medical condition where the blood pressure in the arteries is chronically elevated. Persistent hypertension is one of the risk factors for strokes, heart attacks, heart failure and arterial aneurysm, and is a leading cause of chronic renal failure.
Triglyceride	Triglyceride is a glyceride in which the glycerol is esterified with three fatty acids. They are the main constituent of vegetable oil and animal fats and play an important role in metabolism as energy sources. They contain a bit more than twice as much energy as carbohydrates and proteins.
Risk factor	A risk factor is a variable associated with an increased risk of disease or infection but risk factors are not necessarily causal.
Cholesterol	Cholesterol is a steroid, a lipid, and an alcohol, found in the cell membranes of all body tissues, and transported in the blood plasma of all animals. It is an important component of the membranes of cells, providing stability; it makes the membrane's fluidity stable over a bigger temperature interval.
Diabetes	Diabetes is a medical disorder characterized by varying or persistent elevated blood sugar levels, especially after eating. All types of diabetes share similar symptoms and complications at advanced stages: dehydration and ketoacidosis, cardiovascular disease, chronic renal failure, retinal damage which can lead to blindness, nerve damage which can lead to erectile dysfunction, gangrene with risk of amputation of toes, feet, and even legs.
Stress	Stress refers to a condition that is a response to factors that change the human systems normal state.
Diabetes mellitus	Diabetes mellitus is a medical disorder characterized by varying or persistent hyperglycemia (elevated blood sugar levels), especially after eating. All types of diabetes mellitus share similar symptoms and complications at advanced stages.

Cardiovascular disease	Cardiovascular disease refers to afflictions in the mechanisms, including the heart, blood vessels, and their controllers, that are responsible for transporting blood to the body's tissues and organs. Psychological factors may play important roles in such diseases and their treatments.
Stroke	A stroke or cerebrovascular accident (CVA) occurs when the blood supply to a part of the brain is suddenly interrupted.
Heart attack	A heart attack, is a serious, sudden heart condition usually characterized by varying degrees of chest pain or discomfort, weakness, sweating, nausea, vomiting, and arrhythmias, sometimes causing loss of consciousness. It occurs when the blood supply to a part of the heart is interrupted, causing death and scarring of the local heart tissue.
Diabetes	Diabetes is a medical disorder characterized by varying or persistent elevated blood sugar levels, especially after eating. All types of diabetes share similar symptoms and complications at advanced stages: dehydration and ketoacidosis, cardiovascular disease, chronic renal failure, retinal damage which can lead to blindness, nerve damage which can lead to erectile dysfunction, gangrene with risk of amputation of toes, feet, and even legs.
Artery	Vessel that takes blood away from the heart to the tissues and organs of the body is called an artery.
Medicine	Medicine is the branch of health science and the sector of public life concerned with maintaining or restoring human health through the study, diagnosis and treatment of disease and injury.
Sugar	A sugar is the simplest molecule that can be identified as a carbohydrate. These include monosaccharides and disaccharides, trisaccharides and the oligosaccharides. The term "glyco-" indicates the presence of a sugar in an otherwise non-carbohydrate substance.
Blood	Blood is a circulating tissue composed of fluid plasma and cells. The main function of blood is to supply nutrients (oxygen, glucose) and constitutional elements to tissues and to remove waste products.
Internal medicine	Doctors of internal medicine ("internists") focus on adult medicine and have had special study and training focusing on the prevention and treatment of adult diseases. At least three of their seven or more years of medical school and postgraduate training are dedicated to learning how to prevent, diagnose, and treat diseases that affect adults.
Health	Health is a term that refers to a combination of the absence of illness, the ability to cope with everyday activities, physical fitness, and high quality of life.
Cardiovascular system	The circulatory system or cardiovascular system is the organ system which circulates blood around the body of most animals.
Influenza	Influenza or flu refers to an acute viral infection of the respiratory tract, occurring in isolated cases, epidemics, and pandemics. Influenza is caused by three strains of influenza virus, labeled types A, B, and C, based on the antigens of their protein coats.
Cancer	Cancer is a class of diseases or disorders characterized by uncontrolled division of cells and the ability of these cells to invade other tissues, either by direct growth into adjacent tissue through invasion or by implantation into distant sites by metastasis.
Cardiac arrest	A cardiac arrest is the ceszation of normal circulation of the blood due to failure of the ventricles of the heart to contract effectively during systole.
Coronary	Referring to the heart or the blood vessels of the heart is referred to as coronary.
Coronary heart disease	Coronary heart disease is the end result of the accumulation of atheromatous plaques within the walls of the arteries that supply the myocardium (the muscle of the heart).

Go to **Cram101.com** for the Practice Tests for this Chapter.

HIV	The virus that causes AIDS is HIV (human immunodeficiency virus).
Blood pressure	Blood pressure is the pressure exerted by the blood on the walls of the blood vessels.
Statistics	Statistics is a type of data analysis which practice includes the planning, summarizing, and interpreting of observations of a system possibly followed by predicting or forecasting of future events based on a mathematical model of the system being observed.
Statistic	A statistic is an observable random variable of a sample.
Prognosis	Prognosis refers to the prospects for the future or outcome of a disease.
Angina	Angina pectoris is chest pain due to ischemia (a lack of blood and hence oxygen supply) to the heart muscle, generally due to obstruction or spasm of the coronary arteries (the heart's blood vessels). Coronary artery disease, the main cause of angina, is due to atherosclerosis of the cardiac arteries.
Pain	Pain is an unpleasant sensation which may be associated with actual or potential tissue damage and which may have physical and emotional components.
Angina pectoris	Angina pectoris is chest pain due to ischemia (a lack of blood and hence oxygen supply) to the heart muscle, generally due to obstruction or spasm of the coronary arteries (the heart's blood vessels).
Population	Population refers to all members of a well-defined group of organisms, events, or things.
Outcome	Outcome is the impact of care provided to a patient. They can be positive, such as the ability to walk freely as a result of rehabilitation, or negative, such as the occurrence of bedsores as a result of lack of mobility of a patient.
Acute	In medicine, an acute disease is a disease with either or both of: a rapid onset; and a short course (as opposed to a chronic course).
Blood vessel	A blood vessel is a part of the circulatory system and function to transport blood throughout the body. The most important types, arteries and veins, are so termed because they carry blood away from or towards the heart, respectively.
Atherosclerosis	Process by which a fatty substance or plaque builds up inside arteries to form obstructions is called atherosclerosis.
Older adult	Older adult is an adult over the age of 65.
Risk factor	A risk factor is a variable associated with an increased risk of disease or infection but risk factors are not necessarily causal.
Value	Value is worth in general, and it is thought to be connected to reasons for certain practices, policies, actions, beliefs or emotions. Value is "that which one acts to gain and/or keep."
Chronic disease	Disease of long duration often not detected in its early stages and from which the patient will not recover is referred to as a chronic disease.
Bypass	In medicine, a bypass generally means an alternate or additional route for blood flow, which is created in bypass surgery, e.g. coronary artery bypass surgery by moving blood vessels or implanting synthetic tubing.
Quality of life	Quality of life refers to the perception of individuals or groups that their needs are being satisfied and that they are not being denied opportunities to achieve happiness and fulfillment.
Lifestyle	The culturally, socially, economically, and environmentally conditioned complex of actions characteristic of an individual, group, or community as a pattern of habituated behavior over

Go to **Cram101.com** for the Practice Tests for this Chapter.

	time that is health related but not necessarily health directed is a lifestyle.
Sodium	Sodium is the chemical element in the periodic table that has the symbol Na (Natrium in Latin) and atomic number 11. Sodium is a soft, waxy, silvery reactive metal belonging to the alkali metals that is abundant in natural compounds (especially halite). It is highly reactive.
Stress	Stress refers to a condition that is a response to factors that change the human systems normal state.
Assess	Assess is to systematically and continuously collect, validate, and communicate patient data.
Oxygen	Oxygen is a chemical element in the periodic table. It has the symbol O and atomic number 8. Oxygen is the second most common element on Earth, composing around 46% of the mass of Earth's crust and 28% of the mass of Earth as a whole, and is the third most common element in the universe.
Organ	Organ refers to a structure consisting of several tissues adapted as a group to perform specific functions.
Capillaries	Capillaries refer to the smallest of the blood vessels and the sites of exchange between the blood and tissue cells.
Capillary	A capillary is the smallest of a body's blood vessels, measuring 5-10 micro meters. They connect arteries and veins, and most closely interact with tissues. Their walls are composed of a single layer of cells, the endothelium. This layer is so thin that molecules such as oxygen, water and lipids can pass through them by diffusion and enter the tissues.
Arteriole	An arteriole is a blood vessel that extends and branches out from an artery and leads to capillaries. They have thick muscular walls and are the primary site of vascular resistance.
Venule	A vessel that conveys blood between a capillary bed and a vein is a venule.
Lungs	Lungs are the essential organs of respiration in air-breathing vertebrates. Their principal function is to transport oxygen from the atmosphere into the bloodstream, and to excrete carbon dioxide from the bloodstream into the atmosphere.
Veins	Blood vessels that return blood toward the heart from the circulation are referred to as veins.
Vein	Vein in animals, is a vessel that returns blood to the heart. In plants, a vascular bundle in a leaf, composed of xylem and phloem.
Ventricle	In the heart, a ventricle is a heart chamber which collects blood from an atrium (another heart chamber) and pumps it out of the heart.
Hormone	A hormone is a chemical messenger from one cell to another. All multicellular organisms produce hormones. The best known hormones are those produced by endocrine glands of vertebrate animals, but hormones are produced by nearly every organ system and tissue type in a human or animal body. Hormone molecules are secreted directly into the bloodstream, they move by circulation or diffusion to their target cells, which may be nearby cells in the same tissue or cells of a distant organ of the body.
Enzyme	An enzyme is a protein that catalyzes, or speeds up, a chemical reaction. They are essential to sustain life because most chemical reactions in biological cells would occur too slowly, or would lead to different products, without them.
Microorganism	A microorganism or microbe is an organism that is so small that it is microscopic (invisible to the naked eye).
Toxin	Toxin refers to a microbial product or component that can injure another cell or organism at

Go to **Cram101.com** for the Practice Tests for this Chapter.

	low concentrations. Often the term refers to a poisonous protein, but toxins may be lipids and other substances.
Atrium	The atrium is the blood collection chamber of a heart. It has a thin-walled structure that allows blood to return to the heart. There is at least one atrium in an animal with a closed circulatory system
Tricuspid valve	The tricuspid valve is on the right side of the heart, between the right atrium and the right ventricle. Being the first valve after the venae cavae, and thus the whole venous system, it is the most common valve to be infected (endocarditis) in IV drug users.
Pulmonary vein	The pulmonary vein carries oxygen rich blood from the lungs to the left atrium of the heart. They are the only veins in the adult human body that carry oxygenated blood.
Left atrium	The left atrium is one of four chambers (two atria and two ventricles) in the human heart. It receives oxygenated blood from the pulmonary veins, and pumps it into the left ventricle.
Left ventricle	The left ventricle is one of four chambers (two atria and two ventricles) in the human heart. It receives oxygenated blood from the left atrium via the mitral valve, and pumps it into the aorta via the aortic valve.
Aorta	The largest artery in the human body, the aorta originates from the left ventricle of the heart and brings oxygenated blood to all parts of the body in the systemic circulation.
Pulmonary artery	The pulmonary artery carrys blood from the heart to the lungs. They are the only arteries (other than umbilical arteries in the fetus) that carry deoxygenated blood.
Right ventricle	The right ventricle is one of four chambers (two atria and two ventricles) in the human heart. It receives de-oxygenated blood from the right atrium via the tricuspid valve, and pumps it into the pulmonary artery via the pulmonary valve.
Aortic valve	The aortic valve lies between the left ventricle and the aorta. The most common congenital abnormality of the heart is the bicuspid aortic valve. In this condition, instead of three cusps, the aortic valve has two cusps.
Mitral valve	The mitral valve, also known as the bicuspid valve, is a valve in the heart that lies between the left atrium (LA) and the left ventricle (LV). The mitral valve and the tricuspid valve are known as the atrioventricular valves because they lie between the atria and the ventricles of the heart.
Anatomy	Anatomy is the branch of biology that deals with the structure and organization of living things. It can be divided into animal anatomy (zootomy) and plant anatomy (phytonomy).
Inferior vena cava	The inferior vena cava is a large vein that carries de-oxygenated blood from the lower half of the body into the heart. It is formed by the left and right common iliac veins and transports blood to the right atrium of the heart.
Carbon	Carbon is a chemical element in the periodic table that has the symbol C and atomic number 6. An abundant nonmetallic, tetravalent element, carbon has several allotropic forms.
Carbon dioxide	Carbon dioxide is an atmospheric gas comprized of one carbon and two oxygen atoms. A very widely known chemical compound, it is frequently called by its formula CO_2. In its solid state, it is commonly known as dry ice.
Arrhythmia	Cardiac arrhythmia is a group of conditions in which muscle contraction of the heart is irregular for any reason.
Cerebrovascular accident	Cerebrovascular accident refers to a sudden stoppage of blood flow to a portion of the brain, leading to a loss of brain function.
Congestive	Congestive heart failure is the inability of the heart to pump a sufficient amount of blood

Go to **Cram101.com** for the Practice Tests for this Chapter.

heart failure	throughout the body, or requiring elevated filling pressures in order to pump effectively.
Cholesterol	Cholesterol is a steroid, a lipid, and an alcohol, found in the cell membranes of all body tissues, and transported in the blood plasma of all animals. It is an important component of the membranes of cells, providing stability; it makes the membrane's fluidity stable over a bigger temperature interval.
Calcium	Calcium is the chemical element in the periodic table that has the symbol Ca and atomic number 20. Calcium is a soft grey alkaline earth metal that is used as a reducing agent in the extraction of thorium, zirconium and uranium. Calcium is also the fifth most abundant element in the Earth's crust.
Fibrin	Fibrin is a protein involved in the clotting of blood. It is a fibrillar protein that is polymerized to form a "mesh" that forms a haemostatic plug or clot (in conjunction with platelets) over a wound site.
Hyperlipidemia	Hyperlipidemia refers to the presence of an abnormally large amount of lipids in the circulating blood.
Lipid	Lipid is one class of aliphatic hydrocarbon-containing organic compounds essential for the structure and function of living cells. They are characterized by being water-insoluble but soluble in nonpolar organic solvents.
Sinoatrial node	Sinoatrial node refers to a small mass of specialized muscle in the wall of the right atrium; generates electrical signals rhythmically and spontaneously and serves as the heart's pacemaker.
Coronary artery disease	Coronary artery disease (CAD) is the end result of the accumulation of atheromatous plaques within the walls of the arteries that supply the myocardium (the muscle of the heart).
Coronary arteries	Arteries that directly supply the heart with blood are referred to as coronary arteries.
Coronary artery	An artery that supplies blood to the wall of the heart is called a coronary artery.
Triglycerides	Triglycerides refer to fats and oils composed of fatty acids and glycerol; are the body's most concentrated source of energy fuel; also known as neutral fats.
Triglyceride	Triglyceride is a glyceride in which the glycerol is esterified with three fatty acids. They are the main constituent of vegetable oil and animal fats and play an important role in metabolism as energy sources. They contain a bit more than twice as much energy as carbohydrates and proteins.
Brain	The part of the central nervous system involved in regulating and controlling body activity and interpreting information from the senses transmitted through the nervous system is referred to as the brain.
Theory	Theory refers to an explanatory statement, or set of statements, that concisely summarizes the state of knowledge on a phenomenon and provides direction for further study.
Endothelium	The endothelium is the layer of thin, flat cells that lines the interior surface of blood vessels, forming an interface between circulating blood in the lumen and the rest of the vessel wall.
Inflammation	Inflammation is the first response of the immune system to infection or irritation and may be referred to as the innate cascade.
Protein	A protein is a complex, high-molecular-weight organic compound that consists of amino acids joined by peptide bonds. They are essential to the structure and function of all living cells and viruses. Many are enzymes or subunits of enzymes.

331

Amino acid	An amino acid is any molecule that contains both amino and carboxylic acid functional groups. They are the basic structural building units of proteins. They form short polymer chains called peptides or polypeptides which in turn form structures called proteins.
Folic acid	Folic acid and folate (the anion form) are forms of a water-soluble B vitamin. These occur naturally in food and can also be taken as supplements.
Acid	An acid is a water-soluble, sour-tasting chemical compound that when dissolved in water, gives a solution with a pH of less than 7.
Blood clot	A blood clot is the final product of the blood coagulation step in hemostasis. It is achieved via the aggregation of platelets that form a platelet plug, and the activation of the humoral coagulation system
Vitamin	An organic compound other than a carbohydrate, lipid, or protein that is needed for normal metabolism but that the body cannot synthesize in adequate amounts is called a vitamin.
Lesion	A lesion is a non-specific term referring to abnormal tissue in the body. It can be caused by any disease process including trauma (physical, chemical, electrical), infection, neoplasm, metabolic and autoimmune.
Pathogen	A pathogen or infectious agent is a biological agent that causes disease or illness to its host. The term is most often used for agents that disrupt the normal physiology of a multicellular animal or plant.
Herpes simplex	Herpes simplex refers to two common types of viruses, herpes simplex virus 1 and herpes simplex virus 2. Herpes simplex virus 2 is responsible for the STD known as genital herpes.
Infection	The invasion and multiplication of microorganisms in body tissues is called an infection.
Chlamydia	A sexually transmitted disease, caused by a bacterium, that causes inflammation of the urethra in males and of the urethra and cervix in females is referred to as chlamydia.
Ulcer	An ulcer is an open sore of the skin, eyes or mucous membrane, often caused by an initial abrasion and generally maintained by an inflammation and/or an infection.
Virus	Obligate intracellular parasite of living cells consisting of an outer capsid and an inner core of nucleic acid is referred to as virus. The term virus usually refers to those particles that infect eukaryotes whilst the term bacteriophage or phage is used to describe those infecting prokaryotes.
Herpes simplex virus	The herpes simplex virus is a virus that manifests itself in two common viral infections, each marked by painful, watery blisters in the skin or mucous membranes (such as the mouth or lips) or on the genitals. The disease is contagious, particularly during an outbreak, and is incurable.
Cytomegalovirus	Cytomegalovirus is a genus of Herpes viruses; in humans the species is known as Human herpesvirus 5 (HHV-5). It belongs to the Betaherpesvirinae subfamily of Herpesviridae. The virus especially attacks salivary glands and may also be devastating or even fatal to fetuses.
Free radicals	Free radicals are atomic or molecular species with unpaired electrons on an otherwise open shell configuration.
Carbohydrate	Carbohydrate is a chemical compound that contains oxygen, hydrogen, and carbon atoms. They consist of monosaccharide sugars of varying chain lengths and that have the general chemical formula $C_n(H_2O)_n$ or are derivatives of such.
Lipoprotein	A lipoprotein is a biochemical assembly that contains both proteins and lipids and may be structural or catalytic in function. They may be enzymes, proton pumps, ion pumps, or some combination of these functions.

Syndrome	Syndrome is the association of several clinically recognizable features, signs, symptoms, phenomena or characteristics which often occur together, so that the presence of one feature alerts the physician to the presence of the others
Insulin	Insulin is a polypeptide hormone that regulates carbohydrate metabolism. Apart from being the primary effector in carbohydrate homeostasis, it also has a substantial effect on small vessel muscle tone, controls storage and release of fat (triglycerides) and cellular uptake of both amino acids and some electrolytes.
Glucose	Glucose, a simple monosaccharide sugar, is one of the most important carbohydrates and is used as a source of energy in animals and plants. Glucose is one of the main products of photosynthesis and starts respiration.
Calorie	Calorie refers to a unit used to measure heat energy and the energy contents of foods.
Diabetes mellitus	Diabetes mellitus is a medical disorder characterized by varying or persistent hyperglycemia (elevated blood sugar levels), especially after eating. All types of diabetes mellitus share similar symptoms and complications at advanced stages.
Endocrinologist	An endocrinologist is a doctor who specializes in treating such disorders, particularly disorders of the pituitary, including growth disorders; diseases of the thyroid gland; of the adrenal glands; and of the ovary and testes; and diabetes, a disorder of insulin secretion or sensitivity.
Thrombosis	Thrombosis is the formation of a clot inside a blood vessel, obstructing the flow of blood through the circulatory system. A cerebral thrombosis can result in stroke.
Thrombus	Blood clot that remains in the blood vessel where it formed is called a thrombus.
Embolus	Embolus refers to any abnormal traveling object in the bloodstream, such as agglutinated bacteria or blood cells, a blood clot, or an air bubble.
Circulatory system	The circulatory system or cardiovascular system is the organ system which circulates blood around the body of most animals.
Adaptation	A biological adaptation is an anatomical structure, physiological process or behavioral trait of an organism that has evolved over a period of time by the process of natural selection such that it increases the expected long-term reproductive success of the organism.
Muscle	Muscle is a contractile form of tissue. It is one of the four major tissue types, the other three being epithelium, connective tissue and nervous tissue. Muscle contraction is used to move parts of the body, as well as to move substances within the body.
Angiogenesis	Angiogenesis is the physiological process involving the growth of new blood vessels from pre-existing vessels.
Fibrillation	Fibrillation is the rapid, irregular, and unsynchronized contraction of the muscle fibers of the heart. There are two major classes of fibrillation, atrial fibrillation and ventricular fibrillation.
Tachycardia	Tachycardia is an abnormally rapid beating of the heart, defined as a resting heart rate of over 100 beats per minute. Common causes are autonomic nervous system or endocrine system activity, hemodynamic responses, and various forms of cardiac arrhythmia.
Ventricular fibrillation	Ventricular fibrillation is a cardiac condition that consists of a lack of coordination of the contraction of the muscle tissue of the large chambers of the heart that eventually leads to the heart stopping altogether.
Young adult	An young adult is someone between the ages of 20 and 40 years old.
Illicit drugs	Illicit drugs refers to drugs whose use, possession, cultivation, manufacture, and/or sale

Go to **Cram101.com** for the Practice Tests for this Chapter.

	are against the law because they are generally recognized as harmful.
Lead	Lead is a chemical element in the periodic table that has the symbol Pb and atomic number 82. A soft, heavy, toxic and malleable poor metal, lead is bluish white when freshly cut but tarnishes to dull gray when exposed to air. Lead is used in building construction, lead-acid batteries, bullets and shot, and is part of solder, pewter, and fusible alloys.
Asthma	Asthma is a complex disease characterized by bronchial hyperresponsiveness (BHR), inflammation, mucus production and intermittent airway obstruction.
Trauma	Trauma refers to a severe physical injury or wound to the body caused by an external force, or a psychological shock having a lasting effect on mental life.
Ischemia	Narrowing of arteries caused by plaque buildup within the arteries is called ischemia.
Channel	Channel, in communications (sometimes called communications channel), refers to the medium used to convey information from a sender (or transmitter) to a receiver.
Atom	An atom is the smallest possible particle of a chemical element that retains its chemical properties.
Arrhythmias	Arrhythmias refers to abnormal heart rhythms which may be too slow, too early, too rapid, or irregular.
Anxiety	Anxiety is a complex combination of the feeling of fear, apprehension and worry often accompanied by physical sensations such as palpitations, chest pain and/or shortness of breath.
Bradycardia	Bradycardia, as applied in adult medicine, is defined as a heart rate of under 60 beats per minute, though it is seldom symptomatic until the rate drops below 50 beat/min.
Nicotine	Nicotine is an organic compound, an alkaloid found naturally throughout the tobacco plant, with a high concentration in the leaves. It is a potent nerve poison and is included in many insecticides. In lower concentrations, the substance is a stimulant and is one of the main factors leading to the pleasure and habit-forming qualities of tobacco smoking.
Pneumonia	Pneumonia is an illness of the lungs and respiratory system in which the microscopic, air-filled sacs (alveoli) responsible for absorbing oxygen from the atmosphere become inflamed and flooded with fluid.
Affect	Affect is the scientific term used to describe a subject's externally displayed mood. This can be assesed by the nurse by observing facial expression, tone of voice, and body language.
Fever	Fever (also known as pyrexia, or a febrile response, and archaically known as ague) is a medical symptom that describes an increase in internal body temperature to levels that are above normal (37°C, 98.6°F).
Rheumatic fever	Rheumatic fever is an inflammatory disease which may develop after a Group A streptococcal infection (such as strep throat or scarlet fever) and can involve the heart, joints, skin, and brain.
Chemotherapy	Chemotherapy is the use of chemical substances to treat disease. In its modern-day use, it refers almost exclusively to cytostatic drugs used to treat cancer.In its non-oncological use, the term may also refer to antibiotics.
Radiation	The emission of electromagnetic waves by all objects warmer than absolute zero is referred to as radiation.
Congestion	In medicine and pathology the term congestion is used to describe excessive accumulation of blood or other fluid in a particular part of the body.
Tissue	A collection of interconnected cells that perform a similar function within an organism is

	called tissue.
Murmurs	Murmurs are produced as a result of turbulent flow of blood, turbulence sufficient to produce audible noise.
Cardiology	Cardiology is the branch of medicine dealing with disorders of the heart and blood vessels. The field is commonly divided in the branches of congenital heart defects, coronary artery disease, heart failure, valvular heart disease and electrophysiology.
Joint	A joint (articulation) is the location at which two bones make contact (articulate). They are constructed to both allow movement and provide mechanical support.
Skin	Skin is an organ of the integumentary system composed of a layer of tissues that protect underlying muscles and organs.
Connective tissue	Connective tissue is any type of biological tissue with an extensive extracellular matrix and often serves to support, bind together, and protect organs.
Aneurysm	An aneurysm is a localized dilation or ballooning of a blood vessel by more than 50% of the diameter of the vessel. Aneurysms most commonly occur in the arteries at the base of the brain and in the aorta (the main artery coming out of the heart) - this is an aortic aneurysm.
Transient ischemic attack	A transient ischemic attack (TIA, often colloquially referred to as "mini stroke") is caused by the temporary disturbance of blood supply to a restricted area of the brain, resulting in brief neurologic dysfunction that usually persists for less than 24 hours.
Antibody	An antibody is a protein used by the immune system to identify and neutralize foreign objects like bacteria and viruses. Each antibody recognizes a specific antigen unique to its target.
Bacteria	The domain that contains procaryotic cells with primarily diacyl glycerol diesters in their membranes and with bacterial rRNA. Bacteria also is a general term for organisms that are composed of procaryotic cells and are not multicellular.
Immune response	The body's defensive reaction to invasion by bacteria, viral agents, or other foreign substances is called immune response.
Floating	Floating is a technique used to advance the IV catheter into the vein, whereby the catheter is inserted halfway into the vein and the tourniquet and needle are removed. The cannula hub is then attached to the infusion tubing and the control clamp on the tubing is slowly opened, floating the catheter into the vein with the infusate.
Paralysis	Paralysis is the complete loss of muscle function for one or more muscle groups. Paralysis may be localized, or generalized, or it may follow a certain pattern.
Eye	An eye is an organ that detects light. Different kinds of light-sensitive organs are found in a variety of creatures. The simplest eyes do nothing but detect whether the surroundings are light or dark, while more complex eyes can distinguish shapes and colors.
Rehabilitation	Rehabilitation is the restoration of lost capabilities, or the treatment aimed at producing it. Also refers to treatment for dependency on psychoactive substances such as alcohol, prescription drugs, and illicit drugs such as cocaine, heroin or amphetamines.
Independence	The condition in which one variable has no effect on another is referred to as independence.
Medicaid	Medicaid in the United States is a program managed by the states and funded jointly by the states and federal government to provide health insurance for individuals and families with low incomes and resources. Medicaid is the largest source of funding for medical and health-related services for people with limited income.
Medicare	Medicare refers to government health insurance for those over sixty-five.

Heart rate	Heart rate is a term used to describe the frequency of the cardiac cycle. It is considered one of the four vital signs. Usually it is calculated as the number of contractions of the heart in one minute and expressed as "beats per minute".
Evaluation	The fifth step of the nursing process where nursing care and the patient's goal achievement are measured is the evaluation.
Saturated fat	Saturated fat is fat that consists of triglycerides containing only fatty acids that have no double bonds between the carbon atoms of the fatty acid chain (hence, they are fully saturated with hydrogen atoms).
Predisposition	Predisposition refers to an inclination or diathesis to respond in a certain way, either inborn or acquired. In abnormal psychology, it is a factor that lowers the ability to withstand stress and inclines the individual toward pathology.
Elimination	Elimination refers to the physiologic excretion of drugs and other substances from the body.
Metabolism	Metabolism is the biochemical modification of chemical compounds in living organisms and cells. This includes the biosynthesis of complex organic molecules (anabolism) and their breakdown (catabolism).
Liver	The liver is an organ in vertebrates, including humans. It plays a major role in metabolism and has a number of functions in the body including drug detoxification, glycogen storage, and plasma protein synthesis. It also produces bile, which is important for digestion.
Ratio	In number and more generally in algebra, a ratio is the linear relationship between two quantities.
Trans fat	Trans fat is an unsaturated fatty acid whose molecules contain trans double bonds between carbon atoms, which makes the molecules less kinked compared with those of 'cis fat'.
Egg	An egg is the zygote, resulting from fertilization of the ovum. It nourishes and protects the embryo.
Obesity	The state of being more than 20 percent above the average weight for a person of one's height is called obesity.
Monounsaturated fats	In nutrition, monounsaturated fats are dietary fats with one double-bonded carbon in the molecule, with all of the others single-bonded carbons.
Course	Pattern of development and change of a disorder over time is a course.
Lifestyle changes	Lifestyle changes are changes to the way a person lives which are often called for when treating chronic disease.
Niacin	Niacin, also known as vitamin B3, is a water-soluble vitamin whose derivatives such as NADH play essential roles in energy metabolism in the living cell and DNA repair. The designation vitamin B3 also includes the amide form, nicotinamide or niacinamide.
Sterol	A sterol, or steroid alcohols are a subgroup of steroids with a hydroxyl group in the 3-position of the A-ring. They are amphipathic lipids synthetized from Acetyl coenzyme A.
Housework	Unpaid work carried on in and around the home such as cooking, cleaning and shopping, is referred to as a housework.
Systolic pressure	The force of blood against the walls of the arteries when the heart contracts to pump blood to the rest of the body is systolic pressure.
Diastolic pressure	Diastolic pressure refers to arterial blood pressure during the diastolic phase of the cardiac cycle.
Hypertension	Hypertension is a medical condition where the blood pressure in the arteries is chronically

elevated. Persistent hypertension is one of the risk factors for strokes, heart attacks, heart failure and arterial aneurysm, and is a leading cause of chronic renal failure.

Isolated systolic hypertension	A condition in older adults in which only the systolic blood pressure is high (systolic at or above 140 mm Hg and diastolic under 90 mm Hg) is isolated systolic hypertension.
Diuretic	A diuretic is any drug that elevates the rate of bodily urine excretion.
Salt	Salt is a term used for ionic compounds composed of positively charged cations and negatively charged anions, so that the product is neutral and without a net charge.
Essential hypertension	Essential hypertension refers to a psychophysiological disorder characterized by high blood pressure that cannot be traced to an organic cause.
Adrenal glands	The adrenal glands are the triangle-shaped endocrine glands that sit atop the kidneys; their name indicates that position. They are chiefly responsible for regulating the stress response through the synthesis of corticosteroids and catecholamines, including cortisol and adrenaline.
Adrenal gland	In mammals, the adrenal gland (also known as suprarenal glands or colloquially as kidney hats) are the triangle-shaped endocrine glands that sit atop the kidneys; their name indicates that position.
Adrenal	In mammals, the adrenal glands are the triangle-shaped endocrine glands that sit atop the kidneys. They are chiefly responsible for regulating the stress response through the synthesis of corticosteroids and catecholamines, including cortisol and adrenaline.
Kidney	The kidney is a bean-shaped excretory organ in vertebrates. Part of the urinary system, the kidneys filter wastes (especially urea) from the blood and excrete them, along with water, as urine.
Tumor	An abnormal mass of cells that forms within otherwise normal tissue is a tumor. This growth can be either malignant or benign
Gland	A gland is an organ in an animal's body that synthesizes a substance for release such as hormones, often into the bloodstream or into cavities inside the body or its outer surface.
Diastolic blood pressure	The pressure present in a large artery when the heart is at the resting phase of the cardiac cycle is called diastolic blood pressure.
Base	The common definition of a base is a chemical compound that absorbs hydronium ions when dissolved in water (a proton acceptor). An alkali is a special example of a base, where in an aqueous environment, hydroxide ions are donated.
Host	Host is an organism that harbors a parasite, mutual partner, or commensal partner; or a cell infected by a virus.
Estrogen	Estrogen is a steroid that functions as the primary female sex hormone. While present in both men and women, they are found in women in significantly higher quantities.
Hormone replacement therapy	Hormone replacement therapy is a system of medical treatment for perimenopausal and postmenopausal women, based on the assumption that it may prevent discomfort and health problems caused by diminished circulating estrogen hormones.
Intervention	Intervention refers to a planned attempt to break through addicts' or abusers' denial and get them into treatment. Interventions most often occur when legal, workplace, health, relationship, or financial problems have become intolerable.
Incidence	In epidemiological studies of a particular disorder, the rate at which new cases occur in a given place at a given time is called incidence.

343

Osteoporosis	Osteoporosis is a disease of bone in which bone mineral density (BMD) is reduced, bone microarchitecture is disrupted, the amount and variety of non-collagenous proteins in bone is changed, and a concomitantly fracture risk is increased.
Menopause	Menopause is the physiological cessation of menstrual cycles associated with advancing age in species that experience such cycles. Menopause is sometimes referred to as change of life or climacteric.
Hot flash	A hot flash is a symptom of menopause and changing hormone levels which typically expresses itself at night as periods of intense heat with sweating and rapid heartbeat and may typically last from two to thirty minutes on each occasion.
Trial	In classical conditioning, any presentation of a stimulus or pair of stimuli is called a trial.
Insomnia	Insomnia is a sleep disorder characterized by an inability to sleep and/or to remain asleep for a reasonable period during the night.
Sexual dysfunction	Sexual dysfunction or sexual malfunction is difficulty during any stage of the sexual act (which includes desire, arousal, orgasm, and resolution) that prevents the individual or couple from enjoying sexual activity.
Embolism	An embolism occurs when an object (the embolus) migrates from one part of the body and causes a blockage of a blood vessel in another part of the body.
Deep vein thrombosis	Deep vein thrombosis is the formation of a blood clot ("thrombus") in a deep vein. It commonly affects the leg veins, such as the femoral vein or the popliteal vein or the deep veins of the pelvis.
Pulmonary embolism	A pulmonary embolism occurs when a blood clot, generally a venous thrombus, becomes dislodged from its site of formation and embolizes to the arterial blood supply of one of the lungs.
Hip	In anatomy, the hip is the bony projection of the femur, known as the greater trochanter, and the overlying muscle and fat.
Colorectal cancer	Colorectal cancer includes cancerous growths in the colon, rectum and appendix. It is the third most common form of cancer and the second leading cause of death among cancers in the Western world.
Electrocardi-gram	An electrocardiogram is a graphic produced by an electrocardiograph, which records the electrical voltage in the heart in the form of a continuous strip graph. It is the prime tool in cardiac electrophysiology, and has a prime function in screening and diagnosis of cardiovascular diseases..
Angiography	Angiography is a medical imaging technique in which an X-Ray picture is taken to visualize the inner opening of blood filled structures, including arteries, veins and the heart chambers.
Catheter	A tubular surgical instrument for withdrawing fluids from a cavity of the body, especially one for introduction into the bladder through the urethra for the withdrawal of urine is referred to as a catheter.
Positron emission tomography	Positron Emission Tomography measures emissions from radioactively labeled chemicals that have been injected into the bloodstream. The greatest benefit is that different compounds can show blood flow and oxygen and glucose metabolism in the tissues of the working brain.
Radioactive tracer	A radioactive tracer is a substance containing a radioactive isotope (radioisotope). They can be used to measure the speed of chemical processes and was developed by George de Hevesy.
Cardiac catheterization	Cardiac catheterization is the insertion of a catheter into a chamber or vessel of the heart. A small incision is made in a vessel in the groin, wrist or neck area (the femoral vessels

or the carotid/jugular vessels), then a guidewire is inserted into the incision and threaded through the vessel into the area of the heart that requires treatment, visualized by fluoroscopy or echocardiogram, and a catheter is then threaded over the guidewire.

Intravenous	Present or occurring within a vein, such as an intravenous blood clot is referred to as intravenous. Introduced directly into a vein, such as an intravenous injection or I.V. drip.
Injection	A method of rapid drug delivery that puts the substance directly in the bloodstream, in a muscle, or under the skin is called injection.
Intravenous injection	The introduction of drugs directly into a vein is an intravenous injection.
Progestin	A progestin is a synthetic progestagen. These particular synthetic hormones are most often used in the production of contraceptives.
Secondary prevention	Psychological counseling, psychotropic medications, and other rehabilitation treatment programs designed to prevent repeat offenses are called secondary prevention.
Computed tomography	Computed tomography is an imaging method employing tomography where digital processing is used to generate a three-dimensional image of the internals of an object from a large series of two-dimensional X-ray images taken around a single axis of rotation.
Magnetic resonance imaging	Magnetic resonance imaging refers to imaging technology that uses magnetism and radio waves to induce hydrogen nuclei in water molecules to emit faint radio signals. A computer creates images of the body from the radio signals.
Opioid	An opioid is any agent that binds to opioid receptors, found principally in the central nervous system and gastrointestinal tract. There are four broad classes of opioids: endogenous opioid peptides, produced in the body; opium alkaloids, such as morphine and codeine; semi-synthetic opioids such as heroin and oxycodone.
Migraine	Migraine is a neurologic disease, of which the most common symptom is an intense and disabling headache. Migraine is the most common type of vascular headache.
Angioplasty	Angioplasty is the mechanical, hydraulic dilation of a narrowed or totally obstructed arterial lumen, generally caused by atheroma (the lesion of atherosclerosis).
Longevity	A long duration of life is referred to as longevity.
Receptor	A receptor is a protein on the cell membrane or within the cytoplasm or cell nucleus that binds to a specific molecule (a ligand), such as a neurotransmitter, hormone, or other substance, and initiates the cellular response to the ligand. Receptor, in immunology, the region of an antibody which shows recognition of an antigen.
Insight	Insight refers to a sudden awareness of the relationships among various elements that had previously appeared to be independent of one another.
Genes	Genes are the units of heredity in living organisms. They are encoded in the organism's genetic material (usually DNA or RNA), and control the development and behavior of the organism.
Troponin	A molecule found in thin filaments of muscle that helps regulate when muscle cells contract is referred to as troponin.
Diagnosis	In medicine, diagnosis is the process of identifying a medical condition or disease by its signs, symptoms, and from the results of various diagnostic procedures.
Magnetic resonance angiography	Magnetic resonance angiography is used to generate pictures of the arteries in order to evaluate them for stenosis (abnormal narrowing) or aneurysms (vessel wall dilatations, at risk of rupture).

Blood clotting	A complex process by which platelets, the protein fibrin, and red blood cells block an irregular surface in or on the body, such as a damaged blood vessel, sealing the wound is referred to as blood clotting.
Intolerance	Intolerance refers to a type of interaction in which two or more drugs produce extremely uncomfortable symptoms.
Activator	Activator (proteomics), is a type of effector that increases the rate of enzyme mediated reactions.
Agent	Agent refers to an epidemiological term referring to the organism or object that transmits a disease from the environment to the host.
Unstable angina	Worsening angina attacks, sudden-onset angina at rest, and angina lasting more than 15 minutes are symptoms of unstable angina or acute coronary syndrome. As these may herald myocardial infarction (a heart attack), they require urgent medical attention and are generally treated quite similarly
Assertiveness	Asking for what one wants while demonstrating respect for others is refered to as assertiveness.
Crisis	A crisis is a temporary state of high anxiety where the persons usual coping mechanisims cease to work. This may have a result of disorganization or possibly personality growth.
Living will	A living will, also called will to live, advance health directive, or advance health care directive, is a specific type of power of attorney or health care proxy or advance directive. It is a legal instrument that usually is witnessed or notarized.
Informed consent	The term used by psychologists to indicate that a person has agreed to participate in research after receiving information about the purposes of the study and the nature of the treatments is informed consent. Even with informed consent, subjects may withdraw from any experiment at any time.
Life support	Life support, in the medical field, refers to a set of therapies for preserving a patient's life when essential body systems are not functioning sufficiently to sustain life unaided.
Advocate	An advocate is one who speaks on behalf of another, especially in a legal context. Implicit in the concept is the notion that the represented lacks the knowledge, skill, ability, or standing to speak for themselves.
Registered Nurse	A Registered Nurse is a professional nurse who often supervises the tasks performed by Licensed Practical Nurses, orderlies, medical assistants and nursing assistants. They provide direct care and make decisions regarding plans of care for individuals and groups of healthy, ill and injured people.
Stress management	Stress management encompasses techniques intended to equip a person with effective coping mechanisms for dealing with psychological stress.
Body mass index	Body mass index refers to a number derived from an individual's weight and height used to estimate body fat. The formula is- weight /height' .
Fiber	Fibers used by man come from a wide variety of sources: Natural fiber include those made out of plants, animal and mineral sources. Natural fibers can be classified according to their origin.
Heredity	Heredity refers to the transmission of genetic information from parent to offspring.
Susceptibility	The degree of resistance of a host to a pathogen is susceptibility.
Stent	In medicine, a stent is either an expandable wire mesh or hollow perforated tube that is inserted into a hollow structure of the body to keep it open.

Go to **Cram101.com** for the Practice Tests for this Chapter.

Wellness	A dimension of health beyond the absence of disease or infirmity, including social, emotional, and spiritual aspects of health is called wellness.
Clinician	A health professional authorized to provide services to people suffering from one or more pathologies is a clinician.
Agency for Health Care Policy and Research	The Agency for Healthcare Research and Quality (AHRQ), formerly known as the Agency for Health Care Policy and Research (AHCPR), supports research designed to improve the outcomes and quality of health care, reduce its costs, address patient safety and medical errors, and broaden access to effective services.

Vaccine	A harmless variant or derivative of a pathogen used to stimulate a host organism's immune system to mount a long-term defense against the pathogen is referred to as vaccine.
Cancer	Cancer is a class of diseases or disorders characterized by uncontrolled division of cells and the ability of these cells to invade other tissues, either by direct growth into adjacent tissue through invasion or by implantation into distant sites by metastasis.
Virus	Obligate intracellular parasite of living cells consisting of an outer capsid and an inner core of nucleic acid is referred to as virus. The term virus usually refers to those particles that infect eukaryotes whilst the term bacteriophage or phage is used to describe those infecting prokaryotes.
Diagnosis	In medicine, diagnosis is the process of identifying a medical condition or disease by its signs, symptoms, and from the results of various diagnostic procedures.
Health	Health is a term that refers to a combination of the absence of illness, the ability to cope with everyday activities, physical fitness, and high quality of life.
Infection	The invasion and multiplication of microorganisms in body tissues is called an infection.
Epidemic	An epidemic is a disease that appears as new cases in a given human population, during a given period, at a rate that substantially exceeds what is "expected", based on recent experience.
HIV	The virus that causes AIDS is HIV (human immunodeficiency virus).
Agent	Agent refers to an epidemiological term referring to the organism or object that transmits a disease from the environment to the host.
Prognosis	Prognosis refers to the prospects for the future or outcome of a disease.
Hepatitis B	Hepatitis B is caused by a doublestranded DNA virus formerly called the 'Dane particle.' The virus is transmitted by body fluids.
Antibiotic	Antibiotic refers to substance such as penicillin or streptomycin that is toxic to microorganisms. Usually a product of a particular microorvanism or plant.
Hepatitis	Hepatitis is a gastroenterological disease, featuring inflammation of the liver. The clinical signs and prognosis, as well as the therapy, depend on the cause.
Obesity	The state of being more than 20 percent above the average weight for a person of one's height is called obesity.
Human papillomavirus	Human papillomavirus is a member of a group of viruses in the genus Papillomavirus that can infect humans and cause changes in cells leading to abnormal tissue growth.
Helicobacter pylori	Helicobacter pylori is a bacterium that infects the mucus lining of the human stomach. This bacterium lives in the human stomach exclusively and is the only known organism that can thrive in that highly acidic environment..
Infectious disease	In medicine, infectious disease or communicable disease is disease caused by a biological agent such as by a virus, bacterium or parasite. This is contrasted to physical causes, such as burns or chemical ones such as through intoxication.
Lymphoma	Lymphoma is any of a variety of cancer that begins in the lymphatic system. In technical terms, lymphoma denotes malignancies of lymphocytes or, more rarely, of histiocytes.
Leukemia	Leukemia refers to a type of cancer of the bloodforming tissues, characterized by an excessive production of white blood cells and an abnormally high number of them in the blood; cancer of the bone marrow cells that produce leukocytes.
Sarcoma	Cancer of the supportive tissues, such as bone, cartilage, and muscle is referred to as

353

sarcoma.

Acute lymphocytic leukemia	Acute lymphocytic leukemia is a cancer of the white blood cells, characterized by the overproduction and continuous multiplication of malignant and immature white blood cells (referred to as lymphoblasts) in the bone marrow.
Kidney	The kidney is a bean-shaped excretory organ in vertebrates. Part of the urinary system, the kidneys filter wastes (especially urea) from the blood and excrete them, along with water, as urine.
Tumor	An abnormal mass of cells that forms within otherwise normal tissue is a tumor. This growth can be either malignant or benign
Acute	In medicine, an acute disease is a disease with either or both of: a rapid onset; and a short course (as opposed to a chronic course).
Culture	Culture, generally refers to patterns of human activity and the symbolic structures that give such activity significance.
Affect	Affect is the scientific term used to describe a subject's externally displayed mood. This can be assesed by the nurse by observing facial expression, tone of voice, and body language.
Value	Value is worth in general, and it is thought to be connected to reasons for certain practices, policies, actions, beliefs or emotions. Value is "that which one acts to gain and/or keep."
Mortality rate	Mortality rate is the number of deaths (from a disease or in general) per 1000 people and typically reported on an annual basis.
Mortality	The incidence of death in a population is mortality.
Prostate	The prostate is a gland that is part of male mammalian sex organs. Its main function is to secrete and store a clear, slightly basic fluid that is part of semen. The prostate differs considerably between species anatomically, chemically and physiologically.
Radiation	The emission of electromagnetic waves by all objects warmer than absolute zero is referred to as radiation.
Lung cancer	Lung cancer is a malignant tumour of the lungs. Most commonly it is bronchogenic carcinoma (about 90%).
Colorectal cancer	Colorectal cancer includes cancerous growths in the colon, rectum and appendix. It is the third most common form of cancer and the second leading cause of death among cancers in the Western world.
Epidemiology	Epidemiology is the study of the distribution and determinants of disease and disorders in human populations, and the use of its knowledge to control health problems.Epidemiology is considered the cornerstone methodology in all of public health research, and is highly regarded in evidence-based clinical medicine for identifying risk factors for disease and determining optimal treatment approaches to clinical practice.
National Cancer Institute	The National Cancer Institute (NCI) is the United States federal government's principal agency for cancer research and training, and the first institute of the present-day National Institutes of Health. The NCI is a federally funded research and development center, one of eight agencies that compose the Public Health Service in the United States Department of Health and Human Services. The Institute coordinates the National Cancer Program.
Risk factor	A risk factor is a variable associated with an increased risk of disease or infection but risk factors are not necessarily causal.
Population	Population refers to all members of a well-defined group of organisms, events, or things.

355

Base	The common definition of a base is a chemical compound that absorbs hydronium ions when dissolved in water (a proton acceptor). An alkali is a special example of a base, where in an aqueous environment, hydroxide ions are donated.
Carcinogen	A carcinogen is any substance or agent that promotes cancer. A carcinogen is often, but not necessarily, a mutagen or teratogen.
Immune system	The immune system is the system of specialized cells and organs that protect an organism from outside biological influences. When the immune system is functioning properly, it protects the body against bacteria and viral infections, destroying cancer cells and foreign substances.
Organ	Organ refers to a structure consisting of several tissues adapted as a group to perform specific functions.
Benign tumor	A benign tumor does not invade neighboring tissues and do not seed metastases, but may locally grow to great size. They usually do not return after surgical removal.
Tissue	A collection of interconnected cells that perform a similar function within an organism is called tissue.
Stroke	A stroke or cerebrovascular accident (CVA) occurs when the blood supply to a part of the brain is suddenly interrupted.
Brain	The part of the central nervous system involved in regulating and controlling body activity and interpreting information from the senses transmitted through the nervous system is referred to as the brain.
Blood	Blood is a circulating tissue composed of fluid plasma and cells. The main function of blood is to supply nutrients (oxygen, glucose) and constitutional elements to tissues and to remove waste products.
Biopsy	Removal of small tissue sample from the body for microscopic examination is called biopsy.
Protrusion	Protrusion is the anterior movement of an object. This term is often applied to the jaw.
Acid	An acid is a water-soluble, sour-tasting chemical compound that when dissolved in water, gives a solution with a pH of less than 7.
DNA	Deoxyribonucleic acid (DNA) is a nucleic acid usually in the form of a double helix that contains the genetic instructions specifying the biological development of all cellular forms of life, and most viruses.
Metabolism	Metabolism is the biochemical modification of chemical compounds in living organisms and cells. This includes the biosynthesis of complex organic molecules (anabolism) and their breakdown (catabolism).
Epidemiologist	A epidemiologist specializes in the scientific study of factors affecting the health and illness of individuals and populations, and serves as the foundation and logic of interventions made in the interest of public health and preventive medicine.
Lifestyle	The culturally, socially, economically, and environmentally conditioned complex of actions characteristic of an individual, group, or community as a pattern of habituated behavior over time that is health related but not necessarily health directed is a lifestyle.
Neoplasm	Neoplasm refers to abnormal growth of cells; often used to mean a tumor.
Theory	Theory refers to an explanatory statement, or set of statements, that concisely summarizes the state of knowledge on a phenomenon and provides direction for further study.
Metastasis	The spread of cancer cells beyond their original site are called metastasis.

Go to **Cram101.com** for the Practice Tests for this Chapter.

357

Reproduction	Biological reproduction is the biological process by which new individual organisms are produced. Reproduction is a fundamental feature of all known life; each individual organism exists as the result of reproduction by an antecedent.
Toxin	Toxin refers to a microbial product or component that can injure another cell or organism at low concentrations. Often the term refers to a poisonous protein, but toxins may be lipids and other substances.
Chromosomes	Physical structures in the cell's nucleus that house the genes. Each human cell has 23 pairs of chromosomes.
Genes	Genes are the units of heredity in living organisms. They are encoded in the organism's genetic material (usually DNA or RNA), and control the development and behavior of the organism.
Stress	Stress refers to a condition that is a response to factors that change the human systems normal state.
Lead	Lead is a chemical element in the periodic table that has the symbol Pb and atomic number 82. A soft, heavy, toxic and malleable poor metal, lead is bluish white when freshly cut but tarnishes to dull gray when exposed to air. Lead is used in building construction, lead-acid batteries, bullets and shot, and is part of solder, pewter, and fusible alloys.
Assess	Assess is to systematically and continuously collect, validate, and communicate patient data.
Course	Pattern of development and change of a disorder over time is a course.
Incidence	In epidemiological studies of a particular disorder, the rate at which new cases occur in a given place at a given time is called incidence.
Outcome	Outcome is the impact of care provided to a patient. They can be positive, such as the ability to walk freely as a result of rehabilitation, or negative, such as the occurrence of bedsores as a result of lack of mobility of a patient.
Esophagus	The esophagus, or gullet is the muscular tube in vertebrates through which ingested food passes from the mouth area to the stomach. Food is passed through the esophagus by using the process of peristalsis.
Pancreas	The pancreas is a retroperitoneal organ that serves two functions: exocrine - it produces pancreatic juice containing digestive enzymes, and endocrine - it produces several important hormones, namely insulin.
Pharynx	The pharynx is the part of the digestive system and respiratory system of many animals immediately behind the mouth and in front of the esophagus.
Bladder	A hollow muscular storage organ for storing urine is a bladder.
Alcohol	Alcohol is a general term, applied to any organic compound in which a hydroxyl group (-OH) is bound to a carbon atom, which in turn is bound to other hydrogen and/or carbon atoms. The general formula for a simple acyclic alcohol is $C_nH_{2n+1}OH$.
Larynx	The larynx is an organ in the neck of mammals involved in protection of the trachea and sound production. The larynx houses the vocal cords, and is situated at the point where the upper tract splits into the trachea and the esophagus.
Variable	A characteristic or aspect in which people, objects, events, or conditions vary is called variable.
Gallbladder	The gallbladder is a pear-shaped organ that stores bile until the body needs it for digestion. It is connected to the liver and the duodenum by the biliary tract.
Endometrium	The endometrium is the inner uterine membrane in mammals which is developed in preparation

359

for the implantation of a fertilized egg upon its arrival into the uterus.

Colon	The colon is the part of the intestine from the cecum to the rectum. Its primary purpose is to extract water from feces.
Endometrial cancer	Endometrial cancer involves cancerous growth of the endometrium (lining of the uterus). It mainly occurs after menopause, and presents with vaginal bleeding. A hysterectomy (surgical removal of the uterus) is generally performed.
Rectum	The rectum is the final straight portion of the large intestine in some mammals, and the gut in others, terminating in the anus.
Liver	The liver is an organ in vertebrates, including humans. It plays a major role in metabolism and has a number of functions in the body including drug detoxification, glycogen storage, and plasma protein synthesis. It also produces bile, which is important for digestion.
Hormone	A hormone is a chemical messenger from one cell to another. All multicellular organisms produce hormones. The best known hormones are those produced by endocrine glands of vertebrate animals, but hormones are produced by nearly every organ system and tissue type in a human or animal body. Hormone molecules are secreted directly into the bloodstream, they move by circulation or diffusion to their target cells, which may be nearby cells in the same tissue or cells of a distant organ of the body.
Predisposition	Predisposition refers to an inclination or diathesis to respond in a certain way, either inborn or acquired. In abnormal psychology, it is a factor that lowers the ability to withstand stress and inclines the individual toward pathology.
Ovaries	Ovaries are egg-producing reproductive organs found in female organisms.
Stomach	The stomach is an organ in the alimentary canal used to digest food. It's primary function is not the absorption of nutrients from digested food; rather, the main job of the stomach is to break down large food molecules into smaller ones, so that they can be absorbed into the blood more easily.
Uterus	The uterus is the major female reproductive organ of most mammals. One end, the cervix, opens into the vagina; the other is connected on both sides to the fallopian tubes. The main function is to accept a fertilized ovum which becomes implanted into the endometrium, and derives nourishment from blood vessels which develop exclusively for this purpose.
Ovary	The primary reproductive organ of a female is called an ovary.
Lungs	Lungs are the essential organs of respiration in air-breathing vertebrates. Their principal function is to transport oxygen from the atmosphere into the bloodstream, and to excrete carbon dioxide from the bloodstream into the atmosphere.
Eye	An eye is an organ that detects light. Different kinds of light-sensitive organs are found in a variety of creatures. The simplest eyes do nothing but detect whether the surroundings are light or dark, while more complex eyes can distinguish shapes and colors.
Genome	In biology the genome of an organism is the whole hereditary information of an organism that is encoded in the DNA (or, for some viruses, RNA). This includes both the genes and the non-coding sequences.
Heredity	Heredity refers to the transmission of genetic information from parent to offspring.
Cervical cancer	Cervical cancer is a malignancy of the cervix. Worldwide, it is the second most common cancer of women.
Childbirth	Childbirth (also called labour, birth, partus or parturition) is the culmination of a human pregnancy with the emergence of a newborn infant from its mother's uterus.

Menopause	Menopause is the physiological cessation of menstrual cycles associated with advancing age in species that experience such cycles. Menopause is sometimes referred to as change of life or climacteric.
Menarche	Menarche is the first menstrual period as a girl's body progresses through the changes of puberty. Menarche usually occurs about two years after the first changes of breast development.
Parity	Parity is defined as the number of pregnancies that a woman delivers past 24 weeks. A grandmultiparous woman is a woman who has delivered four or more infants who have achieved a gestational age of 24 weeks or more.
Estrogen	Estrogen is a steroid that functions as the primary female sex hormone. While present in both men and women, they are found in women in significantly higher quantities.
Hormone replacement therapy	Hormone replacement therapy is a system of medical treatment for perimenopausal and postmenopausal women, based on the assumption that it may prevent discomfort and health problems caused by diminished circulating estrogen hormones.
Insulation	The practice of managing our role performances so that role partners cannot observe our behavior in two or more conflicting roles is referred to as an insulation.
Benzene	Benzene is an organic chemical compound that is a colorless and flammable liquid with a pleasant, sweet smell. Benzene is a known carcinogen. It is a minor, or additive, component of gasoline. It is an important industrial solvent and precursor in the production of drugs, plastics, gasoline, synthetic rubber, and dyes.
Arsenic	Arsenic is a chemical element in the periodic table that has the symbol As and atomic number 33. This is a notoriously poisonous metalloid that has many allotropic forms; yellow, black and grey are a few that are regularly seen. Arsenic and its compounds are used as pesticides, herbicides, insecticides and various alloys.
Nickel	Nickel is a metallic chemical element in the periodic table that has the symbol Ni and atomic number 28. Notable characteristicsNickel is a silvery white metal that takes on a high polish. It belongs to the iron group, and is hard, malleable, and ductile. It occurs combined with sulfur in millerite, with arsenic in the mineral niccolite, and with arsenic and sulfur in nickel glance.
Inhalant	Inhalant refers to any substance that is vaporized, misted, or gaseous that is inhaled and absorbed through the capillaries in the alveoli of the lungs.
Radon	Radon refers to a radioactive gas that is formed by the disintegration of radium, radon is one of the heaviest gases and is considered to be a health hazard.
Ionizing radiation	Ionizing radiation is a type of particle radiation in which an individual particle carries enough energy to ionize an atom or molecule. If the individual particles do not carry this amount of energy, it is essentially impossible for even a large flood of particles to cause ionization.
Radiotherapy	Radiotherapy is the medical use of ionising radiation as part of cancer treatment to control malignant cells (not to be confused with radiology, the use of radiation in medical imaging and diagnosis).
Bone marrow	Bone marrow is the tissue comprising the center of large bones. It is the place where new blood cells are produced. Bone marrow contains two types of stem cells: hemopoietic (which can produce blood cells) and stromal (which can produce fat, cartilage and bone).
Uranium	When refined, uranium is a silvery white, weakly radioactive metal, which is slightly softer than steel. It is malleable, ductile, and slightly paramagnetic. Uranium metal has very high density, 65% more dense than lead, but slightly less dense than gold. When finely divided, it

can react with cold water; in air, uranium metal becomes coated with uranium oxide.

Thyroid	The thyroid is one of the larger endocrine glands in the body. It is located in the neck and produces hormones, principally thyroxine and triiodothyronine, that regulate the rate of metabolism and affect the growth and rate of function of many other systems in the body.
Alcoholic	An alcoholic is dependent on alcohol as characterized by craving, loss of control, physical dependence and withdrawal symptoms, and tolerance.
Susceptibility	The degree of resistance of a host to a pathogen is susceptibility.
Solution	Solution refers to homogenous mixture formed when a solute is dissolved in a solvent.
Depression	In everyday language depression refers to any downturn in mood, which may be relatively transitory and perhaps due to something trivial. This is differentiated from Clinical depression which is marked by symptoms that last two weeks or more and are so severe that they interfere with daily living.
Nitrate	Nitrate refers to a salt of nitric acid; a compound containing the radical NO_3; biologically, the final form of nitrogen from the oxidation of organic nitrogen compounds.
Sodium	Sodium is the chemical element in the periodic table that has the symbol Na (Natrium in Latin) and atomic number 11. Sodium is a soft, waxy, silvery reactive metal belonging to the alkali metals that is abundant in natural compounds (especially halite). It is highly reactive.
Botulism	Botulism is a rare but serious paralytic illness caused by a nerve toxin, botulin, that is produced by the bacterium Clostridium botulinum.
Bacteria	The domain that contains procaryotic cells with primarily diacyl glycerol diesters in their membranes and with bacterial rRNA. Bacteria also is a general term for organisms that are composed of procaryotic cells and are not multicellular.
Herbicide	Herbicide refers to a chemical substance that kills plants.
Residue	A residue refers to a portion of a larger molecule, a specific monomer of a polysaccharide, protein or nucleic acid.
Genital warts	A sexually transmitted disease, caused by a virus, that forms growths or bumps on the external genitalia, in or around the vagina or anus, or on the cervix in females or penis, scrotum, groin, or thigh in males are called genital warts.
Wart	A wart is a generally small, rough, cauliflower-like growth, of viral origin, typically on hands and feet.
Human papilloma virus	Human papilloma virus is a member of a group of viruses in the genus Papillomavirus that can infect humans and cause changes in cells leading to abnormal tissue growth.
Ulcer	An ulcer is an open sore of the skin, eyes or mucous membrane, often caused by an initial abrasion and generally maintained by an inflammation and/or an infection.
Viral	Viral phenomena are objects or patterns able to replicate themselves or convert other objects into copies of themselves when these objects are exposed to them.
Miscarriage	Miscarriage or spontaneous abortion is the natural or accidental termination of a pregnancy at a stage where the embryo or the fetus is incapable of surviving, generally defined at a gestation of prior to 20 weeks.
Diethylstilb-strol	Diethylstilbestrol is a drug, a synthetic estrogen that was developed to supplement a woman's natural estrogen production. First prescribed by physicians in 1938 for women who experienced miscarriages or premature deliveries, it was originally considered effective and safe for both the pregnant woman and the developing baby.

365

Chemotherapy	Chemotherapy is the use of chemical substances to treat disease. In its modern-day use, it refers almost exclusively to cytostatic drugs used to treat cancer.In its non-oncological use, the term may also refer to antibiotics.
Body cavity	A fluid-containing space between the digestive tract and the body wall is referred to as body cavity.
Muscle	Muscle is a contractile form of tissue. It is one of the four major tissue types, the other three being epithelium, connective tissue and nervous tissue. Muscle contraction is used to move parts of the body, as well as to move substances within the body.
Connective tissue	Connective tissue is any type of biological tissue with an extensive extracellular matrix and often serves to support, bind together, and protect organs.
Lymphatic system	Lymph originates as blood plasma lost from the circulatory system, which leaks out into the surrounding tissues. The lymphatic system collects this fluid by diffusion into lymph capillaries, and returns it to the circulatory system.
Spleen	The spleen is a ductless, vertebrate gland that is not necessary for life but is closely associated with the circulatory system, where it functions in the destruction of old red blood cells and removal of other debris from the bloodstream, and also in holding a reservoir of blood.
White blood cell	The white blood cell is a a component of blood. They help to defend the body against infectious disease and foreign materials as part of the immune system.
Carcinoma	Cancer that originates in the coverings of the body, such as the skin or the lining of the intestinal tract is a carcinoma.
Oral cavity	The mouth, also known as the buccal cavity or the oral cavity, is the opening through which an animal or human takes in food and water. It is usually located in the head, but not always; the mouth of a planarium is in the middle of its belly.
Melanoma	Melanoma is a malignant tumor of melanocytes. Melanocytes predominantly occur in the skin but can be found elsewhere, especially the eye. The vast majority of melanomas originate in the skin.
Skin	Skin is an organ of the integumentary system composed of a layer of tissues that protect underlying muscles and organs.
Bronchus	A bronchus is a caliber of airway in the respiratory tract that conducts air into the lungs. No gas exchange takes place in this part of the lungs.
Urinary bladder	In the anatomy of mammals, the urinary bladder is the organ that collects urine excreted by the kidneys prior to disposal by urination. Urine enters the bladder via the ureters and exits via the urethra.
Bronchitis	Bronchitis is an obstructive pulmonary disease characterized by inflammation of the bronchi of the lungs.
Pneumonia	Pneumonia is an illness of the lungs and respiratory system in which the microscopic, air-filled sacs (alveoli) responsible for absorbing oxygen from the atmosphere become inflamed and flooded with fluid.
Sputum	The mucous secretion from the lungs, bronchi, and trachea that is ejected through the mouth is sputum.
Pain	Pain is an unpleasant sensation which may be associated with actual or potential tissue damage and which may have physical and emotional components.
Radiation	Treatment for cancer in which parts of the body that have cancerous tumors are exposed to

Go to **Cram101.com** for the Practice Tests for this Chapter.

367

therapy	high-energy radiation to disrupt cell division of the cancer cells is called radiation therapy.
Ratio	In number and more generally in algebra, a ratio is the linear relationship between two quantities.
Mammography	Mammography is the process of using low-dose X-rays (usually around 0.7 mSv) to examine the human breast. It is used to look for different types of tumors and cysts.
Assessment	In clinical practice, the process by which a mental health professional gathers and compiles information about a client for the purpose of describing the person's problems or disorder and developing a plan of treatment is an assessment.
Lymph node	A lymph node acts as a filter, with an internal honeycomb of connective tissue filled with lymphocytes that collect and destroy bacteria and viruses. When the body is fighting an infection, these lymphocytes multiply rapidly and produce a characteristic swelling of the lymph node.
Lymph	Lymph originates as blood plasma lost from the circulatory system, which leaks out into the surrounding tissues. The lymphatic system collects this fluid by diffusion into lymph capillaries, and returns it to the circulatory system.
Saturated fat	Saturated fat is fat that consists of triglycerides containing only fatty acids that have no double bonds between the carbon atoms of the fatty acid chain (hence, they are fully saturated with hydrogen atoms).
Hyperplasia	Hyperplasia is a general term for an increase in the number of the cells of an organ or tissue causing it to increase in size.
Progestin	A progestin is a synthetic progestagen. These particular synthetic hormones are most often used in the production of contraceptives.
Clavicle	In human anatomy, the clavicle or collar bone is a bone that makes up part of the shoulder girdle (pectoral girdle). It is a doubly-curved long bone that connects the arm (upper limb) to the body (trunk), located directly above the first rib.
Hip	In anatomy, the hip is the bony projection of the femur, known as the greater trochanter, and the overlying muscle and fat.
Menstruation	Loss of blood and tissue from the uterine lining at the end of a female reproductive cycle are referred to as menstruation.
Progesterone	Progesterone is a C-21 steroid hormone involved in the female menstrual cycle, pregnancy (supports gestation) and embryogenesis of humans and other species.
Menstrual cycle	The menstrual cycle is the set of recurring physiological changes in a female's body that are under the control of the reproductive hormone system and necessary for reproduction. Besides humans, only other great apes exhibit menstrual cycles, in contrast to the estrus cycle of most mammalian species.
Sigmoidoscopy	Sigmoidoscopy is the minimally invasive medical examination of the large intestine from the rectum through the last part of the colon.
Colonoscopy	Direct visual examination of the large intestine using a lighted, flexible tube is referred to as colonoscopy.
Antigen	An antigen is a substance that stimulates an immune response, especially the production of antibodies. They are usually proteins or polysaccharides, but can be any type of molecule, including small molecules (haptens) coupled to a protein (carrier).
Barium	Barium is a chemical element in the periodic table that has the symbol Ba and atomic number

Go to **Cram101.com** for the Practice Tests for this Chapter.

369

56. A soft silvery metallic element, barium is an alkaline earth metal and melts at a very high temperature. Its oxide is historically known as baryta but is never found in nature in its pure form due to its reactivity with air.

Enema	An enema (plural enemata or enemas) is the procedure of introducing liquids into the rectum and colon via the anus.
Lumpectomy	Lumpectomy is a common surgical procedure designed to remove a discrete lump (usually a tumour, benign or otherwise) from an affected woman's breast.
Mastectomy	Surgical removal of a breast. Radical mastectomy involves removal of the breast, muscle tissue, and lymph nodes in the armpit. Simple mastectomy involves removal of the breast only.
Stool	Stool is the waste matter discharged in a bowel movement.
Colostomy	A colostomy is a surgical procedure that involves connecting a part of the colon onto the anterior abdominal wall, leaving the patient with an opening on the abdomen called a stoma. This opening is formed from the end of the large intestine drawn out through the incision and sutured to the skin.
Referred pain	Referred pain is an unpleasant senzation localised to an area separate from the site of the causative injury or other painful stimulation. Often, referred pain arises when a nerve is compressed or damaged at or near its origin.
Urethra	In anatomy, the urethra is a tube which connects the urinary bladder to the outside of the body. The urethra has an excretory function in both sexes, to pass urine to the outside, and also a reproductive function in the male, as a passage for sperm.
Urine	Concentrated filtrate produced by the kidneys and excreted via the bladder is called urine.
Sperm	Sperm refers to the male sex cell with three distinct parts at maturity: head, middle piece, and tail.
Gland	A gland is an organ in an animal's body that synthesizes a substance for release such as hormones, often into the bloodstream or into cavities inside the body or its outer surface.
Seminal fluid	Semen is composed of sperm and seminal fluid. About 10-30% of the seminal fluid is produced by the prostate gland, the rest is produced by the two seminal vesicles.
Reproductive system	A reproductive system is the ensembles and interactions of organs and or substances within an organism that stricly pertain to reproduction. As an example, this would include in the case of female mammals, the hormone estrogen, the womb and eggs but not the breast.
Orgasm	Orgasm refers to rhythmic contractions of the reproductive structures, accompanied by extreme pleasure, at the peak of sexual excitement in both sexes; includes ejaculation by the male.
Penis	The penis is the male reproductive organ and for mammals additionally serves as the external male organ of urination.
Semen	Semen is a fluid that contains spermatozoa. It is secreted by the gonads (sexual glands) of male or hermaphroditic animals including humans for fertilization of female ova. Semen discharged by an animal or human is known as ejaculate, and the process of discharge is called ejaculation.
Inflammation	Inflammation is the first response of the immune system to infection or irritation and may be referred to as the innate cascade.
Urination	Urination is the process of disposing urine from the urinary bladder through the urethra to the outside of the body. The process of urination is usually under voluntary control.
Pelvis	The pelvis is the bony structure located at the base of the spine (properly known as the caudal end). The pelvis incorporates the socket portion of the hip joint for each leg (in

bipeds) or hind leg (in quadrupeds). It forms the lower limb (or hind-limb) girdle of the skeleton.

Asymptomatic	A disease is asymptomatic when it is at a stage where the patient does not experience symptoms. By their nature, asymptomatic diseases are not usually discovered until the patient undergoes medical tests (X-rays or other investigations). Some diseases remain asymptomatic for a remarkably long time, including some forms of cancer.
False negative	A false negative, also called a Type II error or miss, exists when a test incorrectly reports that a result was not detected, when it was really present.
Hypertrophy	Hypertrophy is the increase of the size of an organ. It should be distinguished from hyperplasia which occurs due to cell division; hypertrophy occurs due to an increase in cell size rather than division. It is most commonly seen in muscle that has been actively stimulated, the most well-known method being exercise.
Herbal preparations	Substances of plant origin that are believed to have medicinal properties are called herbal preparations.
Ultrasound	Ultrasound is sound with a frequency greater than the upper limit of human hearing, approximately 20 kilohertz. Medical use can visualise muscle and soft tissue, making them useful for scanning the organs, and obstetric ultrasonography is commonly used during pregnancy.
Calcium	Calcium is the chemical element in the periodic table that has the symbol Ca and atomic number 20. Calcium is a soft grey alkaline earth metal that is used as a reducing agent in the extraction of thorium, zirconium and uranium. Calcium is also the fifth most abundant element in the Earth's crust.
Selenium	Selenium is a chemical element in the periodic table that has the symbol Se and atomic number 34. It is a toxic nonmetal that is chemically related to sulfur and tellurium. It occurs in several different forms but one of these is a stable gray metallike form that conducts electricity better in the light than in the dark and is used in photocells.
Vitamin	An organic compound other than a carbohydrate, lipid, or protein that is needed for normal metabolism but that the body cannot synthesize in adequate amounts is called a vitamin.
Vasectomy	Vasectomy refers to surgical removal of a section of the two sperm ducts to prevent sperm from reaching the urethra; a means of sterilization in the male.
Squamous cell carcinoma	In medicine, squamous cell carcinoma is a form of cancer of the carcinoma type that may occur in many different organs, including the skin, the esophagus, the lungs, and the cervix.
Basal cell carcinoma	Basal cell carcinoma refers to the most common form of skin cancer that forms in the innermost skin layer.
International unit	International unit refers to a crude measure of vitamin activity, often based on the growth rate of animals. Today these units have generally been replaced by precise measurement of actual quantities in milligrams or micrograms.
Cataract	Opaqueness of the lens of the eye, making the lens incapable of transmitting light is called a cataract.
Melanocyte	Melanocyte cells are located in the bottom layer of the skin's epidermis. With a process called melanogenesis, they produce melanin, a pigment in the skin, eyes, and hair.
Collagen	Collagen is the main protein of connective tissue in animals and the most abundant protein in mammals, making up about 1/4 of the total. It is one of the long, fibrous structural proteins whose functions are quite different from those of globular proteins such as enzymes.
Ozone	Ozone (O_3) is an allotrope of oxygen, the molecule consisting of three oxygen atoms, a

triatomic molecule, instead of the more stable diatomic O_2. Ozone is a powerful oxidizing agent. It is also unstable, decaying to ordinary oxygen through the reaction: $2O_3 \rightarrow 3O_2$.

Ibuprofen	A nonopiate pain reliever that controls pain, fever, and inflammation is referred to as ibuprofen.
Malaise	Malaise is a term used to refer to a general state of discomfort, tiredness, or illness. It is a symptom of many illnesses.
Freezing	Freezing is the process in which blood is frozen and all of the plasma and 99% of the WBCs are eliminated when thawing takes place and the nontransferable cryoprotectant is removed.
Young adult	An young adult is someone between the ages of 20 and 40 years old.
Longitudinal study	Longitudinal study refers to a type of developmental study in which the same group of participants is followed and measured at different ages.
Rotation	Movement turning a body part on its longitudinal axis is rotation.
Genitalia	The Latin term genitalia is used to describe the sex organs, and in the English language this term and genital area are most often used to describe the externally visible sex organs or external genitalia: in males the penis and scrotum, in females the vulva.
Retina	The retina is a thin layer of cells at the back of the eyeball of vertebrates and some cephalopods; it is the part of the eye which converts light into nervous signals.
Dermatology	Dermatology is a branch of medicine dealing with the skin and its appendages (hair, nails, sweat glands etc). A medical doctor who specializes in dermatology is a dermatologist. The surgical practice of dermatology is dermasurgery.
Urticaria	Urticaria or hives is a relatively common form of allergic reaction that causes raized red skin welts. Urticaria is also known as nettle rash or uredo. These welts can range in diameter from 5 mm (0.2 inches) or more, itch severely, and often have a pale border.
Medicine	Medicine is the branch of health science and the sector of public life concerned with maintaining or restoring human health through the study, diagnosis and treatment of disease and injury.
Scrotum	In some male mammals the scrotum is an external bag of skin and muscle containing the testicles. It is an extension of the abdomen, and is located between the penis and anus.
Epididymis	The epididymis is part of the human male reproductive system and is present in all male mammals. It is a narrow, tightly-coiled tube connecting the efferent ducts from the rear of each testicle to its vas deferens.
Abdomen	The abdomen is a part of the body. In humans, and in many other vertebrates, it is the region between the thorax and the pelvis. In fully developed insects, the abdomen is the third (or posterior) segment, after the head and thorax.
Evaluation	The fifth step of the nursing process where nursing care and the patient's goal achievement are measured is the evaluation.
Syndrome	Syndrome is the association of several clinically recognizable features, signs, symptoms, phenomena or characteristics which often occur together, so that the presence of one feature alerts the physician to the presence of the others
Mutation	A change in the structure of a gene is called a mutation.
Fiber	Fibers used by man come from a wide variety of sources: Natural fiber include those made out of plants, animal and mineral sources. Natural fibers can be classified according to their origin.

Cervix	The cervix is actually the lower, narrow portion of the uterus where it joins with the top end of the vagina. It is cylindrical or conical in shape and protrudes through the upper anterior vaginal wall.
Fallopian tube	The Fallopian tube is one of two very fine tubes leading from the ovaries of female mammals into the uterus. They deliver the ovum to the uterus.
Chronic leukemia	Chronic leukemia is distinguished by the excessive buildup of relatively mature, but still abnormal, blood cells. Typically taking months to years to progress, the cells are produced at a much higher rate than normal cells, resulting in many abnormal white blood cells in the blood.
Living will	A living will, also called will to live, advance health directive, or advance health care directive, is a specific type of power of attorney or health care proxy or advance directive. It is a legal instrument that usually is witnessed or notarized.
Atom	An atom is the smallest possible particle of a chemical element that retains its chemical properties.
Magnetic resonance imaging	Magnetic resonance imaging refers to imaging technology that uses magnetism and radio waves to induce hydrogen nuclei in water molecules to emit faint radio signals. A computer creates images of the body from the radio signals.
Computerized axial tomography	Computerized axial tomography is a medical imaging method employing tomography where digital processing is used to generate a three-dimensional image of the internals of an object from a large series of two-dimensional X-ray images taken around a single axis of rotation.
Dietary fiber	Dietary fiber is the indigestible portion of plant foods that move food through the digestive system and absorb water.
Heart attack	A heart attack, is a serious, sudden heart condition usually characterized by varying degrees of chest pain or discomfort, weakness, sweating, nausea, vomiting, and arrhythmias, sometimes causing loss of consciousness. It occurs when the blood supply to a part of the heart is interrupted, causing death and scarring of the local heart tissue.
Cholesterol	Cholesterol is a steroid, a lipid, and an alcohol, found in the cell membranes of all body tissues, and transported in the blood plasma of all animals. It is an important component of the membranes of cells, providing stability; it makes the membrane's fluidity stable over a bigger temperature interval.
Blood clot	A blood clot is the final product of the blood coagulation step in hemostasis. It is achieved via the aggregation of platelets that form a platelet plug, and the activation of the humoral coagulation system
Insulin	Insulin is a polypeptide hormone that regulates carbohydrate metabolism. Apart from being the primary effector in carbohydrate homeostasis, it also has a substantial effect on small vessel muscle tone, controls storage and release of fat (triglycerides) and cellular uptake of both amino acids and some electrolytes.
Sugar	A sugar is the simplest molecule that can be identified as a carbohydrate. These include monosaccharides and disaccharides, trisaccharides and the oligosaccharides. The term "glyco-" indicates the presence of a sugar in an otherwise non-carbohydrate substance.
Adenoma	Adenoma refers to a collection of growths of glandular origin. They can grow from many organs including the colon, adrenal, pituitary, thyroid, etc. These growths are benign, but some are known to have the potential, over time, to transform to malignancy
Antibody	An antibody is a protein used by the immune system to identify and neutralize foreign objects like bacteria and viruses. Each antibody recognizes a specific antigen unique to its target.

Go to **Cram101.com** for the Practice Tests for this Chapter.

377

Monoclonal antibodies	Monoclonal antibodies are antibodies that are identical because they were produced by one type of immune cell, all clones of a single parent cell.
Resistance	Resistance refers to a nonspecific ability to ward off infection or disease regardless of whether the body has been previously exposed to it. A force that opposes the flow of a fluid such as air or blood. Compare with immunity.
Cardiovascular system	The circulatory system or cardiovascular system is the organ system which circulates blood around the body of most animals.
Interferon	Interferon is a natural protein produced by the cells of the immune systems of most animals in response to challenges by foreign agents such as viruses, bacteria, parasites and tumor cells. They belong to the large class of glycoproteins known as cytokines.
Protein	A protein is a complex, high-molecular-weight organic compound that consists of amino acids joined by peptide bonds. They are essential to the structure and function of all living cells and viruses. Many are enzymes or subunits of enzymes.
Measles	Measles refers to a highly contagious skin disease that is endemic throughout the world. It is caused by a morbilli virus in the family Paramyxoviridae, which enters the body through the respiratory tract or through the conjunctiva.
Trial	In classical conditioning, any presentation of a stimulus or pair of stimuli is called a trial.
Immune response	The body's defensive reaction to invasion by bacteria, viral agents, or other foreign substances is called immune response.
Angiogenesis	Angiogenesis is the physiological process involving the growth of new blood vessels from pre-existing vessels.
Blood vessel	A blood vessel is a part of the circulatory system and function to transport blood throughout the body. The most important types, arteries and veins, are so termed because they carry blood away from or towards the heart, respectively.
Oxygen	Oxygen is a chemical element in the periodic table. It has the symbol O and atomic number 8. Oxygen is the second most common element on Earth, composing around 46% of the mass of Earth's crust and 28% of the mass of Earth as a whole, and is the third most common element in the universe.
Enzyme	An enzyme is a protein that catalyzes, or speeds up, a chemical reaction. They are essential to sustain life because most chemical reactions in biological cells would occur too slowly, or would lead to different products, without them.
Inhibitor	An inhibitor is a type of effector (biology) that decreases or prevents the rate of a chemical reaction. They are often called negative catalysts.
Enzyme inhibitor	A chemical that interferes with an enzyme's activity is called enzyme inhibitor.
Anxiety	Anxiety is a complex combination of the feeling of fear, apprehension and worry often accompanied by physical sensations such as palpitations, chest pain and/or shortness of breath.
Anger	Anger is an emotional response often based on a sensation or perception of threat to one's needs.
Inspiration	Inspiration begins with the onset of contraction of the diaphragm, which results in expansion of the intrapleural space and an increase in negative pressure according to Boyle's Law.
Pathogen	A pathogen or infectious agent is a biological agent that causes disease or illness to its host. The term is most often used for agents that disrupt the normal physiology of a

Go to **Cram101.com** for the Practice Tests for this Chapter.

multicellular animal or plant.

Go to **Cram101.com** for the Practice Tests for this Chapter.

Public health	Public health is concerned with threats to the overall health of a community based on population health analysis.
Infection	The invasion and multiplication of microorganisms in body tissues is called an infection.
Condom	Sheath used to cover the penis during sexual intercourse is referred to as condom.
Health	Health is a term that refers to a combination of the absence of illness, the ability to cope with everyday activities, physical fitness, and high quality of life.
Viral	Viral phenomena are objects or patterns able to replicate themselves or convert other objects into copies of themselves when these objects are exposed to them.
Pain	Pain is an unpleasant sensation which may be associated with actual or potential tissue damage and which may have physical and emotional components.
Gonorrhea	Gonorrhea refers to an acute infectious sexually transmitted disease of the mucous membranes of the genitourinary tract, eye, rectum, and throat. It is caused by Neisseria gonorrhoeae.
Bacteria	The domain that contains procaryotic cells with primarily diacyl glycerol diesters in their membranes and with bacterial rRNA. Bacteria also is a general term for organisms that are composed of procaryotic cells and are not multicellular.
Sexually transmitted disease	Infection transmitted from one individual to another by direct contact during sexual activity is referred to as a sexually transmitted disease.
Microorganism	A microorganism or microbe is an organism that is so small that it is microscopic (invisible to the naked eye).
Exogenous	Exogenous refers to an action or object coming from outside a system.
Pathogen	A pathogen or infectious agent is a biological agent that causes disease or illness to its host. The term is most often used for agents that disrupt the normal physiology of a multicellular animal or plant.
Immune system	The immune system is the system of specialized cells and organs that protect an organism from outside biological influences. When the immune system is functioning properly, it protects the body against bacteria and viral infections, destroying cancer cells and foreign substances.
Virus	Obligate intracellular parasite of living cells consisting of an outer capsid and an inner core of nucleic acid is referred to as virus. The term virus usually refers to those particles that infect eukaryotes whilst the term bacteriophage or phage is used to describe those infecting prokaryotes.
Susceptibility	The degree of resistance of a host to a pathogen is susceptibility.
Multifactorial disease	Disease caused by interactions of several factors is called multifactorial disease.
Risk factor	A risk factor is a variable associated with an increased risk of disease or infection but risk factors are not necessarily causal.
Cancer	Cancer is a class of diseases or disorders characterized by uncontrolled division of cells and the ability of these cells to invade other tissues, either by direct growth into adjacent tissue through invasion or by implantation into distant sites by metastasis.
Chronic disease	Disease of long duration often not detected in its early stages and from which the patient will not recover is referred to as a chronic disease.
Population	Population refers to all members of a well-defined group of organisms, events, or things.

383

Epidemic	An epidemic is a disease that appears as new cases in a given human population, during a given period, at a rate that substantially exceeds what is "expected", based on recent experience.
Infectious disease	In medicine, infectious disease or communicable disease is disease caused by a biological agent such as by a virus, bacterium or parasite. This is contrasted to physical causes, such as burns or chemical ones such as through intoxication.
Tuberculosis	Tuberculosis is an infection caused by the bacterium Mycobacterium tuberculosis, which most commonly affects the lungs but can also affect the central nervous system, lymphatic system, circulatory system, genitourinary system, bones and joints.
Influenza	Influenza or flu refers to an acute viral infection of the respiratory tract, occurring in isolated cases, epidemics, and pandemics. Influenza is caused by three strains of influenza virus, labeled types A, B, and C, based on the antigens of their protein coats.
Pandemic	Pandemic refers to an increase in the occurrence of a disease within a large and geographically widespread population .
Cholera	Cholera is a water-borne disease caused by the bacterium Vibrio cholerae, which are typically ingested by drinking contaminated water, or by eating improperly cooked fish, especially shellfish.
Pasteurization	The process of heating milk and other liquids to destroy microorganisms that can cause spoilage or disease is called pasteurization.
Antibiotic	Antibiotic refers to substance such as penicillin or streptomycin that is toxic to microorganisms. Usually a product of a particular microorvanism or plant.
Vaccine	A harmless variant or derivative of a pathogen used to stimulate a host organism's immune system to mount a long-term defense against the pathogen is referred to as vaccine.
Resistance	Resistance refers to a nonspecific ability to ward off infection or disease regardless of whether the body has been previously exposed to it. A force that opposes the flow of a fluid such as air or blood. Compare with immunity.
Endogenous	Originating internally, such as the endogenous cholesterol synthesized in the body in contrast to the exogenous cholesterol coming from the diet is referred to as endogenous. Compare with exogenous.
Host	Host is an organism that harbors a parasite, mutual partner, or commensal partner; or a cell infected by a virus.
Affect	Affect is the scientific term used to describe a subject's externally displayed mood. This can be assesed by the nurse by observing facial expression, tone of voice, and body language.
Anemia	Anemia is a deficiency of red blood cells and/or hemoglobin. This results in a reduced ability of blood to transfer oxygen to the tissues, and this causes hypoxia; since all human cells depend on oxygen for survival, varying degrees of anemia can have a wide range of clinical consequences.
Organ	Organ refers to a structure consisting of several tissues adapted as a group to perform specific functions.
Skin	Skin is an organ of the integumentary system composed of a layer of tissues that protect underlying muscles and organs.
Protein	A protein is a complex, high-molecular-weight organic compound that consists of amino acids joined by peptide bonds. They are essential to the structure and function of all living cells and viruses. Many are enzymes or subunits of enzymes.

Go to **Cram101.com** for the Practice Tests for this Chapter.

Enzyme	An enzyme is a protein that catalyzes, or speeds up, a chemical reaction. They are essential to sustain life because most chemical reactions in biological cells would occur too slowly, or would lead to different products, without them.
Mucus	Mucus is a slippery secretion of the lining of various membranes in the body (mucous membranes). Mucus aids in the protection of the lungs by trapping foreign particles that enter the nose during normal breathing. Additionally, it prevents tissues from drying out.
Eye	An eye is an organ that detects light. Different kinds of light-sensitive organs are found in a variety of creatures. The simplest eyes do nothing but detect whether the surroundings are light or dark, while more complex eyes can distinguish shapes and colors.
Polypeptide	Polypeptide refers to polymer of many amino acids linked by peptide bonds.
Lysozyme	Lysozyme is an enzyme (EC 3.2.1.17), commonly referred to as the "body's own antibiotic" since it kills bacteria. It is abundantly present in a number of secretions, such as tears (except bovine tears).
Fever	Fever (also known as pyrexia, or a febrile response, and archaically known as ague) is a medical symptom that describes an increase in internal body temperature to levels that are above normal (37°C, 98.6°F).
Agent	Agent refers to an epidemiological term referring to the organism or object that transmits a disease from the environment to the host.
Variable	A characteristic or aspect in which people, objects, events, or conditions vary is called variable.
Stress	Stress refers to a condition that is a response to factors that change the human systems normal state.
Misuse	Misuse refers to an unusual or illegal use of a prescription, usually for drug diversion purposes.
Salmonella	Salmonella is a genus of rod-shaped Gram-negative enterobacteria that causes typhoid fever, paratyphoid and foodborne illness. It is motile in nature and produces hydrogen sulfide.
Escherichia coli	Escherichia coli is one of the main species of bacteria that live in the lower intestines of warm-blooded animals, including birds and mammals. They are necessary for the proper digestion of food and are part of the intestinal flora. Its presence in groundwater is a common indicator of fecal contamination.
Interspecies transmission	Interspecies transmission refers to transmission of disease from humans to animals or from animals to humans.
Uterus	The uterus is the major female reproductive organ of most mammals. One end, the cervix, opens into the vagina; the other is connected on both sides to the fallopian tubes. The main function is to accept a fertilized ovum which becomes implanted into the endometrium, and derives nourishment from blood vessels which develop exclusively for this purpose.
Blood	Blood is a circulating tissue composed of fluid plasma and cells. The main function of blood is to supply nutrients (oxygen, glucose) and constitutional elements to tissues and to remove waste products.
Egg	An egg is the zygote, resulting from fertilization of the ovum. It nourishes and protects the embryo.
Vagina	The vagina is the tubular tract leading from the uterus to the exterior of the body in female placental mammals and marsupials, or to the cloaca in female birds, monotremes, and some reptiles. Female insects and other invertebrates also have a vagina, which is the terminal part of the oviduct.

Microscope	A microscope is an instrument for viewing objects that are too small to be seen by the naked or unaided eye.
Light microscope	An optical instrument with lenses that refract visible light to magnify images and project them into a viewer's eye or onto photographic film is referred to as light microscope.
Toxin	Toxin refers to a microbial product or component that can injure another cell or organism at low concentrations. Often the term refers to a poisonous protein, but toxins may be lipids and other substances.
Epidermis	Epidermis is the outermost layer of the skin. It forms the waterproof, protective wrap over the body's surface and is made up of stratified squamous epithelium with an underlying basement membrane. It contains no blood vessels, and is nourished by diffusion from the dermis. In plants, the outermost layer of cells covering the leaves and young parts of a plant is the epidermis.
Wound	A wound is type of physical trauma wherein the skin is torn, cut or punctured, or where blunt force trauma causes a contusion.
Stye	A stye (also spelled sty) is an inflammation of the sebaceous glands at the base of the eyelashes.
Syndrome	Syndrome is the association of several clinically recognizable features, signs, symptoms, phenomena or characteristics which often occur together, so that the presence of one feature alerts the physician to the presence of the others
Shock	Circulatory shock, a state of cardiac output that is insufficient to meet the body's physiological needs, with consequences ranging from fainting to death is referred to as shock. Insulin shock, a state of severe hypoglycemia caused by administration of insulin.
Toxic shock syndrome	Toxic shock syndrome (TSS) is a rare but potentially fatal disease caused by a bacterial toxin. Different bacterial toxins may cause toxic shock syndrome, depending on the situation. The causative agent is Staphylococcus aureus.
Scarlet fever	Scarlet fever refers to a disease that results from infection with a strain of Streptococcus pyogenes that carries a lysogenic phage with the gene for erythrogenic toxin. The toxin causes shedding of the skin. This is a communicable disease spread by respiratory droplets.
Pharyngitis	Pharyngitis inflammation of the pharynx, often due to a S. pyogenes infection.
Stillbirth	A stillbirth occurs when a fetus, of mid-second trimester to full term gestational age, which has died in the womb or during labour or delivery, exits the maternal body.
Bladder	A hollow muscular storage organ for storing urine is a bladder.
Lead	Lead is a chemical element in the periodic table that has the symbol Pb and atomic number 82. A soft, heavy, toxic and malleable poor metal, lead is bluish white when freshly cut but tarnishes to dull gray when exposed to air. Lead is used in building construction, lead-acid batteries, bullets and shot, and is part of solder, pewter, and fusible alloys.
Pneumonia	Pneumonia is an illness of the lungs and respiratory system in which the microscopic, air-filled sacs (alveoli) responsible for absorbing oxygen from the atmosphere become inflamed and flooded with fluid.
Incidence	In epidemiological studies of a particular disorder, the rate at which new cases occur in a given place at a given time is called incidence.
Older adult	Older adult is an adult over the age of 65.
Elderly	Old age consists of ages nearing the average life span of human beings, and thus the end of the human life cycle. Euphemisms for older people include advanced adult, elderly, and senior

Go to **Cram101.com** for the Practice Tests for this Chapter.

389

	or senior citizen.
Isolation	Isolation refers to the degree to which groups do not live in the same communities.
Lungs	Lungs are the essential organs of respiration in air-breathing vertebrates. Their principal function is to transport oxygen from the atmosphere into the bloodstream, and to excrete carbon dioxide from the bloodstream into the atmosphere.
Infiltration	Infiltration is the diffusion or accumulation (in a tissue or cells) of substances not normal to it or in amounts in excess of the normal. The material collected in those tissues or cells is also called infiltration.
Respiratory system	The respiratory system is the biological system of any organism that engages in gas exchange.In humans and other mammals, the respiratory system consists of the airways, the lungs, and the respiratory muscles that mediate the movement of air into and out of the body.
Ventilation	Ventilation refers to a mechanism that provides contact between an animal's respiratory surface and the air or water to which it is exposed. It is also called breathing.
Statistics	Statistics is a type of data analysis which practice includes the planning, summarizing, and interpreting of observations of a system possibly followed by predicting or forecasting of future events based on a mathematical model of the system being observed.
Statistic	A statistic is an observable random variable of a sample.
World Health Organization	The World Health Organization (WHO) is a specialized agency of the United Nations, acting as a coordinating authority on international public health, headquartered in Geneva, Switzerland.
Mycobacterium	Mycobacterium is the a genus of actinobacteria, given its own family, the Mycobacteriaceae. It includes many pathogens known to cause serious diseases in mammals, including tuberculosis and leprosy.
Mycobacterium tuberculosis	Mycobacterium tuberculosis is the bacterium that causes most cases of tuberculosis. Its genome has been sequenced. It is an obligate aerobe mycobacterium (not gram positive/negative) that divides every 16 to 20 hours.
Tissue	A collection of interconnected cells that perform a similar function within an organism is called tissue.
Periodontal disease	A disease located around the teeth or in the periodontiumthe tissue investing and supporting the teeth, including the cementum, periodontal ligament, alveolar bone, and gingiva is referred to as the periodontal disease.
Respiratory tract	In humans the respiratory tract is the part of the anatomy that has to do with the process of respiration or breathing.
Urine	Concentrated filtrate produced by the kidneys and excreted via the bladder is called urine.
Skin test	A skin test is a test to determine reactions to antigens or antibodies. Also used to determine sensitivity to allergens.
Caries	Caries is a progressive destruction of any kind of bone structure, including the skull, the ribs and other bones.
Carrier	Person in apparent health whose chromosomes contain a pathologic mutant gene that may be transmitted to his or her children is a carrier.
Vector	A vector is an organism that does not cause disease itself but which spreads infection by conveying pathogens from one host to another.
Rocky Mountain	Rocky Mountain spotted fever is the most severe and most frequently reported rickettsial

Go to **Cram101.com** for the Practice Tests for this Chapter.

spotted fever	illness in the United States, and has been diagnosed throughout the Americas.
Metabolism	Metabolism is the biochemical modification of chemical compounds in living organisms and cells. This includes the biosynthesis of complex organic molecules (anabolism) and their breakdown (catabolism).
Acid	An acid is a water-soluble, sour-tasting chemical compound that when dissolved in water, gives a solution with a pH of less than 7.
DNA	Deoxyribonucleic acid (DNA) is a nucleic acid usually in the form of a double helix that contains the genetic instructions specifying the biological development of all cellular forms of life, and most viruses.
Protein structure	A protein structure are amino acid chains, made up from 20 different L-α-amino acids, also referred to as residues, that fold into unique three-dimensional structures.
Reproduction	Biological reproduction is the biological process by which new individual organisms are produced. Reproduction is a fundamental feature of all known life; each individual organism exists as the result of reproduction by an antecedent.
Culture	Culture, generally refers to patterns of human activity and the symbolic structures that give such activity significance.
Radiation	The emission of electromagnetic waves by all objects warmer than absolute zero is referred to as radiation.
Incubation	In problem solving, a hypothetical process that sometimes occurs when we stand back from a frustrating problem for a while and the solution 'suddenly' appears is an incubation.
Incubation period	The period after pathogen entry into a host and before signs and symptoms appear is called the incubation period.
HIV	The virus that causes AIDS is HIV (human immunodeficiency virus).
Interferon	Interferon is a natural protein produced by the cells of the immune systems of most animals in response to challenges by foreign agents such as viruses, bacteria, parasites and tumor cells. They belong to the large class of glycoproteins known as cytokines.
Common cold	An acute, self-limiting, and highly contagious virus infection of the upper respiratory tract that produces inflammation, profuse discharge, and other symptoms is referred to as the common cold.
Megadose	Generally an intake of a nutrient in excess of 10 times human need is called megadose.
Theory	Theory refers to an explanatory statement, or set of statements, that concisely summarizes the state of knowledge on a phenomenon and provides direction for further study.
Diarrhea	Diarrhea or diarrhoea is a condition in which the sufferer has frequent and watery, chunky, or loose bowel movements.
Immunity	Resistance to the effects of specific disease-causing agents is called immunity.
Crisis	A crisis is a temporary state of high anxiety where the persons usual coping mechanisms cease to work. This may have a result of disorganization or possibly personality growth.
Infectious mononucleosis	Infectious mononucleosis is a disease seen most commonly in adolescents and young adults, characterized by fever, sore throat and fatigue. It is caused by the Epstein-Barr virus (EBV) or the cytomegalovirus (CMV).
Lymph node	A lymph node acts as a filter, with an internal honeycomb of connective tissue filled with lymphocytes that collect and destroy bacteria and viruses. When the body is fighting an infection, these lymphocytes multiply rapidly and produce a characteristic swelling of the

	lymph node.
Jaundice	Jaundice is yellowing of the skin, sclera (the white of the eyes) and mucous membranes caused by increased levels of bilirubin in the human body.
Spleen	The spleen is a ductless, vertebrate gland that is not necessary for life but is closely associated with the circulatory system, where it functions in the destruction of old red blood cells and removal of other debris from the bloodstream, and also in holding a reservoir of blood.
Lymph	Lymph originates as blood plasma lost from the circulatory system, which leaks out into the surrounding tissues. The lymphatic system collects this fluid by diffusion into lymph capillaries, and returns it to the circulatory system.
Joint	A joint (articulation) is the location at which two bones make contact (articulate). They are constructed to both allow movement and provide mechanical support.
White blood cell	The white blood cell is a a component of blood. They help to defend the body against infectious disease and foreign materials as part of the immune system.
Inflammation	Inflammation is the first response of the immune system to infection or irritation and may be referred to as the innate cascade.
Hepatitis	Hepatitis is a gastroenterological disease, featuring inflammation of the liver. The clinical signs and prognosis, as well as the therapy, depend on the cause.
Liver	The liver is an organ in vertebrates, including humans. It plays a major role in metabolism and has a number of functions in the body including drug detoxification, glycogen storage, and plasma protein synthesis. It also produces bile, which is important for digestion.
Morbidity	Morbidity refers to any condition that causes illness.
Mortality	The incidence of death in a population is mortality.
Acute	In medicine, an acute disease is a disease with either or both of: a rapid onset; and a short course (as opposed to a chronic course).
Hepatitis A	Hepatitis A is an enterovirus transmitted by the orofecal route, such as contaminated food. It causes an acute form of hepatitis and does not have a chronic stage.
Chronic carrier	An individual who harbors a pathogen for a long time is called chronic carrier.
Hepatitis B	Hepatitis B is caused by a doublestranded DNA virus formerly called the 'Dane particle.' The virus is transmitted by body fluids.
Hepatitis C	Hepatitis C is a blood-borne viral disease which can cause liver inflamation, fibrosis, cirrhosis and liver cancer.
Liver failure	Liver failure is the final stage of liver disease. Liver failure is divided into types depending on the rapidity of onset.
Cirrhosis	Cirrhosis is a chronic disease of the liver in which liver tissue is replaced by connective tissue, resulting in the loss of liver function. Cirrhosis is caused by damage from toxins (including alcohol), metabolic problems, chronic viral hepatitis or other causes
Chronic Hepatitis C	Chronic hepatitis C is defined as infection with the hepatitis C virus persisting for more than six months. The course of chronic hepatitis C varies considerably from one person to another.
Prognosis	Prognosis refers to the prospects for the future or outcome of a disease.
Mumps	Mumps is a viral disease of humans. Prior to the development of vaccination, it was a common childhood disease worldwide, and is still a significant threat to health in the third world.

Apathy	Apathy is the lack of emotion, motivation, or enthusiasm. Apathy is a psychological term for a state of indifference where an individual is unresponsive or "indifferent" to aspects of emotional, social, or physical life.
Gland	A gland is an organ in an animal's body that synthesizes a substance for release such as hormones, often into the bloodstream or into cavities inside the body or its outer surface.
Parotid	The parotid gland is the largest of the salivary glands. It is found in the subcutaneous tissue of the face, overlying the mandibular ramus and anterior and inferior to the external
Chickenpox	Chickenpox refers to a highly contagious skin disease, usually affecting 2- to 7-year-old children; it is caused by the varicellazoster virus, which is acquired by droplet inhalation into the respiratory system.
Shingles	A reactivated form of chickenpox caused by the varicella-zoster virus is shingles. It leads to a crop of painful blisters over the area of a dermatome.
Hibernation	Hibernation is a state of regulated hypothermia, lasting several days or weeks, that allows animals to conserve energy during the winter. During hibernation animals slow their metabolism to a very low level, with body temperature and breathing rates lowered, gradually using up the body fat reserves stored during the warmer months.
Measles	Measles refers to a highly contagious skin disease that is endemic throughout the world. It is caused by a morbilli virus in the family Paramyxoviridae, which enters the body through the respiratory tract or through the conjunctiva.
Inhalation	Inhalation is the movement of air from the external environment, through the airways, into the alveoli during breathing.
Rubella	An infectious disease that, if contracted by the mother during the first three months of pregnancy, has a high risk of causing mental retardation and physical deformity in the child is called rubella.
Course	Pattern of development and change of a disorder over time is a course.
Trimester	In human development, one of three 3-mnonth-long periods of pregnancy is called trimester.
Fetus	Fetus refers to a developing human from the ninth week of gestation until birth; has all the major structures of an adult.
First trimester	The first trimester is the period of time from the first day of the last menstrual period through 12 weeks of gestation. It is during this period that the embryo undergoes most of its early structural development. Most miscarriages occur during this period.
Immunization	Use of a vaccine to protect the body against specific disease-causing agents is called immunization.
Kidney	The kidney is a bean-shaped excretory organ in vertebrates. Part of the urinary system, the kidneys filter wastes (especially urea) from the blood and excrete them, along with water, as urine.
Rabies	Rabies refers to an acute infectious disease of the central nervous system, which affects all warmblooded animals, It is caused by an ssRNA virus belonging to the genus Lv.ssaviru.s in the family Rhahdoviridae.
Asymptomatic	A disease is asymptomatic when it is at a stage where the patient does not experience symptoms. By their nature, asymptomatic diseases are not usually discovered until the patient undergoes medical tests (X-rays or other investigations). Some diseases remain asymptomatic for a remarkably long time, including some forms of cancer.
Nervous system	The nervous system of an animal coordinates the activity of the muscles, monitors the organs,

Go to **Cram101.com** for the Practice Tests for this Chapter.

constructs and processes input from the senses, and initiates actions.

Central nervous system	The central nervous system comprized of the brain and spinal cord, represents the largest part of the nervous system. Together with the peripheral nervous system, it has a fundamental role in the control of behavior.
Saliva	Saliva is the moist, clear, and usually somewhat frothy substance produced in the mouths of some animals, including humans.
Pharynx	The pharynx is the part of the digestive system and respiratory system of many animals immediately behind the mouth and in front of the esophagus.
Muscle	Muscle is a contractile form of tissue. It is one of the four major tissue types, the other three being epithelium, connective tissue and nervous tissue. Muscle contraction is used to move parts of the body, as well as to move substances within the body.
Brain	The part of the central nervous system involved in regulating and controlling body activity and interpreting information from the senses transmitted through the nervous system is referred to as the brain.
Unicellular	Microorganisms are often illustrated using single-celled, or unicellular organisms; however, some unicellular protists are visible to the naked eye, and some multicellular species are microscopic.
Fungi	Fungi refers to simple parasitic life forms, including molds, mildews, yeasts, and mushrooms. They live on dead or decaying organic matter. Fungi can grow as single cells, like yeast, or as multicellular colonies, as seen with molds.
Malaria	Malaria refers to potentially fatal human disease caused by the protozoan parasite Plasmodium, which is transmitted by the bite of an infected mosquito.
Sleeping sickness	Sleeping sickness or African trypanosomiasis is a parasitic disease in people and in animals. Caused by protozoa of genus Trypanosoma and transmitted by the tsetse fly, the disease is endemic in certain regions of Sub-Saharan Africa, covering about 36 countries and 60 million people.
Giardiasis	Giardiasis is a disease caused by the flagellate protozoan Giardia lamblia. The giardia organism inhabits the digestinal tract of a wide variety of domestic and wild animal species as well as humans. It is a common cause of gastroenteritis in humans, infecting approximately 200 million people worldwide.
Prion	Prion is an infectious particle consisting of protein only and no nucleic acid which is believed to be linked to several diseases of the central nervous system.
Chemical reaction	Chemical reaction refers to a process leading to chemical changes in matter; involves the making and/or breaking of chemical bonds.
Projection	Attributing one's own undesirable thoughts, impulses, traits, or behaviors to others is referred to as projection.
Cilia	Microscopic, hairlike processes on the exposed surfaces of certain epithelial cells are cilia.
Carbohydrate	Carbohydrate is a chemical compound that contains oxygen, hydrogen, and carbon atoms. They consist of monosaccharide sugars of varying chain lengths and that have the general chemical formula $C_n(H_2O)_n$ or are derivatives of such.
Minerals	Minerals refer to inorganic chemical compounds found in nature; salts.
Vitamin	An organic compound other than a carbohydrate, lipid, or protein that is needed for normal metabolism but that the body cannot synthesize in adequate amounts is called a vitamin.

399

Antibody	An antibody is a protein used by the immune system to identify and neutralize foreign objects like bacteria and viruses. Each antibody recognizes a specific antigen unique to its target.
Antigen	An antigen is a substance that stimulates an immune response, especially the production of antibodies. They are usually proteins or polysaccharides, but can be any type of molecule, including small molecules (haptens) coupled to a protein (carrier).
Immune response	The body's defensive reaction to invasion by bacteria, viral agents, or other foreign substances is called immune response.
Humoral immunity	Humoral immunity is the aspect of immunity that is mediated by secreted antibodies, produced in the cells of the B lymphocyte lineage (B cell). Secreted antibodies bind to antigens on the surfaces of invading microbes, which flags them for destruction.
Lymphocyte	A lymphocyte is a type of white blood cell involved in the human body's immune system. There are two broad categories, namely T cells and B cells.
Bone marrow	Bone marrow is the tissue comprising the center of large bones. It is the place where new blood cells are produced. Bone marrow contains two types of stem cells: hemopoietic (which can produce blood cells) and stromal (which can produce fat, cartilage and bone).
Rejection	Rejection is a response by caregivers where they distance themselves emotionally from a chronically ill patient. Although they provide physical care they tend to scold and and correct the patient continuously.
Lymphatic system	Lymph originates as blood plasma lost from the circulatory system, which leaks out into the surrounding tissues. The lymphatic system collects this fluid by diffusion into lymph capillaries, and returns it to the circulatory system.
Autoimmune	Autoimmune refers to immune reactions against normal body cells; self against self.
Autoimmune disease	Disease that results when the immune system mistakenly attacks the body's own tissues is referred to as autoimmune disease.
Immunodeficiency	Immunodeficiency is a state in which the immune system's ability to fight infectious disease is compromized or entirely absent. Most cases of immunodeficiency are either congenital or acquired.
Defense mechanism	Defense mechanism refers to in psychodynamic theory, an unconscious function of the ego that protects it from anxiety-evoking material by preventing accurate recognition of this material.
Nerve	A nerve is an enclosed, cable-like bundle of nerve fibers or axons, which includes the glia that ensheath the axons in myelin.
Referred pain	Referred pain is an unpleasant senzation localised to an area separate from the site of the causative injury or other painful stimulation. Often, referred pain arises when a nerve is compressed or damaged at or near its origin.
Injection	A method of rapid drug delivery that puts the substance directly in the bloodstream, in a muscle, or under the skin is called injection.
Virulence	The degree or intensity of pathogenicity of an organism as indicated by case fatality rates and/or ability to invade host tissues and cause disease is referred to as the virulence.
Active acquired immunity	Naturally active acquired immunity occurs when the person is exposed to a live pathogen, develops the disease, and becomes immune as a result of the primary immune response.
Passive immunity	Passive immunity refers to temporary immunity obtained by acquiring ready-made antibodies or immune cells; lasts only a few weeks or months because the immune system has not been stimulated by antigens.

Critical period	A period of time when an instinctive response can be elicited by a particular stimulus is referred to as critical period.
Globulin	Globulin is one of the two types of serum proteins, the other being albumin. This generic term encompasses a heterogenous series of families of proteins, with larger molecules and less soluble in pure water than albumin, which migrate less than albumin during serum electrophoresis.
Donor	Blood donation is a process by which a blood donor voluntarily has blood drawn for storage in a blood bank for subsequent use in a blood transfusion.
Breastfeeding	Breastfeeding is the process of a woman feeding an infant or young child with milk from her breasts, usually directly from the nipples, a process called lactation. .
Penicillin	Penicillin refers to a group of β-lactam antibiotics used in the treatment of bacterial infections caused by susceptible, usually Gram-positive, organisms.
Capillaries	Capillaries refer to the smallest of the blood vessels and the sites of exchange between the blood and tissue cells.
Capillary	A capillary is the smallest of a body's blood vessels, measuring 5-10 micro meters. They connect arteries and veins, and most closely interact with tissues. Their walls are composed of a single layer of cells, the endothelium. This layer is so thin that molecules such as oxygen, water and lipids can pass through them by diffusion and enter the tissues.
Hemorrhagic fever	Hemorrhagic fever refers to a fever usually caused by a specific virus that may lead to hemorrhage, shock, and sometimes death.
Bioterrorism	Bioterrorism is terrorism using germ warfare, an intentional human release of a naturally-occurring or human-modified toxin or biological agent.
Antimicrobial	An antimicrobial is a substance that kills or slows the growth of microbes like bacteria (antibacterial activity), fungi (antifungal activity), viruses (antiviral activity), or parasites (antiparasitic activity).
Medicine	Medicine is the branch of health science and the sector of public life concerned with maintaining or restoring human health through the study, diagnosis and treatment of disease and injury.
Meningitis	Meningitis is inflammation of the membranes covering the brain and the spinal cord. Although the most common causes are infection (bacterial, viral, fungal or parasitic), chemical agents and even tumor cells may cause meningitis.
Salmonella enterica	Salmonella enterica is a species of Salmonella bacterium. S. enterica has a number of varieties or serovars. Salmonella enterica Serovar Typhi is the disease agent in typhoid fever
Stomach	The stomach is an organ in the alimentary canal used to digest food. It's primary function is not the absorption of nutrients from digested food; rather, the main job of the stomach is to break down large food molecules into smaller ones, so that they can be absorbed into the blood more easily.
Aerosol	Liquid that is dispersed in the form of a fine mist is called aerosol.
Genes	Genes are the units of heredity in living organisms. They are encoded in the organism's genetic material (usually DNA or RNA), and control the development and behavior of the organism.
Obsession	An obsession is a thought or idea that the sufferer cannot stop thinking about. Common examples include fears of acquiring disease, getting hurt, or causing harm to someone. They are typically automatic, frequent, distressing, and difficult to control or put an end to by

Go to **Cram101.com** for the Practice Tests for this Chapter.

themselves.

Intestine	The intestine is the portion of the alimentary canal extending from the stomach to the anus and, in humans and mammals, consists of two segments, the small intestine and the large intestine. The intestine is the part of the body responsible for extracting nutrition from food.
Chlorine	Chlorine is the chemical element with atomic number 17 and symbol Cl. It is a halogen, found in the periodic table in group 17. As chlorine gas, it is greenish yellow, is two and one half times as heavy as air, has an intensely disagreeable suffocating odor, and is exceedingly poisonous. In its liquid and solid form it is a powerful oxidizing, bleaching, and disinfecting agent.
Salivary gland	The salivary gland produces saliva, which keeps the mouth and other parts of the digestive system moist. It also helps break down carbohydrates and lubricates the passage of food down from the oro-pharynx to the esophagus to the stomach.
Port	A port is a central venous line that does not have an external connector; instead, it has a small reservoir implanted under the skin.
Disorientation	A state of mental confusion with respect to time, place, identity of self, other persons, and objects is disorientation.
Encephalitis	Encephalitis is an acute inflammation of the brain, commonly caused by a viral infection.
Convulsions	Involuntary muscle spasms, often severe, that can be caused by stimulant overdose or by depressant withdrawal are called convulsions.
Paralysis	Paralysis is the complete loss of muscle function for one or more muscle groups. Paralysis may be localized, or generalized, or it may follow a certain pattern.
Tremor	Tremor is the rhythmic, oscillating shaking movement of the whole body or just a certain part of it, caused by problems of the neurons responsible from muscle action.
Elimination	Elimination refers to the physiologic excretion of drugs and other substances from the body.
Necrotizing fasciitis	A disease that results from a severe invasive group A streptococcus infection. Necrotizing fasciitis is an infection of the subcutaneous soft tissues, particularly of fibrous tissue, and is most common on the extremities. It begins with skin reddening, swelling, pain, and cetlulitis, and proceeds to skin breakdown and gangrene after 3 to 5 days.
Communicable disease	A disease associated with a pathogen that can be transmitted from one host to another is a communicable disease.
Centers for Disease Control and Prevention	The Centers for Disease Control and Prevention in Atlanta, Georgia, is recognized as the lead United States agency for protecting the public health and safety of people by providing credible information to enhance health decisions, and promoting health through strong partnerships with state health departments and other organizations.
Syphilis	Syphilis is a sexually transmitted disease that is caused by a spirochaete bacterium, Treponema pallidum. If not treated, syphilis can cause serious effects such as damage to the nervous system, heart, or brain. Untreated syphilis can be ultimately fatal.
Genital herpes	Genital herpes refers to a sexually transmitted disease, caused by a virus, that can cause painful blisters on the genitals and surrounding skin.
Young adult	An young adult is someone between the ages of 20 and 40 years old.
Assess	Assess is to systematically and continuously collect, validate, and communicate patient data.
Chlamydia	A sexually transmitted disease, caused by a bacterium, that causes inflammation of the urethra in males and of the urethra and cervix in females is referred to as chlamydia.

Genitals	Genitals refers to the internal and external reproductive organs.
Pelvis	The pelvis is the bony structure located at the base of the spine (properly known as the caudal end). The pelvis incorporates the socket portion of the hip joint for each leg (in bipeds) or hind leg (in quadrupeds). It forms the lower limb (or hind-limb) girdle of the skeleton.
Nongonococcal urethritis	Any inflammation of the urethra not caused by Neisseria gonorrhoeae is a nongonococcal urethritis.
Urination	Urination is the process of disposing urine from the urinary bladder through the urethra to the outside of the body. The process of urination is usually under voluntary control.
Penis	The penis is the male reproductive organ and for mammals additionally serves as the external male organ of urination.
Blood vessel	A blood vessel is a part of the circulatory system and function to transport blood throughout the body. The most important types, arteries and veins, are so termed because they carry blood away from or towards the heart, respectively.
Arthritis	Arthritis is a group of conditions that affect the health of the bone joints in the body. Arthritis can be caused from strains and injuries caused by repetitive motion, sports, overexertion, and falls. Unlike the autoimmune diseases, it largely affects older people and results from the degeneration of joint cartilage.
Prostate	The prostate is a gland that is part of male mammalian sex organs. Its main function is to secrete and store a clear, slightly basic fluid that is part of semen. The prostate differs considerably between species anatomically, chemically and physiologically.
Vesicle	Membranous, cytoplasmic sac formed by an infolding of the cell membrane is called a vesicle.
Bulbourethral gland	The bulbourethral gland is a small, rounded, and somewhat lobulated body, of a yellow color, about the size of a pea, placed behind and lateral to the membranous portion of the urethra, between the two layers of the fascia of the urogenital diaphragm. They secrete a clear fluid known as pre-ejaculate.
Seminal vesicles	The seminal vesicles are a pair of glands on the posterior surface of the urinary bladder of males. They secrete a significant proportion of the fluid that ultimately becomes semen.
Genital warts	A sexually transmitted disease, caused by a virus, that forms growths or bumps on the external genitalia, in or around the vagina or anus, or on the cervix in females or penis, scrotum, groin, or thigh in males are called genital warts.
Wart	A wart is a generally small, rough, cauliflower-like growth, of viral origin, typically on hands and feet.
Survey	A method of scientific investigation in which a large sample of people answer questions about their attitudes or behavior is referred to as a survey.
Stigma	Stigma refers to a personal characteristic that at least some other individuals perceive negatively because that characteristic is different than those of the general population.
Value	Value is worth in general, and it is thought to be connected to reasons for certain practices, policies, actions, beliefs or emotions. Value is "that which one acts to gain and/or keep."
Anus	In anatomy, the anus is the external opening of the rectum. Closure is controlled by sphincter muscles. Feces are expelled from the body through the anus during the act of defecation, which is the primary function of the anus.
Uterine tube	Also called the oviduct, the tube leading out of the ovary to the uterus, into which the

407

	secondary oocyte is released is referred to as uterine tube.
Miscarriage	Miscarriage or spontaneous abortion is the natural or accidental termination of a pregnancy at a stage where the embryo or the fetus is incapable of surviving, generally defined at a gestation of prior to 20 weeks.
Cervix	The cervix is actually the lower, narrow portion of the uterus where it joins with the top end of the vagina. It is cylindrical or conical in shape and protrudes through the upper anterior vaginal wall.
Pelvic inflammatory disease	Pelvic inflammatory disease is a generic term for infection of the female uterus, fallopian tubes, and/or ovaries as it progresses to scar formation with adhesions to nearby tissues and organs.
Conjunctivitis	Conjunctivitis refers to serious inflammation of the eye caused by any number of pathogens or irritants; can be caused by stds such as chlamydia.
Erythromycin	Erythromycin is a macrolide antibiotic which has an antimicrobial spectrum similar to or slightly wider than that of penicillin, and is often used for people who have an allergy to penicillins.
Tetracycline	Tetracycline is an antibiotic produced by the streptomyces bacterium, indicated for use against many bacterial infections. It is commonly used to treat acne.
Ovaries	Ovaries are egg-producing reproductive organs found in female organisms.
Ovary	The primary reproductive organ of a female is called an ovary.
Substance abuse	Substance abuse refers to the overindulgence in and dependence on a stimulant, depressant, or other chemical substance, leading to effects that are detrimental to the individual's physical or mental health, or the welfare of others.
Infertility	The inability to conceive after one year of regular, unprotected intercourse is infertility.
Ectopic pregnancy	An ectopic pregnancy is one in which the fertilized ovum is implanted in any tissue other than the uterine wall.
Chancre	The primary lesion of syphilis, occurring at the site of initial exposure to the bacterium, often on the penis, vagina or rectum is referred to as the chancre.
Nitrate	Nitrate refers to a salt of nitric acid; a compound containing the radical NO_3; biologically, the final form of nitrogen from the oxidation of organic nitrogen compounds.
Silver	Silver is a chemical element with the symbol Ag. A soft white lustrous transition metal, it has the highest electrical and thermal conductivity of any metal and occurs in minerals and in free form.
Scar	A scar results from the biologic process of wound repair in the skin and other tissues of the body. It is a connective tissue that fills the wound.
Treponema pallidum	Treponema pallidum is a spirochaete bacterium. It is a motile spirochaete that is generally acquired by close sexual contact, entering the host via breaches in squamous or columnar epithelium.
Scrotum	In some male mammals the scrotum is an external bag of skin and muscle containing the testicles. It is an extension of the abdomen, and is located between the penis and anus.
Latent	Hidden or concealed is a latent.
Lesion	A lesion is a non-specific term referring to abnormal tissue in the body. It can be caused by any disease process including trauma (physical, chemical, electrical), infection, neoplasm, metabolic and autoimmune.

Congenital syphilis	Syphilis that is acquired in utero from the mother is referred to as congenital syphilis.
Marriage	A socially approved sexual and economic relationship between two or more individuals is a marriage.
Dementia	Dementia is progressive decline in cognitive function due to damage or disease in the brain beyond what might be expected from normal aging.
Benzathine penicillin	Benzathine penicillin is slowly absorbed into the circulation, after intramuscular injection, and hydrolysed to benzylpenicillin in vivo. It is the drug-of-choice when prolonged low concentrations of benzylpenicillin are required and appropriate, allowing prolonged antibiotic action over 2 4 weeks after a single IM dose.
Solution	Solution refers to homogenous mixture formed when a solute is dissolved in a solvent.
Colposcopy	A colposcopy is a diagnostic procedure in which a colposcope is utilized to examine an illuminated, magnified view of the cervix, vagina, and vulva.
Dysplasia	Dysplasia refers to a change in cell growth and behavior in a tissue in which the structure becomes disordered.
Cervical cancer	Cervical cancer is a malignancy of the cervix. Worldwide, it is the second most common cancer of women.
Cesarean	A caesarean section (cesarean section AE), or C-section, is a form of childbirth in which a surgical incision is made through a mother's abdomen (laparotomy) and uterus (hysterotomy) to deliver one or more babies. It is usually performed when a vaginal delivery would lead to medical complications.
Coronary	Referring to the heart or the blood vessels of the heart is referred to as coronary.
Artery	Vessel that takes blood away from the heart to the tissues and organs of the body is called an artery.
Coronary artery disease	Coronary artery disease (CAD) is the end result of the accumulation of atheromatous plaques within the walls of the arteries that supply the myocardium (the muscle of the heart).
Coronary artery	An artery that supplies blood to the wall of the heart is called a coronary artery.
Cholesterol	Cholesterol is a steroid, a lipid, and an alcohol, found in the cell membranes of all body tissues, and transported in the blood plasma of all animals. It is an important component of the membranes of cells, providing stability; it makes the membrane's fluidity stable over a bigger temperature interval.
Inflammatory response	Inflammatory response refers to a complex sequence of events involving chemicals and immune cells that results in the isolation and destruction of antigens and tissues near the antigens.
Freezing	Freezing is the process in which blood is frozen and all of the plasma and 99% of the WBCs are eliminated when thawing takes place and the nontransferable cryoprotectant is removed.
Fluorouracil	Fluorouracil is a drug that is used in the treatment of cancer. It belongs to the family of drugs called antimetabolites. It is a pyrimidine analog. Its principal use is in colorectal cancer, in which it has been the established form of chemotherapy for decades (platinum-containing drugs are a recent addition).
Candidiasis	Candidiasis, commonly called yeast infection, is a fungal infection of any of the Candida species. Yeast organisms are always present in all people, but are usually prevented from "overgrowth" by naturally occurring microorganisms.
Spermicide	Spermicide refers to a sperm-killing chemical; used for contraceptive purposes.

Menopause	Menopause is the physiological cessation of menstrual cycles associated with advancing age in species that experience such cycles. Menopause is sometimes referred to as change of life or climacteric.
Diabetes	Diabetes is a medical disorder characterized by varying or persistent elevated blood sugar levels, especially after eating. All types of diabetes share similar symptoms and complications at advanced stages: dehydration and ketoacidosis, cardiovascular disease, chronic renal failure, retinal damage which can lead to blindness, nerve damage which can lead to erectile dysfunction, gangrene with risk of amputation of toes, feet, and even legs.
Hormone	A hormone is a chemical messenger from one cell to another. All multicellular organisms produce hormones. The best known hormones are those produced by endocrine glands of vertebrate animals, but hormones are produced by nearly every organ system and tissue type in a human or animal body. Hormone molecules are secreted directly into the bloodstream, they move by circulation or diffusion to their target cells, which may be nearby cells in the same tissue or cells of a distant organ of the body.
Birth control pill	The birth control pill is a chemical taken by mouth to inhibit normal fertility. All act on the hormonal system.
Vulva	The outer features of the female reproductive anatomy is referred to as vulva.
Thrush	Thrush is an infection of the oral mucous membrane by the fungus Candida albicans; also known as oral candidiasis.
Suppository	A suppository is a medicine that is inserted either into the rectum (rectal suppository) or into the vagina (vaginal suppository) where it melts.
Trichomoniasis	A sexually transmitted disease, caused by the protist Trichomonas, that causes inflammation of the mucous membranes than line the urinary tract and genitals is referred to as trichomoniasis.
Catheter	A tubular surgical instrument for withdrawing fluids from a cavity of the body, especially one for introduction into the bladder through the urethra for the withdrawal of urine is referred to as a catheter.
Urinary tract infection	A urinary tract infection is an infection anywhere from the kidneys to the ureters to the bladder to the urethra.
Urethra	In anatomy, the urethra is a tube which connects the urinary bladder to the outside of the body. The urethra has an excretory function in both sexes, to pass urine to the outside, and also a reproductive function in the male, as a passage for sperm.
Vaginitis	Vaginitis is an inflammation of the vaginal mucosa usually caused by a Candida albicans (a yeast), Trichomonas vaginalis (a protozoan) or Gardnerella (a bacterium), and rarely by other pathogens.
Herpes simplex	Herpes simplex refers to two common types of viruses, herpes simplex virus 1 and herpes simplex virus 2. Herpes simplex virus 2 is responsible for the STD known as genital herpes.
Herpes simplex virus	The herpes simplex virus is a virus that manifests itself in two common viral infections, each marked by painful, watery blisters in the skin or mucous membranes (such as the mouth or lips) or on the genitals. The disease is contagious, particularly during an outbreak, and is incurable.
Nerve cell	A cell specialized to originate or transmit nerve impulses is referred to as nerve cell.
Acyclovir	Acyclovir is one of the main antiviral drugs: a synthetic purine nucleoside derivative with antiviral activity against herpes simplex virus.
Base	The common definition of a base is a chemical compound that absorbs hydronium ions when

413

dissolved in water (a proton acceptor). An alkali is a special example of a base, where in an aqueous environment, hydroxide ions are donated.

Genitalia	The Latin term genitalia is used to describe the sex organs, and in the English language this term and genital area are most often used to describe the externally visible sex organs or external genitalia: in males the penis and scrotum, in females the vulva.
Stressor	A factor capable of stimulating a stress response is a stressor.
Anesthetic	Anesthetic refers to a substance that causes the loss of the ability to feel pain or other sensory input, e.g., ether or halothane.
Acquired immunodeficiency syndrome	Acquired Immunodeficiency Syndrome is defined as a collection of symptoms and infections resulting from the depletion of the immune system caused by infection with the human immunodeficiency virus, commonly called HIV.
Human immunodeficiency virus	The human immunodeficiency virus is a retrovirus that primarily infects vital components of the human immune system. It is transmitted through penetrative and oral sex; blood transfusion; the sharing of contaminated needles in health care settings and through drug injection; and, between mother and infant, during pregnancy, childbirth and breastfeeding.
Sarcoma	Cancer of the supportive tissues, such as bone, cartilage, and muscle is referred to as sarcoma.
Diagnosis	In medicine, diagnosis is the process of identifying a medical condition or disease by its signs, symptoms, and from the results of various diagnostic procedures.
Homosexuals	Persons who are sexually attracted to people of their own sex are called homosexuals.
Homosexual	Homosexual refers to referring to people who are sexually aroused by and interested in forming romantic relationships with people of the same gender.
Retrovirus	A retrovirus is a virus which has a genome consisting of two RNA molecules, which may or may not be identical. It relies on the enzyme reverse transcriptase to perform the reverse transcription of its genome from RNA into DNA, which can then be integrated into the host's genome with an integrase enzyme.
National Cancer Institute	The National Cancer Institute (NCI) is the United States federal government's principal agency for cancer research and training, and the first institute of the present-day National Institutes of Health. The NCI is a federally funded research and development center, one of eight agencies that compose the Public Health Service in the United States Department of Health and Human Services. The Institute coordinates the National Cancer Program.
Heterosexual	Referring to people who are sexually aroused by and interested in forming romantic relationships with people of the other gender is referred to as heterosexual.
Addict	A person with an overpowering physical or psychological need to continue taking a particular substance or drug is referred to as an addict.
Perinatal	Pertaining to the time five months before, during, and one month after birth is perinatal.
Semen	Semen is a fluid that contains spermatozoa. It is secreted by the gonads (sexual glands) of male or hermaphroditic animals including humans for fertilization of female ova. Semen discharged by an animal or human is known as ejaculate, and the process of discharge is called ejaculation.
Trial	In classical conditioning, any presentation of a stimulus or pair of stimuli is called a trial.
Cultural norms	Cultural norms refer to norms that are accepted guidelines for behavior. Cultural norms are those that guide interactions within cultural groups.

415

Sexual abuse	Sexual abuse is a relative cultural term used to describe sexual relations and behavior between two or more parties which are considered criminally and/or morally offensive.
Intervention	Intervention refers to a planned attempt to break through addicts' or abusers' denial and get them into treatment. Interventions most often occur when legal, workplace, health, relationship, or financial problems have become intolerable.
Cerebrospinal fluid	Cerebrospinal fluid is a clear bodily fluid that occupies the subarachnoid space in the brain (the space between the skull and the cerebral cortex). It is basically a saline solution and acts as a "cushion" or buffer for the cortex.
Minority group	A group of people who are defined on the basis of their ethnicity or race, is referred to as a minority group.
Denial	Denial is a psychological defense mechanism in which a person faced with a fact that is uncomfortable or painful to accept rejects it instead, insisting that it is not true despite what may be overwhelming evidence.
Alcohol	Alcohol is a general term, applied to any organic compound in which a hydroxyl group (-OH) is bound to a carbon atom, which in turn is bound to other hydrogen and/or carbon atoms. The general formula for a simple acyclic alcohol is $C_nH_{2n+1}OH$.
Tetanus	Tetanus is a serious and often fatal disease caused by the neurotoxin tetanospasmin which is produced by the Gram-positive, obligate anaerobic bacterium Clostridium tetani. Tetanus also refers to a state of muscle tension.
Sterilization	The process of rendering a person infertile, by performing either a vasectomy in the male or tubal ligation in the female, is referred to as sterilization. Also the process by which all microorganisms are destroyed.
Niobium	Niobium is a chemical element in the periodic table that has the symbol Nb and atomic number 41. A rare, soft, gray, ductile transition metal, niobium is found in niobite and used in alloys. The most notable alloys are used to make special steels and strong welded joints.
Gold	Gold is a chemical element in the periodic table that has the symbol Au and atomic number 79. A soft, shiny, yellow, dense, malleable, ductile (trivalent and univalent) transition metal, gold does not react with most chemicals but is attacked by chlorine, fluorine and aqua regia.
Steroid	A steroid is a lipid characterized by a carbon skeleton with four fused rings. Different steroids vary in the functional groups attached to these rings. Hundreds of distinct steroids have been identified in plants and animals. Their most important role in most living systems is as hormones.
Insulin	Insulin is a polypeptide hormone that regulates carbohydrate metabolism. Apart from being the primary effector in carbohydrate homeostasis, it also has a substantial effect on small vessel muscle tone, controls storage and release of fat (triglycerides) and cellular uptake of both amino acids and some electrolytes.
Syringe	A device for injecting drugs directly into the body is a syringe.
ELISA	The Enzyme-Linked Immunosorbent Assay (ELISA for short) is a biochemical technique used mainly in immunology to detect the presence of an antibody or an antigen in a sample. It utilizes two antibodies, one of which is specific to the antigen and the other of which is coupled to an enzyme.
Advocate	An advocate is one who speaks on behalf of another, especially in a legal context. Implicit in the concept is the notion that the represented lacks the knowledge, skill, ability, or standing to speak for themselves.
Inhibitor	An inhibitor is a type of effector (biology) that decreases or prevents the rate of a

Go to **Cram101.com** for the Practice Tests for this Chapter.

chemical reaction. They are often called negative catalysts.

Protease	Protease refers to an enzyme that breaks peptide bonds between amino acids of proteins.
Protease inhibitor	A compound that interferes with the ability of certain enzymes to break down proteins is a protease inhibitor. They can keep a virus from making copies of itself (for example, AIDS virus protease inhibitors), and some can prevent cancer cells from spreading.
Stress management	Stress management encompasses techniques intended to equip a person with effective coping mechanisms for dealing with psychological stress.
Counselor	A counselor is a mental health professional who specializes in helping people with problems not involving serious mental disorders.
Abstinence	Abstinence has diverse forms. In its oldest sense it is sexual, as in the practice of continence, chastity, and celibacy.
Masturbation	Sexual self-stimulation is called masturbation.
Monogamy	A mating system in which one male and one female mate exclusively, or almost exclusively, with each other is referred to as monogamy.
Lifestyle	The culturally, socially, economically, and environmentally conditioned complex of actions characteristic of an individual, group, or community as a pattern of habituated behavior over time that is health related but not necessarily health directed is a lifestyle.
Bronchitis	Bronchitis is an obstructive pulmonary disease characterized by inflammation of the bronchi of the lungs.
Hay fever	Hay fever is a collection of symptoms, predominantly in the nose and eyes, that occur after exposure to airborne particles of dust, dander, or the pollens of certain seasonal plants in people who are allergic to these substances.
Emphysema	Emphysema is a chronic lung disease. It is often caused by exposure to toxic chemicals or long-term exposure to tobacco smoke..
Allergy	An allergy or Type I hypersensitivity is an immune malfunction whereby a person's body is hypersensitized to react immunologically to typically nonimmunogenic substances. When a person is hypersensitized, these substances are known as allergens.
Asthma	Asthma is a complex disease characterized by bronchial hyperresponsiveness (BHR), inflammation, mucus production and intermittent airway obstruction.
Chronic bronchitis	A persistent lung infection characterized by coughing, swelling of the lining of the respiratory tract, an increase in mucus production, a decrease in the number and activity of cilia, and produces sputum for at least three months in two consecutive years is called chronic bronchitis.
Seizure	A seizure is a temporary alteration in brain function expressed as a changed mental state, tonic or clonic movements and various other symptoms. They are due to temporary abnormal electrical activity of a group of brain cells.
Digestion	Digestion refers to the mechanical and chemical breakdown of food into molecules small enough for the body to absorb; the second main stage of food processing, following ingestion.
Chronic fatigue syndrome	Chronic fatigue syndrome is incapacitating exhaustion following only minimal exertion, accompanied by fever, headaches, muscle and joint pain, depression, and anxiety.

419

Multiple sclerosis	Multiple sclerosis affects neurons, the cells of the brain and spinal cord that carry information, create thought and perception, and allow the brain to control the body. Surrounding and protecting these neurons is a layer of fat, called myelin, which helps neurons carry electrical signals. MS causes gradual destruction of myelin (demyelination) in patches throughout the brain and/or spinal cord, causing various symptoms depending upon which signals are interrupted.
Trial	In classical conditioning, any presentation of a stimulus or pair of stimuli is called a trial.
Placebo	A placebo is an inactive substance (pill, liquid, etc.), which is administered as if it were a therapy, but which has no therapeutic value other than the placebo effect.
Cancer	Cancer is a class of diseases or disorders characterized by uncontrolled division of cells and the ability of these cells to invade other tissues, either by direct growth into adjacent tissue through invasion or by implantation into distant sites by metastasis.
Pathogen	A pathogen or infectious agent is a biological agent that causes disease or illness to its host.The term is most often used for agents that disrupt the normal physiology of a multicellular animal or plant.
Lead	Lead is a chemical element in the periodic table that has the symbol Pb and atomic number 82. A soft, heavy, toxic and malleable poor metal, lead is bluish white when freshly cut but tarnishes to dull gray when exposed to air. Lead is used in building construction, lead-acid batteries, bullets and shot, and is part of solder, pewter, and fusible alloys.
Lifestyle	The culturally, socially, economically, and environmentally conditioned complex of actions characteristic of an individual, group, or community as a pattern of habituated behavior over time that is health related but not necessarily health directed is a lifestyle.
Causation	The act of causing some effect is causation. Damage or harn that is caused by a breach of duty.
Health	Health is a term that refers to a combination of the absence of illness, the ability to cope with everyday activities, physical fitness, and high quality of life.
Chronic obstructive pulmonary disease	Chronic obstructive pulmonary disease is an umbrella term for a group of respiratory tract diseases that are characterized by airflow obstruction or limitation. It is usually caused by tobacco smoking.
Dyspnea	Dyspnea or shortness of breath (SOB) is perceived difficulty breathing or pain on breathing. It is a common symptom of numerous medical disorders.
Infection	The invasion and multiplication of microorganisms in body tissues is called an infection.
Bronchitis	Bronchitis is an obstructive pulmonary disease characterized by inflammation of the bronchi of the lungs.
Idiopathic	Idiopathic is a medical adjective that indicates that a recognized cause has not yet been established.
Emphysema	Emphysema is a chronic lung disease. It is often caused by exposure to toxic chemicals or long-term exposure to tobacco smoke..
Asthma	Asthma is a complex disease characterized by bronchial hyperresponsiveness (BHR), inflammation, mucus production and intermittent airway obstruction.
Chronic bronchitis	A persistent lung infection characterized by coughing, swelling of the lining of the respiratory tract, an increase in mucus production, a decrease in the number and activity of cilia, and produces sputum for at least three months in two consecutive years is called

Go to **Cram101.com** for the Practice Tests for this Chapter.

	chronic bronchitis.
Lungs	Lungs are the essential organs of respiration in air-breathing vertebrates. Their principal function is to transport oxygen from the atmosphere into the bloodstream, and to excrete carbon dioxide from the bloodstream into the atmosphere.
Allergen	An allergen is any substance (antigen), most often eaten or inhaled, that is recognized by the immune system and causes an allergic reaction.
Antibody	An antibody is a protein used by the immune system to identify and neutralize foreign objects like bacteria and viruses. Each antibody recognizes a specific antigen unique to its target.
Antigen	An antigen is a substance that stimulates an immune response, especially the production of antibodies. They are usually proteins or polysaccharides, but can be any type of molecule, including small molecules (haptens) coupled to a protein (carrier).
Allergy	An allergy or Type I hypersensitivity is an immune malfunction whereby a person's body is hypersensitized to react immunologically to typically nonimmunogenic substances. When a person is hypersensitized, these substances are known as allergens.
Blood vessel	A blood vessel is a part of the circulatory system and function to transport blood throughout the body. The most important types, arteries and veins, are so termed because they carry blood away from or towards the heart, respectively.
Blood	Blood is a circulating tissue composed of fluid plasma and cells. The main function of blood is to supply nutrients (oxygen, glucose) and constitutional elements to tissues and to remove waste products.
Respiratory system	The respiratory system is the biological system of any organism that engages in gas exchange.In humans and other mammals, the respiratory system consists of the airways, the lungs, and the respiratory muscles that mediate the movement of air into and out of the body.
Oxygen	Oxygen is a chemical element in the periodic table. It has the symbol O and atomic number 8. Oxygen is the second most common element on Earth, composing around 46% of the mass of Earth's crust and 28% of the mass of Earth as a whole, and is the third most common element in the universe.
Activities of daily living	Activities of daily living is a way to describe the functional status of a person.
Mucus	Mucus is a slippery secretion of the lining of various membranes in the body (mucous membranes). Mucus aids in the protection of the lungs by trapping foreign particles that enter the nose during normal breathing. Additionally, it prevents tissues from drying out.
Bacteria	The domain that contains procaryotic cells with primarily diacyl glycerol diesters in their membranes and with bacterial rRNA. Bacteria also is a general term for organisms that are composed of procaryotic cells and are not multicellular.
Eye	An eye is an organ that detects light. Different kinds of light-sensitive organs are found in a variety of creatures. The simplest eyes do nothing but detect whether the surroundings are light or dark, while more complex eyes can distinguish shapes and colors.
Hypersensitivity	Hypersensitivity is an immune response that damages the body's own tissues. Four or five types of hypersensitivity are often described; immediate, antibody-dependent, immune complex, cell-mediated, and stimulatory.
Skin	Skin is an organ of the integumentary system composed of a layer of tissues that protect underlying muscles and organs.
Tissue	A collection of interconnected cells that perform a similar function within an organism is called tissue.

Immune system	The immune system is the system of specialized cells and organs that protect an organism from outside biological influences. When the immune system is functioning properly, it protects the body against bacteria and viral infections, destroying cancer cells and foreign substances.
Hay fever	Hay fever is a collection of symptoms, predominantly in the nose and eyes, that occur after exposure to airborne particles of dust, dander, or the pollens of certain seasonal plants in people who are allergic to these substances.
Fever	Fever (also known as pyrexia, or a febrile response, and archaically known as ague) is a medical symptom that describes an increase in internal body temperature to levels that are above normal (37°C, 98.6°F).
Chronic disease	Disease of long duration often not detected in its early stages and from which the patient will not recover is referred to as a chronic disease.
Diagnosis	In medicine, diagnosis is the process of identifying a medical condition or disease by its signs, symptoms, and from the results of various diagnostic procedures.
Bronchodilator	A bronchodilator is a medication intended to improve bronchial airflow. Treatment of bronchial asthma is the most common application of these drugs.
Wheezing	Wheezing is a continuous, coarse, whistling sound produced in the respiratory airways during breathing. For wheezing to occur, some part of the respiratory tree must be narrowed or obstructed, or airflow velocity within the respiratory tree must be heightened.
Muscle	Muscle is a contractile form of tissue. It is one of the four major tissue types, the other three being epithelium, connective tissue and nervous tissue. Muscle contraction is used to move parts of the body, as well as to move substances within the body.
Pain	Pain is an unpleasant sensation which may be associated with actual or potential tissue damage and which may have physical and emotional components.
Saliva	Saliva is the moist, clear, and usually somewhat frothy substance produced in the mouths of some animals, including humans.
Stress	Stress refers to a condition that is a response to factors that change the human systems normal state.
Tuberculosis	Tuberculosis is an infection caused by the bacterium Mycobacterium tuberculosis, which most commonly affects the lungs but can also affect the central nervous system, lymphatic system, circulatory system, genitourinary system, bones and joints.
Affect	Affect is the scientific term used to describe a subject's externally displayed mood. This can be assesed by the nurse by observing facial expression, tone of voice, and body language.
Alveoli	Alveoli are anatomical structures that have the form of a hollow cavity. In the lung, the pulmonary alveoli are spherical outcroppings of the respiratory bronchioles and are the primary sites of gas exchange with the blood.
Gas exchange	In humans and other mammals, respiratory gas exchange or ventilation is carried out by mechanisms of the lungs. The actual gas exchange occurs in the alveoli.
Air sac	Air sac is an anatomical structure unique to the dinosaur and bird respiratory system that allows unidirectional flow of air into the lungs and through the body
Carbon	Carbon is a chemical element in the periodic table that has the symbol C and atomic number 6. An abundant nonmetallic, tetravalent element, carbon has several allotropic forms.
Carbon dioxide	Carbon dioxide is an atmospheric gas comprized of one carbon and two oxygen atoms. A very widely known chemical compound, it is frequently called by its formula CO_2. In its solid

Go to **Cram101.com** for the Practice Tests for this Chapter.

	state, it is commonly known as dry ice.
World Health Organization	The World Health Organization (WHO) is a specialized agency of the United Nations, acting as a coordinating authority on international public health, headquartered in Geneva, Switzerland.
Incidence	In epidemiological studies of a particular disorder, the rate at which new cases occur in a given place at a given time is called incidence.
Stimulant	A stimulant is a drug which increases the activity of the sympathetic nervous system and produces a sense of euphoria or awakeness.
Intrinsic asthma	Asthma that is caused by pathophysiologic disturbances that do not involve IgE-mediated mechanisms is intrinsic asthma. Symptoms are more likely to be triggered by exercise, emotion or some drugs such as aspirin.
Enzyme	An enzyme is a protein that catalyzes, or speeds up, a chemical reaction. They are essential to sustain life because most chemical reactions in biological cells would occur too slowly, or would lead to different products, without them.
Cardiovascular system	The circulatory system or cardiovascular system is the organ system which circulates blood around the body of most animals.
Inflammation	Inflammation is the first response of the immune system to infection or irritation and may be referred to as the innate cascade.
Antibiotic	Antibiotic refers to substance such as penicillin or streptomycin that is toxic to microorganisms. Usually a product of a particular microorvanism or plant.
Acute	In medicine, an acute disease is a disease with either or both of: a rapid onset; and a short course (as opposed to a chronic course).
Viral	Viral phenomena are objects or patterns able to replicate themselves or convert other objects into copies of themselves when these objects are exposed to them.
Risk factor	A risk factor is a variable associated with an increased risk of disease or infection but risk factors are not necessarily causal.
Sleep apnea	Sleep apnea refers to a sleep disorder involving periods during sleep when breathing stops and the person must awaken briefly in order to breathe; major symptoms are excessive daytime sleepiness and loud snoring.
Diabetes	Diabetes is a medical disorder characterized by varying or persistent elevated blood sugar levels, especially after eating. All types of diabetes share similar symptoms and complications at advanced stages: dehydration and ketoacidosis, cardiovascular disease, chronic renal failure, retinal damage which can lead to blindness, nerve damage which can lead to erectile dysfunction, gangrene with risk of amputation of toes, feet, and even legs.
Apnea	Apnea is the absence of external breathing. During apnea there is no movement of the muscles of respiration and the volume of the lungs initially remains unchanged. .
Brain	The part of the central nervous system involved in regulating and controlling body activity and interpreting information from the senses transmitted through the nervous system is referred to as the brain.
Central sleep apnea	Central sleep apnea are brief periods of complete cessation in respiratory activity during sleep that may be associated with central nervous system disorders. Most awaken often as a result but do not report sleepiness and may be unaware of any problem.
Alcohol	Alcohol is a general term, applied to any organic compound in which a hydroxyl group (-OH) is bound to a carbon atom, which in turn is bound to other hydrogen and/or carbon atoms. The

general formula for a simple acyclic alcohol is $C_nH_{2n+1}OH$.

Obstructive sleep apnea	Most people with sleep disorders have obstructive sleep apnea, in which the person stops breathing during sleep due to airway blockage. Sufferers usually resume breathing within a few seconds. It is more common amongst people who snore, who are obese, who consume alcohol, or who have anatomical abnormalities of the jaw or soft palate.
Blood pressure	Blood pressure is the pressure exerted by the blood on the walls of the blood vessels.
Host	Host is an organism that harbors a parasite, mutual partner, or commensal partner; or a cell infected by a virus.
Nervous system	The nervous system of an animal coordinates the activity of the muscles, monitors the organs, constructs and processes input from the senses, and initiates actions.
Autonomic nervous system	The autonomic nervous system is the part of the nervous system that is not consciously controlled. It is commonly divided into two usually antagonistic subsystems: the sympathetic and parasympathetic nervous system.
Oxygen saturation	Oxygen saturation is a relative measure of the amount of oxygen that is dissolved or carried in a given medium.
Soft palate	The soft palate, is the soft tissue comprising the back of the roof of the mouth. It is movable, consisting of muscle fibers sheathed in mucous membrane, and is responsible for closing off the nasal passages during the act of swallowing.
Uvula	The uvula is a small cone-shaped mass of tissue hanging down from the soft palate, near the back of the throat. The uvula plays an important role in the creation of the sound of the human voice.
Base	The common definition of a base is a chemical compound that absorbs hydronium ions when dissolved in water (a proton acceptor). An alkali is a special example of a base, where in an aqueous environment, hydroxide ions are donated.
Stroke	A stroke or cerebrovascular accident (CVA) occurs when the blood supply to a part of the brain is suddenly interrupted.
Heart attack	A heart attack, is a serious, sudden heart condition usually characterized by varying degrees of chest pain or discomfort, weakness, sweating, nausea, vomiting, and arrhythmias, sometimes causing loss of consciousness. It occurs when the blood supply to a part of the heart is interrupted, causing death and scarring of the local heart tissue.
Depression	In everyday language depression refers to any downturn in mood, which may be relatively transitory and perhaps due to something trivial. This is differentiated from Clinical depression which is marked by symptoms that last two weeks or more and are so severe that they interfere with daily living.
Arousal	Arousal is a physiological and psychological state involving the activation of the reticular activating system in the brain stem, the autonomic nervous system and the endocrine system, leading to increased heart rate and blood pressure and a condition of alertness and readiness to respond.
Rapid eye movement	Rapid eye movement is the stage of sleep during which the most vivid dreams occur. During this stage, the eyes move rapidly, and the activity of the brain's neurons is quite similar to that during waking hours. It is the lightest form of sleep in that people awakened during this time usually feel alert and refreshed.
Predisposition	Predisposition refers to an inclination or diathesis to respond in a certain way, either inborn or acquired. In abnormal psychology, it is a factor that lowers the ability to withstand stress and inclines the individual toward pathology.

Osteoarthritis	Osteoarthritis is a condition in which low-grade inflammation results in pain in the joints, caused by wearing of the cartilage that covers and acts as a cushion inside joints.
Morbidity	Morbidity refers to any condition that causes illness.
Arthritis	Arthritis is a group of conditions that affect the health of the bone joints in the body. Arthritis can be caused from strains and injuries caused by repetitive motion, sports, overexertion, and falls. Unlike the autoimmune diseases, it largely affects older people and results from the degeneration of joint cartilage.
Rheumatoid arthritis	Rheumatoid arthritis is a chronic, inflammatory autoimmune disorder that causes the immune system to attack the joints. It is a disabling and painful inflammatory condition, which can lead to substantial loss of mobility due to pain and joint destruction.
Population	Population refers to all members of a well-defined group of organisms, events, or things.
Migraine	Migraine is a neurologic disease, of which the most common symptom is an intense and disabling headache. Migraine is the most common type of vascular headache.
Cluster headache	Cluster headache sufferers typically experience very severe headaches of a piercing quality near one eye or temple that last for between 15 minutes and three hours. The headaches are unilateral and occasionally change sides.
Diffuse pain	Diffuse pain is pain that covers a large area.
Menstruation	Loss of blood and tissue from the uterine lining at the end of a female reproductive cycle are referred to as menstruation.
Young adult	An young adult is someone between the ages of 20 and 40 years old.
Blind spot	In anatomy, the blind spot is the region of the retina where the optic nerve and blood vessels pass through to connect to the back of the eye. Since there are no light receptors there, a part of the field of vision is not perceived.
Aura	An aura is the perceptual disturbance experienced by some migraine sufferers before a migraine headache, and the telltale sensation experienced by some epileptics before a seizure. It often manifests as a strange light or an unpleasant smell.
Sinus	A sinus is a pouch or cavity in any organ or tissue, or an abnormal cavity or passage caused by the destruction of tissue.
Laboratory setting	Research setting in which the behavior of interest does not naturally occur is called a laboratory setting.
Theory	Theory refers to an explanatory statement, or set of statements, that concisely summarizes the state of knowledge on a phenomenon and provides direction for further study.
Consciousness	Consciousness refers to the ability to perceive, communicate, remember, understand, appreciate, and initiate voluntary movements; a functioning sensorium.
Convulsions	Involuntary muscle spasms, often severe, that can be caused by stimulant overdose or by depressant withdrawal are called convulsions.
Epilepsy	Epilepsy is a chronic neurological condition characterized by recurrent unprovoked neural discharges. It is commonly controlled with medication, although surgical methods are used as well.
Cortex	In anatomy and zoology the cortex is the outermost or superficial layer of an organ or the outer portion of the stem or root of a plant.
Meninges	The meninges are the system of membranes that envelop the central nervous system. The meninges consist of three layers, the dura mater, the arachnoid mater, and the pia mater.

Nerve	A nerve is an enclosed, cable-like bundle of nerve fibers or axons, which includes the glia that ensheath the axons in myelin.
Serotonin	Serotonin is a monoamine neurotransmitter synthesized in serotonergic neurons in the central nervous system and enterochromaffin cells in the gastrointestinal tract. It is believed to play an important part of the biochemistry of depression, migraine, bipolar disorder and anxiety.
Susceptibility	The degree of resistance of a host to a pathogen is susceptibility.
Hypertension	Hypertension is a medical condition where the blood pressure in the arteries is chronically elevated. Persistent hypertension is one of the risk factors for strokes, heart attacks, heart failure and arterial aneurysm, and is a leading cause of chronic renal failure.
Common cold	An acute, self-limiting, and highly contagious virus infection of the upper respiratory tract that produces inflammation, profuse discharge, and other symptoms is referred to as the common cold.
Sugar	A sugar is the simplest molecule that can be identified as a carbohydrate. These include monosaccharides and disaccharides, trisaccharides and the oligosaccharides. The term "glyco-" indicates the presence of a sugar in an otherwise non-carbohydrate substance.
Seizure	A seizure is a temporary alteration in brain function expressed as a changed mental state, tonic or clonic movements and various other symptoms. They are due to temporary abnormal electrical activity of a group of brain cells.
Punishment	An unpleasant stimulus that suppresses the behavior it follows is a punishment.
Stigma	Stigma refers to a personal characteristic that at least some other individuals perceive negatively because that characteristic is different than those of the general population.
Loss of control	The point in drug use where the user becomes unable to limit or stop use is referred to as loss of control.
Narcolepsy	A serious sleep disorder characterized by excessive daytime sleepiness and sudden, uncontrollable attacks of REM sleep is called narcolepsy.
Heredity	Heredity refers to the transmission of genetic information from parent to offspring.
Trauma	Trauma refers to a severe physical injury or wound to the body caused by an external force, or a psychological shock having a lasting effect on mental life.
Tumor	An abnormal mass of cells that forms within otherwise normal tissue is a tumor. This growth can be either malignant or benign
Intervention	Intervention refers to a planned attempt to break through addicts' or abusers' denial and get them into treatment. Interventions most often occur when legal, workplace, health, relationship, or financial problems have become intolerable.
Tremor	Tremor is the rhythmic, oscillating shaking movement of the whole body or just a certain part of it, caused by problems of the neurons responsible from muscle action.
Toxin	Toxin refers to a microbial product or component that can injure another cell or organism at low concentrations. Often the term refers to a poisonous protein, but toxins may be lipids and other substances.
Myelin	Myelin is an electrically insulating fatty layer that surrounds the axons of many neurons, especially those in the peripheral nervous system. It is an outgrowth of glial cells: Schwann cells supply the myelin for peripheral neurons while oligodendrocytes supply it to those of the central nervous system.
Scar	A scar results from the biologic process of wound repair in the skin and other tissues of the

	body. It is a connective tissue that fills the wound.
Remission	Disappearance of the signs of a disease is called remission.
Menstrual cycle	The menstrual cycle is the set of recurring physiological changes in a female's body that are under the control of the reproductive hormone system and necessary for reproduction. Besides humans, only other great apes exhibit menstrual cycles, in contrast to the estrus cycle of most mammalian species.
Cyst	A cyst is a closed sac having a distinct membrane and developing abnormally in a cavity or structure of the body. They may occur as a result of a developmental error in the embryo during pregnancy or they may be caused by infections.
Endometriosis	Endometriosis is a common medical condition where the tissue lining the uterus is found outside of the uterus, typically affecting other organs in the pelvis.
Uterus	The uterus is the major female reproductive organ of most mammals. One end, the cervix, opens into the vagina; the other is connected on both sides to the fallopian tubes. The main function is to accept a fertilized ovum which becomes implanted into the endometrium, and derives nourishment from blood vessels which develop exclusively for this purpose.
Fibroids	Uterine fibroids are the most common neoplasm in females, and may affect about of 25 % of white and 50% of black women during the reproductive years. Fibroids may be removed simply by means of a hysterectomy, but much more favourably by a myomectomy or by uterine artery embolization, which preserve the uterus.
Endometrium	The endometrium is the inner uterine membrane in mammals which is developed in preparation for the implantation of a fertilized egg upon its arrival into the uterus.
Obesity	The state of being more than 20 percent above the average weight for a person of one's height is called obesity.
Abdomen	The abdomen is a part of the body. In humans, and in many other vertebrates, it is the region between the thorax and the pelvis. In fully developed insects, the abdomen is the third (or posterior) segment, after the head and thorax.
Anemia	Anemia is a deficiency of red blood cells and/or hemoglobin. This results in a reduced ability of blood to transfer oxygen to the tissues, and this causes hypoxia; since all human cells depend on oxygen for survival, varying degrees of anemia can have a wide range of clinical consequences.
Cramp	A cramp is an unpleasant sensation caused by contraction, usually of a muscle. It can be caused by cold or overexertion.
Uterine tube	Also called the oviduct, the tube leading out of the ovary to the uterus, into which the secondary oocyte is released is referred to as uterine tube.
Infertility	The inability to conceive after one year of regular, unprotected intercourse is infertility.
Menopause	Menopause is the physiological cessation of menstrual cycles associated with advancing age in species that experience such cycles. Menopause is sometimes referred to as change of life or climacteric.
Estrogen	Estrogen is a steroid that functions as the primary female sex hormone. While present in both men and women, they are found in women in significantly higher quantities.
Hormone	A hormone is a chemical messenger from one cell to another. All multicellular organisms produce hormones. The best known hormones are those produced by endocrine glands of vertebrate animals, but hormones are produced by nearly every organ system and tissue type in a human or animal body. Hormone molecules are secreted directly into the bloodstream, they move by circulation or diffusion to their target cells, which may be nearby cells in the same

Go to **Cram101.com** for the Practice Tests for this Chapter.

tissue or cells of a distant organ of the body.

Hysterectomy	A hysterectomy is the surgical removal of the uterus, usually done by a gynecologist. Hysterectomy may be total (removing the body and cervix of the uterus) or partial. In many cases, surgical removal of the ovaries (oophorectomy) is performed concurrent with a hysterectomy.
Catheter	A tubular surgical instrument for withdrawing fluids from a cavity of the body, especially one for introduction into the bladder through the urethra for the withdrawal of urine is referred to as a catheter.
Ovaries	Ovaries are egg-producing reproductive organs found in female organisms.
Artery	Vessel that takes blood away from the heart to the tissues and organs of the body is called an artery.
Ovary	The primary reproductive organ of a female is called an ovary.
Ultrasound	Ultrasound is sound with a frequency greater than the upper limit of human hearing, approximately 20 kilohertz. Medical use can visualise muscle and soft tissue, making them useful for scanning the organs, and obstetric ultrasonography is commonly used during pregnancy.
Magnetic resonance imaging	Magnetic resonance imaging refers to imaging technology that uses magnetism and radio waves to induce hydrogen nuclei in water molecules to emit faint radio signals. A computer creates images of the body from the radio signals.
Constipation	Constipation is a condition of the digestive system where a person (or other animal) experiences hard feces that are difficult to eliminate; it may be extremely painful, and in severe cases (fecal impaction) lead to symptoms of bowel obstruction.
Diarrhea	Diarrhea or diarrhoea is a condition in which the sufferer has frequent and watery, chunky, or loose bowel movements.
Aerobic	An aerobic organism is an organism that has an oxygen based metabolism. Aerobes, in a process known as cellular respiration, use oxygen to oxidize substrates (for example sugars and fats) in order to obtain energy.
Aerobic exercise	Exercise in which oxygen is used to produce ATP is aerobic exercise.
Organ	Organ refers to a structure consisting of several tissues adapted as a group to perform specific functions.
Progesterone	Progesterone is a C-21 steroid hormone involved in the female menstrual cycle, pregnancy (supports gestation) and embryogenesis of humans and other species.
Digestion	Digestion refers to the mechanical and chemical breakdown of food into molecules small enough for the body to absorb; the second main stage of food processing, following ingestion.
Carbohydrate	Carbohydrate is a chemical compound that contains oxygen, hydrogen, and carbon atoms. They consist of monosaccharide sugars of varying chain lengths and that have the general chemical formula $C_n(H_2O)_n$ or are derivatives of such.
Metabolism	Metabolism is the biochemical modification of chemical compounds in living organisms and cells. This includes the biosynthesis of complex organic molecules (anabolism) and their breakdown (catabolism).
Pancreas	The pancreas is a retroperitoneal organ that serves two functions: exocrine - it produces pancreatic juice containing digestive enzymes, and endocrine - it produces several important hormones, namely insulin.
Insulin	Insulin is a polypeptide hormone that regulates carbohydrate metabolism. Apart from being the

primary effector in carbohydrate homeostasis, it also has a substantial effect on small vessel muscle tone, controls storage and release of fat (triglycerides) and cellular uptake of both amino acids and some electrolytes.

Diabetes mellitus	Diabetes mellitus is a medical disorder characterized by varying or persistent hyperglycemia (elevated blood sugar levels), especially after eating. All types of diabetes mellitus share similar symptoms and complications at advanced stages.
Elderly	Old age consists of ages nearing the average life span of human beings, and thus the end of the human life cycle. Euphemisms for older people include advanced adult, elderly, and senior or senior citizen.
Adolescence	Adolescence is the period of psychological and social transition between childhood and adulthood (gender-specific manhood, or womanhood). As a transitional stage of human development it represents the period of time during which a juvenile matures into adulthood.
Autoimmune	Autoimmune refers to immune reactions against normal body cells; self against self.
Autoimmune disease	Disease that results when the immune system mistakenly attacks the body's own tissues is referred to as autoimmune disease.
Injection	A method of rapid drug delivery that puts the substance directly in the bloodstream, in a muscle, or under the skin is called injection.
Gestational diabetes	A form of diabetes that develops during pregnancy and typically disappears after the baby is delivered is gestational diabetes.
Childbirth	Childbirth (also called labour, birth, partus or parturition) is the culmination of a human pregnancy with the emergence of a newborn infant from its mother's uterus.
Glucose	Glucose, a simple monosaccharide sugar, is one of the most important carbohydrates and is used as a source of energy in animals and plants. Glucose is one of the main products of photosynthesis and starts respiration.
Receptor	A receptor is a protein on the cell membrane or within the cytoplasm or cell nucleus that binds to a specific molecule (a ligand), such as a neurotransmitter, hormone, or other substance, and initiates the cellular response to the ligand. Receptor, in immunology, the region of an antibody which shows recognition of an antigen.
Urine	Concentrated filtrate produced by the kidneys and excreted via the bladder is called urine.
Channel	Channel, in communications (sometimes called communications channel), refers to the medium used to convey information from a sender (or transmitter) to a receiver.
Prognosis	Prognosis refers to the prospects for the future or outcome of a disease.
Assess	Assess is to systematically and continuously collect, validate, and communicate patient data.
Infusion pump	An infusion pump or perfusor infuses fluids, medication or nutrients into a patient's circulatory system. It is generally used intravenously, although subcutaneous, arterial and epidural infusions are occasionally used.
Sodium	Sodium is the chemical element in the periodic table that has the symbol Na (Natrium in Latin) and atomic number 11. Sodium is a soft, waxy, silvery reactive metal belonging to the alkali metals that is abundant in natural compounds (especially halite). It is highly reactive.
Fiber	Fibers used by man come from a wide variety of sources: Natural fiber include those made out of plants, animal and mineral sources. Natural fibers can be classified according to their origin.
Clinical	Although nearly any mood with some element of sadness may colloquially be termed a

Go to **Cram101.com** for the Practice Tests for this Chapter.

439

depression	depression, clinical depression is more than just a temporary state of sadness. Symptoms lasting two weeks or longer in duration, and of a severity that they begin to interfere with daily living.
Kidney	The kidney is a bean-shaped excretory organ in vertebrates. Part of the urinary system, the kidneys filter wastes (especially urea) from the blood and excrete them, along with water, as urine.
Cesarean	A caesarean section (cesarean section AE), or C-section, is a form of childbirth in which a surgical incision is made through a mother's abdomen (laparotomy) and uterus (hysterotomy) to deliver one or more babies. It is usually performed when a vaginal delivery would lead to medical complications.
Cesarean section	A cesarean section is a form of childbirth in which a surgical incision is made through a mother's abdomen and uterus to deliver one or more babies. It is usually performed when a vaginal delivery would lead to medical complications.
Pneumonia	Pneumonia is an illness of the lungs and respiratory system in which the microscopic, air-filled sacs (alveoli) responsible for absorbing oxygen from the atmosphere become inflamed and flooded with fluid.
Vaccine	A harmless variant or derivative of a pathogen used to stimulate a host organism's immune system to mount a long-term defense against the pathogen is referred to as vaccine.
Intolerance	Intolerance refers to a type of interaction in which two or more drugs produce extremely uncomfortable symptoms.
Lactose	Lactose is a disaccharide that makes up around 2-8% of the solids in milk. Lactose is a disaccharide consisting of two subunits, a galactose and a glucose linked together.
Lactose intolerance	Lactose intolerance is the condition in which lactase, an enzyme needed for proper metabolization of lactose (a constituent of milk and other dairy products), is not produced in adulthood.
Stomach	The stomach is an organ in the alimentary canal used to digest food. It's primary function is not the absorption of nutrients from digested food; rather, the main job of the stomach is to break down large food molecules into smaller ones, so that they can be absorbed into the blood more easily.
Lactase	Lactase (LCT), a member of the β-galactosidase family of enzyme, is involved in the hydrolysis of lactose into constituent galactose and glucose monomers. In humans, lactase is present predominantly along the brush border membrane of the differentiated enterocytes lining the villi of the small intestine.
Intestine	The intestine is the portion of the alimentary canal extending from the stomach to the anus and, in humans and mammals, consists of two segments, the small intestine and the large intestine. The intestine is the part of the body responsible for extracting nutrition from food.
Syndrome	Syndrome is the association of several clinically recognizable features, signs, symptoms, phenomena or characteristics which often occur together, so that the presence of one feature alerts the physician to the presence of the others
Irritable bowel syndrome	In gastroenterology, irritable bowel syndrome is a functional bowel disorder characterized by abdominal pain and changes in bowel habits which are not associated with any abnormalities seen on routine clinical testing.
Ulcerative colitis	Ulcerative colitis (UC) is a form of inflammatory bowel disease (IBD) featuring systemic inflammation specifically causing episodic mucosal inflammation of the colon (large bowel).

Go to **Cram101.com** for the Practice Tests for this Chapter.

441

Large intestine	In anatomy of the digestive system, the colon, also called the large intestine or large bowel, is the part of the intestine from the cecum ('caecum' in British English) to the rectum. Its primary purpose is to extract water from feces.
Steroid	A steroid is a lipid characterized by a carbon skeleton with four fused rings. Different steroids vary in the functional groups attached to these rings. Hundreds of distinct steroids have been identified in plants and animals. Their most important role in most living systems is as hormones.
Digestive system	The organ system that ingests food, breaks it down into smaller chemical units, and absorbs the nutrient molecules is referred to as the digestive system.
Stress management	Stress management encompasses techniques intended to equip a person with effective coping mechanisms for dealing with psychological stress.
Antidepressant	An antidepressant is a medication used primarily in the treatment of clinical depression. They are not thought to produce tolerance, although sudden withdrawal may produce adverse effects. They create little if any immediate change in mood and require between several days and several weeks to take effect.
Small intestine	The small intestine is the part of the gastrointestinal tract between the stomach and the large intestine (colon). In humans over 5 years old it is about 7m long. It is divided into three structural parts: duodenum, jejunum and ileum.
Peptic ulcer	Peptic ulcer is an ulcer of one of those areas of the gastrointestinal tract that are usually acidic.
Lesion	A lesion is a non-specific term referring to abnormal tissue in the body. It can be caused by any disease process including trauma (physical, chemical, electrical), infection, neoplasm, metabolic and autoimmune.
Ulcer	An ulcer is an open sore of the skin, eyes or mucous membrane, often caused by an initial abrasion and generally maintained by an inflammation and/or an infection.
Wound	A wound is type of physical trauma wherein the skin is torn, cut or punctured, or where blunt force trauma causes a contusion.
Acid	An acid is a water-soluble, sour-tasting chemical compound that when dissolved in water, gives a solution with a pH of less than 7.
Cholecystitis	Cholecystitis is inflammation of the gallbladder. It is commonly due to impaction (sticking) of a gallstone within the neck of the gall bladder, leading to inspiszation of bile, bile stasis, and infection by gut organisms.
Gallbladder	The gallbladder is a pear-shaped organ that stores bile until the body needs it for digestion. It is connected to the liver and the duodenum by the biliary tract.
Bile	Bile is a bitter, greenish-yellow alkaline fluid secreted by the liver of most vertebrates. In many species, it is stored in the gallbladder between meals and upon eating is discharged into the duodenum where it aids the process of digestion.
Cholesterol	Cholesterol is a steroid, a lipid, and an alcohol, found in the cell membranes of all body tissues, and transported in the blood plasma of all animals. It is an important component of the membranes of cells, providing stability; it makes the membrane's fluidity stable over a bigger temperature interval.
Gallstone	A gallstone is a crystalline body formed within the body by accretion or concretion of normal or abnormal bile components. They can occur anywhere within the biliary tree, including the gallbladder and the common bile duct.
Minerals	Minerals refer to inorganic chemical compounds found in nature; salts.

Go to **Cram101.com** for the Practice Tests for this Chapter.

Calcium	Calcium is the chemical element in the periodic table that has the symbol Ca and atomic number 20. Calcium is a soft grey alkaline earth metal that is used as a reducing agent in the extraction of thorium, zirconium and uranium. Calcium is also the fifth most abundant element in the Earth's crust.
Joint	A joint (articulation) is the location at which two bones make contact (articulate). They are constructed to both allow movement and provide mechanical support.
Cartilage	Cartilage is a type of dense connective tissue. Cartilage is composed of cells called chondrocytes which are dispersed in a firm gel-like ground substance, called the matrix. Cartilage is avascular (contains no blood vessels) and nutrients are diffused through the matrix.
Cardiovascular disease	Cardiovascular disease refers to afflictions in the mechanisms, including the heart, blood vessels, and their controllers, that are responsible for transporting blood to the body's tissues and organs. Psychological factors may play important roles in such diseases and their treatments.
Fusion	Fusion refers to the combination of two atoms into a single atom as a result of a collision, usually accompanied by the release of energy.
Acute pain	Acute pain refers to pain that typically follows an injury and that disappears once the injury heals or is effectively treated.
Shock	Circulatory shock, a state of cardiac output that is insufficient to meet the body's physiological needs, with consequences ranging from fainting to death is referred to as shock. Insulin shock, a state of severe hypoglycemia caused by administration of insulin.
Microorganism	A microorganism or microbe is an organism that is so small that it is microscopic (invisible to the naked eye).
Inflammatory response	Inflammatory response refers to a complex sequence of events involving chemicals and immune cells that results in the isolation and destruction of antigens and tissues near the antigens.
Fibromyalgia	Fibromyalgia refers to a chronic, rheumatoid-like disorder that can be highly painful and difficult to diagnose.
Axial skeleton	The axial skeleton consists of the bones in the head and trunk of a vertebrate body. It is composed of three major parts; the skull, the bony thorax (i.e. the ribs and sternum), and the vertebral column.
Skeleton	In biology, the skeleton or skeletal system is the biological system providing physical support in living organisms.
Palpation	Palpation is a method of examination in which the examiner feels the size or shape or firmness or location of something.
Systemic lupus erythematosus	An autoimmune, inflammatory disease that may affect every tissue of the body is called systemic lupus erythematosus.
Lupus erythematosus	Lupus erythematosus is a rheumatological autoimmune disorder in which antibodies are created against the patient's own DNA. It can cause various symptoms, but the main ones relate to the skin, kidney, joints, blood and immune system.
Scleroderma	Scleroderma is a rare, chronic disease characterized by excessive deposits of collagen.Scleroderma affects the skin, and in more serious cases it can affect the blood vessels and internal organs. The most evident symptom is the hardening of the skin and associated scarring.
Connective	Connective tissue is any type of biological tissue with an extensive extracellular matrix and

445

tissue	often serves to support, bind together, and protect organs.
Shunt	In medicine, a shunt is a hole or passage which moves, or allows movement of, fluid from one part of the body to another. The term may describe either congenital or acquired shunts; and acquired shunts may be either biological or mechanical.
Vasoconstriction	Vasoconstriction refers to a decrease in the diameter of a blood vessel.
Nicotine	Nicotine is an organic compound, an alkaloid found naturally throughout the tobacco plant, with a high concentration in the leaves. It is a potent nerve poison and is included in many insecticides. In lower concentrations, the substance is a stimulant and is one of the main factors leading to the pleasure and habit-forming qualities of tobacco smoking.
Chronic pain	Chronic pain is defined as pain that has lasted 6 months or longer.
Dislocation	Dislocation occurs when bones are forced out of their normal alignment at a joint.
Vertebrae	Vertebrae are the individual bones that make up the vertebral column (aka spine) - a flexuous and flexible column.
Epidemic	An epidemic is a disease that appears as new cases in a given human population, during a given period, at a rate that substantially exceeds what is "expected", based on recent experience.
Rehabilitation	Rehabilitation is the restoration of lost capabilities, or the treatment aimed at producing it. Also refers to treatment for dependency on psychoactive substances such as alcohol, prescription drugs, and illicit drugs such as cocaine, heroin or amphetamines.
Complaint	Complaint refers to report made by the police or some other agency to the court that initiates the intake process.
Excretion	Excretion is the biological process by which an organism chemically separates waste products from its body. The waste products are then usually expelled from the body by elimination.
Hemoglobin	Hemoglobin is the iron-containing oxygen-transport metalloprotein in the red cells of the blood in mammals and other animals. Hemoglobin transports oxygen from the lungs to the rest of the body, such as to the muscles, where it releases the oxygen load.
Red blood cell	The red blood cell is the most common type of blood cell and is the vertebrate body's principal means of delivering oxygen from the lungs or gills to body tissues via the blood.
Red blood cells	Red blood cells are the most common type of blood cell and are the vertebrate body's principal means of delivering oxygen from the lungs or gills to body tissues via the blood.
Thyroid	The thyroid is one of the larger endocrine glands in the body. It is located in the neck and produces hormones, principally thyroxine and triiodothyronine, that regulate the rate of metabolism and affect the growth and rate of function of many other systems in the body.
Conditioning	Processes by which behaviors can be learned or modified through interaction with the environment are conditioning.
Drug abuse	Drug abuse has a wide range of definitions, all of them relating either to the misuse or overuse of a psychoactive drug or performance enhancing drug for a non-therapeutic or non-medical effect, or referring to any use of illegal drug in the absence of a required, yet practically impossible to get, license from a government authority.
Apathy	Apathy is the lack of emotion, motivation, or enthusiasm. Apathy is a psychological term for a state of indifference where an individual is unresponsive or "indifferent" to aspects of emotional, social, or physical life.
Lumbar	In anatomy, lumbar is an adjective that means of or pertaining to the abdominal segment of the torso, between the diaphragm and the sacrum (pelvis). The five vertebra in the lumbar

region are the largest and strongest in the spinal column.

Pelvis	The pelvis is the bony structure located at the base of the spine (properly known as the caudal end). The pelvis incorporates the socket portion of the hip joint for each leg (in bipeds) or hind leg (in quadrupeds). It forms the lower limb (or hind-limb) girdle of the skeleton.
Lymph node	A lymph node acts as a filter, with an internal honeycomb of connective tissue filled with lymphocytes that collect and destroy bacteria and viruses. When the body is fighting an infection, these lymphocytes multiply rapidly and produce a characteristic swelling of the lymph node.
Lymph	Lymph originates as blood plasma lost from the circulatory system, which leaks out into the surrounding tissues. The lymphatic system collects this fluid by diffusion into lymph capillaries, and returns it to the circulatory system.
Virus	Obligate intracellular parasite of living cells consisting of an outer capsid and an inner core of nucleic acid is referred to as virus. The term virus usually refers to those particles that infect eukaryotes whilst the term bacteriophage or phage is used to describe those infecting prokaryotes.
Chronic fatigue syndrome	Chronic fatigue syndrome is incapacitating exhaustion following only minimal exertion, accompanied by fever, headaches, muscle and joint pain, depression, and anxiety.
Typing	Determining a patients blood type is called typing.
Statistics	Statistics is a type of data analysis which practice includes the planning, summarizing, and interpreting of observations of a system possibly followed by predicting or forecasting of future events based on a mathematical model of the system being observed.
Statistic	A statistic is an observable random variable of a sample.
Compensation	Compensation refers to according to Adler, efforts to overcome imagined or real inferiorities by developing one's abilities.
Carpal	In human anatomy, the carpal bones are the bones of the human wrist.There are eight of them altogether, and they can be thought of as forming two rows of four.
Carpal tunnel syndrome	Carpal tunnel syndrome (CTS) is a medical condition in which the median nerve is compressed at the wrist causing symptoms like tingling, pain, coldness, and sometimes weakness in parts of the hand.
Median	The median is a number that separates the higher half of a sample, a population, or a probability distribution from the lower half. It is the middle value in a distribution, above and below which lie an equal number of values.
Immunology	Immunology refers to the branch of science that deals with the immune system and attempts to understand the many phenomena that are responsible for both acquired and innate immunity. It also includes the use of antibodyantigen reactions in other laboratory work .
Anxiety	Anxiety is a complex combination of the feeling of fear, apprehension and worry often accompanied by physical sensations such as palpitations, chest pain and/or shortness of breath.
Health promotion	Any planned combination of educational, political, regulatory, and organizational supports for actions and conditions of living conducive to the health of individuals, groups, or communities is called health promotion.
Epidemiology	Epidemiology is the study of the distribution and determinants of disease and disorders in human populations, and the use of its knowledge to control health problems.Epidemiology is considered the cornerstone methodology in all of public health research, and is highly

	regarded in evidence-based clinical medicine for identifying risk factors for disease and determining optimal treatment approaches to clinical practice.
Public health	Public health is concerned with threats to the overall health of a community based on population health analysis.
Vital statistics	Vital statistics are the information maintained by a government, recording the birth and death of individuals within that government's jurisdiction. These data are used by public health programs to evaluate how effective are their programs and are the cornerstone to public health systems today.
Mortality	The incidence of death in a population is mortality.
Osteoporosis	Osteoporosis is a disease of bone in which bone mineral density (BMD) is reduced, bone microarchitecture is disrupted, the amount and variety of non-collagenous proteins in bone is changed, and a concomitantly fracture risk is increased.
Older adult	Older adult is an adult over the age of 65.
Urinary incontinence	Urinary incontinence is the involuntary excretion of urine from one's body. It is often temporary, and it almost always results from an underlying medical condition.

Dementia	Dementia is progressive decline in cognitive function due to damage or disease in the brain beyond what might be expected from normal aging.
Health	Health is a term that refers to a combination of the absence of illness, the ability to cope with everyday activities, physical fitness, and high quality of life.
Epidemiologist	A epidemiologist specializes in the scientific study of factors affecting the health and illness of individuals and populations, and serves as the foundation and logic of interventions made in the interest of public health and preventive medicine.
Public health	Public health is concerned with threats to the overall health of a community based on population health analysis.
Mental health	Mental health refers to the 'thinking' part of psychosocial health; includes your values, attitudes, and beliefs.
Lifestyle	The culturally, socially, economically, and environmentally conditioned complex of actions characteristic of an individual, group, or community as a pattern of habituated behavior over time that is health related but not necessarily health directed is a lifestyle.
Wellness	A dimension of health beyond the absence of disease or infirmity, including social, emotional, and spiritual aspects of health is called wellness.
Health promotion	Any planned combination of educational, political, regulatory, and organizational supports for actions and conditions of living conducive to the health of individuals, groups, or communities is called health promotion.
Atom	An atom is the smallest possible particle of a chemical element that retains its chemical properties.
Lead	Lead is a chemical element in the periodic table that has the symbol Pb and atomic number 82. A soft, heavy, toxic and malleable poor metal, lead is bluish white when freshly cut but tarnishes to dull gray when exposed to air. Lead is used in building construction, lead-acid batteries, bullets and shot, and is part of solder, pewter, and fusible alloys.
Assess	Assess is to systematically and continuously collect, validate, and communicate patient data.
Life changes	Any noticeable alterations in one's living circumstances that require readjustment are referred to as life changes.
Conception	Conception is fusion of gametes to form a new organism. In animals, the process involves a sperm fusing with an ovum, which eventually leads to the development of an embryo.
Ageism	Prejudice against other people because of their age, especially prejudice against older adults is referred to as ageism.
Gerontology	The interdisciplinary study of aging and of the special problems of the elderly is referred to as gerontology.
Gerontologists	Gerontologists are health care professionals who specialize in working with older adults. They provide their services to people in nursing homes, senior citizen centers, and other similar facilities.
Organ	Organ refers to a structure consisting of several tissues adapted as a group to perform specific functions.
Cardiovascular system	The circulatory system or cardiovascular system is the organ system which circulates blood around the body of most animals.
Arthritis	Arthritis is a group of conditions that affect the health of the bone joints in the body. Arthritis can be caused from strains and injuries caused by repetitive motion, sports, overexertion, and falls. Unlike the autoimmune diseases, it largely affects older people and

	results from the degeneration of joint cartilage.
Obesity	The state of being more than 20 percent above the average weight for a person of one's height is called obesity.
Chronic illness	A chronic illness is a persistent and lasting condition that generally involves progressive deterioration and an increase in symptoms and disability.
Host	Host is an organism that harbors a parasite, mutual partner, or commensal partner; or a cell infected by a virus.
Heart rate	Heart rate is a term used to describe the frequency of the cardiac cycle. It is considered one of the four vital signs. Usually it is calculated as the number of contractions of the heart in one minute and expressed as "beats per minute".
Critical period	A period of time when an instinctive response can be elicited by a particular stimulus is referred to as critical period.
Helplessness	A maladaptive pattern of achievement behavior in which children avoid challenge, do not persist in the face of difficulty, and tend to attribute their failure on tasks to a lack of ability rather than a lack of effort or an inappropriate strategy is referred to as helplessness.
Learned helplessness	A model for the acquisition of depressive behavior, based on findings that organisms in aversive situations learn to show inactivity when their operants go unreinforced are called learned helplessness.
Elderly	Old age consists of ages nearing the average life span of human beings, and thus the end of the human life cycle. Euphemisms for older people include advanced adult, elderly, and senior or senior citizen.
Activities of daily living	Activities of daily living is a way to describe the functional status of a person.
Older adult	Older adult is an adult over the age of 65.
Population	Population refers to all members of a well-defined group of organisms, events, or things.
Construct	Generalized concept, such as anxiety or gravity, which is constructed in a theoretical manner is referred to as construct.
Character	Character is a constellation of enduring motivational and other traits that are manifested in the characteristic ways that an individual reacts to various kinds of challenges.
Healthy aging	The use of lifestyle choices to maximize longevity and increase quality of life is called healthy aging.
Mortality	The incidence of death in a population is mortality.
Medicare	Medicare refers to government health insurance for those over sixty-five.
Chronic disease	Disease of long duration often not detected in its early stages and from which the patient will not recover is referred to as a chronic disease.
Blood pressure	Blood pressure is the pressure exerted by the blood on the walls of the blood vessels.
Cancer	Cancer is a class of diseases or disorders characterized by uncontrolled division of cells and the ability of these cells to invade other tissues, either by direct growth into adjacent tissue through invasion or by implantation into distant sites by metastasis.
Blood	Blood is a circulating tissue composed of fluid plasma and cells. The main function of blood is to supply nutrients (oxygen, glucose) and constitutional elements to tissues and to remove waste products.

Nerve cell	A cell specialized to originate or transmit nerve impulses is referred to as nerve cell.
Muscle	Muscle is a contractile form of tissue. It is one of the four major tissue types, the other three being epithelium, connective tissue and nervous tissue. Muscle contraction is used to move parts of the body, as well as to move substances within the body.
Nerve	A nerve is an enclosed, cable-like bundle of nerve fibers or axons, which includes the glia that ensheath the axons in myelin.
Brain	The part of the central nervous system involved in regulating and controlling body activity and interpreting information from the senses transmitted through the nervous system is referred to as the brain.
Insulin	Insulin is a polypeptide hormone that regulates carbohydrate metabolism. Apart from being the primary effector in carbohydrate homeostasis, it also has a substantial effect on small vessel muscle tone, controls storage and release of fat (triglycerides) and cellular uptake of both amino acids and some electrolytes.
Medical therapies	Any bodily therapy, such as drug therapy, electroshock, or psychosurgery are medical therapies.
Medical therapy	Any bodily therapy, such as drug therapy, electroshock, or psychosurgery are considered a medical therapy.
Embryonic stem cell	An embryonic stem cell is a cultured cell obtained from the undifferentiated inner mass cells of an early stage human embryo (sometimes called a blastocyst, which is an embryo that is between 50 to 150 cells).
In vitro	In vitro is an experimental technique where the experiment is performed in a test tube, or generally outside a living organism or cell.
Egg	An egg is the zygote, resulting from fertilization of the ovum. It nourishes and protects the embryo.
Implantation	Implantation refers to attachment and penetration of the embryo into the lining of the uterus.
Embryo	A prenatal stage of development after germ layers form but before the rudiments of all organs are present is referred to as an embryo.
Advocate	An advocate is one who speaks on behalf of another, especially in a legal context. Implicit in the concept is the notion that the represented lacks the knowledge, skill, ability, or standing to speak for themselves.
Donor	Blood donation is a process by which a blood donor voluntarily has blood drawn for storage in a blood bank for subsequent use in a blood transfusion.
Tissue	A collection of interconnected cells that perform a similar function within an organism is called tissue.
Theory	Theory refers to an explanatory statement, or set of statements, that concisely summarizes the state of knowledge on a phenomenon and provides direction for further study.
Autoimmune	Autoimmune refers to immune reactions against normal body cells; self against self.
Immune system	The immune system is the system of specialized cells and organs that protect an organism from outside biological influences. When the immune system is functioning properly, it protects the body against bacteria and viral infections, destroying cancer cells and foreign substances.
Stress	Stress refers to a condition that is a response to factors that change the human systems normal state.

Go to **Cram101.com** for the Practice Tests for this Chapter.

Mutation	A change in the structure of a gene is called a mutation.
Genes	Genes are the units of heredity in living organisms. They are encoded in the organism's genetic material (usually DNA or RNA), and control the development and behavior of the organism.
Adjustment	Adjustment is an attempt to cope with a given situation.
Adaptation	A biological adaptation is an anatomical structure, physiological process or behavioral trait of an organism that has evolved over a period of time by the process of natural selection such that it increases the expected long-term reproductive success of the organism.
Stimulus	Stimulus in a nervous system, a factor that triggers sensory transduction.
Maladjustment	Maladjustment is the condition of being unable to adapt properly to your environment with resulting emotional instability.
Rosacea	Rosacea is a common but often misunderstood condition that is estimated to affect over 45 million people worldwide. It begins as flushing and redness on the central face and across the cheeks, nose, or forehead but can also less commonly affect the neck, chest, scalp or ears.
Skin	Skin is an organ of the integumentary system composed of a layer of tissues that protect underlying muscles and organs.
Osteoporosis	Osteoporosis is a disease of bone in which bone mineral density (BMD) is reduced, bone microarchitecture is disrupted, the amount and variety of non-collagenous proteins in bone is changed, and a concomitantly fracture risk is increased.
Pallor	Pallor is an abnormal loss of skin or mucous membrane color. It can develop suddenly or gradually, depending of the cause.
Alcohol	Alcohol is a general term, applied to any organic compound in which a hydroxyl group (-OH) is bound to a carbon atom, which in turn is bound to other hydrogen and/or carbon atoms. The general formula for a simple acyclic alcohol is $C_nH_{2n+1}OH$.
Affect	Affect is the scientific term used to describe a subject's externally displayed mood. This can be assesed by the nurse by observing facial expression, tone of voice, and body language.
Life span	Life span refers to the upper boundary of life, the maximum number of years an individual can live. The maximum life span of human beings is about 120 years of age.
Minerals	Minerals refer to inorganic chemical compounds found in nature; salts.
Joint	A joint (articulation) is the location at which two bones make contact (articulate). They are constructed to both allow movement and provide mechanical support.
Calcium	Calcium is the chemical element in the periodic table that has the symbol Ca and atomic number 20. Calcium is a soft grey alkaline earth metal that is used as a reducing agent in the extraction of thorium, zirconium and uranium. Calcium is also the fifth most abundant element in the Earth's crust.
Cartilage	Cartilage is a type of dense connective tissue. Cartilage is composed of cells called chondrocytes which are dispersed in a firm gel-like ground substance, called the matrix. Cartilage is avascular (contains no blood vessels) and nutrients are diffused through the matrix.
Adolescence	Adolescence is the period of psychological and social transition between childhood and adulthood (gender-specific manhood, or womanhood). As a transitional stage of human development it represents the period of time during which a juvenile matures into adulthood.
Skeleton	In biology, the skeleton or skeletal system is the biological system providing physical

Go to **Cram101.com** for the Practice Tests for this Chapter.

	support in living organisms.
Course	Pattern of development and change of a disorder over time is a course.
Testosterone	Testosterone is a steroid hormone from the androgen group. Testosterone is secreted in the testes of men and the ovaries of women. It is the principal male sex hormone and the "original" anabolic steroid. In both males and females, it plays key roles in health and well-being.
Risk factor	A risk factor is a variable associated with an increased risk of disease or infection but risk factors are not necessarily causal.
Menopause	Menopause is the physiological cessation of menstrual cycles associated with advancing age in species that experience such cycles. Menopause is sometimes referred to as change of life or climacteric.
Susceptibility	The degree of resistance of a host to a pathogen is susceptibility.
Vertebrae	Vertebrae are the individual bones that make up the vertebral column (aka spine) - a flexuous and flexible column.
Hip	In anatomy, the hip is the bony projection of the femur, known as the greater trochanter, and the overlying muscle and fat.
Anorexia	Anorexia nervosa is an eating disorder characterized by voluntary starvation and exercise stress.
Anticonvulsant	The anticonvulsant belong to a diverse group of pharmaceuticals used in prevention of the occurrence of epileptic seizures. The goal of an anticonvulsant is to suppress the rapid and excessive firing of neurons that start a seizure.
Glucocorticoid	Glucocorticoid is a class of steroid hormones characterized by the ability to bind with the cortisol receptor and trigger similar effects. They are distinguished from mineralocorticoids and sex steroids by the specific receptors, target cells, and effects.
Vitamin	An organic compound other than a carbohydrate, lipid, or protein that is needed for normal metabolism but that the body cannot synthesize in adequate amounts is called a vitamin.
Skull	Skull refers to a bony protective encasement of the brain and the organs of hearing and equilibrium; includes the facial bones. Also called the cranium.
Urination	Urination is the process of disposing urine from the urinary bladder through the urethra to the outside of the body. The process of urination is usually under voluntary control.
Bladder	A hollow muscular storage organ for storing urine is a bladder.
Urine	Concentrated filtrate produced by the kidneys and excreted via the bladder is called urine.
Urinary incontinence	Urinary incontinence is the involuntary excretion of urine from one's body. It is often temporary, and it almost always results from an underlying medical condition.
Infection	The invasion and multiplication of microorganisms in body tissues is called an infection.
Cataract	Opaqueness of the lens of the eye, making the lens incapable of transmitting light is called a cataract.
Retina	The retina is a thin layer of cells at the back of the eyeball of vertebrates and some cephalopods; it is the part of the eye which converts light into nervous signals.
Lens	The lens or crystalline lens is a transparent, biconvex structure in the eye that, along with the cornea, helps to refract light to focus on the retina. Its function is thus similar to a man-made optical lens.

Go to **Cram101.com** for the Practice Tests for this Chapter.

Elevation	Elevation refers to upward movement of a part of the body.
Glaucoma	Glaucoma is a group of diseases of the optic nerve involving loss of retinal ganglion cells in a characteristic pattern of optic neuropathy.
Nervous system	The nervous system of an animal coordinates the activity of the muscles, monitors the organs, constructs and processes input from the senses, and initiates actions.
Central nervous system	The central nervous system comprized of the brain and spinal cord, represents the largest part of the nervous system. Together with the peripheral nervous system, it has a fundamental role in the control of behavior.
Sphincter	Muscle that surrounds a tube and closes or opens the tube by contracting and relaxing is referred to as sphincter.
Kegel exercises	Factors such as pregnancy, childbirth and being overweight often result in the weakening of pelvic muscles. Kegel exercises are useful in regaining pelvic floor muscle strength in such cases.
Biofeedback	Biofeedback is the process of measuring and quantifying an aspect of a subject's physiology, analyzing the data, and then feeding back the information to the subject in a form that allows the subject to enact physiological change.
Stress incontinence	Stress incontinence is involuntary leaking of urine during activities that increase pressure inside the abdomen, such as coughing, sneezing, or jogging.
Stroke	A stroke or cerebrovascular accident (CVA) occurs when the blood supply to a part of the brain is suddenly interrupted.
Stroke volume	The amount of blood pumped by the left ventricle in each contraction is called stroke volume.
Lungs	Lungs are the essential organs of respiration in air-breathing vertebrates. Their principal function is to transport oxygen from the atmosphere into the bloodstream, and to excrete carbon dioxide from the bloodstream into the atmosphere.
Vital capacity	Vital capacity is the total amount of air that a person can expire after a complete inspiration.
Eye	An eye is an organ that detects light. Different kinds of light-sensitive organs are found in a variety of creatures. The simplest eyes do nothing but detect whether the surroundings are light or dark, while more complex eyes can distinguish shapes and colors.
Pupil	Pupil refers to the opening in the iris that admits light into the interior of the vertebrate eye. Muscles in the iris regulate its size.
Depth perception	Ability to distinguish between near and far objects and to judge their distance is called depth perception.
Farsightedness	Farsightedness is a defect of vision caused by an imperfection in the eye (often when the eyeball is too short or when the lens cannot become round enough), causing inability to focus on near objects, and in extreme cases causing a sufferer to be unable to focus on objects at any distance.
Protein	A protein is a complex, high-molecular-weight organic compound that consists of amino acids joined by peptide bonds. They are essential to the structure and function of all living cells and viruses. Many are enzymes or subunits of enzymes.
Diabetes	Diabetes is a medical disorder characterized by varying or persistent elevated blood sugar levels, especially after eating. All types of diabetes share similar symptoms and complications at advanced stages: dehydration and ketoacidosis, cardiovascular disease, chronic renal failure, retinal damage which can lead to blindness, nerve damage which can

lead to erectile dysfunction, gangrene with risk of amputation of toes, feet, and even legs.

Anterior chamber	The anterior chamber if the fluid-filled space inside the eye between the iris and the cornea's innermost surface, the endothelium.
Optic nerve	The optic nerve is the nerve that transmits visual information from the retina to the brain. The blind spot of the eye is produced by the absence of retina where the optic nerve leaves the eye. This is because there are no photoreceptors in this area.
Nearsightedness	Nearsightedness refers to an inability to focus on distant objects; occurs when the eyeball is longer than normal and the lens focuses distant objects in front of the retina; also called myopia.
Macula	The macula is an oval yellow spot near the center of the retina of the human eye. Near its center is the fovea, a small pit that contains the largest concentration of cone cells in the eye and is responsible for central vision.
Trial	In classical conditioning, any presentation of a stimulus or pair of stimuli is called a trial.
Zinc	Zinc is a chemical element in the periodic table that has the symbol Zn and atomic number 30.
Vagina	The vagina is the tubular tract leading from the uterus to the exterior of the body in female placental mammals and marsupials, or to the cloaca in female birds, monotremes, and some reptiles. Female insects and other invertebrates also have a vagina, which is the terminal part of the oviduct.
Physiological changes	Alterations in heart rate, blood pressure, perspiration, and other involuntary responses are physiological changes.
Sexual dysfunction	Sexual dysfunction or sexual malfunction is difficulty during any stage of the sexual act (which includes desire, arousal, orgasm, and resolution) that prevents the individual or couple from enjoying sexual activity.
Epithelium	Epithelium is a tissue composed of a layer of cells. Epithelium can be found lining internal (e.g. endothelium, which lines the inside of blood vessels) or external (e.g. skin) free surfaces of the body. Functions include secretion, absorption and protection.
Ulcer	An ulcer is an open sore of the skin, eyes or mucous membrane, often caused by an initial abrasion and generally maintained by an inflammation and/or an infection.
Disorientation	A state of mental confusion with respect to time, place, identity of self, other persons, and objects is disorientation.
Diagnosis	In medicine, diagnosis is the process of identifying a medical condition or disease by its signs, symptoms, and from the results of various diagnostic procedures.
Heterogeneous	A heterogeneous compound, mixture, or other such object is one that consists of many different items, which are often not easily sorted or separated, though they are clearly distinct.
Depression	In everyday language depression refers to any downturn in mood, which may be relatively transitory and perhaps due to something trivial. This is differentiated from Clinical depression which is marked by symptoms that last two weeks or more and are so severe that they interfere with daily living.
Fiber	Fibers used by man come from a wide variety of sources: Natural fiber include those made out of plants, animal and mineral sources. Natural fibers can be classified according to their origin.
Predisposition	Predisposition refers to an inclination or diathesis to respond in a certain way, either

Go to **Cram101.com** for the Practice Tests for this Chapter.

	inborn or acquired. In abnormal psychology, it is a factor that lowers the ability to withstand stress and inclines the individual toward pathology.
Inflammation	Inflammation is the first response of the immune system to infection or irritation and may be referred to as the innate cascade.
Virus	Obligate intracellular parasite of living cells consisting of an outer capsid and an inner core of nucleic acid is referred to as virus. The term virus usually refers to those particles that infect eukaryotes whilst the term bacteriophage or phage is used to describe those infecting prokaryotes.
Neurotransmitter	A neurotransmitter is a chemical that is used to relay, amplify and modulate electrical signals between a neuron and another cell.
Chromosomes	Physical structures in the cell's nucleus that house the genes. Each human cell has 23 pairs of chromosomes.
Syndrome	Syndrome is the association of several clinically recognizable features, signs, symptoms, phenomena or characteristics which often occur together, so that the presence of one feature alerts the physician to the presence of the others
Cholesterol	Cholesterol is a steroid, a lipid, and an alcohol, found in the cell membranes of all body tissues, and transported in the blood plasma of all animals. It is an important component of the membranes of cells, providing stability; it makes the membrane's fluidity stable over a bigger temperature interval.
Incidence	In epidemiological studies of a particular disorder, the rate at which new cases occur in a given place at a given time is called incidence.
Sugar	A sugar is the simplest molecule that can be identified as a carbohydrate. These include monosaccharides and disaccharides, trisaccharides and the oligosaccharides. The term "glyco-" indicates the presence of a sugar in an otherwise non-carbohydrate substance.
Liver	The liver is an organ in vertebrates, including humans. It plays a major role in metabolism and has a number of functions in the body including drug detoxification, glycogen storage, and plasma protein synthesis. It also produces bile, which is important for digestion.
Inhibitor	An inhibitor is a type of effector (biology) that decreases or prevents the rate of a chemical reaction. They are often called negative catalysts.
Free radicals	Free radicals are atomic or molecular species with unpaired electrons on an otherwise open shell configuration.
Placebo	A placebo is an inactive substance (pill, liquid, etc.), which is administered as if it were a therapy, but which has no therapeutic value other than the placebo effect.
Alcoholic	An alcoholic is dependent on alcohol as characterized by craving, loss of control, physical dependence and withdrawal symptoms, and tolerance.
Drug interaction	A combined effect of two drugs that exceeds the addition of one drug's effects to the other is a drug interaction.
Medicine	Medicine is the branch of health science and the sector of public life concerned with maintaining or restoring human health through the study, diagnosis and treatment of disease and injury.
Laxatives	Medications used to soften stool and relieve constipation are referred to as laxatives.
Laxative	Laxative refers to a medication or other substance that stimulates evacuation of the intestinal tract.
Metabolic rate	Energy expended by the body per unit time is called metabolic rate.

Go to **Cram101.com** for the Practice Tests for this Chapter.

Metabolism	Metabolism is the biochemical modification of chemical compounds in living organisms and cells. This includes the biosynthesis of complex organic molecules (anabolism) and their breakdown (catabolism).
Alcoholism	A disorder that involves long-term, repeated, uncontrolled, compulsive, and excessive use of alcoholic beverages and that impairs the drinker's health and work and social relationships is called alcoholism.
Illicit drugs	Illicit drugs refers to drugs whose use, possession, cultivation, manufacture, and/or sale are against the law because they are generally recognized as harmful.
Kidney	The kidney is a bean-shaped excretory organ in vertebrates. Part of the urinary system, the kidneys filter wastes (especially urea) from the blood and excrete them, along with water, as urine.
Pharmacist	A pharmacist takes requests for medicines from a physician in the form of a medical prescription and dispense the medication to the patient and counsel them on the proper use and adverse effects of that medication.
Housework	Unpaid work carried on in and around the home such as cooking, cleaning and shopping, is referred to as a housework.
Seta	In plants seta is synonymous with bristle a stiff, strong hair. The term can also be applied to a modified hair-like structure, such as a pappus: a modified calyx in the Asteraceae.
Aerobic	An aerobic organism is an organism that has an oxygen based metabolism. Aerobes, in a process known as cellular respiration, use oxygen to oxidize substrates (for example sugars and fats) in order to obtain energy.
Aerobic exercise	Exercise in which oxygen is used to produce ATP is aerobic exercise.
Stomach	The stomach is an organ in the alimentary canal used to digest food. It's primary function is not the absorption of nutrients from digested food; rather, the main job of the stomach is to break down large food molecules into smaller ones, so that they can be absorbed into the blood more easily.
Resistance	Resistance refers to a nonspecific ability to ward off infection or disease regardless of whether the body has been previously exposed to it. A force that opposes the flow of a fluid such as air or blood. Compare with immunity.
Oxygen	Oxygen is a chemical element in the periodic table. It has the symbol O and atomic number 8. Oxygen is the second most common element on Earth, composing around 46% of the mass of Earth's crust and 28% of the mass of Earth as a whole, and is the third most common element in the universe.
Perimenopause	Perimenopause is the period of time preceding menopause when the menstrual cycle is irregular and menopausal symptoms, hot flashes, night sweats, vaginal dryness, are often experienced.
Absorption	Absorption is a physical or chemical phenomenon or a process in which atoms, molecules, or ions enter some bulk phase - gas, liquid or solid material. In nutrition, amino acids are broken down through digestion, which begins in the stomach.
Comorbidity	Comorbidity refers to the presence of more than one mental disorder occurring in an individual at the same time.
Stigma	Stigma refers to a personal characteristic that at least some other individuals perceive negatively because that characteristic is different than those of the general population.
Respite care	The care provided by substitute caregivers to relieve the principal caregiver from his or her continuous responsibility is respite care.

Go to **Cram101.com** for the Practice Tests for this Chapter.

469

Denial	Denial is a psychological defense mechanism in which a person faced with a fact that is uncomfortable or painful to accept rejects it instead, insisting that it is not true despite what may be overwhelming evidence.
Health	Health is a term that refers to a combination of the absence of illness, the ability to cope with everyday activities, physical fitness, and high quality of life.
Anxiety	Anxiety is a complex combination of the feeling of fear, apprehension and worry often accompanied by physical sensations such as palpitations, chest pain and/or shortness of breath.
Assess	Assess is to systematically and continuously collect, validate, and communicate patient data.
Brainstem	Brainstem refers to a functional unit of the vertebrate brain, composed of the midbrain, medulla oblongata, and the pons; serves mainly as a sensory filter, selecting which information reaches higher brain centers.
Brain	The part of the central nervous system involved in regulating and controlling body activity and interpreting information from the senses transmitted through the nervous system is referred to as the brain.
Concept	A mental category used to class together objects, relations, events, abstractions, or qualities that have common properties is called concept.
Pupil	Pupil refers to the opening in the iris that admits light into the interior of the vertebrate eye. Muscles in the iris regulate its size.
Electroencep-alogram	Electroencephalography is the neurophysiologic measurement of the electrical activity of the brain by recording from electrodes placed on the scalp, or in the special cases on the cortex. The resulting traces are known as an electroencephalogram and represent so-called brainwaves.
Nervous system	The nervous system of an animal coordinates the activity of the muscles, monitors the organs, constructs and processes input from the senses, and initiates actions.
Hypothermia	Hypothermia is a low core body temperature, defined clinically as a temperature of less than 35 degrees celsius.
Barbiturate	A barbiturate is a drug that acts as a central nervous system (CNS) depressant, and by virtue of this produces a wide spectrum of effects, from mild sedation to anesthesia.
Depression	In everyday language depression refers to any downturn in mood, which may be relatively transitory and perhaps due to something trivial. This is differentiated from Clinical depression which is marked by symptoms that last two weeks or more and are so severe that they interfere with daily living.
Central nervous system	The central nervous system comprized of the brain and spinal cord, represents the largest part of the nervous system. Together with the peripheral nervous system, it has a fundamental role in the control of behavior.
Culture	Culture, generally refers to patterns of human activity and the symbolic structures that give such activity significance.
Rejection	Rejection is a response by caregivers where they distance themselves emotionally from a chronically ill patient. Although they provide physical care they tend to scold and and correct the patient continuously.
Autonomy	Self-direction is referred to as autonomy. The ability to function in an independent manner.
Crisis	A crisis is a temporary state of high anxiety where the persons usual coping mechanisims cease to work. This may have a result of disorganization or possibly personality growth.

Hypochondriac	Hypochondriac refers to a person who complains about illnesses that appear to be imaginary.
Infection	The invasion and multiplication of microorganisms in body tissues is called an infection.
Euthanasia	Euthanasia is the practice of killing a person or animal, in a painless or minimally painful way, for merciful reasons, usually to end their suffering.
Pain	Pain is an unpleasant sensation which may be associated with actual or potential tissue damage and which may have physical and emotional components.
Anger	Anger is an emotional response often based on a sensation or perception of threat to one's needs.
Shock	Circulatory shock, a state of cardiac output that is insufficient to meet the body's physiological needs, with consequences ranging from fainting to death is referred to as shock. Insulin shock, a state of severe hypoglycemia caused by administration of insulin.
Extension	Movement increasing the angle between parts at a joint is referred to as extension.
Theory	Theory refers to an explanatory statement, or set of statements, that concisely summarizes the state of knowledge on a phenomenon and provides direction for further study.
Insight	Insight refers to a sudden awareness of the relationships among various elements that had previously appeared to be independent of one another.
Bereavement	The loss or deprivation experienced by a survivor when a loved one dies is referred to as bereavement.
Grief	Grief is a multi-faceted response to loss. Although conventionally focused on the emotional response to loss, it also has a physical, cognitive, behavioral, social and philosophical dimensions.
Mourning	The culturally prescribed behavior patterns for the expression of grief is called mourning.
Older adult	Older adult is an adult over the age of 65.
Developmental task	Developmental task refers to any personal change that must take place for optimal development.
Ritual	Formalized ceremonial behavior in which the members of a group or community regularly engage, is referred to as a ritual. In childbirth it is a repeated series of actions used by women as a way of dealing with the discomfort of labor.
Psychiatrist	A psychiatrist is a physician who specializes in the diagnosis and treatment of psychological disorders.
Insomnia	Insomnia is a sleep disorder characterized by an inability to sleep and/or to remain asleep for a reasonable period during the night.
Susceptibility	The degree of resistance of a host to a pathogen is susceptibility.
Identity	The distinguishing character of the individual: who each of us is, what our roles are, and what we are capable of is called identity.
Attachment	Attachment refers to the psychological tendency to seek closeness to another person, to feel secure when that person is present, and to feel anxious when that person is absent.
Population	Population refers to all members of a well-defined group of organisms, events, or things.
Mortality rate	Mortality rate is the number of deaths (from a disease or in general) per 1000 people and typically reported on an annual basis.
Mortality	The incidence of death in a population is mortality.

Go to **Cram101.com** for the Practice Tests for this Chapter.

Medicine	Medicine is the branch of health science and the sector of public life concerned with maintaining or restoring human health through the study, diagnosis and treatment of disease and injury.
Miscarriage	Miscarriage or spontaneous abortion is the natural or accidental termination of a pregnancy at a stage where the embryo or the fetus is incapable of surviving, generally defined at a gestation of prior to 20 weeks.
Homicide	Death that results from intent to injure or kill is referred to as homicide.
Course	Pattern of development and change of a disorder over time is a course.
Hydration	Hydration can create a hydrate from which water can be reextracted. When hydration occurs in a chemical reaction it is called a hydration reaction, in which water is permanently and chemically combined with a reactant in a way that it can no longer be reextracted.
Intravenous	Present or occurring within a vein, such as an intravenous blood clot is referred to as intravenous. Introduced directly into a vein, such as an intravenous injection or I.V. drip.
Conscious	Conscious refers to the thoughts, feelings, sensations, or memories of which a person is aware at any given moment.
Stomach	The stomach is an organ in the alimentary canal used to digest food. It's primary function is not the absorption of nutrients from digested food; rather, the main job of the stomach is to break down large food molecules into smaller ones, so that they can be absorbed into the blood more easily.
Right to refuse treatment	A legal principle according to which a committed mental patient may decline to participate in treatment is the right to refuse treatment.
Nasogastric tube	A nasogastric tube is a plastic tube, inserted into a nostril through the nose, into the throat, down the oesophagus and into the stomach. The main use of a nasogastric tube is for feeding and for administrating drugs and other oral agents (such as activated charcoal and radiographic contrast material).
Moral	A "moral" may refer to a particular principle, usually as an informal and general summary with respect to a moral principle, as it is applied in a given human situation.
Living will	A living will, also called will to live, advance health directive, or advance health care directive, is a specific type of power of attorney or health care proxy or advance directive. It is a legal instrument that usually is witnessed or notarized.
Life support	Life support, in the medical field, refers to a set of therapies for preserving a patient's life when essential body systems are not functioning sufficiently to sustain life unaided.
Agent	Agent refers to an epidemiological term referring to the organism or object that transmits a disease from the environment to the host.
Constant	A behavior or characteristic that does not vary from one observation to another is referred to as a constant.
Marriage	A socially approved sexual and economic relationship between two or more individuals is a marriage.
Blood	Blood is a circulating tissue composed of fluid plasma and cells. The main function of blood is to supply nutrients (oxygen, glucose) and constitutional elements to tissues and to remove waste products.
Assisted suicide	Physician assisted suicide is where doctors assist terminally ill patients in taking their own life. This is often seen as morally distinct from euthanasia because the physician does not directly cause the patient's death but enables the patient to choose the time and

Go to **Cram101.com** for the Practice Tests for this Chapter.

circumstances of his or her own death.

Legalization	Complete removal of all criminal sanctions for certain behaviors without subsequent regulation, is referred to as a legalization.
Diagnosis	In medicine, diagnosis is the process of identifying a medical condition or disease by its signs, symptoms, and from the results of various diagnostic procedures.
Port	A port is a central venous line that does not have an external connector; instead, it has a small reservoir implanted under the skin.
Terminal illness	Terminal illness is a medical term popularized in the 20th century for an active and progressive disease which cannot be cured and is expected to lead to death. Palliative care is often prescribed to manage symptoms and improve quality of life.
Prognosis	Prognosis refers to the prospects for the future or outcome of a disease.
Psychological disorder	Mental processes and/or behavior patterns that cause emotional distress and/or substantial impairment in functioning is a psychological disorder.
Hospice	Hospice refers to a humanized program committed to making the end of life as free from pain, anxiety, and depression as possible. The goals of hospice contrast with those of a hospital, which are to cure disease and prolong life.
Home care	Home care, also known as domiciliary care, is health care provided in the home by healthcare professionals (often referred to as home health care or formal care) or by family and friends (informal care).
Counselor	A counselor is a mental health professional who specializes in helping people with problems not involving serious mental disorders.
Inpatient	Inpatient refers to a person who enters a healthcare setting for a stay ranging from 24 hours to many years.
Active euthanasia	Active euthanasia refers to a physician painlessly putting to death some persons suffering from incurable conditions or diseases.
Passive euthanasia	Passive euthanasia refers to any act of allowing the patient to die, which may include failing to provide necessary medication as well as taking a patient off life support.
Trauma	Trauma refers to a severe physical injury or wound to the body caused by an external force, or a psychological shock having a lasting effect on mental life.
Conviction	Beliefs that are important to a person and that evoke strong emotion are a conviction.
Quality of life	Quality of life refers to the perception of individuals or groups that their needs are being satisfied and that they are not being denied opportunities to achieve happiness and fulfillment.
Cis	A double bond in which the greater radical on both ends is on the same side of the bond is called a cis.
Eye	An eye is an organ that detects light. Different kinds of light-sensitive organs are found in a variety of creatures. The simplest eyes do nothing but detect whether the surroundings are light or dark, while more complex eyes can distinguish shapes and colors.
Consciousness	Consciousness refers to the ability to perceive, communicate, remember, understand, appreciate, and initiate voluntary movements; a functioning sensorium.
Skin	Skin is an organ of the integumentary system composed of a layer of tissues that protect underlying muscles and organs.
Urine	Concentrated filtrate produced by the kidneys and excreted via the bladder is called urine.

Mantra	A mantra is a religious syllable or poem, typically from the Sanskrit language. Their use varies according to the school and philosophy associated with the mantra. They are primarily used as spiritual conduits, words and vibrations that instill one-pointed concentration in the devotee..
Lead	Lead is a chemical element in the periodic table that has the symbol Pb and atomic number 82. A soft, heavy, toxic and malleable poor metal, lead is bluish white when freshly cut but tarnishes to dull gray when exposed to air. Lead is used in building construction, lead-acid batteries, bullets and shot, and is part of solder, pewter, and fusible alloys.
Stress	Stress refers to a condition that is a response to factors that change the human systems normal state.
Homosexual	Homosexual refers to referring to people who are sexually aroused by and interested in forming romantic relationships with people of the same gender.
Organ	Organ refers to a structure consisting of several tissues adapted as a group to perform specific functions.
Tissue	A collection of interconnected cells that perform a similar function within an organism is called tissue.
Donor	Blood donation is a process by which a blood donor voluntarily has blood drawn for storage in a blood bank for subsequent use in a blood transfusion.
Kidney	The kidney is a bean-shaped excretory organ in vertebrates. Part of the urinary system, the kidneys filter wastes (especially urea) from the blood and excrete them, along with water, as urine.

Mercury	Mercury is a chemical element in the periodic table that has the symbol Hg and atomic number 80. A heavy, silvery, transition metal, mercury is one of five elements that are liquid at or near standard room temperature (the others are the metals caesium, francium, and gallium, and the nonmetal bromine).
Survey	A method of scientific investigation in which a large sample of people answer questions about their attitudes or behavior is referred to as a survey.
Health	Health is a term that refers to a combination of the absence of illness, the ability to cope with everyday activities, physical fitness, and high quality of life.
Population	Population refers to all members of a well-defined group of organisms, events, or things.
Infrastructure	Infrastructure refers to the interface between a sociocultural system and its environment.
Compliance	In medicine, a patient's (or doctor's) adherence to a recommended course of treatment is considered compliance.
HIV	The virus that causes AIDS is HIV (human immunodeficiency virus).
Infectious disease	In medicine, infectious disease or communicable disease is disease caused by a biological agent such as by a virus, bacterium or parasite. This is contrasted to physical causes, such as burns or chemical ones such as through intoxication.
Contraception	A behavior or device that prevents fertilization is called contraception.
Advocate	An advocate is one who speaks on behalf of another, especially in a legal context. Implicit in the concept is the notion that the represented lacks the knowledge, skill, ability, or standing to speak for themselves.
Planning	In agreement with the patient, the nurse addresses each of the problems identified in the planning phase. For each problem a measurable goal is set. For example, for the patient discussed above, the goal would be for the patient's skin to remain intact. The result is a nursing care plan. This is the third step.
Planned parenthood	Planned Parenthood began as the National Birth Control League, which was founded in 1916 under the leadership of Mary Ware Dennett. The organization was later renamed the American Birth Control League under the direction of Margaret Sanger. The League was influential in liberalizing laws against birth control throughout the 1920s and 1930s before changing its name to Planned Parenthood Federation of America, Inc. in 1942.
Solution	Solution refers to homogenous mixture formed when a solute is dissolved in a solvent.
Infanticide	In sociology and biology, infanticide is the practice of intentionally causing the death of an infant of a given species, by members of the same species.
Concept	A mental category used to class together objects, relations, events, abstractions, or qualities that have common properties is called concept.
Sulfur dioxide	Sulfur dioxide refers to a major air pollutant, this toxic gas is formed as a result of burning sulfur. The major sources are burning coal that contain some sulfur and refining metal ores that contain sulfur.
Sulfur	Sulfur is the chemical element in the periodic table that has the symbol S and atomic number 16. It is an abundant, tasteless, odorless, multivalent non-metal. Sulfur, in its native form, is a yellow crystaline solid. In nature, it can be found as the pure element or as sulfide and sulfate minerals.
Mortality rate	Mortality rate is the number of deaths (from a disease or in general) per 1000 people and typically reported on an annual basis.
Mortality	The incidence of death in a population is mortality.

Go to **Cram101.com** for the Practice Tests for this Chapter.

Infant mortality rate	Infant mortality rate refers to proportion of babies born alive who die within the first year.
Infant mortality	Infant mortality is the death of infants in the first year of life. The leading causes of infant mortality are dehydration and disease. Major causes of infant mortality in more developed countries include congenital malformation, infection and SIDS. Infant mortality rate is the number of newborns dying under a year of age divided by the number of live births during the year.
Public health	Public health is concerned with threats to the overall health of a community based on population health analysis.
Incentive	Incentive refers to an object, person, or situation perceived as being capable of satisfying a need.
Carbon	Carbon is a chemical element in the periodic table that has the symbol C and atomic number 6. An abundant nonmetallic, tetravalent element, carbon has several allotropic forms.
Affect	Affect is the scientific term used to describe a subject's externally displayed mood. This can be assesed by the nurse by observing facial expression, tone of voice, and body language.
Ozone	Ozone (O_3) is an allotrope of oxygen, the molecule consisting of three oxygen atoms, a triatomic molecule, instead of the more stable diatomic O_2. Ozone is a powerful oxidizing agent. It is also unstable, decaying to ordinary oxygen through the reaction: $2O_3 \rightarrow 3O_2$.
Lead	Lead is a chemical element in the periodic table that has the symbol Pb and atomic number 82. A soft, heavy, toxic and malleable poor metal, lead is bluish white when freshly cut but tarnishes to dull gray when exposed to air. Lead is used in building construction, lead-acid batteries, bullets and shot, and is part of solder, pewter, and fusible alloys.
Assess	Assess is to systematically and continuously collect, validate, and communicate patient data.
Value	Value is worth in general, and it is thought to be connected to reasons for certain practices, policies, actions, beliefs or emotions. Value is "that which one acts to gain and/or keep."
Heavy metals	The heavy metals are a group of elements between copper and lead on the periodic table of the elements having atomic weights between 63.546 and 200.590 and specific gravities greater than
Lungs	Lungs are the essential organs of respiration in air-breathing vertebrates. Their principal function is to transport oxygen from the atmosphere into the bloodstream, and to excrete carbon dioxide from the bloodstream into the atmosphere.
Agent	Agent refers to an epidemiological term referring to the organism or object that transmits a disease from the environment to the host.
Blood	Blood is a circulating tissue composed of fluid plasma and cells. The main function of blood is to supply nutrients (oxygen, glucose) and constitutional elements to tissues and to remove waste products.
Oxygen	Oxygen is a chemical element in the periodic table. It has the symbol O and atomic number 8. Oxygen is the second most common element on Earth, composing around 46% of the mass of Earth's crust and 28% of the mass of Earth as a whole, and is the third most common element in the universe.
Hydrogen	Hydrogen is a chemical element in the periodic table that has the symbol H and atomic number 1. At standard temperature and pressure it is a colorless, odorless, nonmetallic, univalent, tasteless, highly flammable diatomic gas.
Respiratory	The respiratory system is the biological system of any organism that engages in gas

Go to **Cram101.com** for the Practice Tests for this Chapter.

system	exchange.In humans and other mammals, the respiratory system consists of the airways, the lungs, and the respiratory muscles that mediate the movement of air into and out of the body.
Eye	An eye is an organ that detects light. Different kinds of light-sensitive organs are found in a variety of creatures. The simplest eyes do nothing but detect whether the surroundings are light or dark, while more complex eyes can distinguish shapes and colors.
Bronchitis	Bronchitis is an obstructive pulmonary disease characterized by inflammation of the bronchi of the lungs.
Resistance	Resistance refers to a nonspecific ability to ward off infection or disease regardless of whether the body has been previously exposed to it. A force that opposes the flow of a fluid such as air or blood. Compare with immunity.
Pneumonia	Pneumonia is an illness of the lungs and respiratory system in which the microscopic, air-filled sacs (alveoli) responsible for absorbing oxygen from the atmosphere become inflamed and flooded with fluid.
Asthma	Asthma is a complex disease characterized by bronchial hyperresponsiveness (BHR), inflammation, mucus production and intermittent airway obstruction.
Radiation	The emission of electromagnetic waves by all objects warmer than absolute zero is referred to as radiation.
Susceptibility	The degree of resistance of a host to a pathogen is susceptibility.
Acid Rain	The increased acidity of rainfall which is caused by emissions of sulfur dioxide and nitrogen oxides from power plants and automobile is an acid rain.
Acid	An acid is a water-soluble, sour-tasting chemical compound that when dissolved in water, gives a solution with a pH of less than 7.
Nervous system	The nervous system of an animal coordinates the activity of the muscles, monitors the organs, constructs and processes input from the senses, and initiates actions.
Tissue	A collection of interconnected cells that perform a similar function within an organism is called tissue.
Base	The common definition of a base is a chemical compound that absorbs hydronium ions when dissolved in water (a proton acceptor). An alkali is a special example of a base, where in an aqueous environment, hydroxide ions are donated.
Elimination	Elimination refers to the physiologic excretion of drugs and other substances from the body.
Hydrocarbon	A chemical compound composed only of the elements carbon and hydrogen is called hydrocarbon.
Chemical compound	A chemical compound is a chemical substance formed from two or more elements, with a fixed ratio determining the composition. For example, dihydrogen monoxide (water, H_2O) is a compound composed of two hydrogen atoms for every oxygen atom.
Organic compound	An organic compound is any member of a large class of chemical compounds whose molecules contain carbon, with the exception of carbides, carbonates, carbon oxides and gases containing carbon.
Benzene	Benzene is an organic chemical compound that is a colorless and flammable liquid with a pleasant, sweet smell. Benzene is a known carcinogen. It is a minor, or additive, component of gasoline. It is an important industrial solvent and precursor in the production of drugs, plastics, gasoline, synthetic rubber, and dyes.
Older adult	Older adult is an adult over the age of 65.
Emphysema	Emphysema is a chronic lung disease. It is often caused by exposure to toxic chemicals or

	long-term exposure to tobacco smoke..
Precipitation	The crystallization or suspension of particles that occurs due to the mixing of incompatible solutions or adding solutes to incompatible solutions is called precipitation. This results in the occlusion of an intravenous line.
Leach	To dissolve and filter through soil is to leach.
Crystal	Crystal is a solid in which the constituent atoms, molecules, or ions are packed in a regularly ordered, repeating pattern extending in all three spatial dimensions.
Sulfuric acid	Sulfuric acid refers to the major constituent of acid precipitation. Formed as a result of sulfur dioxide emissions reacting with water vapor in the atmosphere.
Nitric acid	Nitric acid refers to one of the acids in acid rain. Formed by reactions between nitrogen oxides and the water vapor in the atmosphere.
Aluminum	Aluminium is the chemical element in the periodic table that has the symbol Al and atomic number 13. It is a silvery and ductile member of the poor metal group of chemical elements. Aluminium is found primarily as the ore bauxite and is remarkable for its resistance to corrosion (due to the phenomenon of passivation) and its light weight. Aluminium is used in many industries to make millions of different products and is very important to the world economy.
Cadmium	Cadmium is a chemical element in the periodic table that has the symbol Cd and atomic number 48. A relatively rare, soft, bluish-white, toxic transition metal, cadmium occurs with zinc ores and is used largely in batteries.
Cancer	Cancer is a class of diseases or disorders characterized by uncontrolled division of cells and the ability of these cells to invade other tissues, either by direct growth into adjacent tissue through invasion or by implantation into distant sites by metastasis.
Crop	An organ, found in both earthworms and birds, in which ingested food is temporarily stored before being passed to the gizzard, where it is pulverized is the crop.
Toxin	Toxin refers to a microbial product or component that can injure another cell or organism at low concentrations. Often the term refers to a poisonous protein, but toxins may be lipids and other substances.
Ventilation	Ventilation refers to a mechanism that provides contact between an animal's respiratory surface and the air or water to which it is exposed. It is also called breathing.
Variable	A characteristic or aspect in which people, objects, events, or conditions vary is called variable.
Radon	Radon refers to a radioactive gas that is formed by the disintegration of radium, radon is one of the heaviest gases and is considered to be a health hazard.
Fiber	Fibers used by man come from a wide variety of sources: Natural fiber include those made out of plants, animal and mineral sources. Natural fibers can be classified according to their origin.
Central nervous system	The central nervous system comprized of the brain and spinal cord, represents the largest part of the nervous system. Together with the peripheral nervous system, it has a fundamental role in the control of behavior.
Disorientation	A state of mental confusion with respect to time, place, identity of self, other persons, and objects is disorientation.
Fever	Fever (also known as pyrexia, or a febrile response, and archaically known as ague) is a medical symptom that describes an increase in internal body temperature to levels that are

	above normal (37°C, 98.6°F).
Pain	Pain is an unpleasant sensation which may be associated with actual or potential tissue damage and which may have physical and emotional components.
Solvent	A solvent is a liquid that dissolves a solid, liquid, or gaseous solute, resulting in a solution. The most common solvent in everyday life is water.
Uranium	When refined, uranium is a silvery white, weakly radioactive metal, which is slightly softer than steel. It is malleable, ductile, and slightly paramagnetic. Uranium metal has very high density, 65% more dense than lead, but slightly less dense than gold. When finely divided, it can react with cold water; in air, uranium metal becomes coated with uranium oxide.
Radium	Radium is a chemical element, which has the symbol Ra and atomic number 88. Its appearance is almost pure white, but it readily oxidizes on exposure to air, turning black. Radium is an alkaline earth metal that is found in trace amounts in uranium ores. It is extremely radioactive. Its most stable isotope, Ra-226, has a half-life of 1602 years and decays into radon gas.
Lung cancer	Lung cancer is a malignant tumour of the lungs. Most commonly it is bronchogenic carcinoma (about 90%).
Fungi	Fungi refers to simple parasitic life forms, including molds, mildews, yeasts, and mushrooms. They live on dead or decaying organic matter. Fungi can grow as single cells, like yeast, or as multicellular colonies, as seen with molds.
Autoimmune	Autoimmune refers to immune reactions against normal body cells; self against self.
Inhibitor	An inhibitor is a type of effector (biology) that decreases or prevents the rate of a chemical reaction. They are often called negative catalysts.
Syndrome	Syndrome is the association of several clinically recognizable features, signs, symptoms, phenomena or characteristics which often occur together, so that the presence of one feature alerts the physician to the presence of the others
Skin	Skin is an organ of the integumentary system composed of a layer of tissues that protect underlying muscles and organs.
Immune system	The immune system is the system of specialized cells and organs that protect an organism from outside biological influences. When the immune system is functioning properly, it protects the body against bacteria and viral infections, destroying cancer cells and foreign substances.
DNA	Deoxyribonucleic acid (DNA) is a nucleic acid usually in the form of a double helix that contains the genetic instructions specifying the biological development of all cellular forms of life, and most viruses.
Insulation	The practice of managing our role performances so that role partners cannot observe our behavior in two or more conflicting roles is referred to as an insulation.
Aerosol	Liquid that is dispersed in the form of a fine mist is called aerosol.
Chlorine	Chlorine is the chemical element with atomic number 17 and symbol Cl. It is a halogen, found in the periodic table in group 17. As chlorine gas, it is greenish yellow, is two and one half times as heavy as air, has an intensely disagreeable suffocating odor, and is exceedingly poisonous. In its liquid and solid form it is a powerful oxidizing, bleaching, and disinfecting agent.
Atom	An atom is the smallest possible particle of a chemical element that retains its chemical properties.

489

Protocol	Protocol is a document with the aim of guiding decisions and criteria in specific areas of healthcare, as defined by an authoritative examination of current evidence. It details the activities to be executed in specific situations.
Greenhouse gases	Gases such as carbon dioxides, nitrogen oxides, and others that contribute to global warming by trapping heat near the earth's surface are greenhouse gases.
Carbon dioxide	Carbon dioxide is an atmospheric gas comprized of one carbon and two oxygen atoms. A very widely known chemical compound, it is frequently called by its formula CO_2. In its solid state, it is commonly known as dry ice.
Reservoir	Reservoir is the source of infection. It is the environment in which microorganisms are able to live and grow.
Contamination	The introduction of microorganisms or particulate matter into a normally sterile environment is called contamination.
Cryptosporid-osis	Cryptosporidiosis infection with protozoa of the genus Csyptosporidium. The most common symptoms are prolonged diarrhea, weight loss, fever, and abdominal pain.
Dysentery	Dysentery is an illness involving severe diarrhea that is often associated with blood in the feces. It is caused by ingestion of food containing bacteria, causing a disease in which inflammation of the intestines affect the body significantly.
Hepatitis A	Hepatitis A is an enterovirus transmitted by the orofecal route, such as contaminated food. It causes an acute form of hepatitis and does not have a chronic stage.
Hepatitis	Hepatitis is a gastroenterological disease, featuring inflammation of the liver. The clinical signs and prognosis, as well as the therapy, depend on the cause.
Cholera	Cholera is a water-borne disease caused by the bacterium Vibrio cholerae, which are typically ingested by drinking contaminated water, or by eating improperly cooked fish, especially shellfish.
Herbicide	Herbicide refers to a chemical substance that kills plants.
Host	Host is an organism that harbors a parasite, mutual partner, or commensal partner; or a cell infected by a virus.
Phosphorus	Phosphorus is the chemical element in the periodic table that has the symbol P and atomic number 15.
Bacteria	The domain that contains procaryotic cells with primarily diacyl glycerol diesters in their membranes and with bacterial rRNA. Bacteria also is a general term for organisms that are composed of procaryotic cells and are not multicellular.
Leachate	A liquid consisting of soluble chemicals that come from garbage and industrial waste that seeps into the water supply from landfills and dumps is referred to as leachate.
Chlorinated hydrocarbon	Chlorinated hydrocarbon is a broad class of organic chemicals used mainly as solvents but also with many other uses. A chlorinated hydrocarbon is derived from a hydrocarbon molecule where one or more of the hydrogen atoms has been replaced by a chlorine atom.
Dioxin	The group of toxic chlorinated hydrocarbon pollutants is called dioxin.
Polychlorinated biphenyl	Polychlorinated biphenyl is a class of organic compounds with 1 to 10 chlorine atoms attached to biphenyl and a general structure of $C_{12}H_{10-x}Cl_x$.
Liver	The liver is an organ in vertebrates, including humans. It plays a major role in metabolism and has a number of functions in the body including drug detoxification, glycogen storage, and plasma protein synthesis. It also produces bile, which is important for digestion.

Go to **Cram101.com** for the Practice Tests for this Chapter.

491

Infection	The invasion and multiplication of microorganisms in body tissues is called an infection.
Residue	A residue refers to a portion of a larger molecule, a specific monomer of a polysaccharide, protein or nucleic acid.
Correlation	A statistical technique for determining the degree of association between two or more variables is referred to as correlation.
Consensus	General agreement is a consensus.
Carrier	Person in apparent health whose chromosomes contain a pathologic mutant gene that may be transmitted to his or her children is a carrier.
Sleep patterns	The order and timing of daily sleep and waking periods are called sleep patterns.
Blood pressure	Blood pressure is the pressure exerted by the blood on the walls of the blood vessels.
Blood vessel	A blood vessel is a part of the circulatory system and function to transport blood throughout the body. The most important types, arteries and veins, are so termed because they carry blood away from or towards the heart, respectively.
Brain	The part of the central nervous system involved in regulating and controlling body activity and interpreting information from the senses transmitted through the nervous system is referred to as the brain.
Cholesterol	Cholesterol is a steroid, a lipid, and an alcohol, found in the cell membranes of all body tissues, and transported in the blood plasma of all animals. It is an important component of the membranes of cells, providing stability; it makes the membrane's fluidity stable over a bigger temperature interval.
Adrenaline	Adrenaline is a hormone released by chromaffin cells and by some neurons in response to stress. Produces 'fight or flight' responses, including increased heart rate and blood sugar levels.
Hormone	A hormone is a chemical messenger from one cell to another. All multicellular organisms produce hormones. The best known hormones are those produced by endocrine glands of vertebrate animals, but hormones are produced by nearly every organ system and tissue type in a human or animal body. Hormone molecules are secreted directly into the bloodstream, they move by circulation or diffusion to their target cells, which may be nearby cells in the same tissue or cells of a distant organ of the body.
Gland	A gland is an organ in an animal's body that synthesizes a substance for release such as hormones, often into the bloodstream or into cavities inside the body or its outer surface.
Endocrine gland	An endocrine gland is one of a set of internal organs involved in the secretion of hormones into the blood. These glands are known as ductless, which means they do not have tubes inside them.
Hazardous waste	Hazardous waste refers to solid waste that, due to its toxic properties, poses a hazard to humans or to the environment.
Epilepsy	Epilepsy is a chronic neurological condition characterized by recurrent unprovoked neural discharges. It is commonly controlled with medication, although surgical methods are used as well.
Miscarriage	Miscarriage or spontaneous abortion is the natural or accidental termination of a pregnancy at a stage where the embryo or the fetus is incapable of surviving, generally defined at a gestation of prior to 20 weeks.
Compensation	Compensation refers to according to Adler, efforts to overcome imagined or real inferiorities by developing one's abilities.

493

Ionizing radiation	Ionizing radiation is a type of particle radiation in which an individual particle carries enough energy to ionize an atom or molecule. If the individual particles do not carry this amount of energy, it is essentially impossible for even a large flood of particles to cause ionization.
Organ	Organ refers to a structure consisting of several tissues adapted as a group to perform specific functions.
Mutation	A change in the structure of a gene is called a mutation.
Diarrhea	Diarrhea or diarrhoea is a condition in which the sufferer has frequent and watery, chunky, or loose bowel movements.
Anemia	Anemia is a deficiency of red blood cells and/or hemoglobin. This results in a reduced ability of blood to transfer oxygen to the tissues, and this causes hypoxia; since all human cells depend on oxygen for survival, varying degrees of anemia can have a wide range of clinical consequences.
Bone marrow	Bone marrow is the tissue comprising the center of large bones. It is the place where new blood cells are produced. Bone marrow contains two types of stem cells: hemopoietic (which can produce blood cells) and stromal (which can produce fat, cartilage and bone).
White blood cell	The white blood cell is a a component of blood. They help to defend the body against infectious disease and foreign materials as part of the immune system.
Leukemia	Leukemia refers to a type of cancer of the bloodforming tissues, characterized by an excessive production of white blood cells and an abnormally high number of them in the blood; cancer of the bone marrow cells that produce leukocytes.
Culture	Culture, generally refers to patterns of human activity and the symbolic structures that give such activity significance.
Arsenic	Arsenic is a chemical element in the periodic table that has the symbol As and atomic number 33. This is a notoriously poisonous metalloid that has many allotropic forms; yellow, black and grey are a few that are regularly seen. Arsenic and its compounds are used as pesticides, herbicides, insecticides and various alloys.
Allergy	An allergy or Type I hypersensitivity is an immune malfunction whereby a person's body is hypersensitized to react immunologically to typically nonimmunogenic substances. When a person is hypersensitized, these substances are known as allergens.
Learning disabilities	General term for learning disorders, communication disorders, and motor skills disorder is referred to as learning disabilities.
Learning disability	A learning disability exists when there is a significant discrepancy between one's ability and achievement.
Brain tumor	A brain tumor is any intracranial mass created by an abnormal and uncontrolled growth of cells either normally found in the brain itself: neurons, glial cells (astrocytes, oligodendrocytes, ependymal cells), lymphatic tissue, blood vessels), in the cranial nerves, in the brain envelopes (meninges), skull, pituitary and pineal gland, or spread from cancers primarily located in other organs.
Tumor	An abnormal mass of cells that forms within otherwise normal tissue is a tumor. This growth can be either malignant or benign
World Health Organization	The World Health Organization (WHO) is a specialized agency of the United Nations, acting as a coordinating authority on international public health, headquartered in Geneva, Switzerland.
Cohort	A cohort is a group of individuals defined by their date of birth.

494

Control group	A group that does not receive the treatment effect in an experiment is referred to as the control group or sometimes as the comparison group.
Carcinogen	A carcinogen is any substance or agent that promotes cancer. A carcinogen is often, but not necessarily, a mutagen or teratogen.
Clinician	A health professional authorized to provide services to people suffering from one or more pathologies is a clinician.
Conversion	Conversion syndrome describes a condition in which physical symptoms arise for which there is no clear explanation.
Statistics	Statistics is a type of data analysis which practice includes the planning, summarizing, and interpreting of observations of a system possibly followed by predicting or forecasting of future events based on a mathematical model of the system being observed.
Statistic	A statistic is an observable random variable of a sample.
Cesium	Cesium is a chemical element in the periodic table that has the symbol Cs and atomic number 55. It is a soft silvery-gold alkali metal which is one of at least three metals that are liquid at or near room temperature. This element is most notably used in atomic clocks.
Iodine	Iodine is a chemical element in the periodic table that has the symbol I and atomic number 53. It is required as a trace element for most living organisms. Chemically, iodine is the least reactive of the halogens, and the most electropositive halogen. Iodine is primarily used in medicine, photography and in dyes.
Assessment	In clinical practice, the process by which a mental health professional gathers and compiles information about a client for the purpose of describing the person's problems or disorder and developing a plan of treatment is an assessment.
Centers for Disease Control and Prevention	The Centers for Disease Control and Prevention in Atlanta, Georgia, is recognized as the lead United States agency for protecting the public health and safety of people by providing credible information to enhance health decisions, and promoting health through strong partnerships with state health departments and other organizations.
Crisis	A crisis is a temporary state of high anxiety where the persons usual coping mechanisims cease to work. This may have a result of disorganization or possibly personality growth.
Projection	Attributing one's own undesirable thoughts, impulses, traits, or behaviors to others is referred to as projection.

Allergy	An allergy or Type I hypersensitivity is an immune malfunction whereby a person's body is hypersensitized to react immunologically to typically nonimmunogenic substances. When a person is hypersensitized, these substances are known as allergens.
Whistleblower	A whistleblower is an employee, former employee, or member of an organization who reports misconduct to people or entities that have the power to take corrective action. Generally the misconduct is a violation of law, rule, regulation and/or a direct threat to public interest -- fraud, health, safety violations, and corruption are just a few examples.
Arthritis	Arthritis is a group of conditions that affect the health of the bone joints in the body. Arthritis can be caused from strains and injuries caused by repetitive motion, sports, overexertion, and falls. Unlike the autoimmune diseases, it largely affects older people and results from the degeneration of joint cartilage.
Advocate	An advocate is one who speaks on behalf of another, especially in a legal context. Implicit in the concept is the notion that the represented lacks the knowledge, skill, ability, or standing to speak for themselves.
Marriage	A socially approved sexual and economic relationship between two or more individuals is a marriage.
Health	Health is a term that refers to a combination of the absence of illness, the ability to cope with everyday activities, physical fitness, and high quality of life.
Skin	Skin is an organ of the integumentary system composed of a layer of tissues that protect underlying muscles and organs.
Common cold	An acute, self-limiting, and highly contagious virus infection of the upper respiratory tract that produces inflammation, profuse discharge, and other symptoms is referred to as the common cold.
Joint	A joint (articulation) is the location at which two bones make contact (articulate). They are constructed to both allow movement and provide mechanical support.
Placebo effect	The placebo effect is the phenomenon that a patient's symptoms can be alleviated by an otherwise ineffective treatment, apparently because the individual expects or believes that it will work.
Remission	Disappearance of the signs of a disease is called remission.
Placebo	A placebo is an inactive substance (pill, liquid, etc.), which is administered as if it were a therapy, but which has no therapeutic value other than the placebo effect.
Spontaneous remission	Spontaneous remission is a catch-all expression by the medical faculty for any healing with no obvious conventional explanation.
Pharmacist	A pharmacist takes requests for medicines from a physician in the form of a medical prescription and dispense the medication to the patient and counsel them on the proper use and adverse effects of that medication.
Assess	Assess is to systematically and continuously collect, validate, and communicate patient data.
Value	Value is worth in general, and it is thought to be connected to reasons for certain practices, policies, actions, beliefs or emotions. Value is "that which one acts to gain and/or keep."
Sugar	A sugar is the simplest molecule that can be identified as a carbohydrate. These include monosaccharides and disaccharides, trisaccharides and the oligosaccharides. The term "glyco-" indicates the presence of a sugar in an otherwise non-carbohydrate substance.
Population	Population refers to all members of a well-defined group of organisms, events, or things.

Megadose	Generally an intake of a nutrient in excess of 10 times human need is called megadose.
Vitamin	An organic compound other than a carbohydrate, lipid, or protein that is needed for normal metabolism but that the body cannot synthesize in adequate amounts is called a vitamin.
Cancer	Cancer is a class of diseases or disorders characterized by uncontrolled division of cells and the ability of these cells to invade other tissues, either by direct growth into adjacent tissue through invasion or by implantation into distant sites by metastasis.
Managed Care	Managed care is a concept in U.S. health care which rose to dominance during the presidency of Ronald Reagan as a means to control Medicare payouts.
Concept	A mental category used to class together objects, relations, events, abstractions, or qualities that have common properties is called concept.
Affect	Affect is the scientific term used to describe a subject's externally displayed mood. This can be assesed by the nurse by observing facial expression, tone of voice, and body language.
Prognosis	Prognosis refers to the prospects for the future or outcome of a disease.
Medicine	Medicine is the branch of health science and the sector of public life concerned with maintaining or restoring human health through the study, diagnosis and treatment of disease and injury.
Accreditation	Accreditation is the certification by a duly recognized body of the facilities, capability, objectivity, competence, and integrity of an agency, service or operational group or individual to provide the specific service(s) or operation(s) needed.
Antibiotic	Antibiotic refers to substance such as penicillin or streptomycin that is toxic to microorganisms. Usually a product of a particular microorvanism or plant.
Infection	The invasion and multiplication of microorganisms in body tissues is called an infection.
Survey	A method of scientific investigation in which a large sample of people answer questions about their attitudes or behavior is referred to as a survey.
Nervous system	The nervous system of an animal coordinates the activity of the muscles, monitors the organs, constructs and processes input from the senses, and initiates actions.
Sedative	A sedative is a drug that depresses the central nervous system (CNS), which causes calmness, relaxation, reduction of anxiety, sleepiness, slowed breathing, slurred speech, staggering gait, poor judgment, and slow, uncertain reflexes.
Anxiety	Anxiety is a complex combination of the feeling of fear, apprehension and worry often accompanied by physical sensations such as palpitations, chest pain and/or shortness of breath.
Central nervous system	The central nervous system comprized of the brain and spinal cord, represents the largest part of the nervous system. Together with the peripheral nervous system, it has a fundamental role in the control of behavior.
Incidence	In epidemiological studies of a particular disorder, the rate at which new cases occur in a given place at a given time is called incidence.
Tranquilizer	A sedative, or tranquilizer, is a drug that depresses the central nervous system (CNS), which causes calmness, relaxation, reduction of anxiety, sleepiness, slowed breathing, slurred speech, staggering gait, poor judgment, and slow, uncertain reflexes.
Minor tranquilizers	Drugs that produce relaxation or reduce anxiety are referred to as minor tranquilizers.
Trade name	A drug company's name for their patented medication is called a trade name.

501

Miltown	The trade name for meprobamate, one of the principal anxiolytics is referred to as miltown.
Psychotherapy	Psychotherapy is a set of techniques based on psychological principles intended to improve mental health, emotional or behavioral issues.
Antidepressant	An antidepressant is a medication used primarily in the treatment of clinical depression. They are not thought to produce tolerance, although sudden withdrawal may produce adverse effects. They create little if any immediate change in mood and require between several days and several weeks to take effect.
Depression	In everyday language depression refers to any downturn in mood, which may be relatively transitory and perhaps due to something trivial. This is differentiated from Clinical depression which is marked by symptoms that last two weeks or more and are so severe that they interfere with daily living.
Major depression	Major depression is characterized by a severely depressed mood that persists for at least two weeks. Episodes of depression may start suddenly or slowly and can occur several times through a person's life. The disorder may be categorized as "single episode" or "recurrent" depending on whether previous episodes have been experienced before.
Antidepressants	Antidepressants are medications used primarily in the treatment of clinical depression. Antidepressants create little if any immediate change in mood and require between several days and several weeks to take effect.
Serotonin	Serotonin is a monoamine neurotransmitter synthesized in serotonergic neurons in the central nervous system and enterochromaffin cells in the gastrointestinal tract. It is believed to play an important part of the biochemistry of depression, migraine, bipolar disorder and anxiety.
Inhibitor	An inhibitor is a type of effector (biology) that decreases or prevents the rate of a chemical reaction. They are often called negative catalysts.
Reuptake	Reuptake is the reabsorption of a neurotransmitter by the molecular transporter of a pre-synaptic neuron after it has performed its function of transmitting a neural impulse.
Selective serotonin reuptake inhibitors	Selective serotonin reuptake inhibitors are a class of antidepressants. They act within the brain to increase the amount of the neurotransmitter, serotonin (5-hydroxytryptamine or 5-HT), in the synaptic gap by inhibiting its reuptake. It is often prescribed for depression.
Selective serotonin reuptake inhibitor	Selective serotonin reuptake inhibitor is a class of antidepressants for treating depression, anxiety disorders and some personality disorders. These drugs are designed to elevate the level of the neurotransmitter serotonin.
Amphetamine	Amphetamine is a synthetic stimulant used to suppress the appetite, control weight, and treat disorders including narcolepsy and ADHD. It is also used recreationally and for performance enhancement.
Stimulant	A stimulant is a drug which increases the activity of the sympathetic nervous system and produces a sense of euphoria or awakeness.
Blood pressure	Blood pressure is the pressure exerted by the blood on the walls of the blood vessels.
Pulse	The rhythmic stretching of the arteries caused by the pressure of blood forced through the arteries by contractions of the ventricles during systole is a pulse.
Blood	Blood is a circulating tissue composed of fluid plasma and cells. The main function of blood is to supply nutrients (oxygen, glucose) and constitutional elements to tissues and to remove waste products.

Hyperactivity	Hyperactivity can be described as a state in which a individual is abnormally easily excitable and exuberant. Strong emotional reactions and a very short span of attention is also typical for the individual.
Obesity	The state of being more than 20 percent above the average weight for a person of one's height is called obesity.
Ritalin	Ritalin, a methylphenidate, is a central nervous system stimulant. It has a "calming" effect on many children who have ADHD, reducing impulsive behavior and the tendency to "act out", and helps them concentrate on schoolwork and other tasks.
Attention deficit hyperactivity disorder	A learning disability marked by inattention, impulsiveness, a low tolerance for frustration, and a great deal of inappropriate activity is the attention deficit hyperactivity disorder.
Tolerance	Drug tolerance occurs when a subject's reaction to a drug decreases so that larger doses are required to achieve the same effect.
Chemical name	The primary function of chemical nomenclature is to ensure that the person who hears or reads a chemical name is under no ambiguity as to which chemical compound it refers: each name should refer to a single substance. It is considered less important to ensure that each substance should have a single name, although the number of acceptable names is limited.
Course	Pattern of development and change of a disorder over time is a course.
Withdrawal effects	Withdrawal effects refer to the physiological, mental, and behavioral disturbances that can occur when a long-term user of a drug stops taking the drug.
Syndrome	Syndrome is the association of several clinically recognizable features, signs, symptoms, phenomena or characteristics which often occur together, so that the presence of one feature alerts the physician to the presence of the others
Irritable bowel syndrome	In gastroenterology, irritable bowel syndrome is a functional bowel disorder characterized by abdominal pain and changes in bowel habits which are not associated with any abnormalities seen on routine clinical testing.
Colon	The colon is the part of the intestine from the cecum to the rectum. Its primary purpose is to extract water from feces.
Public health	Public health is concerned with threats to the overall health of a community based on population health analysis.
Adverse drug reaction	An adverse drug reaction (abbreviated ADR) is a term to describe the unwanted, negative consequences sometimes associated with the use of medications. ADR is a particular type of adverse effect.
Incentive	Incentive refers to an object, person, or situation perceived as being capable of satisfying a need.
Clinical study	An intensive investigation of a single person, especially one suffering from some injury or disease is referred to as a clinical study.
Analgesic	An analgesic is any member of the diverse group of drugs used to relieve pain and to achieve analgesia. Analgesic drugs act in various ways on the peripheral and central nervous system.
Asthma	Asthma is a complex disease characterized by bronchial hyperresponsiveness (BHR), inflammation, mucus production and intermittent airway obstruction.
Pain	Pain is an unpleasant sensation which may be associated with actual or potential tissue damage and which may have physical and emotional components.

Go to **Cram101.com** for the Practice Tests for this Chapter.

Acetaminophen	Acetaminophen is a common analgesic and antipyretic drug that is used for the relief of fever, headaches, and other minor aches and pains. It is a major ingredient in numerous cold and flu medications and many prescription analgesics. It is remarkably safe in standard doses, but, because of its wide availability, deliberate or accidental overdoses are fairly common.
Ibuprofen	A nonopiate pain reliever that controls pain, fever, and inflammation is referred to as ibuprofen.
Receptor	A receptor is a protein on the cell membrane or within the cytoplasm or cell nucleus that binds to a specific molecule (a ligand), such as a neurotransmitter, hormone, or other substance, and initiates the cellular response to the ligand. Receptor, in immunology, the region of an antibody which shows recognition of an antigen.
Prostaglandin	A prostaglandin is any member of a group of lipid compounds that are derived from fatty acids and have important functions in the animal body.
Hormone	A hormone is a chemical messenger from one cell to another. All multicellular organisms produce hormones. The best known hormones are those produced by endocrine glands of vertebrate animals, but hormones are produced by nearly every organ system and tissue type in a human or animal body. Hormone molecules are secreted directly into the bloodstream, they move by circulation or diffusion to their target cells, which may be nearby cells in the same tissue or cells of a distant organ of the body.
Sodium	Sodium is the chemical element in the periodic table that has the symbol Na (Natrium in Latin) and atomic number 11. Sodium is a soft, waxy, silvery reactive metal belonging to the alkali metals that is abundant in natural compounds (especially halite). It is highly reactive.
Fever	Fever (also known as pyrexia, or a febrile response, and archaically known as ague) is a medical symptom that describes an increase in internal body temperature to levels that are above normal (37°C, 98.6°F).
Inflammation	Inflammation is the first response of the immune system to infection or irritation and may be referred to as the innate cascade.
Stroke	A stroke or cerebrovascular accident (CVA) occurs when the blood supply to a part of the brain is suddenly interrupted.
Blood clotting	A complex process by which platelets, the protein fibrin, and red blood cells block an irregular surface in or on the body, such as a damaged blood vessel, sealing the wound is referred to as blood clotting.
Anticoagulant	A biochemical that inhibits blood clotting is referred to as an anticoagulant.
Heart attack	A heart attack, is a serious, sudden heart condition usually characterized by varying degrees of chest pain or discomfort, weakness, sweating, nausea, vomiting, and arrhythmias, sometimes causing loss of consciousness. It occurs when the blood supply to a part of the heart is interrupted, causing death and scarring of the local heart tissue.
Stomach	The stomach is an organ in the alimentary canal used to digest food. It's primary function is not the absorption of nutrients from digested food; rather, the main job of the stomach is to break down large food molecules into smaller ones, so that they can be absorbed into the blood more easily.
Ulcer	An ulcer is an open sore of the skin, eyes or mucous membrane, often caused by an initial abrasion and generally maintained by an inflammation and/or an infection.
Alcohol	Alcohol is a general term, applied to any organic compound in which a hydroxyl group (-OH) is bound to a carbon atom, which in turn is bound to other hydrogen and/or carbon atoms. The

506

Go to **Cram101.com** for the Practice Tests for this Chapter.

	general formula for a simple acyclic alcohol is $C_nH_{2n+1}OH$.
Young adult	An young adult is someone between the ages of 20 and 40 years old.
Liver	The liver is an organ in vertebrates, including humans. It plays a major role in metabolism and has a number of functions in the body including drug detoxification, glycogen storage, and plasma protein synthesis. It also produces bile, which is important for digestion.
Respiratory tract	In humans the respiratory tract is the part of the anatomy that has to do with the process of respiration or breathing.
Immune system	The immune system is the system of specialized cells and organs that protect an organism from outside biological influences. When the immune system is functioning properly, it protects the body against bacteria and viral infections, destroying cancer cells and foreign substances.
Expectorant	Dry coughs are treated with cough suppressants (antitussives) that suppress the body's urge to cough, while productive coughs (coughs that produce phlegm) are treated with a expectorant that loosen mucus from the respiratory tract.
Gras list	A list of drugs generally recognized as safe, which seldom cause side effects when used properly is a gras list.
Grae list	A list of drugs generally recognized as effective, which work for their intended purpose when used properly is called grae list.
Codeine	Codeine is an opioid used for its analgesic, antitussive and antidiarrheal properties
Diphenhydramine	Diphenhydramine is a first generation antihistamine drug. Despite being one of the oldest antihistamines on the market, it is by and large the most effective antihistamine available.Consequently, it is frequently used when an allergic reaction requires fast, effective reversal of the (often dangerous) effects of a massive histamine release.
World Health Organization	The World Health Organization (WHO) is a specialized agency of the United Nations, acting as a coordinating authority on international public health, headquartered in Geneva, Switzerland.
Insomnia	Insomnia is a sleep disorder characterized by an inability to sleep and/or to remain asleep for a reasonable period during the night.
Antihistamine	An antihistamine is a drug which serves to reduce or eliminate effects mediated by histamine, an endogenous chemical mediator released during allergic reactions, through action at the histamine receptor.
Addiction	Addiction is an uncontrollable compulsion to repeat a behavior regardless of its consequences. Many drugs or behaviors can precipitate a pattern of conditions recognized as addiction, which include a craving for more of the drug or behavior, increased physiological tolerance to exposure, and withdrawal symptoms in the absence of the stimulus.
Lead	Lead is a chemical element in the periodic table that has the symbol Pb and atomic number 82. A soft, heavy, toxic and malleable poor metal, lead is bluish white when freshly cut but tarnishes to dull gray when exposed to air. Lead is used in building construction, lead-acid batteries, bullets and shot, and is part of solder, pewter, and fusible alloys.
Sympathetic nervous system	The sympathetic nervous system activates what is often termed the "fight or flight response". Messages travel through in a bidirectional flow. Efferent messages can trigger changes in different parts of the body simultaneously.
Sympathetic	The sympathetic nervous system activates what is often termed the "fight or flight response". It is an automatic regulation system, that is, one that operates without the intervention of conscious thought.

509

Constipation	Constipation is a condition of the digestive system where a person (or other animal) experiences hard feces that are difficult to eliminate; it may be extremely painful, and in severe cases (fecal impaction) lead to symptoms of bowel obstruction.
Laxatives	Medications used to soften stool and relieve constipation are referred to as laxatives.
Laxative	Laxative refers to a medication or other substance that stimulates evacuation of the intestinal tract.
Stool	Stool is the waste matter discharged in a bowel movement.
Excretion	Excretion is the biological process by which an organism chemically separates waste products from its body. The waste products are then usually expelled from the body by elimination.
Diuretic	A diuretic is any drug that elevates the rate of bodily urine excretion.
Urine	Concentrated filtrate produced by the kidneys and excreted via the bladder is called urine.
Complement	Complement is a group of proteins of the complement system, found in blood serum which act in concert with antibodies to achieve the destruction of non-self particles such as foreign blood cells or bacteria.
Elimination	Elimination refers to the physiologic excretion of drugs and other substances from the body.
Minerals	Minerals refer to inorganic chemical compounds found in nature; salts.
Salt	Salt is a term used for ionic compounds composed of positively charged cations and negatively charged anions, so that the product is neutral and without a net charge.
Eating disorders	Psychological disorders characterized by distortion of the body image and gross disturbances in eating patterns are called eating disorders.
Electrolyte	An electrolyte is a substance that dissociates into free ions when dissolved (or molten), to produce an electrically conductive medium. Because they generally consist of ions in solution, they are also known as ionic solutions.
Potassium	Potassium is a chemical element in the periodic table. It has the symbol K (L. kalium) and atomic number 19. Potassium is a soft silvery-white metallic alkali metal that occurs naturally bound to other elements in seawater and many minerals.
Drug interaction	A combined effect of two drugs that exceeds the addition of one drug's effects to the other is a drug interaction.
Inhibition	The ability to prevent from making some cognitive or behavioral response is called inhibition.
Intolerance	Intolerance refers to a type of interaction in which two or more drugs produce extremely uncomfortable symptoms.
Antagonism	A type of interaction in which two or more drugs work at the same receptor site is called antagonism.
Synergism	Synergism refers to an exaggerated effect that occurs when two or more drugs are used at the same time. One reason why this effect occurs is because the liver or body is busy metabolizing one drug while the other slips through unchanged.
Barbiturate	A barbiturate is a drug that acts as a central nervous system (CNS) depressant, and by virtue of this produces a wide spectrum of effects, from mild sedation to anesthesia.
Hypnotic	Hypnotic drugs are a class of drugs that induce sleep, used in the treatment of severe insomnia.
Morphine	Morphine, the principal active agent in opium, is a powerful opioid analgesic drug. According

	to recent research, it may also be produced naturally by the human brain. Morphine is usually highly addictive, and tolerance and physical and psychological dependence develop quickly.
Heroin	Heroin is widely and illegally used as a powerful and addictive drug producing intense euphoria, which often disappears with increasing tolerance. Heroin is a semi-synthetic opioid. It is the 3,6-diacetyl derivative of morphine and is synthesized from it by acetylation.
Opiate	The term opiate refers to the alkaloids found in opium, an extract from the seed pods of the opium poppy (Papaver somniferum L.). It has also traditionally referred to natural and semi-synthetic derivatives of morphine.
Brain	The part of the central nervous system involved in regulating and controlling body activity and interpreting information from the senses transmitted through the nervous system is referred to as the brain.
Heart rate	Heart rate is a term used to describe the frequency of the cardiac cycle. It is considered one of the four vital signs. Usually it is calculated as the number of contractions of the heart in one minute and expressed as "beats per minute".
Illicit drugs	Illicit drugs refers to drugs whose use, possession, cultivation, manufacture, and/or sale are against the law because they are generally recognized as harmful.
Confidentiality	Confidentiality refers to an ethical principle associated with several professions (eg, medicine, law, religion, journalism,). In ethics, and in law, some types of communication between a person and one of these professionals are "privileged" and may not be discussed or divulged to third parties. In those jurisdictions in which the law makes provision for such confidentiality, there are usually penalties for its violation.
Absorption	Absorption is a physical or chemical phenomenon or a process in which atoms, molecules, or ions enter some bulk phase - gas, liquid or solid material. In nutrition, amino acids are broken down through digestion, which begins in the stomach.
Blocking	A sudden break or interuption in the flow of thinking or speech that is seen as an absence in thought is refered to as blocking.
Birth control pill	The birth control pill is a chemical taken by mouth to inhibit normal fertility. All act on the hormonal system.
Alcoholic	An alcoholic is dependent on alcohol as characterized by craving, loss of control, physical dependence and withdrawal symptoms, and tolerance.
Antabuse	A drug that makes the drinking of alcohol produce nausea and other unpleasant effects is an antabuse.
Enzyme	An enzyme is a protein that catalyzes, or speeds up, a chemical reaction. They are essential to sustain life because most chemical reactions in biological cells would occur too slowly, or would lead to different products, without them.
Physiological Tolerance	Physiological tolerance occurs when an organism builds up a resistance to the effects of a substance after repeated exposure.
Folic acid	Folic acid and folate (the anion form) are forms of a water-soluble B vitamin. These occur naturally in food and can also be taken as supplements.
Acid	An acid is a water-soluble, sour-tasting chemical compound that when dissolved in water, gives a solution with a pH of less than 7.
Calcium	Calcium is the chemical element in the periodic table that has the symbol Ca and atomic number 20. Calcium is a soft grey alkaline earth metal that is used as a reducing agent in the extraction of thorium, zirconium and uranium. Calcium is also the fifth most abundant

Go to **Cram101.com** for the Practice Tests for this Chapter.

element in the Earth's crust.

Protein	A protein is a complex, high-molecular-weight organic compound that consists of amino acids joined by peptide bonds. They are essential to the structure and function of all living cells and viruses. Many are enzymes or subunits of enzymes.
Thyroid	The thyroid is one of the larger endocrine glands in the body. It is located in the neck and produces hormones, principally thyroxine and triiodothyronine, that regulate the rate of metabolism and affect the growth and rate of function of many other systems in the body.
Iodine	Iodine is a chemical element in the periodic table that has the symbol I and atomic number 53. It is required as a trace element for most living organisms. Chemically, iodine is the least reactive of the halogens, and the most electropositive halogen. Iodine is primarily used in medicine, photography and in dyes.
Fluoxetine	Fluoxetine is an antidepressant drug used medically in the treatment of depression, obsessive-compulsive disorder, bulimia nervosa, premenstrual dysphoric disorder and panic disorder. It is sold under the brand names Prozac®, and others.
Sertraline	Sertraline is used medically mainly to treat the symptoms of depression and anxiety. It has also been prescribed for the treatment of obsessive-compulsive disorder, post-traumatic stress disorder, premenstrual dysphoric disorder, panic disorder, and bipolar disorder
Tuberculosis	Tuberculosis is an infection caused by the bacterium Mycobacterium tuberculosis, which most commonly affects the lungs but can also affect the central nervous system, lymphatic system, circulatory system, genitourinary system, bones and joints.
Penicillin	Penicillin refers to a group of β-lactam antibiotics used in the treatment of bacterial infections caused by susceptible, usually Gram-positive, organisms.
Breastfeeding	Breastfeeding is the process of a woman feeding an infant or young child with milk from her breasts, usually directly from the nipples, a process called lactation. .
Fetus	Fetus refers to a developing human from the ninth week of gestation until birth; has all the major structures of an adult.
Outcome	Outcome is the impact of care provided to a patient. They can be positive, such as the ability to walk freely as a result of rehabilitation, or negative, such as the occurrence of bedsores as a result of lack of mobility of a patient.
Trial	In classical conditioning, any presentation of a stimulus or pair of stimuli is called a trial.
Validity	The extent to which a test measures what it is intended to measure is called validity.
Acquisition	The initial learning of the stimulus response link, which involves a neutral stimulus being associated with a UCS and becoming a conditioned stimulus is called acquisition.
Nurse Practitioner	A Nurse Practitioner is a Registered Nurse who has completed advanced education (generally a minimum of a master's degree) and training in the diagnosis and management of common medical conditions, including chronic illnesses.
Malpractice	Medical malpractice is an act or omission by a health care provider which deviates from accepted standards of practice in the medical community and which causes injury to the patient.
Informed consent	The term used by psychologists to indicate that a person has agreed to participate in research after receiving information about the purposes of the study and the nature of the treatments is informed consent. Even with informed consent, subjects may withdraw from any experiment at any time.

Go to **Cram101.com** for the Practice Tests for this Chapter.

Diagnosis	In medicine, diagnosis is the process of identifying a medical condition or disease by its signs, symptoms, and from the results of various diagnostic procedures.
Glaucoma	Glaucoma is a group of diseases of the optic nerve involving loss of retinal ganglion cells in a characteristic pattern of optic neuropathy.
Eye	An eye is an organ that detects light. Different kinds of light-sensitive organs are found in a variety of creatures. The simplest eyes do nothing but detect whether the surroundings are light or dark, while more complex eyes can distinguish shapes and colors.
Oral cavity	The mouth, also known as the buccal cavity or the oral cavity, is the opening through which an animal or human takes in food and water. It is usually located in the head, but not always; the mouth of a planarium is in the middle of its belly.
Theory	Theory refers to an explanatory statement, or set of statements, that concisely summarizes the state of knowledge on a phenomenon and provides direction for further study.
Muscular system	The muscular system is the biological system of animals (including humans) that allows them to move internally and externally. The muscular system in vertebrates consists of three different types of muscles: cardiac, skeletal and smooth.
Registered Nurse	A Registered Nurse is a professional nurse who often supervises the tasks performed by Licensed Practical Nurses, orderlies, medical assistants and nursing assistants. They provide direct care and make decisions regarding plans of care for individuals and groups of healthy, ill and injured people.
Health maintenance organization	A Health Maintenance Organization is a type of Managed Care Organization that provides a form of health insurance coverage in the United States that is fulfilled through hospitals, doctors, and other providers with which the organization has a contract.
Group practice	A group of physicians who combine resources, sharing offices, equipment, and staff costs to render care to patients is called group practice.
Carrier	Person in apparent health whose chromosomes contain a pathologic mutant gene that may be transmitted to his or her children is a carrier.
Outpatient	Outpatient refers to a patient who requires treatment but does not need to be admitted into the institution for those sevices.
Inpatient	Inpatient refers to a person who enters a healthcare setting for a stay ranging from 24 hours to many years.
Acute	In medicine, an acute disease is a disease with either or both of: a rapid onset; and a short course (as opposed to a chronic course).
Tubal ligation	Tubal ligation refers to a means of sterilization in which a woman's two oviducts are tied closed to prevent eggs from reaching the uterus. A segment of each oviduct is removed.
Vasectomy	Vasectomy refers to surgical removal of a section of the two sperm ducts to prevent sperm from reaching the urethra; a means of sterilization in the male.
Abortion	An abortion is the termination of a pregnancy associated with the death of an embryo or a fetus.
Ligation	Ligation refers to enzymatically catalyzed formation of a phosphodiester bond that links two DNA molecules.
Biopsy	Removal of small tissue sample from the body for microscopic examination is called biopsy.
Tissue	A collection of interconnected cells that perform a similar function within an organism is called tissue.

Go to **Cram101.com** for the Practice Tests for this Chapter.

Planning	In agreement with the patient, the nurse addresses each of the problems identified in the planning phase. For each problem a measurable goal is set. For example, for the patient discussed above, the goal would be for the patient's skin to remain intact. The result is a nursing care plan. This is the third step.
Licensure	Licensure refers to the granting of a license, usually to work in a particular profession. Many professions require a license from the government in order to ensure that the public will not be harmed by the incompetence of the practitioners. Nurses, lawyers, psychologists, and public accountants are four examples of professions that require licensure.
Chronic illness	A chronic illness is a persistent and lasting condition that generally involves progressive deteriation and an increase in symptoms and disability.
Crisis	A crisis is a temporary state of high anxiety where the persons usual coping mechanisims cease to work. This may have a result of disorganization or possibly personality growth.
Implementation	The methods by which the goal will be achieved is also recorded at this fourth stage. The methods of implementation must be recorded in an explicit and tangible format in a way that the patient can understand should he wish to read it. Clarity is essential as it will aid communication between those tasked with carrying out patient care.
Mortality rate	Mortality rate is the number of deaths (from a disease or in general) per 1000 people and typically reported on an annual basis.
Certification	A professional certification, trade certification, or professional designation often called simply certification or qualification is a designation earned by a person to certify that he is qualified to perform a job. Certification indicates that the individual has a specific knowledge, skills, or abilities in the view of the certifying body.
Mortality	The incidence of death in a population is mortality.
Assessment	In clinical practice, the process by which a mental health professional gathers and compiles information about a client for the purpose of describing the person's problems or disorder and developing a plan of treatment is an assessment.
Coronary	Referring to the heart or the blood vessels of the heart is referred to as coronary.
Bypass	In medicine, a bypass generally means an alternate or additional route for blood flow, which is created in bypass surgery, e.g. coronary artery bypass surgery by moving blood vessels or implanting synthetic tubing.
Medicare	Medicare refers to government health insurance for those over sixty-five.
Constant	A behavior or characteristic that does not vary from one observation to another is referred to as a constant.
Chiropractic	Chiropractic, or chiropractic care, is a CAM health care profession with an underlying principle that health problems can be prevented and treated using spinal adjustments in order to correct spinal dysfunction, or subluxations.
Acupuncture	Acupuncture is a technique of inserting and manipulating needles into specific points on the body. Accordingly this will restore health and well-being.
Anesthesia	Anesthesia is the process of blocking the perception of pain and other sensations. This allows patients to undergo surgery and other procedures without the distress and pain they would otherwise experience.
Negligence	Under law, negligence is usually defined in the context of jury instructions wherein a judge instructs the jury that a party is to be considered negligent if they failed to exercise the standard of care that a reasonable person would have exercised under the same circumstances.

Medicaid	Medicaid in the United States is a program managed by the states and funded jointly by the states and federal government to provide health insurance for individuals and families with low incomes and resources. Medicaid is the largest source of funding for medical and health-related services for people with limited income.
Elderly	Old age consists of ages nearing the average life span of human beings, and thus the end of the human life cycle. Euphemisms for older people include advanced adult, elderly, and senior or senior citizen.
Chronic disease	Disease of long duration often not detected in its early stages and from which the patient will not recover is referred to as a chronic disease.
Kidney	The kidney is a bean-shaped excretory organ in vertebrates. Part of the urinary system, the kidneys filter wastes (especially urea) from the blood and excrete them, along with water, as urine.
Prospective payment system	Prospective payment system is a comprehensive payment for an episode of care, on the basis of initial problems. There are predetermined rates for certain classifications of diseases.
Immunization	Use of a vaccine to protect the body against specific disease-causing agents is called immunization.
Glucose	Glucose, a simple monosaccharide sugar, is one of the most important carbohydrates and is used as a source of energy in animals and plants. Glucose is one of the main products of photosynthesis and starts respiration.
Preferred provider organization	In health insurance, a preferred provider organization is a managed care organization of medical doctors, hospitals, and other health care providers who have covenanted with an insurer or a third-party administrator to provide health care at reduced rates to the insurer's or administrator's clients.
Denial	Denial is a psychological defense mechanism in which a person faced with a fact that is uncomfortable or painful to accept rejects it instead, insisting that it is not true despite what may be overwhelming evidence.
Capitation	Prepayment of a fixed monthly amount per patient without regard to the type or number of services provided is a capitation.
Interest group	Interest group refers to an organization that attempts to affect political decisions by supporting candidates sympathetic to their interests and by influencing those already in positions of authority.
Interest groups	Groups organized to pursue specific interests in the political arena are referred to as interest groups.
Healthcare system	A healthcare system is the organization by which health care is provided.
Fraud	In the broadest sense, a fraud is a deception made for personal gain, although it has a more specific legal meaning, the exact details varying between jurisdictions.
Managed health care	A term that refers to the industrialization of health care, whereby large organizations in the private sector control the delivery of services is called managed health care.
Alternative medicine	Treatment used in place of conventional medicine is an alternative medicine.

Go to **Cram101.com** for the Practice Tests for this Chapter.
And, **NEVER** highlight a book again!

Acupuncture	Acupuncture is a technique of inserting and manipulating needles into specific points on the body. Accordingly this will restore health and well-being.
Blood pressure	Blood pressure is the pressure exerted by the blood on the walls of the blood vessels.
Blood	Blood is a circulating tissue composed of fluid plasma and cells. The main function of blood is to supply nutrients (oxygen, glucose) and constitutional elements to tissues and to remove waste products.
Euphoria	A feeling of well-being, extreme satiation, and satisfaction caused by many psychoactive drugs and certain behaviors, such as gambling and sex is referred to as euphoria.
Medicine	Medicine is the branch of health science and the sector of public life concerned with maintaining or restoring human health through the study, diagnosis and treatment of disease and injury.
Alternative therapy	Alternative therapy refers to a substance or procedure used as a therapy that has not gone through usual scientific testing in this country.
Syndrome	Syndrome is the association of several clinically recognizable features, signs, symptoms, phenomena or characteristics which often occur together, so that the presence of one feature alerts the physician to the presence of the others
Carpal	In human anatomy, the carpal bones are the bones of the human wrist.There are eight of them altogether, and they can be thought of as forming two rows of four.
Carpal tunnel syndrome	Carpal tunnel syndrome (CTS) is a medical condition in which the median nerve is compressed at the wrist causing symptoms like tingling, pain, coldness, and sometimes weakness in parts of the hand.
Lifestyle	The culturally, socially, economically, and environmentally conditioned complex of actions characteristic of an individual, group, or community as a pattern of habituated behavior over time that is health related but not necessarily health directed is a lifestyle.
Health	Health is a term that refers to a combination of the absence of illness, the ability to cope with everyday activities, physical fitness, and high quality of life.
Statistics	Statistics is a type of data analysis which practice includes the planning, summarizing, and interpreting of observations of a system possibly followed by predicting or forecasting of future events based on a mathematical model of the system being observed.
Statistic	A statistic is an observable random variable of a sample.
Survey	A method of scientific investigation in which a large sample of people answer questions about their attitudes or behavior is referred to as a survey.
Alternative medicine	Treatment used in place of conventional medicine is an alternative medicine.
Biofeedback	Biofeedback is the process of measuring and quantifying an aspect of a subject's physiology, analyzing the data, and then feeding back the information to the subject in a form that allows the subject to enact physiological change.
Antibiotic	Antibiotic refers to substance such as penicillin or streptomycin that is toxic to microorganisms. Usually a product of a particular microorvanism or plant.
Affect	Affect is the scientific term used to describe a subject's externally displayed mood. This can be assesed by the nurse by observing facial expression, tone of voice, and body language.
Cancer	Cancer is a class of diseases or disorders characterized by uncontrolled division of cells and the ability of these cells to invade other tissues, either by direct growth into adjacent tissue through invasion or by implantation into distant sites by metastasis.

Go to **Cram101.com** for the Practice Tests for this Chapter.
And, **NEVER** highlight a book again!

Host	Host is an organism that harbors a parasite, mutual partner, or commensal partner; or a cell infected by a virus.
Culture	Culture, generally refers to patterns of human activity and the symbolic structures that give such activity significance.
Complementary medicine	Complementary medicine refers to treatment used in conjunction with conventional medicine.
Chemotherapy	Chemotherapy is the use of chemical substances to treat disease. In its modern-day use, it refers almost exclusively to cytostatic drugs used to treat cancer.In its non-oncological use, the term may also refer to antibiotics.
Registered Nurse	A Registered Nurse is a professional nurse who often supervises the tasks performed by Licensed Practical Nurses, orderlies, medical assistants and nursing assistants. They provide direct care and make decisions regarding plans of care for individuals and groups of healthy, ill and injured people.
Assess	Assess is to systematically and continuously collect, validate, and communicate patient data.
Chiropractic	Chiropractic, or chiropractic care, is a CAM health care profession with an underlying principle that health problems can be prevented and treated using spinal adjustments in order to correct spinal dysfunction, or subluxations.
Pain	Pain is an unpleasant sensation which may be associated with actual or potential tissue damage and which may have physical and emotional components.
Alternative care	Alternative care is a genral term used to identify various methods of nonhospital healthcare. Some of these included are residential housing, day care, respite care, hospice, and extended-care facilities.
Managed Care	Managed care is a concept in U.S. health care which rose to dominance during the presidency of Ronald Reagan as a means to control Medicare payouts.
Chronic pain	Chronic pain is defined as pain that has lasted 6 months or longer.
Population	Population refers to all members of a well-defined group of organisms, events, or things.
Outcome	Outcome is the impact of care provided to a patient. They can be positive, such as the ability to walk freely as a result of rehabilitation, or negative, such as the occurrence of bedsores as a result of lack of mobility of a patient.
Megadose	Generally an intake of a nutrient in excess of 10 times human need is called megadose.
Vitamin	An organic compound other than a carbohydrate, lipid, or protein that is needed for normal metabolism but that the body cannot synthesize in adequate amounts is called a vitamin.
Acupressure	Acupressure involves placing physical pressure by hand, elbow, or with the aid of various devices on different acupuncture points on the surface of the body.
Traditional Chinese medicine	Traditional Chinese medicine is the name commonly given to a range of traditional medical practices used in China that have developed over the course of several thousand years of history.
Glucosamine	Glucosamine ($C_6H_{14}NO_5$) is an amino sugar that is a important precursor in the biochemical synthesis of glycosylated proteins and lipids. Glucosamine is commonly used as a treatment for osteoarthritis, although its acceptance as a medical therapy varies.
Chromium	Chromium is a chemical element in the periodic table that has the symbol Cr and atomic number 24. Chromium (0) is unstable in oxygen, immediately producing a thin oxide layer that is impermeable to oxygen and protects the metal below.

Go to **Cram101.com** for the Practice Tests for this Chapter.

Muscle	Muscle is a contractile form of tissue. It is one of the four major tissue types, the other three being epithelium, connective tissue and nervous tissue. Muscle contraction is used to move parts of the body, as well as to move substances within the body.
Agent	Agent refers to an epidemiological term referring to the organism or object that transmits a disease from the environment to the host.
Health enhancement	A dimension of health promotion pertaining to its goal of reaching higher levels of wellness beyond the mere absence of disease or infirmity is called health enhancement.

Go to **Cram101.com** for the Practice Tests for this Chapter.

Printed in the United States
86634LV00006B/123-124/A